TOM BROWN'S UNIVERSE

TOM BROWN'S UNIVERSE

The Development of the English Public School in the Nineteenth Century

J. R. de S. Honey

Quadrangle/The New York Times Book Co.

First published in Great Britain in 1977 by Millington Books Limited

Library of Congress Catalog Card Number: 76-56585
International Standard Book Number: 0-8129-0689-6

For Jo, Steven, Lucy
and Anne who bore the brunt.

Contents

Preface

Among the pleasures attaching to the writing of this book have been the number of friendships, the many kindnesses and the hospitality to which the pursuit of these researches gave rise. In this connection I have to mention my special indebtedness to Dr and Mrs T. W. Bamford, to Mr and Mrs E. G. H. Kempson, to Mr and Mrs J. B. Hope Simpson, to the Bishop of Ripon and Mrs Mary Moorman, to Mr and Mrs L. W. Stephens and to Mr and Mrs L. Warwick James. The approachability and helpfulness of many established scholars in the field was a heartening experience for a researcher, and I owe particular thanks to Mr David Newsome and to Professor Frank Musgrove: in both cases their seminal influence will be clearly seen, by those who know their work, in the central themes of this book. An earlier stage of these researches led to the presentation of a doctoral thesis, which had been supervised by the late Mr R. B. McCallum and by Mr A. D. C. Peterson, to the University of Oxford: my examiners, Professor W. H. G. Armytage and the Rev. Dr V. H. H. Green, made many valuable suggestions, some of which I have been able to make use of in the writing of this book. Whilst a member of the staff of the University of Durham I benefited from grants from that university's Research Fund, as also from an S.S.R.C. studentship in 1968–9 which promoted great progress in these researches during a year spent as a Visiting Fellow of that delectable society, University College (now Wolfson College), Cambridge. To my old teacher at Cambridge, the late Prof. David Joslin, I pay tribute for his help and constant encouragement.

On specific points I owe thanks to the following, though as with the foregoing they bear no responsibility for the use I have made of information supplied to me: Mr J. C. Dancy, Mr Gerald Murray, Mr G. F. Lamb, Dr D. P. Leinster-Mackay, Mr S. E. A. Green, Mr L. R. Conisbee, Mr H. L. Brereton, Mr Charles

Brereton, Mr J. H. Brereton, Mr T. H. Simms and the Librarian of Homerton College, Dr G. Kitson Clark, Mr J. H. Avery, Mr J. C. Stredder, Dr Henry Pelling, Mr W. L. King, Mr and Mrs C. G. Browning, Dr C. Rigby, Mr G. P. Maguire, Mr I. T. Ker, Dr R. J. A. Skidelsky, Mr A. R. K. Watkinson, Mr T. R. Butchard, Mr B. Cahalin, Mr E. I. David, Mr M. H. Gleeson-White, Mr V. Ogilvie, Dr J. A. Mangan, the late Dr Ian Weinberg, Prof. G. F. A. Best, Mr Patrick G. Scott, Mr Peter Laslett, Mr H. Badger, Prof. E. L. Edmonds, Mr F. R. Thompson and Mr D. Hunt. Among products of the Victorian public school whom I was privileged to interview personally were Mr F. B. Malim (then in his nineties) who was a master at Marlborough in 1895 and later head of three leading schools; and an eccentric Cambridge don (Rossall, 1898) who consented in 1969 to be interviewed in the men's cloakroom of Cambridge University Library.

INTRODUCTION

The Irresistible Tides

This book is about what Winston Churchill called the *irresistible tides*[1]—the pressures which together constituted that remarkable phenomenon identified with the Victorian period whereby a whole section of British society began, as a matter of regular custom, to send away its sons to school, often at a tender age (young Churchill was seven), with the result that—as another 'victim' put it—*successive generations passed ten of the most imaginative and impressionable years of their lives under influences other than those of their parents.*[2] The book explores this topic as the background to the story of the development of the institutions which were the recipients or beneficiaries of this strange new traffic—the public schools, which, together with the preparatory schools which grew up to service the first part of the process, emerged or adapted themselves during the century in such a way as to constitute a *system*, an articulated and coherent set of schools serving a common set of social functions.

Because of these functions, the public schools assumed certain characteristics, some of which were related to a highly developed conception of the school as a community. Because they were part of a system or 'community' of schools, they assumed certain other characteristics. Like the Victorian family, on which no definitive study yet exists, there is still a great deal of basic research to be done on the histories of individual schools and, still more, on the thorough study of the historical development of the individual 'working parts' of the 'machinery' of the Victorian public school—the prefect system, the house system, and so on. At one time it looked as though the researches on which this book is based would cover that ground, but it became clear that the emphasis would have instead to be adapted to take note of the shape which was imposed on these institutions by the fact of being part of a 'system'.

Tom Brown's Universe represents, then, not the immediate world of the Victorian public-school boy, but rather the wider firmament whose nature and functions must be analysed before the particular environment of any one school can be understood. This book contains little in the way of general description of the day-to-day lives of Victorian schoolboys, their living conditions, hours of working and sleeping, their studies, recreations, sorrows and hopes, but rather it looks out from the close horizons of individual schools to see what generalisations can be made about the total functioning of the system of which these schools were a part; but it is also true that a great deal of information about 'day-to-day' school life will in fact emerge in the course of this kind of discussion of the system's functions. Though 'Tom Brown', as the imaginative creation of Thomas Hughes, was at one particular school (Rugby) at the very beginning of the Victorian period, he is taken as a representative of the recipients of the kind of schooling which reached its complete development later in the Victorian period: in fact, many of the generalisations made in this book—liable, as are all such statements, to much qualification and exception—derive from the second half of the Victorian period, when the 'system' had become fully established. Similarly, the dividing line between the Victorian and the Edwardian public school is an artificial one, which it has not always been possible to observe rigidly. 'Tom Brown' also happened to be the real name of an important and in some respects representative public-school assistant master,* and since the present writer believes (by contrast with one well-known twentieth-century pundit, Mr C. S. Lewis†) that the qualities of schoolmasters are as important for the character of schools as those of the schoolboys who attend them, much attention is given throughout this book to the aims and achievements of these men, and an entire chapter at the end is devoted to a discussion of aspects of the schoolmaster profession.

*The Rev. T. E. Brown, assistant master and housemaster at Clifton for nearly thirty years until 1892, is now remembered chiefly as a Manx poet.[3]

† "It is difficult for parents (and more difficult, perhaps, for schoolmasters) to realise the unimportance of most masters in the life of a school."[4]

The contemporary English conception of the 'school' is a complex one: in the 1970s it is confused by presuppositions of enormous size and overtones of intractable discipline problems and crises of values and 'standards', which derive from a decade and more of 'comprehensivisation'. Until very recently it was true to say that the overwhelming formative influence upon the English concept of the 'school' was the model furnished by the boys' 'public' boarding-school which grew up in Victorian times; and even as this influence recedes, one only has to look at the house systems, prefect systems and a host of similar institutions and conceptions grafted on to the secondary modern schools of yester-year, and on to Borstals, and now indeed on to comprehensive schools too, to be forced to concede the pervasiveness of this influence. Probably in no country of the world has this conception of the 'school' been so fully and so powerfully developed, to the point of creating an institution of enormous pretensions and self-consciousness, ready to take upon itself tasks in relation not just to the formal schooling but to the whole lives of its pupils. The analysis of this self-consciousness, these pretensions and the 'machinery' through which they operate is a part of what is called, technically, 'the sociology of the school', and this book represents the sort of exercise which results when a historian strays into the territory of the sociologist.

The starting-point in sociological theory was in Durkheim's *L'Education Morale* (1925), where he considered the need for the study of the school as a social entity:

> With the exception of the school, there is no longer in this country [sc. France] any society intermediate between the family and the State . . . Communal life is now impoverished and holds a very secondary place in our consciousness . . . this state of affairs constitutes a serious crisis . . . For morality to have a sound basis the citizen must have an inclination towards collective life . . . it is precisely at this point that the role of the school can be considered. . .

and later,

> Such phrases as *the class*, the *spirit of the class*, and the *honour of the class* must become something more than abstract

> expressions in the pupil's mind . . . when one says of a class that it is good or bad, that it has a good or bad spirit . . . it is the collective individuality that is being judged or qualified. What gives it this character are the conditions under which it is recruited and the extent to which it is morally and intellectually homogeneous.[5]

Durkheim is thus addressing himself not so much to the social origins of pupils as determinants of their attitudes and values (though these of course are important) as to the characteristics of the "collective individuality"—the class or school—of which the pupils become members; and, beyond that, to the role which is allowed to, or expected of, the school alongside such institutions as the family and other educative agencies. It is thus the wider sociological role of the Victorian public school, and the institutions which were devised to help it fulfil that role, which are the subjects of the present study. It begins with a re-examination of the life and work of Thomas Arnold, whose posthumous reputation did so much for the expansion of public schooling in England—the main point of the re-examination being to see how far the very grand idea of the school, with the pretensions (and their consequences for the family) that have been referred to, are identifiable in Arnold's own thought and practice, or in those of his close disciples. We then follow the course of the great expansion of public-school education, again trying to track down the source of this developing concept of the school. In the course of this, two figures are dealt with who are important in the history of Victorian education—one well remembered, the other now almost entirely forgotten. Their contributions to the expansion of public-school provision throw interesting light on the process we are trying to trace. The great mid-Victorian efflorescence of the system is then examined in some detail, and its various functions exposed—or so it is here claimed; and the description of the 'system' is completed by an attempt at a delimitation of it, in terms of the institutions which by the end of the century could authoritatively be said to have belonged to it.

For not entirely arbitrary reasons, this book concerns itself exclusively with *boys'* schools. On the one hand the enormous literature on both boys' and girls' education argued for a demarcation on grounds of manageability of material; on the other hand it can be argued that girls' public schools served different functions—at least in terms of the ends which emerge in the course of this study—from those of boys' schools.

One last point. In writing of ideologies and of the process whereby they are imparted, it is useful to make a distinction between the conscious imparting of values by way of certain institutions or 'machinery' designed for this purpose; and the possibility that values *inhere* (as it were) in the 'machinery' of the process itself. This is a distinction which this book, in its discussion of the development of the institutions and values of the Victorian public school, does not always make clear, and it is one over which its author recognises that he may be at fault.

NOTE: Certain terms used in this book have been standardised: thus, *headmaster* for 'Master', 'High Master', 'Principal', 'Warden', 'Chief Master', etc.; *prefect* for 'monitor', 'praepostor', etc.; *governors* for members of the Board of Directors, the Council, Trustees, etc.

CHAPTER ONE

The conception of the School in Arnold and in the first new Victorian Public Schools

In the first four decades of the nineteenth century the nine English schools which were generally recognised as public schools were the object of fierce attacks among an important section of public opinion.[1] Yet the next forty years were not only a period of survival and indeed prosperity for these schools, but numbers of new schools were founded in imitation of them, and a further number of endowed schools were remodelled in such a way as to resemble the original public schools in many points.

Credit for this recovery and expansion is generally given to Thomas Arnold; and the régime he developed at Rugby was certainly a seminal influence. G. G. Coulton was to describe the Rugby tradition as "probably the greatest educational movement of nineteenth-century Europe".[2] The educational achievements of Thomas Arnold, his underlying conception of the school and the key ingredients of his system must therefore be examined.

Arnold left behind him few specifically educational writings. His reputation was mediated to the Victorians by two extremely influential books: Stanley's *Life* and Hughes's *Tom Brown's Schooldays*, and his twentieth-century reputation had the dubious benefit of further mediation by the portrait of Arnold in Lytton Strachey's *Eminent Victorians*. The picture of Arnold the educationist in Stanley's *Life* reflected both the pupil's exalted degree of hero-worship of his master and the special position Stanley had enjoyed at school, insulated from the harsher realities of general school life such as are only too graphically portrayed in the much more realistic *Tom Brown*, but even here Hughes's account is coloured by his own developed views about the virtues of school life at Rugby as he chose to remember them. Thus, to distil the essence of Arnoldism *pur sang* it is necessary to get behind the 'legend' which these so different disciples helped to propagate, and which was further developed by the work of other headmasters and assistants who could claim to be Arnoldians; though we must also recognise that for us the reality of any connection between the Arnold reality and the Arnold legend is a question suitable for academic discussion, whereas for Victorian society it was the practical results of the legend which mattered.

There is the further difficulty that Arnold's ideas developed gradually, and it is difficult to know whether the later Arnold would have taken responsibility for ideas expressed in an earlier period.[3] Stanley admits that Arnold's system did not "at once attain full maturity" though some aspects of his thought were consolidated by 1834.[4] Arnold himself wrote in 1833 as if he recognised room for fluidity in his ideas.[5] It was said of him that he awoke every morning with the impression that everything was an open question, though Stanley also claimed that as far as his educational system was concerned, this was true only in matters of detail, for his general principles remained fixed.[6] Nevertheless Stanley acknowledged a great change in Arnold's general outlook in his last two years.[7] (Insofar as graphology is any guide at all, the great change in Arnold's handwriting in the letters of those last years[8]—the meticulous and precise hand had become careless and headlong—perhaps absolves Arnold from any entire consistency of outlook and utterance throughout his adult life.)

But the most important reservation we must make about Arnold the educational theorist is that he did not regard himself as primarily, or even essentially, an educationist at all: his major concerns were ecclesiastical, political, and social problems. He was a college Fellow who had originally taken up private tuition—work he considered useful but somewhat beneath him[9]—because he needed money to pay his bills (including the expenses of foreign travel) and in order to get married, in his middle twenties, with no means and several dependent relatives, to a wife who would bring with her no private fortune.[10]

Then, when happily settled at Laleham, money tempted him to apply for the headmastership of Rugby, when he had many doubts about his effectiveness in such a post. Even while at Rugby he continued to hanker after quite different kinds of work—to go abroad (to India or New Zealand) or to return to Oxford, or even to resume private tuition.[11] He narrowly missed appointment to several bishoprics, and even one archbishopric,[12] but refused the Wardenship of the Collegiate Church and College at Manchester—"a situation", as his wife wrote, "with two thousand pounds a year and no long residence requisite"—partly because of the big drop in salary it would have involved.[13]

Arnold's view of the school as a community can only be seen, then, in the context of a man who happened to find himself in charge of a public school which presented an opportunity[14] to try out in a practical form views about the nature of society in general and about the means whereby it was to be Christianised.

For Arnold, society was pervaded by sin. In England he felt surrounded by a "mass of evil" a thousand times worse than "all the idolatry of India".[15] In contrast to personal successes in 1840 the state of society "pierced through all [his] private happiness" and "haunted him daily like a personal calamity", and the general prevalence of sin and suffering in the world made the reading of newspapers almost unbearable to him.[16]

His own boyhood radicalism gave way to a cautious liberalism which saw law and religion as the "great sanctions and securities" of a society which was at best half-Christian, though he saw a general social reform as urgent in 1830 and the improvement of the physical condition of the people as a vital precondition of their being educated.[17]

In 1832 he demanded a degree of reform which would be "deep, searching, and universal"; it must "extend to church and state, to army, navy, law, trade and education; to our political and social institutions; to our habits, principles and practice both as citizens and men". His fire was trained on the aristocracy—landed and moneyed—but the whole of the upper class, in fact "the whole class of gentlemen", had failed to do their duty to the poor, and only "a reform in the ways and manners of every parish" could cure it. Yet, as he recognised five years later, the popular revolution he feared was averted by the comparative security offered by stable government and an aristocracy which was not so flagrantly corrupt that it did not know how to come to terms in some degree with the people. His aim was not to overturn an aristocracy of birth, which he deeply admired, but to force it to justify its power by competing with the middle classes whose rival exertions would "fully excite" the higher classes " to their great and honourable duty".[18]

The problem for Arnold was that the competition between the upper and the middle classes, and the condition of the masses, all threw into relief the problem of the diversity of values in society, which was further reflected in religious divisions. How was society to be penetrated with the right values so that these moral and social evils could be overcome? One method was propaganda: he wanted journals like the *Quarterly Review* to be "disciplined to a uniformly Christian spirit",[19] and he later started a political journal of his own[20] to achieve political reform through

> moral and intellectual Reform, which would be sure to work out political reform in the best way, and my writing on politics will have for its end not the forwarding of any political measure, but the so purifying, enlightening, sobering and in one word *Christianising* men's notions and feelings on political matters, that from the improved tree may come hereafter a better fruit.[21]

But his main plan for purifying social and political institutions according to the Gospel pattern, and establishing the Kingdom of God in England, was a reform of the Church. Its main principle was a re-assertion in some form of the identity of Church and State by an accommodation of dissenters and by a number of changes such as the revival of the order of Deacons, the revival of daily church services, frequent communions, a modified form of religious orders, and so forth.[22]

Arnold's ideas on Church reform involved him in great controversy and at least temporarily embarrassed his ecclesiastical career, though their opponents, especially High Churchmen, reassured themselves that such undesirable schemes would be defeated by their impracticality. They ridiculed Arnold's idea of a "Christianised state" as "Lambeth and Downing Street in one":

> The sum of his cravings, in short, was to unconsecrate or secularise the priest, and make him a mere government functionary . . .; his fusion of all sects was simply a dream about a religious democracy. By what magic he was to bring Churchmen and the followers of Irving, whom he expressly condemns, or Quakers, or Mormonists together under one roof he has perhaps never considered in detail.

This critic, writing after Arnold's death, went on to accuse Arnold of having theorised on the narrowest premises, and rejoiced that he had had "no power to *act* mischievously, but died, happily for his fame, ruling over boys".[23]

Nevertheless, Arnold's view of the Church and the Christianised community is important for a consideration of his educational ideas, since Stanley specifically tells us that it lay behind his teaching and government of Rugby School;[24] and it is in that sphere where his "power to act mischievously" had practical scope.

Stanley tells us that Arnold himself recognised the analogy between the ideals of the Christian school and those of the Christian state, and that he accepted that the school was an acceptable sphere of action for a man fit to be a statesman. Yet to turn this 'great empire' which he governed into a Christian community required a great contest with evil.[25] If sin and evil were generalised terms Arnold used to describe the unreformed condition of unchristianised society, so in his dealings with his pupils he used these terms partly to indicate individual defects and partly to refer to unredeemed aspects of boy-society in general.

Normally Arnold uses (in a school context) the terms *sin*, *evil* and *vice* in a generalised sense—and with such emphasis and frequency that his daughter Jane in re-publishing his sermons in 1878 felt constrained to apologise for him;[26] but in his sermon on "Christian Schools" he specified[27] the forms of "actual evil which may exist in a school" as direct sensual wickedness (especially drunkenness), systematic lying and cruelty, active disobedience, general idleness, and a spirit of evil combination.[28] (This was the famous sermon in which he discussed and accepted the charge that the public schools were "the very seats and nurseries of vice".) It is clear that Arnold regarded most of these as communal rather than private vices—lying, for example, in the sense of a conspiracy to deceive the masters; and cruelty, in its form of bullying (persecution in which a section of the boy-community acquiesced).

Active disobedience, idleness, and evil combination are symptoms of the powerless disciplinary condition of public schools in the late eighteenth century and onwards, for just as one of Arnold's great fears for society at large was a proletarian upheaval, public-school headmasters of that period lived and worked under the threat of rebellion. The late eighteenth and early nineteenth centuries had been a period of recurrent and very serious disorders at Rugby, Harrow and Eton: at the latter school rebellions had been so common as to have provoked George III to tease Eton boys on the subject,[29] and Gladstone's elder brother had twice narrowly escaped expulsion for his part in rebellions in 1818 and 1819.[30] The troubles of the headmaster, Keate, continued, and he faced another rebellion in 1832—within Arnold's own time at Rugby. Arnold's own old school, Winchester, had seen disorders in 1770, 1774, 1778 and 1793; in the decade after Arnold left, the prefects led a rebellion against Dr Gabell in 1818 in which the boys took over part of the school, barricaded themselves in for twenty-four hours and withstood a summons by a magistrate attended by the constabulary. Only after the militia had been called out did the boys surrender, and a number of prefects and other participants were expelled.[31]

Mass flogging, for which Dr Keate at Eton was notorious, was, with expulsion, the only weapon against the 'spirit of evil combination' bred by a system in which disaffection was a natural reaction to a solidly classical curriculum which had no appeal to the majority of boys, an absence of organised recreation, and the expectation of hostility between boys and masters, who, frequently derided for their lower social class origins, were regarded by their pupils as spies.

Arnold could readily see, as an extension of Aristotelian principle, that "a society formed exclusively of boys, that is of elements each separately weak and imperfect, becomes more than an aggregate of their several defects; the amount of evil in the mass is greater than the sum of evil in the individuals". But if the 'distinct society' of the boarding public school provided enormous opportunities for evil, so might it also provide opportunities for good; and though Arnold felt that the amount of good must be less in the mass than in individuals, nevertheless reform though difficult,[32] must be attempted.

He conceived of the process of reforming or Christianising a school and its pupils in the same terms as he did the process of "purifying, enlightening, sobering and in one word *Christianising*" them in political matters, only here he used the anglicised Greek work 'sophronise' which could be translated as *purifying* or *sobering*.[33]

The historian David Newsome summarises the five key points of Arnold's educational methods as (1) the assertion of the headmaster's independence from the governors in matters of school routine and discipline; (2) his concept of the status and pastoral role (within the school) of the assistant masters; (3) his emphasis, in various ways, on the corporate identity of the school; (4) his ruthless policy of removing unsuitable pupils; and (5) his transformed use of the prefect system.[34]

All of these can be accepted as important elements of Arnold's system, though Arnold's conception of the corporate identity of the school—his view of the school as a community—needs some qualification; and there were other elements, some of which may have been no less important than those specified.

One essential element of Arnold's method was symbolised by his assumption of the chaplaincy in 1831. Previously the roles of headmaster and chaplain had been distinct at Rugby, as at other public schools. Their union under Arnold was to establish one of the key institutions by which the Victorian public school aimed to impart its distinctive set of values, by means of the chapel sermon and by preparation for confirmation.

Another feature was the new spirit which infused Arnold's conservative curriculum. Arnold introduced no new subjects, certainly not science—in fact he effectively deprived his pupils of access to what little science teaching had been made available by visiting lecturers in previous years. His reason seems to have been his inability to conceive of science being taught for its moral content—at least this was impossible unless it was to become a major subject in the curriculum at the expense of subjects which Arnold regarded as more central. Lytton Strachey, in a famous passage,[35] made great sport with Arnold's conviction about the special value of the Latin and Greek languages in forming the human mind in youth. This was certainly providential and convenient for Arnold the teacher, said Strachey; otherwise "Dr Arnold, who had spent his life in acquiring those languages, might have discovered that he had acquired them in vain". But in fact Arnold was not convinced of the exclusive value of the classics, and he certainly considered the possibility of an alternative pabulum for the less academic pupil. Lord Denbigh, one of the Rugby trustees, wrote for his advice about a private school at Cheam run on strict evangelical lines by a disciple of Pestalozzi, Dr Mayo—a school of which Arnold knew little at that time, though Mayo thought highly of Arnold and made his death the subject of a special sermon at the school prayers in 1842.[36]

In a letter, as yet unpublished, Arnold replied:

> With regard to the other subject on which you have done me the honour to ask my opinion I am afraid that I am not enough acquainted with the details of Dr Mayo's school to form a judgement of its merits. I suppose that he does not carry Pestalozzi's system to its full extent, for if I mistake not, the pupils there were actually taught various kinds of manual labour, which I should think would hardly do for the state of society in England. But I am certainly of the opinion that a more enlarged system than that which generally prevails in our schools is highly desirable for the generality of boys, possessing only ordinary abilities. I think if my own children gave promise of considerable power, and of a fondness for reading, I should send them to a good classical school, because to such minds the classical seems to me to afford the best possible discipline, whilst their own natural vigour, and curiosity, which is merely the appetite of a healthy understanding, would lead them to seek for varied information of other kinds, which is in itself more effective than the study of language. But if my boys were of ordinary talents, with no marked fondness for reading, or in other words with a feeble intellectual appetite, then I should think that another kind of treatment was best for them; that a weak curiosity should be

> stimulated by a more agreeable knowledge, and that while the mind was incapable of receiving the benefits of a classical education, precious time and opportunities would be wasted by obstinately forcing upon light soil a crop which requires the strongest and richest. This seems to me the principle on which the classical system is unfitted for general use; but unless there be any great economy of time and very able superintendence, boys cannot be expected to make the same progress in classical knowledge where their attention is partly given to other things as where *that* is the most exclusive study. And consequently when going to a public school where classical knowledge is the test of merit, they will appear to a disadvantage; although they may really be better educated than boys who are considered their superiors. The fact is that the public schools necessarily influence the system followed at private ones, and are themselves influenced by the universities, and with these last therefore the reform should properly begin, as they will act downwards even upon the smallest schools in the kingdom. But till this reform does take place, the question seems to be, how far other things can be taught at preparatory school without putting a boy to a disadvantage when he goes to a public school. I am satisfied that with able management the two things are not incompatible; and then the advantage of such a plan is manifest. But I have no means of judging how far Dr Mayo does combine good classical instruction with other matters, and that is a point on which his usefulness under present circumstances must I think mainly depend.[37]

His principle, therefore, would seem to be that so long as universities required a classical curriculum of the schools, it behoved classical schools like Rugby to pursue that curriculum single-mindedly; but less academic pupils ought to have separate schools where a non-classical curriculum should not deter them from higher education. Personally, like so many of the Victorian intellectuals after him, Arnold was deeply convinced of the pre-eminence of classical study as a vehicle of culture. He was genuinely distressed, on meeting a nonconformist lawyer who was with Wordsworth, to note that a man who had acquired an admirable philosophical and literary education through long residence in Germany still showed

> the original defects of his education; for instance, his want of Greek, which a dissenting school fifty years ago was in no position to give. I could not have had a better instance of the mischief done by driving dissenters to separate places of education which must always be second rate, than by observing the effects of such a system on an acute and active mind. . .[38]

If Arnold helped to perpetuate the predominance of classics in the Victorian public school, his view of these subjects as vehicles for moral ideas was an innovation. "He was the first Englishman who drew attention in our public schools to the historical, political and philosophical value of philology and of the ancient writers, as distinguished from the mere verbal criticism and elegant scholarship of the last century".[39] Yet the degree of his disgust for moral evil, which he could hope to provoke by "the black cloud of indignation which passed over his face when speaking of the crimes of Napoleon, or of Caesar, and the pause which followed, as if the acts had been committed in his very presence", was most obviously a function of his own personality and was the most impermanent feature of his system. Not all of his disciples had the same conception of the use of classical studies, nor had indeed the degree of earnestness of manner which could convey such lessons indirectly. For the vast majority of pupils in public schools in the nineteenth century, and even for most of Arnold's own Rugby pupils, classics were a dull linguistic grind.

How far Arnold saw the school as a corporate unit with its own special character capable of imparting the desired values by its generalised influence, is very difficult to assess. It is true that Arnold used to regard Rugby as "a little commonwealth", and exerted himself to procure for the school some form of honour "analogous to a peerage".[40] But his system was heavily dependent on the personal qualities of individuals—masters, prefects, above all the headmaster himself—and Stanley admitted that "the separate existence of the school" was almost merged in him; Arnold spoke of Rugby as 'our great self'.[41]

In his masters, Arnold required qualities of first-class intellect and wide culture—sustained by reading and foreign travel—liveliness of spirit, and liking for boys.[42] His ban on their combining their post with a curacy[43] in the locality emphasised their pastoral role within the school, which was given further scope by the process of abolishing Dames' houses, which had flourished in this town since the 1740s, and putting them in the charge of assistant masters—four of them were thus transferred in 1831.[44] Stanley suggests that Arnold regarded every house as "an epitome of the whole school", but it is clear that his original aim was partly by means of the profits of boarding to increase the salaries needed to recruit masters of a calibre he required, and partly to extend the degree to which the boys could be "sophronised" by increasing the hours of contact between boys and masters. Only by such means could he hope to rival the evil effects of spontaneous associations among the boys themselves—the knot of "vicious and careless" boys around the schoolhouse fire, among whom he imagined he could see the Devil himself.[45]

Prefects were the keystone of his whole system: not a set of officials, as they had tended to be at Winchester, nor as in some schools a group who represented simply the institutionalisation of the tyranny of the big and the strong over the small and the weak, but the headmaster's moral agents, his fellow-workers in the task of infusing superior elements into the society of boys.[46] But despite the stated priority, among the ideals Arnold sought to impress upon his pupils, of "1st, religious and moral principle, 2ly, gentlemanly conduct, 3rdly, intellectual ability",[47] in fact Arnold's pupils were chosen primarily by intellectual criteria—by vesting the privileges and responsibilities of power in the "highest class or classes"—the select group of thirty boys who constituted the Rugby Sixth. Arnold justified the selection of this group as being "probably . . . at once the oldest and the strongest and the cleverest".[48] Victorian public-school headmasters—even professed Arnoldians—were to surrender the priority of intellect, as a qualification to rule, in favour of more obvious qualities of leadership, especially games ability.

The rationale of Arnold's selection later worried H. H. Almond, who by methods which placed a strong emphasis on muscularity was to transform a Scottish private school, Loretto, on public-school lines. In 1900 Almond wrote:

> I do not perceive how anyone can read Arnold's letters and not see how his great spirit was mysteriously cut off in the early spring of his reforming work. Many have said since that they were "imitating Arnold" when they were stuck fast on the last step of his arrested progress . . . Can we doubt that if Arnold had lived . . . he would have discovered the folly of choosing school officers solely by intellectual attainment.[49]

But in fact Arnold had early discovered some impracticalities in that policy. In a letter to his brother-in-law in 1839—which his biographer, if indeed he ever saw it, understandably did not print in the *Life*—Arnold wrote of the state of evil at Rugby and of the difficulty of ensuring "a combination of leading qualities for good among the principal boys such as I suppose the average of human nature forbids us to hope for often". Among his sixth form were two such good and able boys, but they lacked the physical qualities which ensure a practical influence for good:

> Never were there at Rugby better or more noble-minded boys than the two Walronds: but they want the two qualities without which goodness amongst boys does but provoke the hatred of evil, without having the power to quell it: they have not the high ability which in Stanley's case made up even in the boys' notions for his diminutive size—and they are unhappily scarcely five feet six in height, and are not strong. One smiles at this climax [but] it is really a very serious evil in practice.[50]

Already by 1837 Arnold had amended his system to the extent that where a boarding-house contained no member of the Sixth, the headmaster formally invested the highest boys in that house with power as prefects.[51] A boy who entered the school in Arnold's last year was later invested with the privileges of the Sixth for an act of bravery.[52]

Arnold's system placed an enormous emphasis on the role of the headmaster, both within and outside the immediate community of the school, and invested this role with a *charisma* which has deeply affected the English notion of the school (and the headmaster) down to the present day. His own effectiveness in the pulpit was attested by many witnesses, and even in their published form his sermons enjoyed a wide influence. Years before Stanley had ensured Arnold's special fame, the young Gladstone had developed the habit of reading Arnold's sermons aloud,[53] and they were later a favourite of Queen Victoria.

Arnold was a gifted, if awe-inspiring, teacher, who exercised a formative intellectual influence on the small proportion of the Rugby pupils who reached the Sixth. There, the ablest ones might notice that as a scholar he was, though good, not of the first rank; at least one of his assistant masters, J. Prince Lee, was regarded as his superior in that respect.[54] We have the reported opinion (in 1855) of Halford Vaughan, who was Head of School in Arnold's first year and who later sat on the Clarendon Commission, for whose report he wrote the section on Rugby. Halford Vaughan

> seems to have felt very strongly the influence of [Arnold's] earnest, excellent character and the change from the routine and formality of the former master and the vital spirit Dr Arnold waked up: but he thinks he was not a first-rate scholar, though very frank about his own deficiences, so that they never did him any harm with the boys; and as to his efforts where we should think them most essential, Mr Vaughan merely says that he does not see that Dr Arnold's system has produced finer characters than that which went before.[55]

For the average Rugby boy, as he would not reach the sixth form, his only classroom contact with Arnold would be as examiner, fulfilling with sometimes terrifying effectiveness a function which has been lost by the post-Victorian English headmaster, with the broadening of the curriculum and the growth of external examinations. Whether teaching the Sixth or in examining the lower forms, Arnold's control of the academic standards of the school was personal and decisive.

The circumstances of his position at Rugby, in particular the nature of his governing body, gave him a degree of independence vital to a reformer but denied to, for example, the headmaster of Winchester, whose hands were tied by his subordinate position to the Warden and Fellows.[56] Stanley tells us that

Arnold from the first maintained that in the actual working of the school he must be completely independent. The wide scope of the freedom which he regarded as the prerogative of the headmaster "of every endowed school in England" is illustrated by Stanley's publication of Arnold's proud letter of refusal to hold himself answerable in 1836 to one of the school's Trustees, Lord Howe, for his political writings.[57] Stanley does not print the letter,[58] of whose existence he was probably unaware, in which Arnold in 1832 had promptly and in great detail answered a similar enquiry from another trustee, Lord Denbigh. Since that time, however, Arnold had begun to feel his strength. As he wrote from Rugby in 1834, "I have happily more power than Lord Grey's Government".[59] The degree of independence, including freedom to engage in political and religious controversy, which he was in the long run to assert, nearly brought about his dismissal in 1836, but his ultimate vindication of this position helped to establish the principle that a public-school headmaster's fame—or even notoriety—outside the school world might contribute to the prosperity of his school.

The operation of three of Arnold's educational principles helped to foster an idea of a school community. We may call them *emulation*, *identification*, and *consolidation*. Emulation, especially in the sense of competition as a motive for academic achievement, was a fairly novel feature in an educational period in which serious examinations for honours had only lately been introduced at the universities. Only in 1829 had the Newcastle Scholarships been founded at Eton to give a far greater impetus to learning than the sixth form's weekly exercises had done.[60]

Arnold saw the need to encourage the boys to realise the importance of success in competitive examinations:

> What was accounted great learning some years ago is no longer reckoned such; what was in the days of our fathers only an ordinary and excusable ignorance is esteemed as something disgraceful now. In these things, as in all others, never was competition so active—never were such great exertions needed to gain success. Those who are in the world know this already; and if there are any of you who do not know it, it is fit that you should be made aware of it. Every profession, every institution in the country, will be strung up

to a higher tone; examinations will be more and more searching; the qualifications for every public honourable officer will be raised more and more. All this *will* be certainly; and no human power can stop it; and I think also, that it ought to be.[61]

Thus Arnold from the pulpit in 1831 saw the evolution of competition as one of the organising principles of English education, and indeed of English society, in the Victorian period; and his appraisal was echoed in the attitude to emulation of his more thoughtful pupils.[62]*

Even if he recognised that the cultivation of brilliance was not the chief aim of education, Arnold delighted in the university honours gained by his pupils, and the triumph of one of them in the Balliol scholarship earned public thanks for its effect on the honour of the school. The excellence of the same pupil's verses for a school poetry prize was made the occasion for a half holiday, and his beating an Etonian in the Scholarship examination made him a school hero.[64]

Arnold attempted to consolidate Rugby school in terms of ability, age and social class, as though it was only in a relatively homogeneous community that his ideals could possibly be put across effectively. The curriculum was designed, as we have seen, for the able boy, and boys that showed signs that they could not benefit from it were ruthlessly superannuated. Dr T. W. Bamford has shown[65] how Arnold systematically sabotaged the Lower School, the junior department of Rugby school and the sole means whereby the local boys—the category for whom the school was mainly founded—could hope to enter the main school. This can be seen as a device by which Arnold, who thought that no boy should be in a public school before he was twelve and thus encouraged the development of preparatory schools,[66] could limit the age range of his school community. If Arnold's treatment of the Lower School effectively deterred some boys of the lower classes, e.g. sons of tradesmen, from entering Rugby, he also discouraged the aristocracy—their sons, too, were "almost impossible to sophronise".[67]

*Including, of course, the poet Clough, with his well-known lines:
"Thou shalt not covet, but tradition
Approves all forms of competition."[63]

In a charming letter to her sister in 1839, Mrs Arnold described how her husband had dealt with the Duchess of Sutherland, who in the course of a visit to nearby Leamington had sent a note to make the acquaintance of Dr Arnold and to hear him preach:

> I believe I did not tell you in the summer, but through Lady Hall my husband was asked his opinion of the Duchess's son's coming here, which she was induced to wish by her acquaintance with him through his sermons. He very earnestly advised *not*, and that he should rather go to Eton, where he would meet with others of his own rank, while here he would certainly be considered as being of a rank so different from the sons of gentlemen of moderate fortune, who formed the mass of our boys. His letter entered fully into the subject, and I suppose from the present visit, she did not the less wish to make his acquaintance. It is not exactly that I should choose to receive Duchesses, but I cannot but be pleased at such a tribute to my husband, and, as to the proprieties, I rest very content with the feeling that I can be as attentive as I can whether it is to a Duchess or to a *Mrs.*[68]

The principle of *identification* underlay Arnold's choice of assistant masters, for he recognised the extent to which a master's effectiveness was related to the way a boy identified with and modelled himself on the master.[69] This was *a fortiori* the case in the relations between headmaster and pupil. After his first encounter with Arnold in the sixth form Stanley wrote home, "He is certainly a splendid man. I feel as if he could magnetise one directly".[70] If many boys did leave school without having any personal contact with him, Arnold maintained his contacts with many of the able boys of the Sixth after they had left school, and on them continued to exercise an influence, which was in some cases so strong "that they would have been willing to die for his sake".[71] The role of the headmaster as referent in the lives of his pupils and Old Boys was to be a continuing feature of the Victorian public school.

The relationship between the school and the family, as conceived by Arnold, and the character and roles he would have ascribed to each, are difficult to define.

As an illustration, in October 1835 the second number of the school's *Rugby Magazine* appeared, containing an anonymous article (in fact by A. P. Stanley) entitled "School a Little World", which posed and answered the question as to the meaning of that phrase:

> It is meant that as instruction is or ought to be a part only and not the whole of education, so the idea of a school, much more of a public school containing two or three hundred boys, implies not only a place where boys are receiving knowledge from masters, but a place also where they form a complete society among themselves—a society in its essential points similar, and therefore preparatory, to the society of men.

What then, the author asks, is a world? In a sense, he suggests, it is a series of ever-widening circles—"from the first home of childhood to the highest conceivable range of future glory, or the lowest conceivable range of future misery". The world of school is, next to the home, the innermost of these successive spheres.

> It remains, therefore, for us, by entering more into details, to show that this is not a vague fancy, but a substantial reality; that when we enter upon, and contemplate, this our world with its inhabitants, it is at once felt that it is for a time our country and commonwealth, of which each member of the school is a citizen and in which, as we have often thought, all the chief workings of society might be advantageously viewed as in the Kingdoms of Lilliput or Laputa or in the truer mirror of ancient history . . .

Emphasising that "we speak of the boys in relation to themselves only, and not to the masters", he goes on to "touch on those points in which all schools of size and antiquity have at least a semblance of history and therefore a portion of the outward pomp and circumstance of a state". Through its founder, the Elizabethan grocer Lawrence Sheriff, "whose confections may have touched the lips of Cecil, and whose sugar sweetened the possets of Leicester", the present generation of the school is connected with past ages. Furthermore,

> We have, in the most perfect degree, that visible representation of all the functions of a state, which Greece exhibited in those altar hearths which burnt in every Prytaneum—the schoolhouse, the chapel, and the playground, forming as they do one united group, become a tangible focus, in which the whole of our school existence is, as it were, symbolically consecrated.

The school's history has for the writer all the authentic characteristics of a state's, including even revolutions. "We have to tell of those intellectual and physical contests—those public festivals, which in the interest excited by them through the whole community might fairly vie with the Dionysiac or the Olympic Games of Greece". The school has a constitution and laws; further,

> . . . we have various gradations of rank, of power, of responsibility; we have the connection of patron and client, as well as the broad distinction of patrician and plebeian: we have changes of administration—effected, indeed, more by the natural decease of its members every year than by any pressure from without or schisms from within—but still changes, of which every member of the society is more or less conscious: we have contending parties on whose points of difference we do not further touch, for the party-politics of school are subjects as dangerous in a magazine as the party politics of England. . .

Finally, the school community even has its legislative and judicial assemblies, and forms of taxation: even "in troublous times . . . National Conventions, and Committees of Public Safety".

> This may sound exaggerated to those who have forgotten their school-lives; but we appeal to our school-fellows and those who have examined the subject whether all that they feel and know . . . of our Speeches, of our cricket and football matches, of our occasional rows, of our system of fagging and shirking, and of the various privileges of different forms, of praepostors and sixth-form levies—together with the minor arrangements of subscriptions and of protégés, does not bear out all that has been said.[72]

This society of boyhood, the schoolboy author goes on, will of necessity be analogous to the society of men whose moral and intellectual character is not fully cultivated—whose nation is at its earliest stages—"the stages, namely, of barbarism". The analogy between the state of boyhood and the childhood of the human race was a favourite theme of Arnold himself.[73] The young Stanley enlarged on the similarities between the society of school and earlier stages of civilisation: the predominance in both "of feeling over reason, a respect paid to physical rather than intellectual excellence", superstition, "a rudeness and heartiness of intercourse", and so on. "Can any one," he asks, "read accounts of the feudal ages without being reminded of scenes at school . . . ? What is the [schoolboy moral] code but the very image of the system which once bound together the aristocracy of Christendom".[74]

In a striking passage Stanley indicates his belief in the power of the school's set of values, which he calls 'school patriotism', to work for good; for it is open to every boy in the school to influence those values for good:

> In no subsequent period [*i.e.* of his life] has an individual such power of benefiting those around about him, or himself; in no other place are the good and the evil so little mixed up with secondary considerations and counter-balancing circumstances: and (looking upon the school only under the aspect now in question, viz. as preparatory for manhood) from no other place or time may such important results be expected.

Yet school is only a *little* world, though connected with "the greater one which follows it" in various ways, such as "the communion between those who go and those who are left". But if, on the one hand, this is merely a world of boys—boys at school, "so on the other hand we must bear in mind that we form a complete social body—a society not only of scholars but of human beings—not only of individuals but of citizens—a society in which, by the nature of the case, we must not only learn, but act and live; and act and live not only as boys, but as boys who will be men".[75]

This article enunciated what was, in the climate of opinion about public-school education in the 1830s, a quite novel idea of the school: a boy republic—distinct from the family—which, independently even of master influence,[76] nevertheless contained in its own institutions, and above all in the influence of individual boys, the power to promote the desired values. How far did this reflect Arnold's own view?

A quarter of a century after Stanley's article appeared, the headmaster's son Matthew corresponded with Stephen Hawtrey, an enterprising mathematical master at Eton who had in the 1840s started, on the side, a small private school, St Mark's, at Windsor. Although originally started for "boys of humble condition in life", St Mark's was to develop by the end of the century into a small boarding-school on public-school lines. Hawtrey's principle was to promote, on the analogy of the family, personal contact between "human living souls"—the fraternal relationship between boys, the filial relationship between boy and masters.[77] In support of his proposition "that the family is the type of the school" Hawtrey would cite Stanley's commentary on the Epistle to the Corinthians:

> Sympathy is the secret of power. No artificial self-adaptation, no merely official or pastoral relation, has an influence equal to that produced by the consciousness of a human personal affection in the mind of a teacher towards his scholars, of a general towards his soldiers, of an apostle towards his converts.[78]

He also named Dr Arnold as his authority for this analogy. Writing to Hawtrey in 1863, Matthew Arnold disagreed:

> It seems to me that you lay too much stress on the family and parental relation in school life. It does not seem to me, I confess, that it is through this relation that Eton is strongest, nor do I think that it conveys my father's real mind to say that the type of the family was the ideal type for the public school to follow. "School a little *world*" would have been more his notion, and I remember a paper with this title, and working over the notion, by Arthur Stanley in the old *Rugby Magazine* years ago which my father used to read and speak of with peculiar approbation.

Matthew Arnold went on to develop his own application to mid-Victorian society of the idea which his father had applauded:

> It seems to me that the public school has a different aim to follow at present according to the class which frequents it; to the upper class it has to teach (besides mere book-learning) the notion of a sort of republican fellowship, plain life in common, and self help; to the middle class, largeness of soul and personal dignity; to the lower class, humanity, feeling, and gentleness. No doubt it will best teach its aim with this class by presenting as nearly as possible the type of the family, and your labours at St Mark's have been so excellent and fruitful because you have applied your idea just in the right place for it.[79]

Matthew was to reproduce part of this letter—perhaps that is why a copy of it was preserved among the Arnold family papers—in his essay "A French Eton", published a year later. In this he elaborated his list of the respective qualities which a school could appropriately induce in the sons of the various classes. He further added a word of qualification to his support of Hawtrey's idea that in a school of the humbler orders the imitation of family relationships could compensate these children for the lack of tenderness in their own homes: this principle "must not be used too absolutely or too long", otherwise "the energy and manliness, which he values as much as anyone, run perhaps some little risk of etiolating".[80]

Which of these models was more authentically Thomas Arnold's—that of the school as some kind of alternative family, which by imitating certain family relationships, strives (against the greater difficulties inherent in an aggregation of wicked boyhood) to reproduce the values generated by the best kind of family life? Or that of a kind of a republican community which has important compensatory functions—such as the fostering of necessary social values which the family itself is not adequate to engender?

Thomas Arnold was himself a family man. He was at his warmest and most human when relaxing within the bosom of his family. In a sense he regarded the boarding-house of which he had charge as an extension of his family. Constantly he held up before his pupils the ideals of family and home in contrast to those of the institution which had power to corrupt new boys "within one short month", though he admitted that boys could bring with them evil as well as good from home.[81] From the pulpit he deplored "the effects of the public schools of England to weaken the connection between parent and child" and the boys' tendency to "feel ashamed of indulging [their] natural affections, and particularly of being attached to their mothers and sisters and fond of their society".[82] If he saw his own function, and that of his assistants, as that of being *in loco parentis*, he did not consciously set up the teacher as a rival to the parent, though he recognised that there might be areas in which the teacher's judgement was superior to that of the parent.[83]

Yet Arnold never had any confidence in public-school education. Advising Sir Thomas Pasley in 1835 as between public and private schools, he strongly deprecated private schools of over thirty pupils: "The choice lies between public schools, and an education whose character may be strictly private and domestic".[84] But four years later he was doubtful of the viability of that first alternative when the mass of evil frustrated the masters' efforts. Writing to his brother-in-law, a country parson, he pointed out:

> one difference as it seems to me between your position and mine . . . if your parish goes on ill, there is nothing to be done but to do your best towards mending it, and work on, leaving the rest to God; because there must be parishes and people in them to the end of the world. But our English system of public school education has no such necessity; it is almost peculiar to England, and even here other systems are succeeding to it daily. I have believed, and do believe, that in a good state it is the best possible education; but if bad, I think it the worst. Now if its good state is only a happy accident, requiring a combination of circumstances which occur only rarely, and if its bad state be the rule, as I confess my experience at Rugby seems to show to me, then I think that the system is mischievous, and I should be unwilling to labour on in the hope merely of mitigating the evils which need not exist at all. When I say that the bad state is the rule, I mean that no possible care of the master in our present system can hinder a spirit of low principle from prevailing in a school and from yearly corrupting a number of new boys who come comparatively innocent, unless there be a com-

> bination of leading qualities for good among the principal boys, such as I suppose the average of human nature forbids us to hope for often.[85]

In an earlier letter addressed to his brother-in-law, intended to be opened after his own death, Arnold set out his intentions for the education of his own sons. If he lived, the boys should go to Harrow under his friend Longley: "If I die the best thing would be for Mary to settle somewhere where they could go to school as day-boys, and be under her care at other times. I am a coward now about trusting them to a public school, much more so, if I were gone".[86] In the event he "with trembling"[87] sent the four boys to public schools, finally to be under him at Rugby.

Arnold's ambivalent attitude towards public schools arose from his conviction about the essentially sinful state of boyhood, his conviction that school life presented a valuable testing ground for character, and his lack of confidence that the public school possessed the machinery to ensure the triumph of virtue. Membership of some kind of community he thought essential as a check on vice;[88] he was

> inclined to think that the trials of a school are useful to a boy's after character, and thus I dread not to expose my boys to it; while on the other hand the immediate effect of it is so ugly, that, like washing one's hands with earth, one shrinks from dirtying them so grievously in the first stage of the process.[89]

But how to ensure that in that evil state, good had a chance to triumph over evil? It might seem he had as much confidence in the "call of God"[90] as he had in any "machinery" or in the "happy accident" of there being enough boys of the right character to influence school opinion in the required direction. It helped if one could find a device which would hasten the transition from boyhood to manhood; this, in fact, was one of the aims of the prefect system, and the responsibilities, which Arnold invested formally in the Sixth, he expected God to exact informally from other older and influential boys below the Sixth.[91] He watched, anxiously, for the signs of such a transition in his own sons, and Mrs Arnold shared his misgivings at their delay in manifesting themselves:

> This is our dear Matt's birthday. The present holidays will show us whether there is really any more manliness of character and thoughtfulness than there has been. At sixteen it seems time that there should be more than increased bodily stature. May God bless him and keep him and make him His . . .[92]

Arnold's view of his success in penetrating the evil state of boyhood at Rugby fluctuated considerably; in general, he seemed to expect as little success in this as he expected from any attempt to enlighten and uplift the lower orders of society. How successful, in fact, was Arnold educationally in his own time?

Stanley's biography, written "in a glow of repressed enthusiasm" lest his style should be carried away by his own hero-worship of Arnold, gave a picture of Arnold's effectiveness at Rugby which, as had been indicated, was conditioned by the biographer's own special position in the school, protected by his ability and idiosyncrasies from the rough-and-tumble of school life.[93]

The picture in *Tom Brown's Schooldays* (1857) was much more recognisable to the majority of Arnold's pupils. It showed scenes of bullying, tossing, drinking, "roasting" of fags, ridicule of boys at prayer at their bedsides in the dormitory; the petting and pampering of pretty little boys "by some of the big fellows who wrote their verses for them, taught them to drink and use bad language, did all they could to spoil them for everything in this world and the next".[94] We also see evidence of the supposition that it is ethical to lie to a master but not to a fellow pupil. There is plenty of further evidence from other sources that discipline under Arnold was precarious and the authority of his prefects fragile.[95] Nevertheless, Arnold does seem to have had considerable success in establishing a new relationship of trust between masters and boys, especially senior boys, and this helped to perpetuate in English schools in the nineteenth century the popular distinction between the terms 'public' and 'private' school as indicating the difference between schools in which pupils were trusted to govern themselves through a hierarchy of prefects and fags, and schools in which discipline was maintained only by the constant supervision of masters.[96]

"The spirit of combination", "active disobedience",

"general idleness"—those aspects of generalised evil against which Arnold constantly thundered from the pulpit, and which represented his basic concern for disciplinary security—were successfully contained, in the sense that no serious upheavals took place during his reign. The reported prevalence of drunkenness justified his repeated reference to this example of "profligacy"[97]—one of the few 'vices' that he ever specified, but one "so degrading and so fatal".[98] (For much of the nineteenth century, and in some schools even after 1900, beer was provided for the boys at meal-times, as being less noxious than impure drinking water. In some cases, schools brewed their own supply, generally a rather weak form, and commonly known as 'swipes'; until stricter discipline became enforceable after mid-century, this was supplemented from various unofficial sources by stronger forms of drink.) If it is true that sexual "sins" were common, the boys received little guidance from the pulpit, for apart from a few passing references to purity or impurity there was none of the harping on sexuality which characterised the sermons of later Victorian headmasters. Boys who thought they knew what Arnold meant by unspecified references to "evil thoughts and desires" which "rise constantly within us",[99] or "the indulgence in our lowest appetites" must have been bewildered when other references to "vice" or "sin" or "temptation" or "moral evil", if he went on to define them at all, turned out to mean drunkenness, or getting into debt or unbelief and uncharitableness.[100] In two sermons on 'The Death of Sin' his main examples were the sin of wasting time or money, and the neglect of duty—the latter a persistent theme.[101] A sermon on "Excitement"[102] (a present-day public-school preacher would have called it "Living for Kicks") turned out to be about immoderate intellectual or physical exercise, and about drunkenness again. In a sermon on "Whom does Christ pronounce clean?" the imperfections* he specified are ambition, violence, and worldly-mindedness.[104] Arnold's reticence,

* The prayer Arnold wrote for use on Sunday evenings at Rugby contains a section specifically listing "our particular temptations here", for help in the struggle with which, the assembled school interceded. These were: being ashamed of God and of our duty; fear of one another; idleness and thoughtlessness; falsehood and lying; unkindness and selfishness".[103]

which surely can not have been caused merely by a feeling of delicacy,* is in such contrast to the pointedness of some of his successors that one is forced at least to consider whether Arnold's attitude to schoolboy sexuality was that these sins, in any case far less serious than the collective evils of hostility to authority and discipline, were an almost irremediable aspect of the stage of boyhood which, if not made too much of, might disappear in manhood.

The general effectiveness of Arnold's impact on the religious tone of the school, though it may have been patchy, is observable in the increased number of boys coming forward for confirmation and taking communion. Its results were also noticed among that minority of his pupils who went up to the universities, especially Oxford. But Arnold's "grand self-confidence and imperious volition", which the *Spectator* was to cite years afterwards as the secret of Arnold's "power to reform the whole tenor of our school life",[106] did not have the effect of casting his pupils' views, theological or otherwise, in a uniform mould. From Rugby Arnold watched one of his Old Boys at Oxford "becoming fast a Newmanite", another "is as decidedly become Evangelical";[107] the only characteristic they may have had in common was a quality of moral precocity against which some of them later reacted.

2

Further clues to the effectiveness of Arnold's educational system can be seen in the later careers of his pupils. Even more significantly, we can examine in the case of those who chose a career in education the extent to which they implemented any conception of the school which is recognisably Arnoldian.

*At any rate we know that his attitude cannot be related to any naiveté or unworldliness in Arnold himself, in view of the evidence we now have of the skeletons in his own family cupboard: an illegitimate half-brother born to his father by "an undesirable woman from Hoxton", and a brother who married a prostitute.[105]

The Rugby School *Register*[108] contains a reasonable amount of detail on the majority of boys attending the school in Arnold's time. If we take the period which began in 1822 (the year in which Halford Vaughan, Head of School in Arnold's first year in it, entered, but omitting those boys who appear to have left before Arnold arrived) and which ended in 1842, the year of his death, we may estimate that some 1500–1600 boys came into some form of contact with Arnold, though in the case of the later entrants this was bound to be slight. (Boys known to have gone on to other schools are disregarded.)

At least three hundred of these—that is, between one-sixth and one-fifth—took Holy Orders, most of them becoming parish priests (a handful became bishops in the missionary or colonial field; a very small number defected to Rome; at least two resigned their Orders after 1870). J. D. Collis, headmaster of Bromsgrove, liked to boast that out of the thirty boys in Arnold's sixth form in 1834, he was one of a total of eighteen who became schoolmasters.[109] But not all of these—not even Collis himself—made education their life's work nor even spent any length of time in teaching. At least eighteen of all the boys under Arnold are traceable as having become headmasters, as did four of his own Rugby staff. A further dozen of Arnold's pupils became assistant masters, but several of these did not make schoolmastering their career and went on to do something else. Theodore Walrond left in 1853 after five years as a housemaster at his old school, and his life's work lay with the Civil Service Commission, though he was a candidate for the headmastership in 1869. Richard Congreve left after a shorter spell as a housemaster at Rugby in 1848 to return to Wadham College, Oxford, where he later resigned his tutorship to found a positivist community in London in the late 1850s. Matthew Arnold also taught briefly on the Rugby staff before leaving to combine the life of a man of letters with the work of an H.M.I., in which two capacities he influenced educational thinking and practice, but not in any sense that would be easy to relate to his father's thinking on the sociology of the school. His brother Edward Penrose Arnold was another of at least eight of Arnold's Rugbeians who spent considerable periods as H.M.I.s or in teacher-training. Several of these (though not Matthew) were in Orders.

At least a dozen more—including three very close to Dr Arnold: his sons Thomas and William and his pupil J. P. Gell—became educational administrators, inspectors or schoolmasters in India, Tasmania, New Zealand, Australia or Canada, where in some cases they did work which was important but of a character which is impossible to analyse in terms of our present enquiry into the Arnoldian conception of the relationship between the school and other institutions in English society. Some of Arnold's pupils who became parsons did important work for elementary education in their localities. This was certainly true of Francis Thornton (a member of the Clapham family of Thorntons, who was a canon in Benson's diocese of Truro). There were also important public men who had power to influence the development of education on a national level. Among these were R. A. Cross, Home Secretary and Chairman of a Government Commission reporting on the progress of elementary education between 1870 and 1888; the 15th Earl of Derby (an exception to Arnold's custom of discouraging aristocrats at Rugby), who was in any case said to have been "not much influenced by Arnold";[110] and W. H. Waddington, Minister of Public Instruction in France in 1873 and later Prime Minister there. A close study of the political achievements of these men, especially where they had any bearing on education, might reveal traces of ideas of the school which might be related to Arnold, but apart from the educational reformer J. L. Brereton, who is considered below (Chapter II), it is only those of Arnold's pupils or assistant masters who became headmasters, with some power to embody in their system of school organisation, teaching, and discipline, a conception of a school which might have derived from Arnold, that we can profitably consider here.

Some of these men headed small, essentially local, schools where the scope to develop Arnold's machinery was in any case extremely limited—J. H. Moor at Kingsbridge School, J. Wright at Sutton Coldfield Grammar School, E. H. Price at Maidenhead, and J. R. Crawford at Berkhamsted (who died before his powers or ideas could be judged). Two Rugbeian headmasters in succession totally failed to make any mark on Carlisle Grammar School: W. Bell from 1856 to 1861 and T. C. Durham from 1861 to 1876. At Sherborne, the twenty-nine-year-old C. T. Penrose, who was Mrs Arnold's nephew, was appointed headmaster in 1845, the year after Stanley's effective piece of propaganda was published; he had been an unsuccessful candidate to succeed his uncle at Rugby in 1842. A distinguished classic but a sick man, he did little, in the five years before illness and falling numbers forced his retirement, to indicate his Arnoldian origins, his changes being virtually limited to an increase of study accommodation for senior boys and the introduction of Rugby-style football in 1846.[111] Another Penrose, John, once Arnold's assistant master, moved on to run a private school at Exmouth. In two short years as Headmaster of Lancing, H. Walford, who encouraged his pupils to believe he was the original of one of the characters in *Tom Brown*, had little time to demonstrate his conception of a school, though organised games and a form of house system did begin to develop.[112] In any case the role of headmaster at Lancing was narrowly circumscribed by Woodard in a form discussed in a later chapter. Two Rugbeian headmasters in succession (Burbridge and Parry) made little impact on the character of a proprietary school, Leamington College, which actually foundered under the latter's headmastership but which was later revived; from it one of their successors, Wood, moved on to the headmasterships of Tonbridge and Harrow.

R. G. Bryan (1819–1912) was a clergyman with brief teaching experience in Malta before, at the age of fifty-six, he took charge of Monkton Combe School, near Bath, as its second principal. For nearly twenty years until he retired at the age of seventy-five Bryan ran what was until the end of the century a privately-owned coaching establishment with sometimes as few as forty pupils: at one stage it was actually owned by a boy in the school. It catered primarily for the sons of overseas missionaries, with a sprinkling of sons of African converts—boys who might be as old as twenty-two or twenty-three. Though Bryan did create a prefect system, neither this nor Bryan's own credentials as a pupil of Thomas Arnold were proof against the complete collapse of discipline involved in the school's 'rebellion' of 1900.[113]

A. H. Wratislaw had left Rugby before the end of his normal school career, possibly because of the quarrel between his father and Dr Arnold over the rights of local boys.[114] At Cambridge he was a distinguished classic, a Fellow of Christ's, and later a prolific Slavonic scholar. Appointed in 1852 to the headmastership of the tiny Felsted school in Essex, the constitution of which was newly reformed under a Chancery scheme, Wratislaw "started at once to make it a little Rugby". Among the twenty-two boys, none of them yet in their teens, the prefect system was instituted and provision made for cricket and for the Rugby form of football.[115] But after three years the trustees' disinclination to expand the school to one hundred and fifty, as originally promised, induced him to apply for the headmastership of the larger Bury St Edmund's school where he reigned for twenty-four years. Here the larger numbers gave more scope for his gifts as a scholar and teacher, and the many pupils sent up to university to capture classical honours represented his main success as a headmaster.

This teaching function was also the outstanding characteristic of the headmastership of Arnold's assistant, James Prince Lee at King Edward's, Birmingham (1839–47). The circumstances of a school largely for day boys (where, however, there was a small boarding element until the 1860s)[116] in a big industrial city were so different from Rugby that "even if he had been disposed to import Rugby traditions and Arnoldian methods he would have had to adapt and modify them very considerably to suit the special conditions of a large grammar school".[117] It is not recorded that he made any significant use of the prefect system at King Edward's; it seems that he made no provision for games in a school which had no proper playing field nor gymnasium. The school's historian remarks that he continued the "tradition" begun by his predecessor of regarding the school and its headmaster as important elements in the life of Birmingham, and that under him the school was beginning to take a proper pride in itself. His former Rugby pupil C. J. Vaughan later observed of Lee's Birmingham headmastership that "as a schoolmaster, at the head of a great system, he was wonderful".[118] Yet it is to be doubted whether Prince Lee's greatness and success as a schoolmaster lay in any generalised "system"; his strength lay in his own qualities as a scholar and above all as an inspiring teacher who fired a comparatively small proportion of his pupils—a *corps d'élite*[119]—to a procession of what one historian justifiably calls "astonishing academic successes"[120] at the universities, notably Cambridge. The variety of religious backgrounds of his pupils limited the extent of the generalised religious influence this headmaster could expect to exert, though his influence on individual boys in his own form was profound. His pupils, among whom were a future Archbishop of Canterbury, Benson, and the future Bishops Lightfoot and Westcott, repaid him with a loyalty and regard amounting almost to adoration.* Prince Lee's 'system' was, in fact, even more than Arnold's, a personal spell. Another highly personal educative influence which he harnessed was friendship between individual boys; his attitude to this is referred to in a later chapter.

At another big-city school, the Liverpool Royal Institution, Arnold's pupil Dawson W. Turner (headmaster 1846–74) took over a regime geared to the production of scholars on the Shrewsbury model, and within five years he and his able assistants had raised numbers from thirty to one hundred and forty. He seems to have made no special use of prefects, but he breathed Arnoldian fire into the classical curriculum, resisting the introduction of science but emphasising history (for its moral lessons) and English literature. As an enthusiast for school cricket he urged the moving of the school out into "green fields", but the opposition of the governors frustrated a development which might have allowed the school, in a more spacious setting, to have imitated changes in other schools which would have enabled it to develop into a public school, and indeed to survive.[122]

The strong personality of Arnold's pupil J. D. Collis helped to attract a wider clientele to Bromsgrove during his headmastership there (1843–67). A school chapel was built, but Collis was a wretched preacher, and though he built separate classrooms to replace the one "big school" characteristic of so many schools in the early Victorian period, he was an uninspiring teacher. Whereas he was a good businessman and the

* Unlike Arnold, Prince Lee took pains not to let his own prejudices influence his pupils. As Benson wrote to Lightfoot on their old headmaster's death: ". . . with such honour he abstained from biassing us in politics or religion (when a word from him would have held us) and saw contentedly such different opinions from his own springing up in all of us . . ."[121]

school grew in numbers, Collis could not be described as a single-minded professional schoolmaster with a strong pastoral conception of his task. Furthermore, after presentation to the living of Stratford-on-Avon he started there a private school, Trinity College, whose rivalry nearly caused the extinction of Bromsgrove, though both schools still flourished at the end of the century. If Bromsgrove had by then earned a place—though it was not a leading place—among the public schools, it was the work of the later headmaster, H. Millington (1873–1901), who was responsible for introducing most of the institutions by then characteristic of public schools, but whose chief source of influence in a small school was his superb quality as a teacher, to which a procession of scholars to the universities (among them A. E. Housman) bore witness.[123]

Besides Prince Lee, another member of Arnold's own Rugby staff who went on to a headmastership was the Rev. Herbert Hill, a Fellow of New College who moved to Rugby in 1833 to tutor the Doctor's sons. Arnold then steered other pupils to him at what became a small preparatory school for Rugby, before he was taken on to the Rugby staff itself. A year after Arnold's death Hill began his thirty-three years (1843–76) as Headmaster of Warwick school, where he imported a few Winchester traditions and built up a fine record of scholarships by his able teaching. But it was one of his successors, W. Grundy (1880–85), an old Rossallian, who established the prefect system and began the process which the school's historian, A. F. Leach, described as the "remaking of the school" along public-school lines.[124] Five other public-school headmasters who had strong Rugby associations remain to be noticed: Vaughan, Cotton, Bradby, Highton and Bradley. The characters of their reigns are referred to later in this book; what must be noticed at this point is that, apart from Vaughan (a pupil of Arnold), the other four (of whom all except Cotton had been boys at the school under Arnold) were members of the Rugby staff in the *post-Arnold* period, and they were therefore subject to the influence of a more developed model of the public school than those who had only known Rugby, as boy or master, during Arnold's lifetime.

Several[125] of Arnold's pupils became dons, especially at Oxford, but it is difficult to discern among them, in their capacity either as university teachers or as would-be reformers, any consistent ideas of the nature of universities or of individual colleges as communities. Arnoldian principles are more obvious in the attitudes of these academics to the function of the universities as promoters of truth, and, by fostering social mixture, as agents of social stability; and finally, by the inclusion of dissenters, as forces for the triumph of Christianity.[126]

It remains to examine the great expansion of upper-class boarding-school education in the 1840s to see to what extent the founders of the new schools were conscious of Arnoldian ideals and methods, and to what extent they aimed to reproduce any such model of the school community as, during his lifetime, they might have associated with Arnold.

3

The spread of railways was obviously a precondition of any great extension of boarding school education, involving as it would the movement of boys four times a year (six, when the three-term year became general in the 1870s), but its effect on the founding of new schools was often indirect.

At Cheltenham it helped to augment in the town the element of well-to-do Irish who were to form a strong contingent in the new 'college' by mid-century. By these and by the other gentlefolk in the town the decayed local grammar school was regarded as practically useless for the education of their sons, and a meeting of local residents in November 1840 initiated a plan to establish "a proprietary grammar school on the plan of those so successfully established in other parts of the country". These people solicited advice from the Stockwell, the Kensington, and the Blackheath Proprietary Schools. A meeting of the provisional committee under Mr Fenton Hort decided that the names of would-be shareholders (who would have the right to nominate pupils for admission) must be subject to approval by the committee, and that "no person should be considered as eligible who shall not be moving in the circle of Gentlemen. No retail trader being allowed under any circumstances to be so considered".[127]

This concern for relative social homogeneity was one of the few traces discernible in the schemes of the founders of anything approaching an Arnoldian idea—if indeed it was even that. The school was organised as two separate departments, the classical and the modern (later civil and military)—the latter designed to prepare "the sons of military and naval officers, or of parents connected with the India service, to follow the same profession as their parents".[128] Each department had its own 'headmaster', and set over both was the 'Principal'. Though originally intended as a day school, the houses first rented for the school had a surplus of accommodation. This was available for boarders, who could also be put up in the houses of men and women who were responsible not to the Principal but to the Directors, a body who also maintained discipline in their own hands and appointed and dismissed the assistant masters. Most of the founders were evangelical, and at an early stage they invited those of "the parochial clergy of Cheltenham and immediate vicinity" who might be shareholders to join the committee. This gave Francis Close his chance. A narrow evangelical and a highly successful popular preacher, Close used his pulpit and his position as a leading citizen of Cheltenham after 1826 to campaign against horse-racing, dancing, theatrical amusements, alcohol and tobacco, and he was soon exerting a dominant influence in the counsels of the new governing body, whose meetings now began and ended with prayer. As their Vice-President for the first twenty-one years of the new foundation—a post he retained for a while even after he had succeeded Tait as Dean of Carlisle in 1856—Close was responsible for writing the annual reports of the Directors and was clearly the man behind the arrangement whereby the school's Principal, though he was in Orders, had only general oversight of the religious teaching, which was actually carried out by a special Theological Tutor answerable direct to the governing body. In the absence of a school chapel the boys attended a local church.

Francis Close had himself been educated at Merchant Taylors'; the two army officers who are regarded as co-founders of the school had been respectively at Eton and at Merchant Taylors'. Close explained, at the public meeting held in the town to inaugurate the college in 1841, that the Directors wanted not to discourage the work of existing private schools in

Cheltenham, but "merely to try the adaptation of a new power, or rather the new adaptation of an old power—the power of combination to the principle of education".

> He wished, however, particularly to observe that the school must not be viewed as a public school; it was nothing of the kind, it is, as its designation suggests, strictly private property. If two or three parents care to join together for the purpose of securing a particular kind of education for their children, what had the public to do with it? The principle is the same whether the number be two, or 200 or 300.
> ... The Board of Directors hoped ... by the adoption of the principle of combination to secure many advantages, and escape many evils, which too frequently were attached to public schools. He confessed his belief that on an intellectual point of view, great advantages accrued from the association of 100 or 200 boys in a good system of education. A public school education appeared to be to a certain extent necessary to future success at the learned Universities ... honours were almost invariably carried away by those who had been educated at our great public schools. The reason was plain; in public schools there was more competition, more emulation, and more variety of talent, and each of these was a powerful agent in stimulating the mind to exertion. To the residents of Cheltenham this institution offered a day school possessing all these advantages, while it still preserved for the pupil the blessing and protection of the domestic circle.[129]

The principle of emulation was one which Arnold would have applauded; the diversified curriculum and the combination of a sizeable school with the "protection of the domestic circle" was an experiment which might well have had his private support. But the limitation of the powers of the headmaster ('Principal') would have been regarded by him as totally inimical to the headmaster's proper role, as indeed it proved. The first Principal, who previously with more power had had little success in coping with the state of a new-established boarding school in the Isle of Man, King William's College—conditions at which were later to be depicted in Farrar's *Eric*—soon found the "division of management" unworkable, and resigned. His successor, Dobson, an old Carthusian with no school experience after his Cambridge fellowship, coped well with a situation in which he had no direct authority over the playground[130] or the boarding houses, where discipline was maintained by independently appointed 'drivers' who might or might not be assistant masters. But from the start Dobson was successful in ensuring that if he himself were to have no direct responsibility for discipline out of school hours, he would remove from the masters the duty of constant surveillance over the boys in their play hours, which "must have a tendency to destroy or at least weaken the independence and manliness of character, the formation of which is among the principal advantages of a large school". And he went on, in language which in January 1845 might well have sounded odd to anyone who had not read the biography of Arnold which had made its appearance in the previous half-year: "I believe that when boys are trusted, much reliance may be place upon their *honour*".[131]

Ten years later, when he and his colleagues were urging upon the Board of Directors the building of a school chapel, the name of Arnold was quoted in their arguments, which included the stressing of the value of corporate worship. Even the success of this campaign could not prevent the resignation of Dobson, tired out by the "vexations, annoyances and turmoil"[132] occasioned mainly by the limitation of his authority over all aspects of the school-community. His successor's reign (1859–62) is important because the Rev. Henry Highton was a pupil of Arnold who had maintained close relations with his old headmaster after he left school and had soon rejoined him on the Rugby staff, on which he taught, with one short break, for eighteen years. He was a better mathematician than a classicist and was unusual in his interest in various forms of practical science—his experiments and inventions in wireless telegraphy won him medals from scientific societies. His slightly unorthodox theological views were tempered by strong evangelical sympathies. He took over a school which in nearly thirty years had grown from two hundred to six hundred boys and was now second in size only to Eton. Yet though there was now a chapel Highton had, as Principal, no control over chapel services (this was vested in the Chaplain); he did not appoint the Theological Tutors, nor license the boarding houses, and had no power of expulsion, which was reserved to the Directors.[133]

After a crisis produced by the strains inherent in this situation, Highton resigned and retired into private life to continue his scientific work. The crisis forced the Directors to call in a committee of outside advisers, the main outcome of whose recommendations was the enlargement and consolidation of the Principal's powers and the reorganisation of the governing body. What is significant is that Highton had acquiesced in the earlier dispersal of authority; and that in his three years he had made no attempt even to start a prefect system. So much for the essential machinery of Arnoldism! It would seem that he thought that the Arnoldian aims, such as the building of trustworthy character, could be achieved without such elementary safeguards. In his farewell speech to the boys in 1862 Highton reminded them how

> ever since he had occupied the position as Principal amongst them, *disregarding the many traditions of Public Schools*, he had endeavoured to govern them in a way in which he himself would desire to be governed. That principle of government had clearly been responded to with cordiality and goodwill on their part. They would bear him witness that he had removed every annoying restriction upon their liberty and that he had given them all the freedom possible consistent with their welfare.[134]

4

The development of railways ruined the old coaching inn on the main London–Bath route through Marlborough, and a fine building came on the market just at the time when a group of clergy, led by the Rev. G. H. Bowers, Rector of St Paul's, Covent Garden, were looking for a site for a school which would supply first-class education at low cost for the sons of clergymen. The only respect in which any of the founders are known to have been aware of Arnold the educationist was in connexion with a long memorandum in reply to the founding committee's circular of January 1842. In this a correspondent whose identity is now unknown (but who seems to have been a clergyman educated at Rugby under Dr James in the 1790s) referred in passing to Arnold in a section in which he urged upon the promoters the necessity of limiting the age-range of the proposed school by requiring that entrants give evidence of an elementary standard in Latin and Greek, writing, multiplication and the catechism, and of "habits of attention already formed in some degree"; otherwise valuable staff would be wasting their time:

> Setting a scholar to begin with these eight-year-old Jackies is turning Columbus into a galley slave. He cannot do it. And so well is Dr Arnold, the present Master, aware of the fact from his short experience, that he has encouraged a man in the town not at all concerned with his school to take the little boys in preparation for him.[135]

Later that year, in response to the advertisement of the headmastership, G. E. L. Cotton wrote to Bowers to ask for the details of the post, such as the dates for sending in testimonials, and the date of the election; whether the salary of £600 in a school of two hundred was fixed or would double if numbers doubled; and he went on to enquire:

> Will the Headmaster have the appointment of the other assistant masters, besides the Second Master?
> Will the whole internal disciplinary arrangements of the school be under his authority?
> Is it intended that the Headmaster should preach and perform Divine Service for the boys?
> Will there be a school Chapel?[136]

These questions give an important clue as to what at that stage of the development of Arnoldism were regarded by a close disciple as the essential pre-conditions of Arnoldian rule. Unfortunately we do not have Bowers's answer, nor do we know whether it even persuaded Cotton to apply in 1842–43. In the event, the headmaster chosen was the Rev. Matthew Wilkinson, lately fellow of Clare College, Cambridge, headmaster of the Kensington Proprietary School. Neither of these qualifications could have equipped him to cope with the situation created by the cheapness and consequent attractiveness of the new school.

Having no experience of school management, the founders based their estimates of running costs on replies to their enquiries to a London club and to two Charity schools, deducting a proportion from the latter in respect of twelve weeks' holidays. In 1843 two hundred boys presented themselves in the course of the school's first half-year, and by 1847 there were five hundred boarders, a large proportion being sons of clergy, who paid reduced fees—thirty guineas a year compared with fifty guineas for sons of laymen. The school soon boasted its own chapel, as well as "a bathing place and buildings for carrying on manly exercises", yet the Chaplain was not the headmaster but one of his assistants. Wilkinson appointed prefects, but they do not seem to have been very effective: their failure in one of the special functions Wilkinson ascribed to them in 1846, of acting as carvers in Hall, led to a financial crisis over wastage of food.[137] There were soon complaints from the governors about the insufficient superintendence given by the masters to pupils out of school—masters who undertook the chore of supervising the boys in the dormitories which constituted the new school's vast hostel system were granted special bonuses.[138] The strong undercurrent of indiscipline Wilkinson had to face is exemplified in reports from the school's surveyor on the damage caused when boys took the fire-irons supplied for every classroom, heated them red-hot*, and ran them through floors, ceilings and woodwork; and in the elaborate arrangements necessary to have a new porter's lodge built during the holidays, since even a fence could not protect the half-finished structure from the depredations of the boys in term-time.[140]

The school's finances, based on estimates of running costs which turned out to be too low, worsened when numbers fell

*They had other uses, too, for these. In 1850 a new boy, aged eight, was taken, tied to a bench in Upper School where there were throngs of boys present, and branded on the forearm by means of a red-hot poker: for the rest of his life (and he lived to his hundredth year) he carried the scar, a mark extending from the forearm to the wrist. For his tormentors "there was, so far as the victim was aware, no punishment, though he had to spend three weeks in the Sick House. The mentality of these boys was such that they collected in gangs to beat frogs to death . . . and to fill buckets with their bodies. They poached, and they thieved through the countryside. In the midst of this world the Rev. Matthew Wilkinson, Headmaster, preached edifying sermons on Christian doctrine, couched in rounded periods of piety and propriety."[139]

away after 1848: the governors looked, for a remedy, to minute control of discipline and house-keeping. A member of the domestic staff was rewarded with a £5 gratuity for his invention of a machine for cutting butter, from which "a considerable annual saving was expected"; but the governors found that a static or falling number of mouths to feed resulted in no economy of consumption—indeed, exactly the reverse. The consumption of an extra 18,000 lbs of meat per half year, and a proportionate additional amount of bread, must, they found, have been due at least in part to "insufficient superintendence during meals".[141]

Wilkinson attempted to correct this by formalising the duties of the resident masters, who were now to offer special superintendence, advice, and protection to a group of boys in each house, and not least in Hall at dinner time (which masters must now attend as a duty, "to preserve order and prevent waste"). If they were gratified by the £10 a year increase in salary, some of the masters looked upon the new conception of their role as involving a sense of "degradation". It pained Wilkinson that their protests on this score "overlooked such things as the increased sympathy of boys with masters [and] the comfort to both classes from increased intercourse". This was surely the wrong moment psychologically for Wilkinson to abolish the use of the cane by assistant masters, on the grounds that some of them had used it indiscriminately;[142] shortly before this he had confessed to the chairman of the governors that he was unable to think of any adequate substitute for this use of the cane by the assistant masters "save that of the wholesale flogging" by the Headmaster "which I dare say your Lordship recollects was the use [? case] at Eton".[143]

To a parent who recommended a measure of compulsory exercise for the boys as some remedy for general indiscipline, Wilkinson pointed out, among other things, the problems of supervision:

> With regard to the enforcement of exercise—I fear it would be very distasteful in the way you propose even to those intended to be benefited by it. There are very few boys here I think who do not like being put on what they would probably consider a *private school* system.[144]

With a ratio of masters (several of them by now disaffected) to boys of less than one to thirty—a ratio half as favourable as a boarding public school in the 1960s with fully-fledged house and prefect systems—such supervision was in any case impracticable.

In 1851 there occurred the events which are now commonly described by educational historians as the last great public school rebellion.[145] The chapter on the "Great Rebellion of 1851" in the standard history of the school[146] gives an undoubtedly exaggerated picture of the extent of the disorders, which was challenged by at least one Old Boy who had been a prefect at the time and later wrote a pamphlet exposing the "marvellous fictions" in a "grotesquely absurd account".[147] What is not in dispute is that in October 1851 there were demonstrations involving stone-throwing against the school porter, whose vigilance in reporting misdemeanours was widely resented. Then, unable to identify the culprits, Wilkinson in November punished the whole upper school. As a result, there were demonstrations against him and the staff, the breaking-up of desks and the throwing of fireworks. Some seventy-seven boys were interrogated for their actions during the disorders; their ages ranged from nine to eighteen, but most were aged thirteen. Twenty-five boys were exonerated, six were expelled: of the remainder some were flogged and some reproved. But throughout these events school work went on as usual, and its standard actually improved. The diary of one of the boys—an eighteen-year-old prefect—which is mostly concerned with accounts of birds-nesting and comments on the weather, has a few perfunctory references to "a great row in evening prep", to fireworks let off, and to a boy's being sent away for buying fireworks, but it seems that this prefect spent the evenings of the critical first week of November reading Stanley's *Life of Arnold*.[148] Yet Wilkinson has only himself to blame for the use of the term "rebellion". The carbon book survives[149] of his letters to the parents of miscreants in which he informs them of their sons' expulsions for "heading a confederacy of insurgents", "taking a very active part in an outrageous rebellion", "mutinous outrages", and so on. Significantly, his use of the words "evil" and "immorality" parallels Arnold's attitude to indiscipline. Writing to the parent of a boy whom he identifies as the ringleader of the early troubles, Wilkinson explains that "the evil has gone to great lengths and now wears a mutinous aspect".[150]

These events, the governors' refusal to support his expulsions because of the loss of fees involved (at a time of financial crisis), and the consequent demoralisation of his staff, confirmed Wilkinson in his "private opinion that I was always better fitted for parochial work than for school education",[151] and he left to combine a country living with private tuition of "three or four young men on high terms". Two points must be followed up in a later chapter: the methods by which his Arnoldian successor, Cotton, transformed the school, and the extent to which Marlborough's rebellion was the last such serious upheaval in a public school in the nineteenth century.

5

Cheltenham, Marlborough and Rossall were all founded on a modified proprietary basis, by which shareholders had certain rights to nominate boys for entry. In practice, however, they relied on fees and endowments to pay for running costs, building, interest on borrowed capital, and scholarships; and in the course of the century they bought out their shareholders, who had in few cases received any interest on their shares. The foundation of Rossall (1844) resulted indirectly from the speculations of Sir Peter Hesketh Fleetwood, Bt., "Squire of the Fylde", who invested every penny he could raise on the mistaken expectation of a boom for the town and harbour of Fleetwood when reached by the railway. Monsieur Vantini, a Corsican courtier who in preference to joining his master Napoleon at St Helena had come to England to develop railway hotels, devised a scheme for educating all England on the basis of insurance. On the calculation that half the children born died before reaching the age of twelve, he reckoned that those that lived could be educated at the cost of those who died. The vicar of Fleetwood, Mr St Vincent Beechey, cunningly diverted the schemes of Vantini, and the interest of a public meeting called to discuss them, into the foundation of a "Northern Church of England School" as a public boarding-school for two hundred clergymen's and gentlemen's sons in the buildings and grounds of Rossall Hall, in which the embarrassed Sir Peter could no longer afford to live. Pending the preferment of Bowers (one of the founders of Marlborough) to the Deanery of Manchester, which made him more accessible as adviser to the new foundation, there was constant correspondence between Beechey and the authorities at Marlborough—as the founders of Brighton College were soon to look to Cheltenham—on matters of school organization and domestic economy. There is even a letter from Vantini, full of mis-spellings and gallicisms, among the Marlborough archives. Marlborough equipped Rossall with copies of all its printed papers, rules and regulations, and even gave the new school one of its Matrons.[152]

In all this there was, of course, no mention of Arnold or his ideas. In the month in which Stanley's *Life* was to appear, Beechey was writing to Bowers to ask for advice on the choice of headmaster among the four names short-listed from the twenty-five applicants. One of these was the headmaster of the (then) small school at Uppingham; another was Arnold's nephew and pupil, J. C. Penrose, "reported to be", stated Beechey, "the best man who ever left Rugby",[153] but the governors let slip this opportunity to appoint a man whose credentials might have carried a lot more weight a year later when Stanley's *Life* had had time to make its effect. Instead they appointed the Rev. John Woolley, who at that time was Headmaster of King Edward VI School, Hereford.

Woolley was an able scholar with (it turned out) a strong notion of the importance of prefects in school organization. He soon caused to be printed and circulated a compendium of the rules of the "Northern Church of England School", which set forth the basis of his system of school government in the high-flown language of a political proclamation:

> Whereas the end and purpose of this society, is the advancement of the glory of God, and the training up of its members in such principles of learning and piety as may qualify them to serve Him and to extend His Kingdom, in the several stations to which they may hereafter be called.
> And whereas, both by natural religion, and by the Christian law of Charity, every member of such society is obliged by

> every means in his power to promote the welfare and improvement of those with whom he is connected;—and since in societies, as in individuals, the principle of moral improvement must come from within, and the hearts of its members must be engaged to the love of Honour and Christian Duty, not so much by positive laws and institutions, as by the example and authority of those amongst their associates whose age, character or station, add influence to their actions.
> And since in all political bodies, rewards and privileges are wont to be given for the encouragement and support of those who are called to the difficult and responsible office of guiding and improving others. These things being considered, and in order that so great an assistance may not be wanting to the furtherance of the design for which we are here assembled, it has been determined that the members of the Highest Form in the School shall be invested under the name of Prefects with certain powers, immunities and privileges, which may enable them effectually to co-operate with their Masters, in the maintenance of necessary discipline, and in promoting a spirit of strict integrity, gentlemanly feeling, and Christian principles among their companions generally.[154]

The powers and privileges of the prefects were then elaborated, and the document ends with a long declaration to be signed by each prefect, pledging himself by his authority and example "to discourage all tyranny and oppression; improper language or practices, disingenuousness, lying and evasion, and what is unbecoming in a gentleman", and undertaking to report to the headmaster, if other means should fail, cases of 'vice' or disobedience.

Woolley had had no experience, as pupil or schoolmaster, in any public school. Only one source is traceable for some very Arnoldian elements in his "rules". After graduating from Exeter College, Oxford, he had been a Fellow of University College, where he became a close friend of A. P. Stanley, who could thus have mediated to him some elements of Arnoldism, especially perhaps the analogy between a school and a political society. That Woolley, for all his rules, should have turned out a poor disciplinarian and a weak and indecisive headmaster, illustrates the dependence of Arnoldian institutions like the prefect system on the forceful character of the headmaster; just as Woolley himself recognized in his lengthy preamble that the personal qualities of the prefects themselves were more important than "positive laws and institutions". After five years Woolley resigned, to the relief of the founders, and was appointed—perhaps through the influence of Stanley (whose father was Bishop of Norwich)—to the headmastership of Norwich (Grammar) School, whence he passed on to the Principalship of Sydney University.

The twenty-year reign of his successor, the Rev. W. A. Osborne, established Rossall as a public school. The second of three distinguished scholars and teachers who had been Captains of the School at St Paul's in the 1820s and '30s (J. Prince Lee, Osborne, and Benjamin Jowett), Osborne has joined that school the year after Prince Lee's captaincy and held that office himself four years before Jowett. At Trinity he became Senior Classic, Craven Scholar and Senior Medallist, and if his teaching was not as brilliant as Prince Lee's, more than a hundred of his pupils gained awards to Oxford and Cambridge, where twenty-two got Firsts and eight received fellowships. He dealt peremptorily with the prefects (monitors) when they attempted to continue exercising the degree of independence they had achieved under Dr Woolley, and when they resigned *en bloc* after he had assigned to them "some duty in the way of discipline which . . . savoured of undue espionage over the other boys",[155] Osborne settled the matter simply: "Gentlemen, you are monitors and you will continue to be monitors". It was Osborne who introduced to Rossall the rudiments of a house system, recruited a first-rate staff, established organised games and provided scholarships to and from Rossall; he inaugurated the Corps, the preparatory school, the school magazine; he raised the numbers to nearly four hundred and put up a range of buildings for them, including a new chapel.[156] But apart from his own schooldays at St Paul's and his previous Headship at Macclesfield (Grammar) School, the only other possible formative influence on his conception of a school and its organization was his period at Trinity College, Cambridge. As Senior Classic he must have known well such Trinity contemporaries as G. E. L. Cotton, who was 8th Classic in the same year, and C. J. Vaughan, who was Porson Prizeman in that year and Senior

Classic two years later; but there is no evidence that he was especially intimate, or later maintained any close contact, with either of these two men whose bosom friendship led to Cotton's being offered a post at Rugby under Arnold.

6

Arnold dimly perceived the potentialities of the engine he was helping to create. The efforts of his disciples at the universities, and pre-eminently of A. P. Stanley, in fostering his reputation, served, together with Thomas Hughes's very different kind of propaganda, to create the Arnold 'legend' which undoubtedly helped to popularize public school education, to increase demand, and to promote expansion. Then, as indicated in a later chapter, a more advanced model of the public school, developed from the 1850s and 1860s onwards by Arnoldians such as Cotton and Bradley but also by many others, assisted a further expansion of public school education. Yet it is important to stress that the *original* expansion of upper-class education, i.e. in the 1840s, which produced schools soon to compete as public schools comparable to Rugby, owed virtually nothing to Arnold or the Rugby model. And it must further be noticed that the attempts by Woodard and others from the late 1840s to extend public-school education to a wider sector of society than just the upper middle-class were first conceived of in terms of the *early* model of the Arnoldian public school, not the later model as it developed in mid-Victorian England with its more elaborate machinery of house systems, athleticism, etc., and its more self-conscious idea of community. To these attempts of Woodard and others we must now turn our attention.

CHAPTER TWO

Public Schools for the middle classes: Woodard and Brereton

The second half of the nineteenth century saw the development of two movements whose aim was to extend the provision of public-school education to a very much wider section of the middle classes. Both of these, the Woodard schools and the County School movement initiated by J. L. Brereton, were inspired by churchmen whose concern for education was partly religious.

Throughout the whole of the century churchmen exhibited, to a degree which increased as rival forms of educational provision became more and more available, a concern for the education of the mass of the population by means of elementary schools. But between the popular level and the schools founded on church principles for the more prosperous middle classes—Radley, Marlborough, Cheltenham, etc.—the efforts of churchmen were sporadic. The Rev. Edward Monro, incumbent of Harrow Weald, founded in 1846 St Andrew's College, a boarding-school for farmers' sons—"for the transmutation of raw ploughboys into sweet choristers and good scholars", as Mozley put it.[1] The school collapsed when he left for a parish in the north, and his ideas for the extension of education—especially agricultural education—to the farming middle class were never taken up.[2] More lasting was the achievement of a London clergyman, the Etonian William Rogers, who had, as incumbent of St Thomas, Charterhouse, from 1845, opened day schools for the children of the street traders of his educationally neglected parish; before 1862 he had also opened a 'middle class' school for a higher class of pupil requiring an essentially commercial education, in which Greek was an optional subject. After serving on the Newcastle Commission and becoming in 1863 Rector of St Botolph's, Bishopsgate, he and Alderman W. S. Hale, Lord Mayor of London, initiated the Corporation for Middle Class Education, with the Bishop of London as Visitor. "Much had been done [by 1863] for the children of the poor . . . but what about those whose parents touched upon a higher social stratum, clerks, for instance, and tradesmen with moderate resources?" London swarmed with private academies of a generally inefficient nature; his new Corporation aimed to build in London "schools for children of clerks, tradesmen and others in the same rank of life for whom no adequate system of education existed".[3] This led to the opening in October 1866, of his "Middle Class" school in Bath Street, which soon had seven hundred boys; a second "City of London Middle Class School" was established at Cowper Street. Despite Rogers' pride in the *esprit de corps* which developed in them, these day schools were never self-supporting[4] and had no pretensions to being 'public schools'. Nor had the many other 'middle class schools' whose foundation, especially in London and other cities, was a feature of the educational history of the second half of the century.[5]

But an important by-product of Rogers' main efforts was in connexion with the re-organisation after 1857 of Alleyn's Charity, of which he became a Governor in 1858 and later Chairman. An Act of 1857 had created an "Upper School" of one hundred and fifty boys and a "Lower School" of ninety boys of "the industrial and poorer classes". But as Rogers himself said, the real "founders of Dulwich College" were the London, Chatham & Dover and the London, Brighton & South Coast Railway Companies who in the 1860s needed to run their lines through the Alleyn's estate. The Governors drove a hard bargain, getting £100,000 for some one hundred acres, so that when a new scheme in 1882 turned the Upper School into Dulwich College it already had magnificent buildings in forty-five acres, seven hundred boys (including some boarders)[6] and an impressive record in University scholarships and Army and Civil Service examinations: by 1888 its income was around £20,000 a year.[7] The Lower School ("Alleyn's") benefitted by buildings costing £12,000 for its four hundred and fifty boys.

Arnold's warnings, as early as 1832, about the inadequacy of middle-class education had not, by mid-century, yielded any general movement to supply this lack, which was to become even more marked as the advance of the century brought with it an increase in the numbers of the middle classes, reflected in the great expansion of those vocations for which contemporaries used the term "middle class"[8]—with the exception only of agriculture. Nathaniel Woodard is important not only for identifying the need and devising educational provision for it, but also for his conception of it as being an opportunity to re-assert the educational authority of the Established Church.

Woodard had not himself been at a public school. The son of a country gentleman of limited means, he had been educated privately before he went in 1834 to Oxford, where his academic career, interrupted by marriage, was undistinguished. During his first curacy in London (1843) he was in trouble with his diocesan over a sermon on confession, and it was from the obscurity of an assistant curacy at New Shoreham in Sussex that he issued in 1848 his *Plea for the Middle Classes*, the first statement of the plan which was to lead to the establishment of a whole system of public boarding-schools designed to cover the country.

Woodard's definition of the "middle classes" for whom education was to be provided mentioned two groups: (1) "Gentlemen with small incomes, solicitors and surgeons with limited practice, unbeneficed clergymen, naval and military officers", etc., and (2) the "trades-class"—"from the small huckster who obtains his livelihood by his dealings with the poor, up, step by step through third and second rate retail shops, publicans, gin-palace keepers etc., to the highly influential and respectable tradesman, whose chief dealings are with the higher ranks of society".[9] Later his definition was to be refined into three groups as the clientele of the three types of school he established took in more professional men and even noblemen at the top end, and mechanics at the bottom. But his basic conception reflected both senses in which Victorians used the phrase "middle class", i.e. not only those who mixed socially with the professional classes and even the gentry at the top, but also all those at the bottom above the level of labourer and unskilled artisan—especially the category of small farmer, tradesman and clerk. Though Woodard conceived the clientele of his three types of school as divisible in terms of income—the third grade of school as being for parents with income of up to £150 a year[10]—in fact, occupation was his main criterion, as, in effect, it was also to be for the Taunton Commissioners, whose divisions into three grades of schools by leaving age, eighteen, sixteen or fourteen, reflected gradings of parental occupation almost identical to Woodard's.[11]

Whereas all public schools in the early nineteenth-century, and many other schools providing a classical education, had some proportion of the lower-middle class, as represented by the trades class, etc., the idea of a public school specifically for boys of this class was novel for this century, though Woodard's plan that his schools above the lower-middle class level (i.e. those in the first of the two grades of school envisaged by his *Plea* in 1848) should conform "to the rule of Winchester as it was at first"[12] reflects a pre-Victorian idea of social mixture.

Woodard saw the stratification in three levels of school not as a device to perpetuate social division but as a means of promoting social unity. Not only would the schools promote cohesion among the pupils coming from the limited range of occupational backgrounds represented in each, but the schools would also function as part of a grand scheme of inter-relationship between the strata. Pupils from the lowest stratum would be able to use the system as a ladder leading to the universities and thus to the top of the social scale. Above all, the schools were to be provided with mechanisms to blend these elements together in the service of a common ideal—the beliefs and practices of the Church of England as interpreted by the High Churchman Woodard and his supporters.

Woodard's ideas and plans were elaborated between 1848 and 1869. The impracticality of a diocesan basis for the national system of middle-class schools became increasingly obvious as the varying prejudices of diocesan bishops for or against the Anglo-Catholic character of the Woodard schools came out into the open. Instead, Woodard developed the idea of a religious corporation made up of five regional divisions (North, South, East, West, Midlands), each consisting of a Provost and Fellows engaged in establishing, administering, or teaching in, three levels of public boarding-schools in their division.

The individual schools were conceived of as communities whose strong pastoral ethos and secure Anglo-Catholic ideals were reflected in the closely defined roles of the staff, especially the chaplain. The association of Provost and Fellows in each regional division was designed to have the character of a religious brotherhood, sustained by regular meetings and common devotions; in practice, however, the ideal of the common religious life took second place to the needs of teaching and administering schools, and to fund-raising. Financially, the higher levels of school were to support the lowest, but this ideal was not adhered to in practice.

Thus, upon a hierarchy of schools which were individual communities was superimposed a community of clergymen, praying, teaching, and working together for an explicit set of ideals. Another form of community which was envisaged was that of the assistant masters, for whose recruitment and training to teach in Woodard schools there was special provision.[13]

Woodard's first school was for his first level of the middle classes—"the upper portion",[14] which, as we have seen, he had identified in the *Plea* as "the sons of gentlemen of small incomes, solicitors, surgeons in limited practice" and so on.[15] The school began in a small way in the Vicarage at New Shoreham in 1848, five months after he had issued the *Plea*; its first three masters in 1849 were all graduate parsons. Originally known as SS. Mary and Nicholas Grammar School, it moved in 1858 to Lancing, by which name it was to be generally known. To begin with it charged £30 a year for board and tuition, but it proved difficult to provide an education to the "upper middle classes" at such a fee. By 1857 this had gone up to £52 and by the late 1870s it was £58. Although its numbers in the 1870s were over one hundred and twenty (all boarders) it was still not full. The reason for this was explained to Woodard by the headmaster, Sanderson:

> This school is below all other schools in its rank and cost in the material machinery which the parents of boys, rightly or wrongly, consider essential to a well-ordered school.[16]

As the fees went up, so did the specifications of the clientele it sought to attract. Between 1850 and 1859 it was describing itself as "for the sons of clergymen and noblemen of limited means", and in 1873 it was "for the sons of noblemen, clergymen, professional men and others". The fees had risen to £73 by 1902, and some paid even more than this. Only a minute proportion of boys from titled families attended Lancing in the nineteenth century;[17] the largest single class of parents were Anglican clergy. That the numbers at Lancing did not increase as predicted was a disappointment to Woodard and "a reproach to Lancing for 50 years", as an Old Boy wrote in 1913.[18] Its buildings, including a magnificent chapel designed as a sort of cathedral for the Woodard Corporation, were not completed until the twentieth century. Woodard learnt the lesson that the first level of public school was of no great benefit to his scheme, and he planned no more such schools for his other divisions.[19]

His "second-level" school was established at Hurstpierpoint in 1850, originally styled "St John's Middle School" and designed for "tradesmen, farmers and clerks". With fees at eighteen guineas per annum, it was to be the "first genuinely middle class boarding school".[20] Numbers rose from two hundred in the late 1850s to three hundred in the late 1870s, but the fees also rose from eighteen guineas to thirty-three guineas.

Woodards's third level of school was to be, in terms of numbers of pupils, the most successful. As his first school vacated its temporary buildings in 1858 to go to Lancing, Woodard used them to establish St Saviour's Lower Middle School (afterwards Ardingly, with its own buildings in 1870) for the sons of small shopkeepers, farmers, mechanics, clerks and others of limited means.[21] The low fees—thirteen guineas a year—attracted large numbers of boarders, and although fees were increased to fifteen guineas a year in the 1870s the numbers went on rising and there were well over four hundred boarders throughout the 1880s.

Even before the establishment of these three levels of school had been completed in what was to be his "Southern Division", Woodard had turned his attention to other regions. The offer of a site at Denstone in Staffordshire led to the foundation in 1868 of a second-level school on the model of Hurstpierpoint and named "St Chad's Middle School", which in the absence of any first-level school in that region became the centre of a newly established Midlands Division under his faithful lieutenant, E. C. Lowe. Denstone's fees in the 1870s and 1880s were slightly higher than Hurst's thirty-three guineas. A third-level school, on the model of Ardingly, but smaller, was established at Ellesmere in 1884, with fees, at eighteen guineas, rather higher than Ardingly's; and another at Worksop opened in 1895 after Woodard's death.

The education of girls had no central place in Woodard's schemes, but the enthusiasm of some of his supporters led him to allow a girls' school at Hove (later moved to Bognor) to be allied to the Southern Division; and to sanction, if reluctantly, the foundation of two girls' schools in the Midlands Division, for which Lowe, the Provost, planned that there should be seven girls' schools.[22] Not only in the matter of girls' schools did Lowe show his independence of aim from Woodard; he also favoured day schools, for which Woodard with his admiration of the public school model had little enthusiasm. St Augustine's Grammar School was started on Lowe's initiative as a day school in Dewsbury in Yorkshire in 1884; with fees at between £5 and £7.10. a year, its early progress was satisfactory. But a rival grammar school was established in Dewsbury with funds from a local educational charity after these funds had first been offered by the Trustees to the Woodard School and refused because of the insistence by the Charity Commissioners that a conscience clause should operate in the school—a condition intolerable, of course, to Woodard. This competition was soon fatal to St Augustine's, which closed in 1889.[23]

An opportunity to extend his operations into the West of England was held out by the failure of a proprietary school in Taunton which had acquired some useful sixteenth-century endowments and had for a while flourished under the headmastership of the Rev. W. Tuckwell,[24] until he fell out with the Directors. Woodard bought the land and buildings for less than a third of their value, and in 1880 King's College, Taunton, was established as a second-level school on the model of Hurst and with boarding fees of thirty-four guineas. But the idea of establishing a new Western Division, to be based on Taunton, and of pushing ahead with further schools, was held back during his lifetime by the failure of King's College to attract numbers—a failure due perhaps to the more intense competition of "middle class" schools in the South West than in the Midlands, and the experience reinforced the caution of Woodard against the danger of over-expansion. This caution had led him to refuse opportunities to take over on behalf of the Woodard Corporation a number of boys, schools in the 1870s and 1880s, including two which were, in fact, taken over after his death—Bloxham (in 1896) and St Edward's, Oxford (1922–27 only).[25]

Thus by the end of the century a network of schools had been created which included eight boarding public schools for boys. The efforts of Woodard and his supporters had raised, by the time of his death in 1891, perhaps half a million pounds,[26] all of which was expended on the buildings and property or on the endowment of scholarships and fellowships. The motives of Woodard in creating these schools, the ideals which the schools were created to transmit, and the machinery whereby his school system was designed to transmit them, constitute a highly significant development of the Victorian conception of the school as a community.

The original impulse moving Woodard to found his schools had been social and political: as he confessed to Lowe in 1848".[27] Like Arnold, he was horrified by the precarious state of public order in the times in which he lived, and he looked to education as a means of averting a proletarian upheaval. In Woodard's view, the education of the poor was taken care of by the "National" and parish schools: in any case, he felt, until the middle classes were educated, money spent on the education of the poor was virtually wasted because of the influence over working men of the employers, for it is with their employers that working men "spend their whole life, hear the opinions on every subject, watch their habits and mode of life, and in time come to think as they think . . . By neglecting the employer you are, in the present state of civilisation, hastening on a very general state of barbarism".[28] "Till the Church do educate and train up the middle class, *she can never effectually educate the poor*."[29]

The progressive extensions of the franchise would make the education of these classes an even more urgent political necessity for Woodard—but who was to undertake this process? To a High Churchman it was obvious that this was the duty of the Church rather than that of any government, especially so since the political danger represented by the uneducated middle classes derived from their debased morality—which in turn was rooted in their lack of religion—or from what seemed to

Woodard almost as great a threat, the seductions of Dissent. His system of schools had therefore three main aims: the promotion of political stability, the improvement of the morals (in the general sense) of the middle classes, and their conversion to the Church of England, as represented by the Anglo-Catholic wing to which he belonged.

His conception of the moral tasks of the school was illustrated in language which made more explicit than any other Victorian educationist the social function of public-school communities. They must be boarding-schools, for, as Woodard put it in his *Plea*: "The chief thing that is to be desired is to remove the children from the noxious influence of home". (This was language to be used, of course, not in speaking to prospective parents but rather to the general supporters of his scheme.) Woodard had little patience with the conception of education as a partnership between parents and schools, a partnership for which in any case he was unfitted by his own autocratic temperament which brooked no interference in the running of his schools from parents, outsiders, or even Old Boys. The controlled moral and religious atmosphere of the public school was to be substituted for the degrading family life among tradesmen. Its superiority was to be guaranteed by two distinctive features of the public-school community he established: Anglo-Catholic worship, including confirmation and the practice of confession; and the religious commitment of the schools' staffs.

Woodard's system of schools exemplified in its strongest form a conviction which increased in the face of increasing government activity in education, and growing pressure that education should have a non-sectarian or even a secularist character. Religion and education were believed to be inseparable and the Church of England could only discharge its teaching responsibilities by maintaining its own schools. Anglo-Catholic teaching and worship in Woodard's schools were designed to restore the middle classes to their allegiance to the Church of England. Together with preparation for confirmation, the practice of confession was designed to improve their standard of morality, a term which in this context had a specifically sexual connotation:

> the people of this country [wrote Woodard] have an undeserved *reputation for chastity*; when, notoriously, the whole land is drenched in the sin of uncleanness and most of our youth into life familiarised and reconciled to living in the most deadly sin.[30]

It would be the work of his school chaplains to help save boys "from this source of misery and desolation."[31] But Woodard did not force confession upon the boys in his schools: it was to be a voluntary act, and the encouragement which his chaplains could give to it was hedged around with specific directions laid down by Woodard, and in any case it could only be administered with parents' consent. Some of Woodard's supporters, though only a few of the influential ones, were uneasy about the practice of confession. Woodard himself had got into trouble over confession in his early days as a parson, and for all his tastes in Gothic architecture and plain-song he was in some ways nearer to the old fashioned High Churchman than to the advanced Ritualists, though several of the members of his staff were more advanced. Certainly the popular reputation of his schools, fanned by the press generally and especially the evangelical wing, was of popish seminaries in which confession was compulsory.

The chaplaincy for each school was a key post: a non-teaching appointment responsible to the Provost and Fellows, not to the headmaster, but with religious and pastoral functions so wide as to encroach on the sphere of all the teaching staff and even the headmaster himself.[32] Critics like Thring and Benson foresaw[32] that this must produce friction, and they were right. An able Lancing headmaster (McKenzie, later of Uppingham) resigned on this point in 1894, and the school was in decline until the new headmaster in 1901 insisted on the roles of headmaster and chaplain being re-defined, at the expense of the latter.

Woodard's ideal was for a staff for each school entirely composed of men in Anglican Orders; more realistically he laid down that a specific proportion of them should be ordained. He was successful in recruiting to his cause well-qualified men, even fellows of colleges, at the pitifully low salaries he could offer—one young man was offered £25 a year—and the early staff at Lancing had the character of a teaching order. Perhaps if Woodard had turned his "Fellowships" in each "Division" into a fully-fledged teaching order, he might have capitalised on the potential demand for religious vocations which undoubtedly existed among Anglo-Catholics in nineteenth-century England. But celibacy was not attractive to Woodard personally, and without an obligation of celibacy such an order would have lost the feature most attractive to an educational empire-builder—dedicated, able men available at a pittance. This was the problem inherent in all efforts to extend secondary education of a 'middle-class' character in the nineteenth century, for graduates at Oxford and Cambridge were expensive to train: expenses for a 3- or 4-year university course might come to £600–800,[33] which was clearly beyond the reach of many in his first-level schools and of nearly all in the rest of his schools. Even if schemes could be devised to make Oxford and Cambridge education available on cheaper terms, it could hardly be expected that that source would provide all the men who would be needed for the network of cheap Anglo-Catholic boarding-schools which he had in mind. For this reason Woodard was forced to undertake the training of teachers himself, and a training department was attached to Hurstpierpoint whose products qualified for the "A.S.N.C."—Associateship of St Nicholas' College.

Woodard's conception of a public school was of a boarding-school in which three hundred or four hundred boys lived and worked together. Community life would mould them "into habits of self-control and moderation by the laws of the small world in which they lived, and by the mutual wants of one another".[34] The competitive character of community life (what Woodard called "lawful rivalry") would help train middle-class boys in the desirable aristocratic "habits of honour, integrity and self-restraint".[35] The effectiveness, at least in Woodard's eyes, of these three items of "machinery"—i.e. the elevating nature of life in a community, the influence of the staff and the practice of religion, especially confession and confirmation—may be gauged in his boast in 1857 that Lancing was "the most moral school in England".[36] The relation of the constituent schools to each other was expressed in a number of ways. There was a certain interchange of staff between them, and schools in each division played each other at games. But Woodard's aim—to create a ladder which would enable boys from the lowly school for "servitors" attached to Hurstpierpoint, or from "National" schools, to move up by means of scholarships through each level of Woodard's schools, and finally to get access to Oxford or Cambridge—was in practice frustrated by resistance from headmasters of schools below the first level (Lancing) to being "creamed" of any talent which would make their schools academically prestigious; although the very conservative curricula in all three grades of school, with their emphasis on Latin, should have facilitated such mobility. Thus the "fraternal character"[37] originally envisaged for his system of schools was to that extent limited.

2

Quite independently of Woodard, another admirer of the public-school model started in 1850 a parallel movement to extend the benefits of such schools to a wider section of the middle classes. This was J. L. Brereton, whose biography (unlike that of Woodard and indeed some far less important figures of the nineteenth century) has never been written, so that today he and his "County Education" movement of the nineteenth century are almost totally neglected.[38]

Joseph Lloyd Brereton (1822–1901) was the third son of the Rev. C. D. Brereton, Rector of Little Massingham in Norfolk from 1820 to 1867 and a writer on Poor Law matters. Young Brereton was a day-boy at the Islington Proprietary School under Jackson (later Bishop of London), but at the age of fifteen he transferred to Arnold's Rugby, where he was in "The Twenty" under Bonamy Price and then in Arnold's Sixth:

> I have often [he later wrote] held the candle for Arnold in the Schoolhouse Hall at Rugby when he read either the prayer printed in Stanley's *Life*, or one hastily written for the day. I recollect the reverential feeling, to say no more, that interrupted for those few minutes the careless and not always

> innocent flow of our thoughts and conversation . . . Across the recollection of more than 30 years, few more real religious influences recur to me than those short and earnest utterances of his simple faith, by the strong, brave, and wise teacher, among his childish but would-be-manly scholars.[39]

Yet the influence of Arnold was not, for Brereton, an exclusively religious one. As he explained, even under Arnold Rugby was, as all public schools then were, a rough school, and the tenderly brought-up boy almost begged his father to remove him.[40]

> In the day school I had indeed seen some indications of the very worst side of boys' nature. Some acts of cruel bullying, and some devilish attempts to deprave and pollute, had revealed to me the impotence even of the most excellent of masters to discover and deal with the most vicious instincts which may be drawn out by the contact and companionship of boys though meeting only in the hours of daylight. But my first experience of roughness and badness at Rugby was without mitigation and intensely painful. Within the first few hours I was brutally struck, and might have been almost fatally injured, by one of the biggest boys in the school, who was in a state of maddened intoxication. In the boarding house to which I first belonged I found a prevalence of coarseness and tyranny that would probably have imbued my recollections of Rugby with disappointment and disgust that I should still retain, if I had not found myself at last not only placed in the Sixth Form, but removed by the Headmaster into the Schoolhouse, which was under his own charge and contained then over 70 boys. There I had the opportunity of learning not merely how good may be seen to come out of evil by patient waiting, but how what is truly good may be designed and encouraged and enabled to resist, to control, and to overcome, even what is truly and unmitigatedly evil.[41]

Addressing himself to those who claimed that the evil inherent in boarding-schools is greater than the good that also belongs to them, Brereton went on to consider what in his view was Arnold's "chief work as headmaster":

> The evils are very real that may result from a congregation of boys at a distance from their homes, in a common school, where, besides the teaching and learning, the daily and nightly life of the community is isolated into a boys' world. These evils may be controlled, chastised, and to some degree suppressed by the constant and effective vigilance of the schoolmasters. But they can never be expurgated, and replaced by good and healthy life, except by an active spirit of self-government and self-discipline animating the boys' world itself. To rely by deliberate design and purpose on this purging and invigorating spirit, to encourage and sanction this action, and to give it, by authorised though unwritten laws, power to make a stand against the evil tendencies of congregated boys' life—this was Arnold's great work as Headmaster of a great school.

From Rugby Brereton went up to University College, Oxford, where his tutor was A. P. Stanley, who "allowed me then and afterwards to feel that I might approach him with the full confidence of an attached pupil".[42] After ordination and curacies in London, he became Rector of West Buckland in Devon in 1852. Here he also took an active interest in agricultural matters and gained the Presidency of the Barnstaple Farmers' Club and the close friendship of a neighbouring landowner, Hugh, later 3rd Earl Fortescue (1818–1905). With Fortescue he had a common interest in the improvement of local government and public health, especially in Poor Law reform—an interest derived by Brereton from his father, and by Fortescue from having been Secretary to the Poor Law Board from 1847 to 1851. Known by the courtesy title of Lord Ebrington from 1841 until he succeeded to the Earldom in 1861, Fortescue sat in the House of Commons as a Whig MP 1841–52 for Plymouth and for Marylebone 1854–1859, and was a Junior Minister in the 1840s, though an infection that cost him the sight of one eye later led to his withdrawal from an active political career after he reached the Lords. Fortescue was also an admirer of Arnold, though not as a pupil (for he had been at Harrow),[43] but it was he who had on Lord Melbourne's behalf corresponded with Arnold over the conditions of his appointment to the Regius Professorship at Oxford in 1841.[44] On the publication of

Stanley's *Life* in 1844 Ebrington had written to the author to describe the intensity of his interest and admiration:

> I cannot resist writing you one line to tell you how much pleasure (and I hope something more than pleasure) I have derived from the perusal of your book, and how judiciously and well I think you have executed the labour of love which you undertook. I have no doubt it will be very useful and I think I need only mention that I read the first volume through the night I received it (after 11 o'clock), to prove that to me at least it was deeply interesting. I could not stop and I finished by daylight what I had begun by candlelight. What a delightful picture it gives of . . . a man who was not less great than good . . . I for one, though I can hardly say that I had the happiness of knowing him, feel painfully the blank left by his death, but God will doubtless in His own good time raise up other instruments to do His appointed work.[45]

Even while he as at Oxford Brereton had begun to reflect on Arnold's anxiety for the serious lack of middle-class education in England and to "cherish the hope (like 'a beam in darkness') that I might do something myself towards the solution of this problem".[46] Whether Fortescue regarded Brereton after 1852 as God's chosen instrument (in the sense in which he had written in 1844) is not certain, but the two men were to devote the next fifty years to the cause of public schools for the middle classes—in the case of Brereton, as the almost exclusive preoccupation of the rest of his long life.

Around 1853 Fortescue conceived the idea of a system of public examinations and prizes for farmers' sons in the West of England as a stimulus to the improvement of education and as a channel to higher education. Hardly had the scheme begun to take a practical form in 1855 than it was taken up—and taken over—by T. D. Acland and led directly to the foundation (as a result of the efforts of Acland and Temple) of the Oxford and Cambridge Local (or 'Middle Class') examinations.[47] Brereton elaborated his own scheme of annual 'public county examinations', at which youths of sixteen to twenty-four years could qualify for a "County Degree" and compete for "County Honours"; but this part of his plan received no general support (the universities were implacably opposed to it), and he fell back on the Oxford and Cambridge local examinations—which were always to be a key feature of the public schools he established—as fulfilling the need for a "goal for competition and a standard of requirements".[48]

In 1856 the first of a series of pamphlets was published, in which Brereton and Fortescue developed the case for what they called "county education". Besides the use of local examinations, the two essentials of the 'county system' which they proposed to establish were public proprietary schools in each county and a "county college" for more advanced students. Their conception of the middle class was a very wide one, as Brereton wrote in 1874:

> At the present time there are to be found about a million paupers, or half-slavish class, and there may be another million who are in this exceptional sense free men, that they have more than enough to live on without working at all. But between those that have nothing to lose and those who have enough for every want and to spare, there are, perhaps, twenty millions who with more or less reserve of capital are earning their living by services rendered to others. In one sense all these are the 'Middle Class' of England.

The typical member of this class was, for Brereton, the small farmer:

> If I were asked to pick out the midmost man in England I should be disposed to point my finger at a farmer occupying between 200 acres and 300 acres. There is a man whose place is almost equidistant from the two extremes of English society. His relations and dealings, domestic and public, connect him in a very direct manner with every other class, implying such mutual obligation and respect. The Education which that man has received, or can procure for his sons, would seem to me the true measure of general English Education.

He went on to argue that while the highest and the lowest classes were respectively catered for, the absence of any specific educational provision for the farmer (whose average income would be about £200) left him isolated and "embarrassed in his necessary dealings with those above, below and around him."[49]

The wide range of the middle class caused him to propose

three grades of school for the different gradations of that class. The 'midmost family' such as he described would require a second-grade school; below that a third-grade school would provide for 'smaller farmers, tradesmen and artisans', and here very low boarding fees would be counterbalanced by the schools' organising some agricultural employment for the boys;[50] and there would also be first-grade schools, whose clientele was not defined, but which would be built and run on more economical lines than the great public schools, especially in respect of the expenses of boarding. The third-grade school might have only fifty to one hundred boys; the other two types perhaps two hundred each.

The schools were all designed primarily as boarding-schools and must have a 'public' character insofar as they were to be under the control of responsible, independent, and eminent men whose qualities would guarantee the qualifications of the masters. According to Brereton, only such a school would have the character to provide the stimulus of open competition and public reward which were essential in order to overcome the indolence of youth or the indifference of parents—especially farming parents whose lives (he claimed) are isolated from the enlightening influences of public opinion and who tend to undervalue education.[51]

Envisaging a wide extension of his schools, Brereton made the county the basis of his scheme, rather than the parish or the diocese, because he explicitly recognised that ecclesiastical units no longer corresponded with national needs. Both he and Fortescue were inspired by deep Christian convictions. Brereton in his admiration for Arnold's conception of an effective public school recognised that the basic principle of Arnold's system was a religious one:[52] but it was a principle which stressed accommodation rather than divisions between Anglicans and other Christians, especially nonconformists, and the County Schools were designed to be unsectarian in character and teaching, "inviting and welcoming the co-operation of nonconformists with Churchmen".[53] Both Fortescue and Brereton were strongly opposed to any scheme which attempted to divorce education from religious teaching, and this contributed to their hostility to activity on the part of the government in secondary education. The other reason for this hostility was the fear that such activity would be a dangerous increase in the power of the state.

The financial basis of Brereton's County Schools was a combination of the commercial and the endowment principles. Brereton rather fancied himself as a practical economist, and his pamphlets are littered with computations of comparative costs of tuition, boarding, salaries, buildings, etc., and of the amounts that could be raised on the proprietary principle. By this system, capital for building and equipping schools was to be raised by the sale of shares in a limited liability company; part of the profits would be reserved for endowing scholarships, etc., and the rest would be distributed as a dividend to the shareholders. Further endowments might be provided by benefactors, but the main capital would be provided by the profitability of the school:

> The tendency of endowment is to become negligent and stagnant; and that of commercial speculations to grasp too much at private and immediate, rather than public and permanent, results. But if the two can be worked together, it may be hoped that they will counteract each other's faults, while retaining their respective virtues of patience and vigilance.[54]

Brereton's first school, The Devon County School at West Buckland, was established in 1858 before Brereton had refined his economic statistics—indeed it was started "without any definite estimate of cost"[55]—but his experience of the finances there and in his second school were to become the basis of the estimates of the whole of his schemes. The Devon County School began with three boys and a master, who were lodged and boarded by one of the farmers of the parish of West Buckland. Numbers grew rapidly, and farmhouses and other buildings were soon added and converted,[56] though other schoolmasters in the locality did not take kindly to this new competitor, one of them seizing on Brereton's principle of economy to attack the cheapness and, even more, the element of farm labour with which the school, as originally planned, was intended to operate. He made comparisons with Dickens's Dr Squeers—"such an attempt to introduce juvenile slavery into this county . . . can never be successful".[57]

In 1860 the Devon County School Association was established on a joint stock basis: shareholders included the Rt. Hon. Sir T. D. Acland, the Rt. Hon. Sir John Heathcote Amery, Brereton, Ebrington himself, his father the 2nd Earl Fortescue, Lord Robartes, the Duke of Bedford and the Earl of Devon—though the shareholdings for most of these men, apart from Fortescue, Brereton and the banker, Foster, were very small. Probably the main work of Hugh, 3rd Earl Fortescue, for the "county education" movement consisted in his tireless efforts* to interest men of influence: great magnates or liberal politicians, several of them his relatives—Robartes (Viscount Clifden), Harrowby, Ducie, Marlborough, the Duke of Devonshire, Stafford Northcote (Lord Iddesleigh), Speaker Brand—and leading curchmen and academics, including Stanley, Farrar and Lightfoot. Temple at Exeter (and later at Lambeth) looked kindly on the Devon County School, though Benson at Truro and afterwards at Lambeth was of little help.

In 1864 new buildings for one hundred and twenty boarders were built, and by 1867 numbers at the Devon County School had risen to ninety-eight. The Association declared no dividend until 1866, and then it was a very modest one to allow for investment in buildings. Brereton estimated that a school like the Devon County School should involve a capital outlay of £9,000 or £75 per boy when full (i.e. with one hundred and twenty boys).

About the curriculum of their proposed schools little was said by the originators of the County School movement, beyond an emphasis on scientific instruction (notably in its application to agriculture) and the assumption that, except in their first-grade public schools, the curriculum would be non-classical. The 1860s saw the establishment of a number of other middle-class boarding-schools which exhibited some or all of the features proposed by Brereton and Fortescue.

Framlingham was founded as the Albert Middle Class College on the initiative of Fortescue's friend,[58] Sir Edward Kerrigan, Bt., MP. who was the largest original benefactor; a

* These efforts are documented in Fortescue's letters to Brereton from the 1860s onwards, especially between Brereton's departure from Devon in 1867 and his death in 1901. Copies of these, together with a mass of materials relating to the County School movement, have been deposited in a library in Cambridge.

number of other East Anglian landowners gave more nominal support. Its proprietary character was limited to the right of donors and subscribers to make nominations, and it received valuable land transferred by Pembroke College, Cambridge, on the re-organisation of the Hitcham Bequest of 1636 by the Charity Commissioners. It opened in 1865 with two hundred and sixty-eight boys in the first term, nearly all Suffolk boys who gained a £6 reduction in the £36 boarding fees. As befitted a college intended as a memorial to the late Prince Consort, who had in the 1850s expressed a concern for the improvement of facilities in "the purely agricultural districts" for middle-class education, the original curriculum stressed English subjects and science (including agricultural chemistry) rather than the classics, and Greek was, together with dancing and piano-forte, an optional extra. To those who had passed the Cambridge local examination the rules extended the sixth-form privilege of wearing a mortar board.[59] The religious character of the school was Anglican but with specific allowance for the sons of dissenters. Woodard regarded this policy of comprehensiveness with suspicion, and those who framed it as "those Suffolk impostors".[60]

At Cranleigh, the originators of the Surrey County School were the local rector, Canon Sapte, and the local MP (1860–1892), Mr George Cubitt. Cubitt belonged to an immensely successful London building family: his father had built on the Duke of Westminster's estate in Belgravia and the Duke of Bedford's estates in Tavistock Square and Gordon Square, and his uncle became Lord Mayor of London. After being educated privately, George Cubitt went to Trinity, Cambridge, where he formed a lifelong friendship with E. W. Benson, who in 1863 (by now headmaster of Wellington) was elected to the newly formed Council of the Surrey County School. In 1892 Cubitt became Lord Ashcombe, receiving one of eight peerages recommended by Lord Salisbury on leaving office. The school was founded by donations, and its object was "to provide a sound and plain education in accordance with the principles of the Church of England and on the public school system" for "the sons of persons engaged in farming, trading and other occupations".[61]

Buildings to accommodate one hundred and fifty boarders were erected at a cost of £9,000 a mile from Cranleigh station;

the school started in 1865 with only twenty-two boarders and four day boys, but within six months it was full, and two years later the Council were pressing ahead with buildings to accommodate three hundred. Among the early benefactors were the Duke of Cambridge and the King of the Belgians.[62]

In addressing the school on Speech Day in 1867, Sir Stafford Northcote (fresh from his labours on the Taunton Commission) urged the building of a chapel to help make "this institution what it ought to be, a great Church of England Middle Class College in this part of the country".[63] That summer £5,000 was given for a chapel by a benefactor who hoped the boys would be taught "in a straightforward Church of England spirit, those truths which alone make them the best members of society".[64] One of the boys who in the 1870s enjoyed the benefits of this teaching was Prince Kofi, son of King Kofi of Ashanti, who had been placed in the school "in accordance with treaty engagements" and was described as being "very gentlemanly, especially at table. He is, of course, dressed like those around him and appears to be quite one of them".[65]

The non-classical, and indeed rather elementary, character of the original curriculum was modified in 1869, when Greek became a regular subject rather than an optional extra. The school "held aloof"[66] from the Oxford and Cambridge Local Examinations, though it entered boys for the London Matriculation and for the South Kensington Science and Art Examinations.

By the time the Taunton Commission, to which both Brereton and Fortescue had given evidence, produced its report, it could give details about a number of other middle-class boarding-schools as well as the Devon County School, Cranleigh and Framlingham. The earliest imitator of the Devon County School was the East Devon County School, founded in 1860 at Sampford Peverell by the Rev. C. S. Bere, one of Cotton's earlier appointments at Marlborough—he taught there briefly before going off to become in due course Rector of Uplowman (1858–1885), whence he established the school for farmer's sons with fees at around £30 a year. The school was of a proprietary character and Fortescue became a shareholder, but it did not long flourish. The Taunton Commission found thirty-five boarders and fifteen day-boys in 1868.[67] By 1873 there were eighty boarders, and the school was appealing for funds to build for one hundred and twenty.[68] But by 1882 its total numbers were down to thirty-two, and its fortunes did not revive despite the appointment in 1883 of a new headmaster, one of the products of Woodard's teacher-training department at Hurstpierpoint,[69] who aimed to reproduce at Sampford the aims and methods of Hurstpierpoint (and presumably to reverse the liberal tendency of its religious instruction which the Taunton Commission had noted).[70] Bere closed it in 1886,[71] with a debt of over £2,000. There was also a Dorset County School, founded in 1864, which catered for the sons of yeomen, tradesmen, merchants and professional men, and in 1868 had seventy-five boarders who paid between £30 and £34 per annum.[72] At Wellington, Somerset, a small private school which had begun in 1842 was bought by William Corner and later passed into the hands of a company of local men, under whom by 1879 it was styling itself the West Somerset County School,[73] by which name it was still known at the turn of the century. It offered an essentially non-classical education, with an emphasis on agricultural science and handicrafts. In the twentieth century this school became, as Wellington School, Somerset, a Direct Grant school.

The 8th Duke of Bedford was a considerable benefactor to education: he had given land and money for schools both in Bedfordshire and in Tavistock[74] and was a benefactor of the Devon County School. When in 1866 a group of landowners and others—including W. H. Whitbread, Lord Charles Russell, James and Charles Howard (ironmasters)—established a limited company to found a "Bedford County School", the Duke took £10,000 worth of shares.[75] The school opened on 16th August, 1868, with seventy pupils, and numbers rose steadily, though after the Duke died, his cousin who succeeded as 9th Duke fell out with the directors and withdrew from his association with the school in 1874. The school was in debt and had not so far declared a dividend,[76] yet its fortunes recovered, and in the favourable educational environment of the town of Bedford, flourished under a succession of able headmasters.[77]

Apart from the East Devon County School, of which Fortescue was an active supporter and which acknowledged its connection with Brereton, and the Bedford County School, whose directors consulted Brereton at the early stages, these other schools of the "county school" movement were founded and managed independently of the two men to whose ideas and propaganda they owed their inspiration. But Fortescue and Brereton followed their fortunes with interest and concern and took pride in their successes, which they felt could only do good to their own schools.[78] Brereton's services to education were the specific ground of his being rewarded in 1858 by presentation to a prebendal stall by Phillpotts, Bishop of Exeter—an honour, he was to claim, "which I highly value and the more that it carries no emolument beyond an honourable approval".[79] But the truth was that to a man with a large and growing family—more than eleven children survived infancy—emoluments were very much what he needed. He had already, at West Buckland, combined private tutoring with his active farming, parochial and educational interests, a combination which at times threatened to injure his health;[80] in 1867 he returned to Norfolk to take over from his ailing father the family living of Little Massingham, a parish which he retained until his own death in 1901. The stipend, around £500 in the 1880s, would have been moderately comfortable for the average Victorian country parson, but it allowed no indulgence in the fertile schemes of an educationist[81] who believed in educational ventures based upon the 'commercial principle'. In 1862 he had presumed upon his close friendship with Fortescue by borrowing £5,000 at a low rate of interest, "to be repaid when I succeed to family money".[82] When he moved to Massingham he found he could not recover some thousands which he had invested in the East Buckland glebe without the security of proper leases.[83] In 1886 his father lost heavily in the failure of the Agra Bank,[84] and when his father died soon after the Prebendary took over the family living, the son's inheritance was complicated by a division of the estate among widow and children which led to family quarrels and prolonged litigation. Nevertheless Brereton went ahead with fresh schemes. Proposals for County Schools in Shropshire[85] and in Cambridge[86] came to nothing; but in 1871 Fortescue learnt from a newspaper report that Brereton had founded a small "Norfolk County School" at Massingham, and wrote in some surprise, begging Brereton to be careful about undertaking fresh liabilities.[87]

Although the Devon County School Association declared a

modest dividend in 1870,[88] Fortescue recognised that the charges were too low, that the school was undercapitalised, and that there was no margin for contingencies, such as the need for increasing the accommodation for masters and boys;[89] and in 1872 he even toyed with the idea of disposing of the school.[90] He disagreed with the low priority that Brereton gave to the need for Devon County School to "become decidedly solvent":[91] if some of his fellow directors were cautious, Brereton's temperament, Fortescue felt, was "over-sanguine".[92] There was renewed prosperity at the Devon County School, which had more than one hundred and fifty boys in 1876 and an impressive record in the University Local examinations and the Science and Art examinations; and there was the prospect of the establishment of an Oxfordshire County School under the patronage of the Duke of Marlborough,[93] and of a Hampshire County School supported by Lord Northbrook.[94] Apparent progress on all these fronts only served to stimulate Brereton's optimism, which had already transformed the embryonic Norfolk County School at Massingham into a full-blown, first-grade, county boarding-school financed by capital raised by the issue of shares in the Norfolk County School Association; and Brereton was encouraged to develop further stages of his scheme.

Following the publication in 1871 of a public letter by J. L. Brereton, addressed to the Lord Lieutenant of the Country, and proposing a Norfolk County School, an Association had been formed by 1872 under the Joint Stock Companies Act "to establish one or more schools or colleges in Norfolk, with a capital of £10,000 in £10 shares". The first undertaking was to be a boarding-school for two hundred boys charging not more than forty guineas per annum.[95] In August that year, a meeting of Trustees and Directors at the Earl of Leicester's town house in Grosvenor Square unanimously chose for its site Elmham, near East Dereham in Norfolk, as proposed by Sir T. S. Buxton and the Bishop of Norwich. The Earl of Leicester took £1,000 worth of shares, and the Prince of Wales, "as a Norfolk landowner at Sandringham", laid the foundation stone of a fine new building in 1874 in grounds which extended to over fifty acres.[96] The building, pleasantly situated on the summit of a hill overlooking Lord Sondes' beautiful park, was "Early English Domestic" in style, the exterior being of flint, with red brick dressings, large dormers and weather tiling at intervals. "The roof is covered with red and black banded tiles", wrote the *Illustrated London News*:[97] later writers made comparisons with a French chateau or a battleship.[98] Brereton's architect, who had corresponded with Thring[99] on the possibility of houses connected by arcades as an alternative to the barrack system, contrived to avoid "large barrack-like dormitories" and to provide rooms with between six and twelve beds, within a total cost of £8,000 for three hundred boys—a feat reckoned as a triumph for "the promoter, Mr Brereton [who] contended that £30 per boy in a school of three hundred boys should furnish the building proper".[100] According to its prospectus, the Norfolk County School aimed "to provide at a moderate cost boys of the middle class with a sound liberal education on public school principles". It combined "the commercial and endowment principles by limiting the dividend to 5%, by offering in scholarships a preferential dividend of 5% on the Endowment shares, and by vesting in permanent trustees the appointment and removal of the headmaster". The school was "established on lines which the National Church generally approves, while parents not themselves belonging to the Church of England may feel that their own wishes will be, in every instance, scrupulously regarded".[101]

When the chapel was built for Elmham in 1883, Brereton enlarged on the school's religious status:

> When I am asked whether Elmham is a Church of England school I own that I am obliged to answer, 'It is, and it is not'. It is, for the headmaster is a clergyman; the Bishop of the Diocese is one of the trustees, who can appoint or remove the headmaster; I am myself the Chairman of the Governing Body. There has always been a Church of England service in the school, because the parish church was not convenient. There is now a chapel opened and approved by the Bishop. It is not a Church of England school in the sense that some would give to 'Church schools'—viz. that no one but a clergyman or a conformist can be appointed as a master; that none but churchmen can be trustees; that none but the sons of churchmen can be received as pupils. As a County school it invites and welcomes the co-operation of non-conformists with churchmen.[102]

The Rev. William Watson, who had been chaplain at the Devon County School till brought over to Massingham to start the Norfolk County School, moved in as headmaster with a handful of boys to the new building. On the Opening Day he promised an emphasis on English, mathematics, science, French and, above all, the Bible. At the same ceremony Lord Fortescue observed:

> Now there is one feature of the Norfolk County School, and a most valuable feature it is . . . Other County Schools have been provided by the Landlords for the farmers, this magnificent building has originated with the farmers. (Applause)[103]

In fact, support was not forthcoming from either farmers or landowners to the extent Brereton had led Fortescue to hope, but the establishment of his first-grade school in such auspicious circumstances emboldened Brereton to elaborate his schemes for County Education in a book published in 1874.

In *County Education: a Contribution of Experiments, Estimates and Suggestions*, Brereton enlarged on and extended his already published plans for a national system of county schools, consisting now of third-grade "middle" schools, i.e. middle-class, mainly boarding-schools, with boarding fees up to fifteen guineas a year, for each group of parishes totalling around 20,000 souls;[104] second-grade "middle" schools of the type the Devon County School had become, with fees up to £32, for each county (around 400,000 souls), the pupils staying until sixteen for the Junior Local exams; and a first-grade school for each 'division' of three or more associated counties (1,200,000)—with boarding fees of up to £52. His case here was illustrated by reference to the character and achievements of the Devon County School and the new Norfolk County School, and he followed it up with further pamphlets based on later accounts for these schools, in 1875 and 1876.

The "first-grade" schools were to be connected direct to the universities through a provincial organisation and by means of a 'County College'; provincial educational centres would be established in Cambridge, Oxford, London and a northern university town, and "from each University centre a complete series of local examinations [would] traverse the country"; the provincial educational organisation would be extended to take in the education of girls, to combine with endowed schools, and even possibly to operate in the field of elementary education, where the operation of the commercial principle of "County Education" ought, he claimed, to be able to bring down costs and increase efficiency. All the elements of his 'effective system' should "(1) cover the ground; (2) be self-supporting; (3) maintain the claim of public education in England to be religious and Christian, and (4) avoid the dangers of an over-reaching centralism, or a stagnant local independence".

The idea of a 'County College' had been put forward by Brereton as far back as 1864 when he circularised farmers and magistrates in the West Country[105] to gain support, on the limited commercial principle of shares earning interest of up to 5%, for a Country College to be established at West Buckland "for the sons of farmers and others in the Western Counties, who have left school but wish to continue their studies", especially in practical mathematics, natural science, and farming.[106] Though this proposal came to nothing, by 1869 his increasing awareness that the training of schoolmasters for middle-class schools would be the crucial problem, his fear lest government action might be invoked to meet this need, and the admission to Oxford and Cambridge of "non-collegiate" students, all combined to spur on his advocacy of a county college. This institution was designed "mainly for youths of the age of Arnold's Sixth form" and was needed "to draw to a higher stage the more advanced schoolboy, and to assist those willing and competent to become teachers to prepare themselves for the growing requirements of public tuition". Experience had convinced him "how very difficult indeed it is to find teachers who can be relied upon to teach what they profess, and still more to sustain a high, as distinct from a sentimental, tone of honour in schools where there is such an admixture of rank, and the social standard is necessarily at a moderate level", and that "it [was] of the very greatest importance that one of these such institutions should, if possible, be placed within the precincts of an old university" where "education has always meant something more than certified knowledge; and the advantages of educational residence implied in their degrees have been hitherto thoroughly recognised by the upper classes of this country".

What was needed was "some modified system of residence, partly local and partly at the University . . . combined with the existing examinations". Accordingly in 1872 he had urged upon Cambridge and Oxford the establishment of associations of shareholders with capital of £24,000 each, in order to open in each case a college connected with the 'middle-schools' in the various counties, so that residence in them should be reckoned as part of the county college course and lead to a 'county degree'. The essentials were to give facilities for obtaining an early and inexpensive degree by educating boys at age sixteen at rates far cheaper than the established colleges; to raise the standard, and increase the supply, of masters, and to give special preparation for various branches of professional life.[107]

Oxford rejected the whole idea, but at Cambridge, though the principle of 'county degrees' was not accepted, a syndicate of the Senate in March 1873 reported favourably on the proposal to found a 'County College'. Brereton had anticipated such a move by the establishment of an embryonic 'County College'—a house in Panton Street, Cambridge, leased by Brereton to accommodate his eldest son and some other non-collegiate students—and this he was able to transfer to the County College Association which was formed in April 1873 in order to collect, by the issue of shares, the capital required to start building.

To the chagrin of Brereton and Fortescue the reaction among schoolmasters was unfavourable in precisely that quarter where they expected most support. The Vice-Chancellor of Cambridge was petitioned by the headmasters[108] of five middle-class schools, including Hurstpierpoint and two "County Schools" (but none of Brereton's own schools), who saw that the proposed County College threatened to cream off those able pupils whose remaining at school over the age of sixteen would ensure for their schools a "first-grade" character. So it was rather among the established schools of the H.M.C. that the County College got somewhat unexpected support[109]—at the 1876 Conference the chairman, Jex-Blake of Rugby, quoted a letter from Brereton which commended the new County College to the H.M.C. as having been "founded, in no spirit of hostility to the Great Schools of the Country, with the object of putting university training and university degrees in reach of those who cannot give so many years to studies that do not bear immediately upon their work in the world". Jex-Blake commented that the new college, even before it was founded, had had his best wishes; he referred to its function of "popularising without vulgarising education" and regretted that his own university, Oxford, did not advance "step by step" with Cambridge in this.[110]

By persuasion and persistence Brereton and Fortescue enlisted the support of a number of influential people for their Association and its appeal for capital in the form of shares. The Speaker of the House of Commons was persuaded to lend his house for meetings of supporters, who included W. H. Smith and Sir Stafford Northcote.[111] At Cambridge its main supporters were Thompson (Master of Trinity), Liveing (Professor of Chemistry) and the theologian J. B. Lightfoot—men enlisted by bold letters of invitation, the one addressed to "Canon and Mrs Lightfoot" producing a reply in which the Canon "who turns out not to be married . . . thanks me [wrote Fortescue] for my invitation to Mrs Lightfoot as she is a 'potentiality', though not yet existing".[112] Soon Lightfoot and Fortescue were going through building plans for the new college together.[113] Brereton's *coup* was the adhesion of the Chancellor of the University, the 7th Duke of Devonshire, who became a £1,000 shareholder in 1874,[114] but the Duke advised against Brereton's original intention to name the new college after Thomas Arnold: "I fear that the connexion between the work and life of Dr Arnold, and the objects of the college, would not be sufficiently obvious".[115] In due course he consented as president of the County College Association that his own family name, Cavendish, should be adopted for the college, for whose new buildings he laid the foundation stone in 1876 on a site of ten acres bought for £4,000 from Trinity College in what is now Hills Road, Cambridge. So large an area was justified on the grounds that

> it would afford room for the cultivation on a garden scale of little plots of corn and other crops to illustrate lectures, while the situation held out a reasonable probability of some arrangements being made with a farmer of land adjoining . . .

for allowing the students the opportunity of watching or even taking part in agricultural operations.[116]

The Wardenship established in 1876 was given to the Rev. T. J. Lawrence, a Downing don, who with two graduate tutors taught and supervised the small number of students who moved into the first of the new buildings at the beginning of the Michaelmas term. By what procedures were these men to turn the farmers' lads and sixteen-year-olds of similar background into the "well-toned" schoolmasters,[117] or honours graduates, or useful members of the various professions? Was there an Arnoldian answer? In 1877 Fortescue reported to Brereton a "longish talk" which he had had with Matthew Arnold in which Matthew

> observed truly that while it was of great importance to have middle class students there, it was hardly less so to keep it gentleman-like, and secure from the ban of caste, by having sons of poor clergy and officers[118]

—but as to precisely how these objects should be achieved Mathew Arnold had been very unhelpful: acknowledging a copy of *County Education* in 1874 which he had read "with interest", he informed Brereton:

> I am not very particular how things in the way of school establishment are done provided they are done well and thoroughly.[119]

The Warden found the new kind of educational community daunting:

> The college has no tradition to appeal to. Its members are drawn in great part from classes who have had no public school or university education; they are at that most difficult age between boyhood and manhood when they can enter fully into the feelings of neither; and it is a work of the greatest difficulty to teach them the principles of corporate action,[120]

and he resigned later that year.

Despite the expectation in Brereton's *County Education*

(1874) that the Warden would be a member of the National Church,[121] a nonconformist, John Cox, who had been educated at the City of London School (where he was a close friend of Asquith) and at Trinity, was appointed to succeed, and it was in the hope of calming the suspicions among churchmen at this move that the Duke of Devonshire approved the invitations to Dean Stanley, Canon Farrar, and Dr Lightfoot to the laying of a foundation stone to a new wing in 1876.[122] But the growth in numbers of students was extremely disappointing. The financial prospects of the college brightened when a new treasurer of the Association was recruited, in the person of Samuel Morley, wealthy nonconformist, Liberal MP and admirer of Dr Arnold, who made a business of giving away money, but the Duke of Devonshire recognised that support from a few large shareholders was useless unless the college gained more support "from the agricultural and commercial classes"; "strenuous effort to raise capital [was] . . . of pressing importance".[123] In 1878 the Duke attributed the slow progress in numbers of students "to Mr Lawrence's retirement and to Cox's nonconformity",[124] but there were other reasons—among them the principle of economy on which the college was run, which resulted in the single rooms being sparsely furnished and in complaints of poor food.

Morley held meetings, in Nottingham (1878) and elsewhere, to increase support for shares for Cavendish, but the response was disappointing. In reporting this to Brereton in 1878 he passed on to him a letter from a Derbyshire rector, which made the significant suggestion that if Cavendish would only incorporate as a fully-fledged college in the University, as Keble College had done at Oxford, it would fill up and become a large college. As Keble was High Church, so Cavendish should [he urged] be made distinctive as a resort of holders of the distinctive reformation principles of Ridley, Simeon, etc. Poor clergy like himself, he claimed, would hail a college like Cavendish if only the difficulty were removed that it was in no sense like one of the old colleges: "our young people don't like to be looked down on, and why should they?"[125]

The improving academic reputation of the college was signalled by a Cavendish student's getting a first in the Natural Sciences Tripos in 1882. A good proportion of the students were reading science or mathematics,* about a third of them preparatory to medicine; others were destined for the Church, law, or teaching. Whereas in its early days the college had attracted numbers of students who did not matriculate in the university but came and went from term to term, the proportion of matriculants had increased. Ten entrance scholarships had been founded by 1883, including one for an intending teacher.[127]

A much surer method of getting recognition was afforded by success on the river. Morley and the Duke of Devonshire bought a rowing eight for the college, which won its oars in 1881 and 1882. P. L. Hunt, a Cavendish undergraduate who had been a boy at Highgate School, coxed a Cambridge crew which contained the great oarsman, Steve Fairbairn, in the Boat Race two years running, in 1882 and 1883.[128] Brereton's son, Frank, was one of four boys from the Norfolk County School who were up at Cavendish in 1881. Three of them rowed for the College VIII which made thirteen bumps in sixteen races that year. Speaking on behalf of Old Boys at a Speech Day at Elmham, Frank said of Cavendish:

> Now I am sure I am not exaggerating when I say that, if not its success, at any rate its hearty recognition by the other colleges, is largely due to the success of its boat.[129]

A new measure of official recognition was given in the form of the granting of the status of Public Hostel, so that Cavendish men were indicated on Tripos Lists by "*H. Cav.*" just as Selwyn men would for many years (and indeed until 1923) appear as "*H. Selw*". The foundation of Selwyn was itself a blow. By 1883 Cavendish was just emerging from a period in which about as many of its students migrated to other colleges as proceeded to degrees through Cavendish—such were the social and material handicaps of the new foundation. But the twenty-two students of 1878 had risen to ninety-six by 1883, and if the annual number of entrants could be sustained at thirty-six[130] or improved, and if increasing social recognition could help to stem migrations, the college could hope to reach one hundred and twenty students. This was the minimum at which the college was

* J. J. Thompson was a tutor at Cavendish in these subjects, lecturing for three hours on three mornings a week in the early 1880s.[126]

reckoned to pay its way—compared with the full three hundred for which Brereton had planned it. But the new specifically Anglican foundation, Selwyn, was intended to offer a cheaper university education than the older colleges to young men of similar backgrounds and, as Fortescue recognised, would "in spite of the university feeling against it . . . take away a certain number of Lay, and almost all Clerical, Churchmen", though he was sanguine enough to think that the controversy over its foundation would benefit Cavendish in the sense of drawing attention to the needs of 'middle-class' university education generally.[131]

From its high point of ninety-six students in 1883, numbers dropped to seventy-eight in 1886. In that year the college suffered another blow in the death of Samuel Morley. He had supported the Association as a major shareholder and as a guarantor of its escalating mortgages—contracted to pay for new buildings—but he had many calls on his generosity: the college was only one of more than ninety organisations represented at his funeral, and the bulk of his great fortune was bequeathed to his children. It would only have been human if Brereton or Fortescue had toyed with the conjecture that with a stroke of his pen Morley could have cured Cavendish's financial problems and ensured its prosperous survival, but for Brereton at least this would have been an admission of the failure of the commercial principle basic to the "County Education" movement, and when this principle was indeed abondoned at Cavendish, Morley was not alive to help. With only fifty-four students in 1887 the interest on the mortgages could not be paid, and the bankers forbade further advances. The university supporters of Cavendish, led by Professor Liveing, persuaded the Duke of Devonshire that the commercial or proprietary principle would have to be jettisoned and that the college could only be saved by an appeal for endowments. The crisis over these principles was ventilated in the correspondence columns of the *Times*; Brereton resigned the Chairmanship of the County College Association, which went into voluntary liquidation and its assets, including the college, passed to a new company, the Cavendish College Association. The Duke of Devonshire put up the money for big extensions to the buildings, and Cox, who had resigned, was succeeded by a new warden.

Even in its new guise the social disadvantages of Cavendish made it vulnerable. The *Pall Mall Gazette*, which in 1874[132] had attacked—among other things—the commercial principle involved in the proposed County College, now renewed its attack on the social and educational pretensions of the college which was now appealing for endowments. It quoted as Cambridge's opinion of the College a phrase later identified as emanating from Oscar Browning—as a place "where the young farmer of sixteen gets at very moderate charges what his fond parents believe to be a university education". The *Pall Mall Gazette* went on:

> No one grudges to the 'young farmer' the value attaching to his B.A. degree as an intellectual diploma, for that is nil; but that degree has a real value of another kind, and, in so far, it is a fraudulent label as attached to the alumnus of Cavendish. To begin with: the isolated brick building which stands like a fever hospital apart from the desolate outskirts of new Cambridge, was intended all along to cut off its inmates from the culture of various social contact. It has succeeded, and the youth of Cavendish mix only with one another. This advantage they enjoyed equally before their removal from some good 'middle class school'. Of course they do get something. And there may be much virtue in a good butter-substitute turned out cheaply and in a hurry. But if its special recommendation lies in being got up to look superficially like prime Dorset, though its customers may like their margarine in that form, the patrons of the higher butter can scarcely be expected to subsidise its manufacture. We are all for the ideal of popularising the universities; but we would rather see '£10,000' raised for the growing local extension system, which has already done more towards the object than Cavendish College is likely to achieve if it stands till the blank brick walls begin to crumble.[133]

Of the replies this provoked, one, from an "M.A. (Cavendish)" threw interesting light on the social character of the college:

> Even supposing Cavendish were full of young farmers, is it to be therefore damned? But, as a matter of fact, most of its students are the sons of professional men. During the three years I spent there as an undergraduate I only knew of two

farmers' sons among my fellows. The remainder were chiefly the sons of parsons, lawyers and doctors.*

It may be that a mistake was made when Cavendish College was built so far from the town. But to say that its inmates are "cut off from the culture of various social contact" is also a mistake. No doubt the students mix more with themselves [*sic*] than with the men of other colleges; but in this they only conform to the universal rule. All the men have friends in other colleges. The companionship of the river and the athletic grounds, the culture of the university lecture rooms and library, and of musical and other societies, are open to and enjoyed by them. Surely in these things they have more opportunities than men who are only able to take advantage of the University Extension lectures, and even in the mere matter of learning mathematics, classics, or science, they are at least as well off as if they studied in distant towns.[134]

This sort of exchange did nothing to stem the decline at Cavendish under the new régime from 1888 onwards, not did the new buildings. If the nonconformist Cox had been unbusinesslike and a lax disciplinarian, the new warden, Mr Flather of Emmanuel, who had been bursar and tutor under the old régime, was objected to as not being distinguished as a scholar;[135] in pointing this out the journal *The Private Schoolmaster* (August 1888) was "not sure that the importation of new ability would not have been more advisable". Having by now severed all connection with the college, Fortescue and Brereton watched its decline with some detachment. In July 1891 Fortescue wrote that Cavendish was "in a very failing state, and threatened with extinction",[136] and at the end of December the college closed.† Ten days earlier its eponymous patron, the Duke, had died. The empty buildings were bought by the Congregational Board of Education to house its training

* School registers for the period show there was at least a sprinkling of public-school Old Boys at Cavendish, even some from major schools like Harrow, Merchant Taylors', etc.

† Many of its students were absorbed into other colleges. One such, an Open Classical Scholar of Cavendish who graduated from Christ's, went on to become headmaster of a public school (S. E. Longland, Glenalmond 1913–23).

college, Homerton College, which moved to Cambridge from its inadequate site in North East London (Middlesex) in 1894.[137]

Fortescue identified[138] as the causes of Cavendish's failure the establishment of Selwyn and the revival of the smaller colleges. The popularity of educational institutions conducted on Church principles rather than suspect unsectarian ones had already exhibited itself in the success of Woodard's schools and of Cranleigh compared with other 'middle-class' boarding-schools. At Oxford the strongly ecclesiastical character of the proposed Keble College had clearly stimulated the enthusiasm which caused over £30,000 to be subscribed for its establishment in 1870 in buildings soon to be described by the *Spectator* as "one of the most beautiful structures of modern England, and even of the city of Oxford itself".[139] (Not all shared this taste.) Hertford College, Oxford, reorganised in 1874, offered by 1883 thirty scholarships of £100 a year (compared with Cavendish's ten of £30 a year in 1883), and some of them, newly endowed by Mr Thomas Baring, were exclusively for Anglicans.[140] Cavendish had had the early support of J. B. Lightfoot, but on becoming Bishop of Durham in 1879 Lightfoot accepted a place on the Council of Selwyn. Though he continued to assert that "the principles of the two colleges are different . . . but legitimate,[141] the move symbolised the weakness of the non-Anglican alternative. The ancient universities, only recently opening up fully to nonconformists, were not yet ready to welcome a collegiate community whose membership blurred the lines between the Church and dissent, and, in the person of its longest-reigning warden, overstepped them. Even its friends outside the university were less passionate in their support than they would have been for a more extreme cause. Morley warned Fortescue not to expect too much popular support for Cavendish—"it is too wise, moderate, unsectarian, and unparty to excite enthusiasm",[142] and he himself seemed to exemplify this moderation when, as Fortescue said of him (in the year before Morley died) that where he would put down £1 for Cavendish he would "put down £5.10. for some regular nonconformist institution".[143]

Cambridge's student population rose from 1,526 in 1862 to 2,979 in 1886.[144] J. A. Venn's charts of Oxford and Cambridge matriculations show Cambridge falling off from the high point of just under 1,000 in 1886 and 1888 to 900 in 1904, while Oxford's matriculations went on rising steadily. Oxford's advantage in the last decade of the century has been seriously attributed to Oxford's nine-year sequence of victories in the Boat Race.[145] Keble was founded when Oxford's matriculations were very much on the upgrade—solidly from 1862 to 1879 (when they grew from about 450 to about 750 a year), a growth to which the new college of course contributed in a small way. Selwyn, too, had the advantage of starting in the period of a strong upward surge which was uninterrupted until 1887. Cavendish was being founded just at the time when for the moment the numbers of Cambridge matriculations were overtaking Oxford's.

It was not just the fortunes of new colleges which gave rise to these increases. At Cambridge the rise reflected (as Fortescue recognised) the growth of smaller colleges such as Jesus College which, under outstanding tutors and with a strong *esprit de corps* sustained by rowing successes,[146] had risen from around fourteen entries a year in the late 1850s, to around sixty in the early 1880s, although this fell to around thirty-two a year at the end of the century. At Pembroke, where in 1858 only one freshman had matriculated—and then promptly migrated to Caius—the tutorship of C. E. Searle marked a new era in the history of the college,[147] characterised by a rise in admissions to about fifty a year in the early 1880s. The recession in admissions which helped to sweep away Cavendish also hit some of the larger colleges—matriculations at St John's slumped from over one hundred in 1884 to below seventy in the early years of this century, though Trinty's continued to rise.[148]

The initial choice of an old-established college in preference to Cavendish might, therefore, have been influenced by doctrinal or ecclesiastical considerations (an ordinand, for example, might need to note that the new foundations had no ecclesiastical partronage to offer) or by the prejudices of schoolmasters.[149] Once entered at Cavendish, a man who later decided to migrate was more likely to have been influenced by its social disadvantages. Brereton had been at pains to stress that no "ascetic principle" lay behind the "economical discipline", which was rather to prevent "contracting habits of luxury". But it was one thing to offer members of "the most educated and the best-bred English families", "the less cultured but ever-rising middle ranks", and "the increasing numbers which may be expected to emerge from the elementary schools" an opportunity of "securing a place among the best certified scholars and gentlemen of the land",[150] and quite another thing to locate them in a building variously likened to a "fever hospital" or a "lunatic asylum",[151] in which these principles of economy were rendered even less palatable by inefficient management. As we have seen, loyal Cavendish men proclaimed that none of these disadvantages prevented their enjoyment of all the academic and social privileges of the university; others claimed that self-discipline, Dr Arnold's prerequisite of public-school education, was the principle fostered by the régime of life and work at the college.[152] But there were others still who voted with their feet.

Women students at Cambridge had to put up with long distances between their colleges and the centres of university activities because they had no alternative. But even the proctors found the comparative remoteness of Cavendish too much for their normal circuit,[153] and when the college gained its 'recognised' status in 1882 its members had to observe a curfew after 10 p.m. If Cavendish had survived for a few more years these disadvantages would have been greatly reduced. F. W. Pethick-Lawrence, who went up from Eton to Trinity in 1891, described in his autobiography how during his period of residence in Cambridge

> . . . the safety bicycle created a revolution in university life. The old 'penny farthing' had never, of course, been a practical means of locomotion, and in consequence we walked everywhere. But the 'safety' could be mounted at any time in any clothes and left anywhere. It saved time and enabled sports grounds to be much further out from the colleges . . .[154]

3

The County College had been the keystone of Brereton's whole structure of "County Education" and was as important a complement to the middle-class schools as was William of Wykeham's New College to his school at Winchester. Characteristically, Brereton had pressed ahead with its establishment before the rest of the framework of contributory schools were either numerous or successful,[155] but Fortescue joined him in thinking that the creation of this apex of the system was "more important at present"[156] than the expansion of County Schools; in Brereton's own County Schools the existence of Cavendish was seen as essential to their own success, as a place where they might send on perhaps as many as twenty boys a year.[157] Yet Brereton's involvement, from his Norfolk Rectory, in the fluctuating fortunes of Cavendish had not prevented the proliferation of further schemes.

An opportunity was presented by the activities of the Rev. B. L. Dwarris,[158] a Tyneside rector who had been a contemporary of Sir Stafford Northcote at Eton. On his initiative a committee was founded in 1869, in connection with the University of Durham, "for the purpose of improving middle class education in the Northern counties". After a plan to use the funds of the Shaftoe Foundation at Haydon Bridge, Northumberland, as the basis of a "Northumberland County School" had fallen foul of the inhabitants of that town, Dwarris was approached by the Trustees of the late Benjamin Flounders, a timber merchant and active supporter of the Stockton and Darlington railway, who had left more than £30,000 for "the general encouragement and promotion and extension of education . . . among classes of every religious denomination (except Roman Catholics)".[159]

Meanwhile the trustees of St John's Hospital, Barnard Castle, a thirteenth-century chantry foundation which in 1864 was producing an income of about £250, were considering the establishment of a school in their own town. In 1882 a scheme under the Endowed Schools Act consolidated these two endowments and allowed for the establishment of a "County School" on condition that at least £10,000 be raised by voluntary subscription for the buildings, which the activities of Dwarris's Committee and the support of Earl Grey soon achieved. Dwarris's admiration for the County School movement was reflected in the choice by the Governors (an imposing body which included the Lords Lieutenant of Durham,

Northumberland and the North Riding, and representatives of Durham University, etc.), of a headmaster for the new school: they chose Brereton's son, Frank, who, after being educated at the Norfolk County School, had graduated at Cavendish and then been ordained. The foundation stone of buildings costing nearly £30,000 was laid in 1883 by Lord Fortescue at a ceremony at which Warden Cox of Cavendish and Bishop Lightfoot of Durham were present, the latter also attending as the main guest at the formal opening in 1886 of the "North Eastern County School".

Longley, the Chief Charity Commissioner, advised Brereton in 1881 that the provision of girls' education would be safer than that of boys' education in arousing less hostility and jealousy from schoolmasters.[160] *County Education* had in 1874 already proposed some such provision in due course, and Brereton saw in the undoubted profitability of some girls' school ventures[161] in the 1880s an opportunity to recoup his family fortunes, in which hope Fortescue sympathised with him. Brereton was still involved in lengthy and costly litigation with his brothers and cousins over his parents' estate and his own trusteeship of it. Before he knew the outcome of a lawsuit over a serious railway accident which had injured him in 1881 (and for which he was ultimately awarded £4,000, against which he had already raised loans), Brereton plunged into the promotion of the "Graduated County Schools Association". Its aims were to found or to take over girls' schools (though boys' schools might follow) on a proprietary basis and on the gradations proposed by *County Education* (1874) and with some provision for higher education by way of a women's hostel in a university town.[162] In 1881 the Duke of Devonshire wrote that at seventy-three he was unwilling to connect himself with a new undertaking involving unfamiliar and unforeseen responsibilities. He observed that Brereton seemed to have no definite promises of financial assistance and questioned the expediency of proceeding—indeed of starting *immediately*, as Brereton proposed—without a wide basis of assured support,[163] but in 1885 he was willing to give his name as a supporter of the principles of the G.C.S.A.[164] Morely was not prepared to do even that[165] and "resolutely repudiated an interest in the Association".[166] Between 1880 and 1887 Brereton swept into his educational empire a collection of girls' schools at Darlington, Barnard Castle, Worcester Park, Taunton, Bayswater, King's Lynn, Blackheath and Uffcolme, the last-mentioned under a separate "Devon and Somerset County School for Girls Association".[167]

From a temporary base at Darlington, within reach of his son Frank at Barnard Castle, Brereton attempted to persuade the northerners to take shares in his association, but he had miscalculated both the support they would give[168] and the margin of capital that would be needed to cater for an emergency in any of the schools—whether an epidemic or a scandal.[169] As if in desperation, Brereton launched yet another enterprise, a Gloucester County School Association[170] which created a Gloucester County School to be overseen by another son, Henry, a Cavendish graduate who had a Gloucester curacy. Here too the creditors were soon pressing.[171] In 1887, as Brereton put it, "the storm burst".[172] The failure of the proprietary principle which led in that year to the reconstitution of Cavendish without Brereton led also to the collapse of G.C.S.A. in a blaze of recriminations in which the word "swindler" was used of Brereton by his fellow directors.[173] Fortescue had invested heavily in Brereton's schemes, not in the hope of gain, but that they might prove a "*tabula in naufragio*" for his friend's luckless family;[174] he lost more than £1,600 in the G.C.S.A.[175] Brereton seemed more concerned about Fortescue's doubts about such essential doctrines of county education as the commercial principle than about his own—or the Earl's—financial losses, and a rift, serious but short-lived, developed between the two men.[176]

After his very successful start at the "North Eastern County School", Frank Brereton had transferred to the headmastership of the Norfolk County School in 1887, but the agricultural depression starved it of both capital and pupils, and in May 1891 the Brereton régime at Elmham collapsed. The Directors, who included the Earl of Leicester and the Bishop of Norwich, arranged to carry on the school on condition that J. L. Brereton withdrew from the Association and his son Frank from the headmastership; in 1893 the Norfolk County School, despite grants from the Norfolk County Council for science teaching, finally went into liquidation.[177] Meanwhile the Gloucester

County School Association and its boys' school had disappeared virtually without trace.

By 1892 those parts of the County School movement directly connected with Brereton lay largely in ruins. Other schools of the type still flourished. Of his own schools and colleges, however, only the Devon County School survived precariously and the North Eastern County School at Barnard Castle flourished, but in other hands, as an endowed school under independent governors and a new headmaster imported from Repton—a former Captain of the Cambridge University Boat Club.

Even before he and his son had been ousted from Elmham in 1891 Brereton had established a new "County College" at nearby Massingham, planning a building which Fortescue warned him would be "in the wise old Duke of Wellington's words . . . the raw material of his ruination". Joined by his parson sons Frank and Harry, after their withdrawal respectively from the County Schools of Norfolk and Gloucester, the rector of Massingham and his two curates[178] carried on with private tuition. The sudden death of the Reptonian oarsman left a vacancy for a headmaster at Barnard Castle. With a little help from Fortescue, who used his influence with one of the governors (the new Bishop Westcott of Durham, who had taught Fortescue's son at Harrow), Frank was re-appointed in 1893, and his brother Harry joined him as second master in 1897.[179]

At West Buckland, the Devon County School had nearly closed in 1891 after a steady decline in numbers, and although these rose again in 1892 (from about thirty-eight to eighty-three)[180] it was clear that a drastic remedy was necessary. Fortescue's son and heir, Lord Ebrington, was a member of the Devonshire County Council; unlike Brereton's sons, he had long lost any enthusiasm he had ever shared with his father for the County School movement.[181] But with his fellow-councillor, Acland, he suggested that the Devon County School should apply to the Council for a grant out of the Government provision for technical instruction[182]—the famous "whisky money" made available as a result of the Local Taxation (Customs and Excise) Act of 1890. It became obvious that such a grant could only be made if the commercial principle were abandoned; it was also obvious that the Devon County School could not compete with other schools that benefited from this provision in science unless its governors consented to this change. Fortescue deplored the inevitable consequence of "this innocent false step of the Tories", that "the wisest and most practical scheme for the diminution of drunkeness, when applied to promote Technical Education, would accelerate enormously the government's practical control through the County Councils and similar bodies over secondary education". Yet he was obliged to note a "growing feeling in the middle class, and especially of the farmers, now in favour of aid from rates and taxes" and an "acquiescence in Government inspection and in Government control of secondary education". "Nothing but theological ardour," he felt, "can be arrayed with success on the other side", yet, as he observed ruefully but pointedly, "schools on the soundest principles are useless without scholars".[183]

The required change in the constitution of the school involved the replacement of shares by mortgage debentures with interest limited to 4½%.[184] This surrender of a vital proprietary principle and the acceptance of the often reviled public money was a bitter pill, though swallowed more readily by the realistic Fortescue than by Brereton. Fortescue "recognised that the tide of public opinion was steadily setting in favour of Government grants, involving of course Government interference", while still agreeing with Brereton that public opinion and a succession of governments were mistaken in ignoring the part which the commercial principle could have played in the provision of secondary education.[185]

The "undesirably modified shape" of Brereton's first great handiwork[186] brought with it a measure of control by the Devon County Council over the fees chargeable and also the institution of three day-boy scholarships for boys from elementary schools within six miles of the Devon County School.[187] This gave rise to fears among

> some middle class parents at the large influx of elementary school boys as Devon County Council Scholars. But [the headmaster] had no fear for the tone of the school having suffered in consequence. He thinks on the contrary, *post* not *propter*, hoc, that it has on the whole improved.[188]

Nor did a measure of 'government' control and financial aid in itself ensure the school's stability. A fresh crisis arose at the end of the century when an able headmaster disagreed with the Governors over his wife's handling of the domestic side and resigned, set up a rival school at Barnstaple and took away about fifty of the boys from Devon County School with him.[189] Disaster was only averted by fresh financial guarantees from leading trustees and from the new headmaster himself, and by the device whereby Fortescue ostentatiously sent off telegrams to other members of the governing body from the local post office—"School prospects now excellent"—to allay rumours in the neighbourhood that the school was about to close.[190]

To the end, Brereton never abandoned hope of the recovery of Elmham as a school or college.[191] His disappointments over the surrender at the Devon County School and its later difficulties were balanced by his pleasure in the continuing success of the North Eastern County School which, under his sons Frank and Harry, for the first time reached three hundred pupils in the year of Brereton's death.[192]

The preoccupations of Brereton's last years—pursued in the correspondence columns of the *Times* and in lectures and papers—were proposals, in which Fortescue supported him, for training colleges,[193] and for the "revival of the diaconate of the primitive church". The order was to be created or re-created in the Anglican and other Christian churches,[194] and thrown open to teachers as a means of ensuring avowedly Christian instruction and of binding to the service of the churches men whose professional status would be dignified by the title of "Reverend".[195] He died in August 1901, leaving his children to cope with the large residue of debt which had nearly caused his bankruptcy at the time of the crises of Cavendish, the G.C.S.A. and the Norfolk County School, and which included £5,000 owed to Fortescue on which no interest had been paid since 1862.[196] The latter's losses in many of Brereton's schemes, together with declining rents on his estates in Lincolnshire and confiscations in Ireland, had forced him to sell his London house and to shut up all but a wing of the family home at Castle Hill in Devon.[197]

4

The essentials of the County School movement were that its schools and colleges were designed for the middle classes; and that they were to be proprietary, unsectarian, and cheap. The movement largely failed because, as the benefit of hindsight now enables us to realise, each one of these four principles was inappropriate for Victorian society.

Almost all of Brereton's working life was spent in rural England—in East Anglia and in the South West—and it was natural for him to consider the problems of educational provision in mid-century in terms of the "midmost man". Yet England's farmers were the least education-conscious of any group in the wider middle classes. The Taunton Commissioners in 1868 noted the report of their Assistant Commissioner for Devon and Somerset:

> I was most struck in my enquiries with the general indifference of parents to the education of their sons. This especially was the case with the smaller farmers. The only spur which goaded them into a languid activity was the growing consciousness that the labourers were being better educated than their own sons.[198]

Nearly thirty years later this "indifference" was reported as "hostility" by the Assistant Commissioner for Devon to the Bryce Commission on Secondary Education: a hostility which extended even to technical agricultural education. He noted that farmers did not hesitate to reduce the amount allotted to school fees when harvests were bad.[199]

Brereton had been warned of this by the landowners whom he circulated in 1864 in support of his first County College, in Devon. The Earl of Devon wrote that he doubted "if tradesmen and farmers would be disposed to leave their children at school after fifteen or sixteen".[200] A Frome farmer warned him that Somerset farmers were "so economical a race, and so distrustful of the value of a really good education", and in his next letter went on to make the significant comment, "I had not understood from your programme that you wished to create a want rather than to satisfy one".[201]

Brereton pressed ahead, but these warnings were confirmed in the experience of the Norfolk County School. Despite Fortescue's proud claim in 1874 that the magnificent buildings "originated with the farmers", these same farmers were slow in supporting the school either with capital or with their sons, as his correspondence with Brereton frequently complains: by 1895 the older middle-class independence, especially of farmers, had been replaced by "an eager scrambling for public assistance".[202] The Bryce Commissioners noted the fine site and flourishing state of the Surrey County School at Cranleigh by 1895; they also noted that the school intended for farmers and tradesmen's sons "would have disappeared if it had depended on the farmers".[203] Brereton and Fortescue had always recognised that farmers undervalued education and had looked to the challenge of the Local Examinations to overcome this;[204] experience taught them the painful lesson that the imposing Local Examination record of all their County Schools made no impact on the farmers at all. The great farming depression of later Victorian England which was to hit at rent rolls and banks and college revenues (and Fellows' dividends)—not least at Cambridge—would hit hardest of all those institutions specifically designed for a farming clientele.

We do not know how far the 'commercial' or 'proprietary' principle would have succeeded if left alone in the field. As it happened, the idea was overtaken by what Brereton and Fortescue regarded as unfair (indeed "mischievous") competition—the creation of a rival system of secondary education as a result of the work of the Endowed Schools Commissioners, government provision of elementary (and in some cases post-elementary) schools, and the activities of religious enthusiasts.[205] They viewed the extension of "state" activity with mounting alarm, partly because at the elementary level it represented "the unfair forcing on of labourers' children (at the expense of farmers' children) at the public expense"; partly because at the secondary level it involved both waste and secularisation, and partly because any new schools threatened the survival of their own. Even rival "county schools" in the South West, such as the West Somerset County School (Wellington, Somerset) were seen as dangers,[206] while Woodard's new King's College, Taunton, was both dangerous and foolish—the opening of a brand new school intended for the same class as was the one that had failed was "a fresh specimen of Somersetshire folly" as well as an attempt to extend bigotry.[207]

Because of this competition from 'state' provision, it is impossible to use the County Education movement as a test of the controversial thesis which has been advanced[208] that the extent of voluntary provision of education in the nineteenth century made state intervention (from 1870 onwards) unnecessary, if not actually undesirable. Nevertheless the fact that the voluntary principle as exemplified in Brereton's 'proprietary' schemes suffered not merely a disappintment but a rout, seems to offer little support to that argument. At this distance, Brereton's financial computations look very unsound. For many of his contemporaries they must have been compromised by his over-optimism, even recklessness, and possibly also by his tendency to regard his schools as openings for employment for his own numerous sons and daughters—a flagrant example was his proposal in 1881 that young Frank, who had graduated at seventeen from Cavendish, should be dispensed from having to wait till the canonical age of ordination in order that he might almost immediately become Chaplain of the college.[209]

That the cheapness which should have been one of the strongest points of Breretons' programme became one of its weak points, illustrates the founders' failure to grasp the true nature of the Victorian concept of the public school or of the university collegiate community. The three grades of County Schools were designed to be "public schools"—the prospectus of the Norfolk County School emphasised that the school was "arranged on practically the same lines as Marlborough and Wellington Colleges"[210]—and they all developed at least rudimentary house systems, with an emphasis on *esprit de corps* and prefects and organised games. But if the boys behaved like public-school boys and "indulged in precisely the same larks as Rugby boys",[211] or demanded similar recreational facilities to those of public-school boys, Fortescue's indignation and scorn knew no bounds. Of the headmaster of Devon County School he wrote:

> I have always thought [that] Thompson, mis-reading *Tom Brown* and its lessons, thought it rather fine to have County

> School boys @ £25 a year breaking windows, tearing books and wasting food, exactly as public school boys do, foolishly and wrongly, whose parents pay from £150 to £300 for them.[212]

He later complained that Thompson insisted on costly *covered* fives courts at Devon County School, as if the D.C.S. "should provide (for £30 p.a.) everything for the boys that Eton and Harrow do for £200".[213] The boarding costs of the three grades of County School, and of the County College, were geared to the more economical styles of life of the various gradations of the middle class,[214] but in a period when schools (and colleges at the university) were being used to obtain and confirm social status it was a fallacy to suppose that one could advertise one's cheaper style of life and still gain social acceptance—as Cavendish men found. It is significant that there was pressure from both parents and masters at County Schools that the schools should move upwards through the gradations: Devon County School started as a grade III school with its own farm, became second-grade, and was at one time being considered for elevation to the status of a first-grade school; at Norfolk County School Brereton originally "had difficulty in getting assent to fixing the charge to parents no higher than 40 gns".[215] Woodard's schools, as we have seen, demonstrated a similar "upward" tendency.

Nowhere is the connection between cheapness and the barriers to social acceptance seen more obviously than in the case of staff. Without any distinctive religious ethos to appeal to, the men who were found for the County Schools and the County College were only as good as the founders could afford to pay. J. H. Thompson, a bluff Yorkshireman, had started up the Devon County School with three boys in 1858 when he was twenty-one and later interrupted his headmastership to graduate at Cambridge in his late twenties. His rough manners repelled the farmers and professional men of North Devon and were an obstacle to the school's gaining social respectability.[216] When the collapse of the West of England Bank swept away his provision for retirement he could not be expected to retire (since Brereton's schemes made no provision for pension) unless a living could be found for him—he had been ordained a deacon after graduating but only proceeded to the priesthood after nearly thirty years as headmaster. By contrast, Woodard could recruit for his schools some good graduates of impeccable social origin whose Anglo-Catholic dedication would reconcile them to low salaries, and at the "churchy" Cranleigh the flourishing numbers in 1875 sustained a salary of £900 for a headmaster of high calibre.[217] The warden's low stipend[218] at Cavendish furnished the college with a man who, for all he was "a thorough gentleman",[219] had neither the character nor the social connections such as helped the first warden of Keble College, Oxford, to overcome the initial hostility[220] which had attended its establishment. At Keble, exactly the same prejudices[221] had been ventilated as were to haunt Cavendish—including even the suggestion at Keble that an austere régime at the university was "morally undesirable"[222] (whatever that meant), whereas the mixing of richer and poorer men, it was argued, could better be contrived within existing colleges. With an aristocratic background that was combined with connections with the Lytteltons and the Gladstones, Edward Talbot was at twenty-five appointed warden of Keble from a Studentship at Christ Church. Undergraduates from all colleges found him a charming and inspiring companion with a "genius for fellowship"; his wife (a Lyttelton) brought to her social relations with the Keble undergraduates a sparkling grace, and Talbot exercised a concern to bring his undergraduates in touch with public men in Church and State. A procession of famous figures who were invited to stay with the warden—Stubbs, Acton, Newman, Dean Church, Archbishop Benson, Lord Halifax, Jowett, Goldwin Smith, Salisbury, Gladstone, Arthur Balfour, Archbishop Tait, even the young Curzon—helped bring prestige to the "upstart college".[223] The brilliant band of Keble tutors he collected around him included the future Sir Arthur Acland (1847–1926), Liberal politician and Education minister.[224] Like Cavendish, Keble chose the games field and the river as an avenue to acceptance in the university—a policy which the college was to carry to even greater lengths in the twentieth century. Talbot was bitterly disappointed when the College Eight, which rose rapidly from the bottom to be Head of the River, was bumped on the third night—Bishop Abraham testified that Talbot cared quite as much as any undergraduate how the Eight was doing, and it is recorded that in the course of a really grave illness from which he was not expected to recover he sent for the Keble score book from the cricket captain.[225]

Even by 1874 Fortescue recognised that, in the competition between the "comparatively unendowed County Schools" and the "newly revived Endowed schools", the unsectarian principle was at a disadvantage in the struggle with "Ritualists and Secularists". "Enlightened Christians, liberal but not radical, Broad Church but not sceptical, lack the energy within and the support from without that violent partisanship secures".[226] Besides the secularism which he felt was implicit in the extension of Government activity in secondary education, he recognised that his chief enemy was Woodard, though any extreme of "churchiness" had its dangers, not least in the competition among schools to which it gave rise—it was the intense "churchiness" of Bishop Benson, and more particularly of Mrs Benson and the episcopal entourage at Truro, which Fortescue saw as responsible for provoking the establishment of a Wesleyan school at Truro which threatened to lure away an average of twenty boys a year from the Devon County School.[277] Yet he rejoiced when, out of range of competition with the Devon County School, the evangelical Trent College (under the patronage of the Duke of Devonshire and Fortescue's uncle, Lord Harrowby) was founded in opposition to Denstone by local men alarmed "for the future of the race" [*sic*] by the "Oxford movement as embodied in Dr Woodard".[228]

Brereton's educational ideas, even his scheme for three grades of schools for the gradations of the middle classes, seem to have been little influenced by Woodard, whose original manifesto in 1848 was privately circulated rather than published.[229] References to Woodard (often spelt Woodward, as was common even among the latter's supporters) throughout the extensive Fortescue-Brereton correspondence from the 1860s onwards are virtually limited to despairing reactions to the comparative success of the rival whose system embodied the key element that was so repugnant to their own principle of unsectarian Christianity. Yet as well as such differences, there were many points of similarity between the County School movement and Woodard's system, and indeed between the two men. Both men conducted their educational campaigns from their positions as fairly obscure Victorian parsons. Neither was a distinguished public speaker,[230] though Brereton as a writer had a graceful style. Neither had any school experience as classroom teacher or headmaster. Both devoted immense energies to circularising possible supporters by public or private letters and subscription lists, and propagandising their schemes by public meetings, school ceremonies, and items in the press.[231] A major objective for both was to secure the adhesion of influential people, and both were rewarded for their efforts by a measure of ecclesiastical recognition secured by the intervention of an influential supporter on their behalf. Woodard was promoted to a Canonry of Manchester in 1870 and later became Sub-Dean, a D.C.L. of Oxford, and Proctor in Convocation; and Lowe was recommended to Gladstone for preferment by a supporter of the movement.[232] Brereton was made a Prebendary of Exeter after only ten years in Orders and might have achieved further preferment if his supporters (or indeed his schemes) had been more successful. Early in 1873 Fortescue had written to Brereton:

> I do hope and trust that you personally are in a fairer way of having your great public services recognised a little, though your views and acts are hardly those which a Puseyite Radical, such as Gladstone is now, with a Government comprising many secularists, would best appreciate . . .[233]

and the following year Fortescue expressed his indignation that

> Confessional Woodward receives a magnificent recognition of his very minor services and your far greater ones are ignored

—and went on to reflect that this was because Palmerston "died before your work had at all conspicuously extended, and Gladstone naturally turned away from a Protestant to a Romanising parson".[234] Fortescue's father, the 2nd Earl, had strongly recommended Brereton to Palmerston for a canonry, and Lord Taunton had asked for a similar preferment for him; Fortescue himself, together with Sir Stafford Northcote, had recommended Brereton for the new Bishopric of Truro.[235] In the event, the only palpable result of Fortescue's influence was in persuading Temple to procure Brereton's appointment as Select Preacher at Oxford.[236] Even Bishop Jackson refused to bestow a lucrative London living on his former pupil, on the grounds that there were already in the diocese "600 unbeneficed and for the most part expectant clergy" with a prior claim.[237]

Woodard's rejection of the commercial principle on which Brereton had relied was vindicated by his success in raising huge sums and securing them by a cautious policy of "making our way sure as we go along by backing up our results . . . with marketable property".[238] His one failure in his lifetime was a military and commercial college at Leyton, whose collapse after eight years in 1858 may have made him, if anything, over-cautious; his planned chapel at Lancing was unfinished at his death, but it seems he expected this. By contrast all Brereton's schemes were undercapitalised, and he seemed to learn nothing from their collapse, pressing ahead with fresh proposals amid the ruins of the earlier ones and doggedly reluctant to adjust his principles in the light of new forms of competition after 1869—competition from which Woodard also suffered[239] but which he was in a better position to survive.

As to religious education, the two men were united only in their conviction that increasing state activity must take a form which was inimical to the survival of Christianity among the people. Both their systems of schools were attended by the sons of dissenters, but those few who went to Woodard's had parents who were prepared to risk their indoctrination in order to secure a good education. Both men were forced by the laws of supply and demand to make provision for the training of teachers, Woodard with his own form of teachers' diploma (A.S.N.C.), Brereton in his County College and, after the collapse of Cavendish, by reviving his earlier proposal deriving from Arnold, of a teaching diaconate. Both were concerned with the problem of making university education available to the less well-off student, but after tentatively proposing to found his own college at Cambridge in 1879,[240] Woodard left the field clear for Cavendish (which was popular with Woodard's products) and later Selwyn, and, of course, Keble College at Oxford. While Brereton provided a practical curriculum for his middle-class pupils, Woodard's schools retained an emphasis on Latin. Brereton's reliance on university local examinations at which schools like the Devon County School sustained a high rate of success (though with small effect on recruitment), was not shared by Woodard, who disliked forms of certification which could not measure religious or moral qualities. (Lowe, however, differed with him on this.)

Brereton and Fortescue never committed themselves to the thorough-going view of the transfer of function between school and parents which was implicit in Woodard's view of the role of his schools in transforming the values of the middle classes. Like Woodard, Brereton and Fortescue were political conservatives who looked on their system of schools as a means of securing social and political stability. It was precisely because they saw in the lack of public provision for the middle classes compared with their social inferiors[241] a threatened "inversion of the actual order of society" that Brereton and Fortescue sought to make good that want by appealing to the pride and independence—and the financial contributions—of the middle classes to found and support a system of public schools. From time to time Fortescue's private suspicions of the middle classes showed through, as when he confided to Brereton in 1882 his distrust of that class "which I fear from all I hear is becoming constantly sharper and less scrupulous in its practices and less ashamed of fraud of all kinds, and especially adulterations and lies . . ."[242] But there is little sign that the schools they founded were designed to supersede parental influence, as in part Woodard conceived his. In 1868 Fortescue expressed to Brereton his agreement with an (unidentified) speech by C. J. Vaughan:

> I mean to take up the tone [of that speech], which led me to become a Sanitary Reformer 25 years ago, [which was] that influences of the home affect the religious and moral (as well as ex hypothesi the physical) wellbeing of the population more than Schools . . .[243]

and though this may only have been at a popular level, there is enough evidence for the conclusion that, at least in religious matters, Brereton regarded the schoolmaster as "the trusted representative of the parents".[244]

Starting out from the belief in the co-extensiveness of Church and State, Woodard was forced away from reliance on the diocesan basis because of episcopal prejudices and the disarray of ecclesiastical authority symbolised by the Gorham judgement and its repercussions. Brereton, with no such starting point, looked to a county basis for his system: a basis with no obvious rationale except to an enthusiast for a kind of local government reform very different from that which actually took shape in the later nineteenth century. At the outset of Brereton's County College schemes the Duke of Devonshire had questioned the logic of founding a new system on the "county" principle at the very moment when "the recent tendency at the Universities" had been to abolish the "county" and "local" character of higher education.[245] In fact, Brereton looked to *locality* to foster interest in middle-class education as a partnership between home and school. The system was never sufficiently well-established to indicate to us how he would have reacted to a conflict of values between the two, though in the last analysis the force of religion was probably regarded as the great solvent—but without the powerful apparatus of indoctrination provided for in Woodard's schools: only one of Brereton's schools (Elmham) had its own chapel. Apart from this, we only know that, like Woodard, Brereton identified three grades of social class and, like Woodard, devised for them severally a range of boys' boarding-schools[246] which in both systems developed, as Victorian public schools must, most of the characteristic machinery of prefects, houses, games etc.; and also that, almost as an afterthought, both systems made some provision for girls' education.

Within a general framework of political and social stability, both Brereton's and Woodard's systems were designed to promote a measure of social mobility. The success of Woodard's schools in achieving this was modified by the tendency the schools showed when they became prosperous and academically successful to become more exclusive socially. There is no reason to suppose that Brereton's schools would not have done the same if they had had similar success. The County College, in giving higher education to boys from all levels of the contributory school structure, had a most obvious function to promote social mobility. The difficulty was in designing a means of achieving this—of striking the balance between the two aims of stimulating higher university standards by introducing increasing numbers of socially mobile middle-class students, on the one hand, while on the other hand of avoiding the danger of "so many of the middle class being introduced, as sensibly to lower the tone and social position of the universities, instead of, as at present, [its] being raised to a higher level".[247] Brereton saw as a third function of the County College the wider diffusion of the culture of the élite, and in 1878 he looked forward to the time when, after twenty years of success at Cavendish, university men would no longer "find it difficult to retain their raised literary tastes when merged in the chaos of great cities, or scattered in provincial towns and villages . . . University men . . . will not be a reserved clique in any county or neighbourhood".[248] The collapse of Cavendish showed that the failure of that third aim was bound up in the failure to design and create a community which could reconcile the other two.

5

Professor W. B. D. Heeney sees Woodard as "a grand failure"; as one who bore witness to a forgotten ideal—of the church as educator of the nation.[249] Yet Woodard left behind him a network of schools and a band of enthusiastic disciples who would increase their prosperity and expand his system. The schools inspired hundreds of men to a life of service according to the values they fostered—whether in Holy Orders, teaching, or any of the various careers into which public school men[250] would enter—and the appeal of their "churchiness" was far greater than Brereton's alternative. Brereton in this was ahead of his time, whereas in other respects—the acknowledgements of government action, for example—he was overtaken by events. None of the schools of the County Schools movement which survived adhered to his principles. Cranleigh and Framlingham went on to become orthodox public schools with a conventional clientele; by the end of the Victorian period Cranleigh had gained acceptance among what were perhaps the top fifty public schools, while Framlingham lagged a little further behind. The Bedford County School abandoned the 'commercial principle' on which it had been founded when, in 1898, the proprietorship passed from the Company to its headmaster, the Rev. C. S.

Farrar, an Anglican of Methodist origin who taught at Manchester Grammar School before becoming Headmaster of Bedford County School in 1893. (His brother, Sir George Farrar, had made a fortune on the Rand before the Jameson Raid, and some of this may have been made available to help with the purchase:[251] a strong contingent of boys from South Africa attended the school during his headmastership.) Farrar was an able preacher and public speaker, and his prominent position as a citizen of Bedford both reflected and supported the flourishing state of the school under him, in numbers, in scholarship and, not least, in cricket. An indication of the school's standing by 1912 was the selection of one of its boys to play for the Public Schools' Eleven in that year.[252] In 1907 Farrar changed the school's name to Elstow, after John Bunyan's village on the outskirts of Bedford in which it stood, in order to avoid confusion with the new "county schools" established by local authorities. In 1916 the school's buildings were requisitioned by the War Office for use as a military college, and his own failing health, after twenty-three years as headmaster, reconciled Farrar to the closure of the school* in that year.[254] Its rather ornate building did duty as a warehouse for a firm which specialised in the manufacture of dustless chalk for schoolmasters before it was pulled down in the 1960s.

A witness to the Bryce Commission in 1895 considered that if special trains were laid on to bring day boys from Dereham to Elmham, the Norfolk County School might be revived.[255] Brereton, whose speculations had included investments in railways in Norfolk, had early persuaded the Great Eastern Railway to make a special County School Station† for Elmham, and special trains at the beginning and end of term were serving the school by 1874. But it was now too late; the buildings were bought by a Mr G. H. Watts of London and presented to Dr Barnardo's organisation to serve as a school for boys intended for the merchant navy and the R.N.[256] into which it sent on many hundreds of boys for nearly sixty years until it closed in 1953 on

*Among its pupils in its later years was J. A. Steers, later Professor of Geography at Cambridge; among its masters was the formidable F. J. Shirley, later headmaster of the King's School, Canterbury.[253]

† One of only three stations located primarily to serve schools. The others were Wellington and Radley.

grounds of economy.[257] It passed to a London demolition and development firm for £15,000 in 1957,[258] and, after the main building had been demolished, the outbuildings were converted into a broiler farm and the chapel into a centrally-heated piggery.[259] The County School Station is still marked on modern maps of the area.

Frank Brereton sustained the success of the North Eastern County School until he retired in 1924 to succeed his brother in the family living at Little Massingham. "Barnard Castle School" accepted Direct Grant status, and after the Second World War his successor as headmaster was elected to the HMC. The Devon County School likewise became (as "West Buckland School") a Direct Grant school but did not achieve HMC status until the 1960s. Of J. L. Brereton's grandsons, one became joint-headmaster and later warden of Gordonstoun; another became warden of a Cambridgeshire village college—a venture inspired by an ideal similar to Brereton's, of extending the intellectual and cultural horizons of the local community in rural areas.

CHAPTER THREE

The development of the system and its functions: some implications of 'community'

1. Rise of the games cult.

Cotton's rescue and transformation of Marlborough, and the methods which helped him achieve this, are symbolic of a new phase in the development of the Victorian public school.

Six weeks after Cotton's assumption of the headmastership in August 1852, a Marlborough boy entered a terse note in his diary. "Capital speech from Cotton. The Sixth form are to govern the school."[1] The anxious governors had asked Cotton for an assurance that he would allow no boys to go out except in pairs with a master. Cotton replied that he would make the school govern itself by means of prefects or he would resign. The boys "must either submit to the prefects, or be reduced to the level of a private school, and have their freedom ignominiously curtailed".[2]

A prefect system, complete with prefects' courts, already existed. What Cotton did was to transform it by enlarging the prefects' functions, increasing their privileges and making them responsible directly to himself. At the same time bounds were codified in such a way as to increase the freedom of all the boys. Significantly, since it was the spirit and not the form of the institution that mattered, Cotton actually abolished the formal oath which Wilkinson (like Woolley at Rossall) had exacted from his prefects on entering office.[3]

Though not athletic himself (he had, as a Westminster boy, displayed a distaste for games)[4] Cotton responded to a demand which came from the boys themselves[5] by arranging for the provision of organised games—"constant and wholesome recreation for the boys"[6]—for which he circularised the parents for subscriptions. By means of games Cotton helped to break down the unofficial but powerful system of "tribes" which had grown up among the boys[7] and to divert them from birds-nesting, poaching and other more undesirable recreations which had been characteristic of Wilkinson's Marlborough, though it must also be noted that football (unorganised, of course) was being played during Wilkinson's time and furthermore had gone on as usual throughout the period of the 1851 rebellion.[8]

Cotton persuaded friends and former pupils to join his staff at the reduced salaries made necessary by the school's straitened finances. He himself gave the lead in transforming the distant relationship between boys and staff which had been the rule under his predecessor, at first by the simple device of entertaining boys to tea or dinner in his house. As the schoolboy diarist noted in 1854:

> Went with Smith to tea with Cotton—he made himself remarkably pleasant and showed us pictures of Thorne, etc. Brawn and bacon.[9]

Fifteen years later another boy, who had entered with Cotton in 1852, looked back on the transformation:

> Gradually but very surely the old conservative masters took themselves off to other fields, and one after another came dropping in some new and young faces, inspiring all with confidence, and something very like affection . . .
> . . . Marlborough's great transformation was accomplished in her games. These young brave masters came among us and reformed our cricket in a slight degree; they altogether reformed our football, turning it from a private farce into a great school institution . . . they helped us to build our racket court and fives courts . . . But not only in the cricket and football field, in the courts and in the music-room, did this great work of reformation march along. After chapel, when the day

was done, in those quiet cosy little rooms of theirs, over pleasant pots of tea and large pots of jam, these young masters proved . . . how much we had to be thankful for in their friendship . . . they turned their rooms into bear-gardens in our account, and a few of us were initiated into the art of drop kicking in their very rooms . . .[10]

Another entry in a schoolboy diary illustrates the readier expression of emotions (so untypical of the public school half a century later) which surrounded the new relationship between boys and masters. It touchingly describes how C. S. Bere, one of Cotton's young masters, who became a Devon rector and originator of the East Devon County School, took leave of his form:

> Bere made his fellows a very affecting speech this morning, it being his last time of coming into school, and sent them all away blubbing, and he himself rushed out of school in the same predicament.[11]

It remains to examine how general this kind of transformation was to prove among Victorian public schools, but what is certain is that Cotton had discovered in organised games, and in the new master-boy relationship, effective institutions to cope with the old fear of persistent general indiscipline amounting to a state of rebellion. The danger was not yet completely stamped out: Mitchinson, able headmaster of King's School, Canterbury, and a pioneer of the HMC, had to face at the end of his reign a rebellion in 1873 which involved the hissing of the prefects and a cannonade of missiles against their study doors, the singing of the *Marseillaise*, and plans for a mutiny involving at least thirty-five boys who made preparations to withstand a siege. Only the amnesty occasioned by Mitchinson's appointment to an overseas bishopric avoided the necessity for a mass expulsion.[12] Earlier, at Radley, where relations between the head and the boys had always been close, a planned rebellion against his severity was only prevented by a reconciliation between Sewell and the conspirators.[13]

The International College in Isleworth had opened in 1867 as an expensive boarding-school on public-school lines, with fees of up to ninety guineas. Its sponsors, who included Kay-Shuttleworth, Cobden and T. H. Huxley, intended it to contribute to understanding between nations, and it attracted a polyglot clientele. In addition to pupils from all over Britain it contained boys from Germany, France, Spain, Portugal, India, and a large contingent from North and South America. Assimilation proved impossible, and indiscipline was a serious problem: when provoked to a demonstration the Brazilians and Chileans were only too ready with the knife. In 1879 the neighbourhood was shaken by the "Great College Revolt", which was finally quelled only with the help of the police. The young Delius, who had come on to the school after beginning his education in Bradford, composed his first song in the school sanatorium after having been hit on the head with a cricket stump during the disturbances. Though the school achieved the dignity of having its headmaster elected to the HMC, it never solved the problems of discipline or assimilation, and closed in 1890.[14]

It is easy to understand how, at Wellington in 1859, when a group of boys deceived by very bright moonlight imagined that dawn had arrived and rose at 3 a.m., their new headmaster's first thought was that a rebellion had broken out.[15] The later Victorian public-school headmaster, however, could begin to feel that with the developed machinery of games, house loyalties, prefects and improved boy-master relations, discipline was secure. The only serious jolts to this growing sense of security came at the turn of the century at the Leys School and at Monkton Combe. As we have seen, there were serious disorders at the latter school, but as a small private school it may have had little influence, even as a cautionary example. The heads of public schools would, however, have taken much more note of events at the Leys School at about the same time. Here, in defiance of a new headmaster who had disallowed the time-honoured custom of a holiday on the Queen's birthday, numbers of boys barracked the head, assaulted a prefect, and overpowered a master who attempted to control them. The headmaster called in the mounted police, who were driven out by the boys. Eventually the rebels were starved into submission, and the collapse of the rebellion was sealed by floggings and expulsions.[16] But rebellions on this scale were becoming rare, indeed exceptional. The worst that now tended to happen was a demonstration, such as the hissing of the headmaster by a group of boys or even the whole school. A weak headmaster of Radley in the 1870s suffered a succession of such public insults; his much stronger successor faced, and ignored, a similar demonstration by the whole school in 1880 and had no further trouble.[17] Two years after becoming headmaster of Wellington in 1893, Pollock, who had incurred unpopularity by the manner of his investigation of a case of immorality, was hissed by a section of the school in the great hall after an evening concert. Pollock met this crucial test of his authority by ordering that the culprits, who included a school prefect, be caned by the Head Boy, and there was no more trouble.[18]

At Haileybury in 1900 there were demonstrations against Lyttelton's refusal of a half-holiday to mark the relief of Ladysmith, and two hundred and fifty boys including sixth-formers deserted their lessons and paraded round the neighbourhood singing patriotic songs. Though the press made something of the event, in fact Lyttelton and his prefects had the situation in hand, and the affair ended with some formal floggings, some impositions, and a hearty 'three cheers' for the headmaster proposed by the Head Boy.[19]

Nevertheless the fears of the school authorities during the main part of the Victorian period had been fully justified. Lyttelton himself had only to think of his own schooldays, which had coincided with a transition from "open barbarism" to "something like decorum" at Eton. In the early 1870s one Eton housemaster had actually gone in fear of his life—a boy attempted to blow up the house with gunpowder—and a notorious period of rowdiness and "shameless defiance" of their housemaster ended only with the expulsion of fourteen boys in 1875. The new "decorum" of the late 1870s at Eton was attributed by Lyttelton largely to the pastoral zeal of new masters,[20] who carried on the tradition of close relations with boys which Cory had tried to establish. Manifestations of 'student unrest', of which even advanced countries have had a taste in the 1960s and 1970s, were sufficiently close to the experience of Victorian headmasters for us to be able to understand the sentiments expressed by a man whose move from Uppingham to Durham had given Thring his chance. Henry Holden, in his farewell speech on retiring in 1882 after nearly thirty successful years as headmaster of Durham School, uttered a heartfelt "Thank God" that he had had no rebellions in his time there.[21]

Cotton's achievement at Marlborough was to add to the developing model of the public school new elements whose effect was to strengthen control by the authorities over the boys. Still more elements were to be added later. But while this new model could cope more powerfully with indiscipline, the very effectiveness of its new elements gave it the power to generate a loyalty to the institution itself. Secondly, the strengthening of the *esprit de corps* gave rise to new forms of boy tribalism (the house, the team, etc.) to replace the unofficial sort which had existed in the early days of the school. This new element could only be used to serve the ideals of the school authorities if masters could continue to be recruited who had the qualities —youth, vigour, and sympathy—required to exercise influence over the boy-community. Even when the model of the Victorian public school might be said to have been complete, having developed all the institutions of school life which had come to be expected of the public school, the qualities and influence of its teaching staff were a decisive factor. To this extent the history of the Victorian public school is the story of the men who served that institution, which is why we are obliged to give some attention to the development of that sector of the academic profession in the final chapter of this book.

Cotton's transformation of Marlborough by Arnoldian methods, and in particular his post-Arnoldian developments, the encouragement of athleticism and of closer boy-master relations, have been treated as significant for the development of the Victorian public school. Yet it must be admitted that it is difficult to explain how these new elements can have spread. They were not accompanied by any propaganda—even posthumous—and unlike Thring, Cotton did not write books setting forth his educational ideas, except in respect of India, where he went on as a bishop after a bare six years at Marlborough (only to die in slightly mysterious circumstances in 1866). Not many of his staff went on to headships elsewhere. Among those who did were Farrar, who after an assistant mastership at Harrow later returned to Marlborough as head, and Jex-Blake who moved on to Rugby as assistant master and later headed Cheltenham and Rugby in turn. Another who went on to a headship was Ellis, who became the first headmaster (1863–79) of Weymouth College, a proprietary school founded by evangelicals. In his sixteen years there he does not seem to have founded a prefect system—admittedly in a small school—but he did make provision for organised games.[22]

About as many boys left Marlborough early under Cotton as had done so under Wilkinson, but for the more respectable reason in Cotton's case that the school was being used as a preparatory school for other public schools, and these leavers may have carried with them the expectation of the games provision they had been used to at Marlborough. But Cottonism really became influential under the man he had himself nominated to succeed him at Marlborough, G. G. Bradley, pupil of Arnold 1837–40 (and the prototype of 'Tadpole' in *Tom Brown's Schooldays*), who added to the foundations of the system Cotton had already laid at Marlborough the benefit of his own twelve years on the Rugby staff. His reign established Marlborough's outstanding record for university scholarships and also saw a refinement of Marlborough's house system—out-college houses added to the existing 'hostel' type of in-college houses, and put in the hands of assistant masters as a specific[23] means of augmenting their salaries by the profits of boarding; there was a similar development at other new public schools, such as Wellington and Haileybury.

The responsibility of Cotton and his successor for the development of athleticism in English schools must not of course be exaggerated. What was growing up in public schools coincided with tendencies already becoming apparent at the universities. Here the growth of athleticism was already noticeable in the 1850s and '60s, and at Oxford was publicly deplored by Mark Pattison in 1868.[24] Its progress was facilitated by the purchase by the colleges of playing-fields and by the moving back of the hour of dinner in hall in colleges from 3 o'clock to 4 o'clock and then to 5 or even later, which in some colleges had already taken place by 1850 but which in other colleges was to result partly from the demand for playing-time during daylight hours.[25]

L. R. Farnell, who went up to Exeter College as an undergraduate in 1874, claimed to have been "a sympathetic watcher" of the early stages of the growth of athleticism—"the first symptom of mania was the taking over of games by the clergy as a proper theme for the pulpit"—which had already begun in the mid-'70s.[26] Ince, sub-rector of Exeter and later Regius Professor of Divinity, suggested in a college chapel sermon that the ill-success of the College VIII was displeasing to God.[27] D. H. Newsome has documented the transition in values in Victorian public schools and universities from Arnold's "godliness and good learning" to a cult of manliness associated with athleticism, which was fostered by forces and by individuals both inside and outside the schools.[28] By the 1890s some Oxford colleges were vying with each other to secure promising athletes by awarding them exhibitions or scholarships purely on games ability; prominent games-players became "chartered libertines" when it came to getting leave to play in matches. 'Away' fixtures became a major impediment to serious studies, and the timing of cricket matches to begin at 12 noon effectively cut down the number of lectures which could be attended to one per morning.[29] The universities were soon sending back into the schools men who had acquired a taste for the playing-field or the river which the world of school gave excellent opportunities for them to pursue. The remark ascribed to the Duke of Wellington about Waterloo's being won on the playing-fields of Eton had referred mainly to the semi-organised brawls and fisticuffs—on at least one occasion involving a boy's death[30]—at that school in the early part of the century, though cricket, rowing and forms of football and fives did exist at Eton even then. What changed was the degree of recognition, encouragement, and finally participation, by the *masters*. R. A. H. Mitchell, a cricketer of prodigious promise,[31] who was captain of the Oxford XI for three successive years and whose chances of a century in the Balliol-Christ Church match were the subject of a bet between Jowett[32] and the Principal of Brasenose College*, returned to his own school (Eton) as a master in 1866 and coached more than a

* i.e. Dr Cradock, a keen supporter of games-playing, during whose Principalship of Brasenose (1853–86) "anyone who had been in the Eton Eight or in the cricket Eleven of any public school was accepted as an undergraduate without any fuss as to a matriculation examination".[33]

generation[34] of outstanding cricketers, while making (unlike most of his colleagues) no attempt to dilute his athleticism.[35]

Moberly, headmaster of Winchester (1835–66) had as his Second Master the Rev. Charles Wordsworth (later Warden of Glenalmond), an outstanding all-rounder at games, who had been one of the founders both of the Oxford *vs.* Cambridge cricket match in 1827 and of the Boat Race in 1829, at a time when it was held that "no man in a racing boat could live to the age of thirty"[36]—a fallacy later exposed by the longevity of Bishop Charles Wordsworth (who died at eighty-six) and of a number of septuagenarian rowing fanatics such as Steve Fairbairn. But Moberly gave little scope to his Second Master's athletic enthusiasms. Though there was an hour a day for cricket or football from 12 to 1 o'clock with compulsory participation of juniors (forced to retrieve the ball as a fagging chore), the main form of exercise at Winchester was a compulsory excursion "up hills" two or three days a week,[37] and Moberly stubbornly resisted the exaltation of athleticism.[38] Though as an undergraduate he had been active in the organisation of cricket at Oxford, Moberly spoke of "the idle boys, I mean the boys who play cricket".[39] It was under his successor George Ridding, (headmaster 1866–84) whose view was "Give me a boy who is a cricketer, and I can make something of him",[40] and under Ridding's "devoted but more limited housemasters",[41] that organised games, including rowing, shooting, rackets and fives, were quickly established at Winchester.[42]

At Harrow under Arnold's pupil C. J. Vaughan (1845–59), football was compulsory,[43] but the relief offered from time to time by the proclamation of "whole holidays without exercise" was abolished[44] by his successor H. M. Butler (1859–85), during whose reign the influence of housemasters like Edward Bowen gave powerful support to the new cult. By 1864 the Clarendon Commission found that a Harrow boy might spend, on average, fifteen hours a week at cricket.[45]

A newly established school, Fettes (1870) won early recognition as a public school by the games exploits of its Old Boys at Oxford and Cambridge.[46]* Loretto under H. H. Almond had a

* Of the forty-one Fettes Rugger blues at Oxford and Cambridge between 1878 and 1914, more than a quarter were also Open Scholars of their colleges.[47]

similar reputation: in 1884, when the school had just over a hundred boys, there were seven Old Lorettonians at Oxford, and they had nine blues among them; all seven were in the Oxford Rugger XV.[48] At the nonconformist public school, The Leys, established by Methodists at Cambridge in 1875 in the gap (Lord Fortescue claimed) left by the failure of attempts to found a county school for Cambridgeshire in 1872, there were by 1876 complaints in the school magazine that boys could be called upon to play football on four days a week, exclusive of matches. But the complainant went on to concede that football has "two moral virtues principally—pluck and the merging of one's individual interests in those of the whole".[49] Those sentiments might have come straight from *Tom Brown*. At the Devon County School in 1868 Lord Fortescue established prizes for games and athletic sports "to enlist the diligence of those who are too idle or backward to hope for distinction in learning, as well as those who have already attained it".[50]

Changes at the universities in the 1870s and '80s, including the abolition of the obligation of celibacy on college fellows, meant that the men sent out into the schools from Oxford and Cambridge would be less likely to be of the type of the singleminded unathletic scholar such as had staffed the early Marlborough. The culmination of this tendency was the appointment of men on games ability alone, illustrated by the story told in *The Contemporary Review* in 1900 of a university 'blue'* who on completing his century in the university cricket match received telegrams from five different headmasters with offers of posts.[52]

But to the end of the century many smaller schools still made do with a drill sergeant in charge of games—there was one at the Norfolk County School; it was the preparatory schools pre-eminently which were the refuge of the "gentlemanly failures"[53] at the universities who had few credentials apart from their ability to supervise small boys at games. Yet the very in-

* The 'full-blue' was first awarded at Oxford and Cambridge to those who took part in the Boat Race. It was then extended to cricket and athletics. In 1883 Oxford granted it for both Rugby and Association football. Early in 1885 a university meeting at Cambridge to ratify a similar extension was ratified by twelve hundred voters.[51]

crease of preparatory schooling from 1870 onwards meant that boys were being sent on to public schools with experience of organised games, and in some cases with developed skills, to reinforce the pressures for athleticism already there.

Thus there was a general tendency in public schools for games to become organised, by about 1860; and between 1880 and 1900 for them to become compulsory. At Bedford School by 1899 it was noted that "all those who like to participate [in games] may participate, and all others *must*".[54] A further development already noticeable in some schools before the end of the period was for spectatorship at matches to become compulsory. Much of the responsibility for the organisation of games was left to the boys themselves,[55] though once the stage was reached where a school's reputation came to depend in part on its games record, final control had to rest with the masters.

Critics of athleticism were not lacking, even among public-school masters. Headmasters like Edward Lyttelton (of Haileybury and later of Eton) and Lionel Ford (Repton, later Harrow) who were themselves distinguished cricketers*, attacked the excesses of the cult, but protests were futile when athleticism had the support not only of boys and of so many masters but also of parents, who in general shared their sons' scale of values which set the fantasy of a century at Lord's above the dream of a Balliol scholarship. Welldon of Harrow complained of the difficulty of getting iambics or hexameters out of boys in view of the pressure on them from parents and other adults towards athletics, and he quoted a case of a boy promised a guinea for each run he made and five pounds for each wicket, who made £50 in a week.[58] Lyttelton spoke of boys sent off to school "primed since the nursery with the idea that amusement is to be sought at school, and that a boy, if he is worth anything, will find it and make the most of it";[59] though at some schools amusement was already going out of school games as 'play' was turned into 'work', and games-playing was treated as though it were the main business of life.[60]

* Canon Lyttelton once confessed to a nephew that he "never walked up the aisle of a church or cathedral without bowling an imaginary ball down it and wondering whether it would take spin";[56] he was also quoted as saying that making a first-rate pentameter was comparable to the joy of a fine off-drive at cricket.[57]

Stimulated by press attention to games events at schools and universities, public interest increased. Lyttelton recalled that in the 1850s and 1860s there were scarcely enough spectators at the Eton-Harrow cricket match to form a continuous line round Lord's cricket ground, and it was not found necessary to use ropes until 1864, whereas by 1880 "such is the importance of [this] annual pageant that it affects the duration of the London season".[61] *Wisden* recorded that, in each of the years 1872 and 1873, 27,000 people paid their shilling to watch the Eton-Harrow match at Lord's.[62] Over the same period there was a similar increase in public interest in the Boat Race, so that by the 1880s "the minutest facts connected with the play of each oarsman's muscles are anxiously picked up on the spot, form a paragraph in the daily papers, and are telegraphed to the Antipodes".[63]

The effects of this preoccupation among the products of the schools and universities were far-reaching, giving rise to a new connotation of the word 'sport' to replace the old associations of grouse-shooting and the turf, and placing skill at handling various sizes of ball high among the lists of the expected 'accomplishments' of a gentleman. The 1850s saw the establishment by public-school Old Boys, especially from Eton and Harrow, of clubs for holiday and country-house cricket, such as 'I Zingari' founded by two brothers of Charles Gore's mother Lady Kerry, and the 'Quidnuncs'.[64] The emphasis was on not just the skill of play but the experience of organisation. "I have known," wrote a public-school master who was himself a product of Victorian Rugby, "grave scholars and efficient civil servants carry into advanced years a habit of imaginary team-building which they contracted in the years when games were the most pressing business of life".[65] No more explicit statement of the widely alleged connection (which was claimed even by the Clarendon Commission)[66] between the qualities cultivated by public-school life (and especially the experience of games) and the qualities needed to carve out and govern an Empire, can be found than in the Cliftonian Henry Newbolt's *Vitai Lampada*, with its refrain "Play up, play up, and play the game!", and headmasters openly averred that "England owed her Empire far more to her sports than to her studies".[67] Others credited athletics with the improvement of the morals "not only of individuals but of whole classes", which they claimed could be noticed in public schools and universities since Arnold, and which had helped to alter "the bestial habits of the well-born and well-to-do" and which if further extended "may gradually improve the habits of the very poorest".[68]

At Cheltenham's Speech Day in 1898 both the headmaster and the guest speaker (Dean Pigou) quoted the envy, among certain French observers, of English public-school games "which taught the lessons of brotherhood" and which they wanted to import into French schools. Dean Pigou went on to point out the contrast between "the poor puny lads turned out by lyceums there and the healthy and strong lads turned out by our English public schools"—a difference which had been illustrated in a picture which (he claimed) French susceptibilities had not allowed to be exhibited in France, showing a tug-of-war between one English boy ("a Cheltenham boy, I expect") and half a dozen French boys.[69]

As to athleticism at the universities, it was argued that team games were a great solvent of social-class differences, and we have seen how this process had begun to operate in favour of Cavendish College. In fact, the early organisation of university sport was by public-school men on a public-school basis, Old Etonians and Old Westminsters at Trinity College (Cambridge) even forming their own club (Third Trinity) for cricket and football in the 1890s,[70] and the products of certain well-known public schools virtually monopolizing places in the University cricket team at Cambridge before 1890.[71] But these particularist distinctions were already breaking down in the late Victorian period, at least in the direction of a preference for the products of public schools *in general* over the other schools. In any case, college society was already fragmented into 'sets' often reflecting public-school education.

A. J. Balfour, a pupil of Cory at Eton and a graduate of Trinity College, Cambridge, spoke to a university audience at the end of the century of the functions of athleticism in the university:

> A University [he said] gave a man all through his life the sense that he belonged to a great community in which he spent his youth, which indeed he had left but to which he still belonged

> ... That feeling might be fostered—was fostered, no doubt—by a community of education, by attending the same lectures, by passing the same examinations, but no influence fostered it more surely and more effectively than that feeling of common life which the modern athletic sports, as they had been developed in modern places of learning, gave to all those who took an interest in such matters, whether as performers or spectators.[72]

Balfour's remarks about the power of athleticism to foster attachment to an educational community, referring on this occasion to a university, must apply *a fortiori* to a school, and this was certainly the effect in public schools which the games cult produced.

2. Transformation and expansion.

Athleticism was one of the few new institutions of the late Victorian public school which was typical and universal, though the extent of its hold of course varied. The difficulty in assessing the prevalence of any such institution regarded as characteristic of the late Victorian public school is that no school conformed to the stereotype, which was rather the product of the great industry of school fiction which sprang from *Tom Brown's Schooldays* and Dean Farrar's very different *Eric* and *St Winifred's*. Soon the school story itself would become more or less standardised:

> ... Take a juvenile athlete as your chief ingredient, add a wit, a bully, a persecuted fag, an awkward scholar, a faithful friend, a dangerous rival and a batch of distorted pedagogues; mix them up in an atmosphere of genial romanticism; insert a smoking scandal, a fight, a cribbing scene, sundry rags, a house-match or two; bring them all to the boiling point when the hero scores the winning try or does the hat-trick; serve the whole hot and with a title associating the dish with an establishment with which the initiated can identify; and the suburbs will raid the libraries for the result;[73]

and in the last decades of the century the *Boys' Own Paper* and a multitude of other papers published by Brett or

Harmsworth—like *Marvel, Pluck, Union Jack, Herald*, and *The Boy's Friend* gave to generations of elementary and private schoolboy readers a glimpse of boarding-school life at St Jim's or some such imagined (in some respects caricatured) public school.[74] Even public school headmasters, like Welldon of Harrow and Gilkes of Dulwich, themselves contributed novels in this genre, the earliest of the type Farrar had done. In addition to this flood of fiction there was a spate of books—descriptions, histories, and reminiscences of school life—about individual public schools or groups of them: the quantity of Etoniana alone which was published between the 1860s and 1900 fills several shelves and must have served a reading public far wider than just Etonians and their families.

But the real world of public schools in the later Victorian period contained a wide variety of types, all exhibiting in varying degrees some of the institutions which characterise the hypothetical model. Chief among them were the seven boarding schools examined by the Clarendon Commission (1861–4), the main result of whose deliberations was the reform of their governing bodies. Alongside these, the new public schools of the 1840s onwards in many cases benefitted from the colonisation by the Rugby staff-room of the post-Arnoldian period, which sent Benson to create Wellington and Percival to create Clifton in something very like the image of Rugby, and more than fourteen others went off to headmasterships in Britain between 1860 and the end of the century. The first three head-masters of the new (1862) Haileybury had Rugby associations—A. G. Butler and Robertson as former Rugby masters, and Bradby as a former pupil of Arnold's. Others still, from the Rugby staff, went out to public schools in India and Australia. In 1877 a 'Public School' founded by Bishop Colenso in Natal appointed as headmaster a man whose only claim to any kind of academic qualification was that he had been a boy at Rugby under Temple, whose sermons he read out to the boys among whom he had promptly instituted Rugby football and the prefect system.[75] Rugby influence and some of its characteristic institutions came to the reorganised Bath College after 1878 by way of one of Percival's masters at Clifton, T. W. Dunn, whose predecessor S. C. Voules (ten years a Marlborough schoolboy under Cotton and Bradley and then a master at both

Rossall and Marlborough) had not instituted prefects or compulsory games.[76] Winchester influence was discernible at Radley, Bradfield, Glenalmond and Malvern.[77]

Pioneers whose organisation seemed to owe little to existing models found scope in the transformation of old endowed grammar schools. Foremost among these was Edward Thring, an Etonian with no teaching experience beyond an elementary school during his curacy in Gloucester, who took over Uppingham when Holden was appointed to Durham and remoulded it according to a well-articulated and explicit concept of the school community and what he called its "machinery".[78] Less famous was H. D. Harper, who achieved a scarcely less spectacular transformation of Sherborne, where he was appointed in 1850 in preference to the Rugbeian A. H. Wratislaw and the former Harrow housemaster J. W. Colenso. There was nothing in Harper's background—Christ's Hospital boy, Scholar and Fellow of Jesus College, Oxford—to enable us to identify the sources of the ideas whereby he refashioned first Cowbridge Grammar School and then Sherborne, the latter into a public school of some standing by the time of his election to the Principalship of Jesus College in 1877. His most obvious assets were his "tact, drive and keen business sense"; his "brilliant powers of organisation"[79] were drawn on heavily by his colleagues on the HMC, of which he was one of the originators. In the transformation of another endowed grammar school, Repton, into a public school with a sizeable non-local boarding element, the inspiration was ultimately Rugbeian—Pears (headmaster 1854–74) had been a Harrow master under Arnold's pupil C. J. Vaughan, and his Second Master Messiter was another of Arnold's Rugbeians.[80]

Throughout the first half of the Victorian period grammar schools could thrive and attract a non-local clientele, essentially by the brilliance of the classical teaching which could send on both local and non-local boys to the university and into elite occupations. This was the service performed by schools such as Richmond (Yorks) Grammar School, which in the first part of the century flourished under James Tate the Elder, who, assisted by one 'usher', sent one hundred and fifty boys (by 1833) to the universities, where they gained a formidable total of firsts, prizes, and fellowships and established the reputation of Richmond as one of the leading classical schools in England.[81] But this success, like that of other schools such as Ipswich, was heavily dependent on the successful teaching of one man, and under less able successors the school's reputation dwindled: what later Victorian parents demanded by way of a school was a more complex community. The Endowed Schools Act of 1869, and the work of reorganisation by the Endowed Schools Commissioners (after 1874 the Charity Commissioners) to which it gave rise, facilitated the extension of the public-school model to a larger number of old-established but essentially local schools, though the far wider scope these reforms gave to the headmasters of the schools continued to place a heavy premium, for the reorganised school's prosperity, on the qualities of the individual head.

3. Community and consolidation.

As has been suggested, few of the institutions which would have to be specified for any model of the later Victorian public school were universal, even in schools whose general claim to be regarded as public schools would never have been questioned by that date. The term 'prefect system' embraces a variety of forms of authority, the most obvious distinction being between Arnold's original conception of authority bestowed upon boys of intellectual ability, and the surrender in some schools to the institutionalisation of the natural authority of senior boys who were good at games. The right of the top scholar in the Sixth to be head boy—Percival of Clifton made him Captain of Football as well[82]—was difficult to sustain with the increasing repectability (if not actual worship) of athleticism: the rationalisation that being a prefect was valuable training for future positions of responsibility made it imperative to give such experience to the all-rounder who seemed more likely than the unathletic intellectual to go on to command a battalion or administer a colony. Replacing the general authority of the Sixth at Repton by a new system of appointed prefects, Lionel Ford explained: "I don't want to *teach* my Sixth form boys responsibility: I want to teach those with responsibility how to *use* it".[83]

The authority, as school prefects at Harrow, of the scholarly J. Addington Symonds[84] in the 1850s, of Charles Gore[85] in the

1860s, and of Montague Rendall[86] in the late 1870s, had been fragile, though at times the recipe worked. Gore's contemporary, Walter Leaf, was invited at fifteen to become head of a boarding-house being taken over by F. W. Farrar. "The ordeal for the small, short-sighted and scholarly boy was terrifying, but Leaf faced it, insisted on order, caned a miscreant twice his age, and conquered".[87] Yet the scholarly priorities even of H. M. Butler were to accommodate a modification of the prefect system at Harrow by a limited recognition of the athlete. In a school like Charterhouse, developing new traditions as an enclosed community after its removal to the Surrey countryside in 1872, the process was carried to an extreme when athletic accomplishments were more important credentials for school prefects than scholarly ability;[88] and below these powerful prefect figures, who had powers of corporal punishment officially denied to the masters, there was a further rung of athletic 'bloods' with complicated sets of privileges defined by school convention.[89] The fact that the prefect régime at any one time in a given public school might reflect any point on the wide spectrum between the rule of the scholar and that of the 'blood' undermines sweeping generalisations about the significance of the prefect system. Theories which relate the system to training in selfless exercise of power need to take account of the fact that the system of payments to prefects at Winchester in the 1840s[90] still existed when the Clarendon Commission reported in 1864,[91] and as late as 1890 prefects were being paid for supervising evening prep. at Marlborough.[92] Facile correlations of public-school attendance and preparation for 'leadership' tend to overlook the fact that not all schools had prefect systems. Even St Paul's, which under Walker educated the future Field-Marshal Montgomery, had during that period only the most nominal prefect system, in which there was no organised or effective delegation of authority, and a similar situation prevailed in some other public schools.[93] The modern functioning of the prefect system, by which a boy will often enjoy this position only for his final year at school, and a head boy only for one term, is very different from that in the mid-nineteenth century, when a boy might be a prefect for his last three years, and we know of at least one case of a boy who was head boy for his last four years.[94]

So, too, must any generalisation about the functions of any of the characteristic institutions of the late Victorian public school take into account the fact that conditions in a school might vary from decade to decade and indeed from house to house. Thus H. A. James carried to Rossall in 1875 from the Marlborough of Bradley and Farrar the concept of a house system which had developed under Bradley, as part of a system in which a key ingredient was the quality of boy-master relations at Marlborough as established by Cotton. James firmly established his house system at Rossall on the rudimentary foundations laid by Osborne a quarter of a century before. During James's headmastership his recruitment and encouragement of enthusiastic young masters, who cultivated closer relationships with the boys, gave life to his system. Unfortunately economy did not allow either for the marriage of his housemasters or for their early retirement; many of the men James appointed in the 1880s were still housemasters twenty or even thirty years later, and the ageing and by now staid bachelors no longer enjoyed the kind of influence among the boys for which they had been appointed.[95] Similarly, after the house system was established at Radley in 1879, three of the first six housemasters appointed stayed in their houses for thirty-five years each, and a fourth for thirty.[96] One Charterhouse housemaster did a forty-two year stint from 1869,[97] and a Haileybury housemaster did thirty-seven years from 1862.[98] At schools where housemasters themselves financed their boarding-houses by arrangement with the school, and where (as in most public schools) there was no limit to tenure, such a situation was to be expected and must have operated against close relations between boys and masters, except in the case of unusual men of the type of Trant Bramston, an outstanding Winchester housemaster for forty years.[99] (Rugby and Cheltenham were in a small minority among public schools in the Victorian period in limiting a housemaster's tenure—normally to fifteen years—in 1894 and 1896 respectively.)[100]

Thus it is extremely dangerous to generalise sweepingly about the extent to which, by the last thirty years of the century, the relationships between master and pupils had been transformed. Modified, yes, in practically all public schools, but a real transformation did not come, for some schools, until well into the twentieth century, despite house systems and the common participation in games of boys and staff. There was very little feeling of real sympathy—still less *cameraderie*—between the still largely "pedagogue"-type masters and the boys at Rugby in the 1870s,[101] and a man who had entered Rugby as a boy in 1897 and returned on the staff in 1913 reported that it was not until 1919 that he noticed that "boys were beginning to talk to masters as if they were both human beings."[102] Another Rugby witness gives exactly similar dates for the process whereby "the old aloofness and mutual suspicion" between masters and boys "had given way to something more human and natural".[103] Another observer with a special knowledge of Harrow, Charterhouse and Rossall over the period 1890–1920 wrote around 1960 that "sixty years ago relations [between boys and masters] had progressed up to a point, but had a good deal further to go to reach the standard of today", and he identified as the main barrier to better relationships the dullness and irrelevance of the teaching.[104] Furthermore, even the centrality of the house system as a key institution of the later Victorian public school is open to question. Dr J. H. Skrine was one of Thring's closest lieutenants, who after the latter's death took over the headship of Glenalmond and in fourteen successful years raised that school to a high place among public schools. Yet by the time of his retirement in 1902, though he had achieved all he set out to do and despite opportunities provided by the expansion of buildings and numbers, he had made no attempt to introduce a house system, which was in fact the work of his successor fifteen years later.[105]

The sense of community in the later Victorian public school was fortified by a process of consolidation on lines inherent in Arnold's own practice, in terms of age and social-class background, but to a much lesser extent of ability. Thring was aware that his highly developed notion of a school community was related to "similarity for the most part of social sympathies among his pupils";[106] like Arnold, he also had definite ideas about the limitation of size of his school, though such limitations were not observed by other Victorian headmasters or even by his successors at Uppingham, any more than was Arnold's decreed limit of two hundred and sixty observed under later headmasters at Rugby.[107] A properly documented study of the social origins of Victorian public-school boys, an enormous task in itself, would be of real benefit if it could uncover the status of grandfathers, since one of the functions of the leading schools was undoubtedly to dignify a process of upward social mobility which had already taken place and which is concealed behind the status and place of residence of the father at the time of the boy's admission. The tendency of the period was for the leading schools—certainly the Clarendon boarding-schools and many endowed schools reorganised by the Endowed Schools Act—to become more exlusive by closing their doors to the local poor. The abolition of free education for the poor was justified by the argument that the free working of the laws of competition would operate in the best interests of the poorer classes[108] and create a ladder for the ascent of the gifted few among them into the ranks of privilege. In addition, 'consolation' schools were established alongside the great schools, for the benefit of the classes from whom the original form of the endowments had been alienated (the Lower School of John Lyon at Harrow, the Lawrence Sheriff School at Rugby, etc.). This was done in response to a counter-attack against that process of alienation—a counter-attack led by members of the lower-middle classes wanting continued access to the great schools for themselves, and certainly not for the poorest classes in whose name they might claim to speak.[109] By thus hiving off into separate schools the bulk of lower-class boys for whose probable future occupations the schools' classical curricula were in any case inappropriate, such schools made it possible for those who remained, especially if they were academically successful, to be more readily assimilated, and the prejudices between 'scholars' and non-scholars tended to be reduced in most schools in the late Victorian period. At Shrewsbury, the historic feud between boarders and day-boys, in accordance with which the latter were not spoken to, nor walked or played with, and were compelled to use separate playing-fields, was healed in the mid-1870s, and the two groups successfully integrated.[110]

Yet if the tendency was for most of the leading public schools to become more socially exclusive, new schools grew up to give public-school education to a wider range of social classes, though, significantly, none of their originators visualised educating the various ranks they identified in one single school. The phenomenon of 'sojourners', *i.e.* widows or grass-widows of Britons in India or the colonies, or retired (or even active) professional men, who settled in a public-school town like Rugby, Harrow or Sherborne "for benefit of the school" (*i.e.* for cheap or free day-school education as quasi-locals), continued throughout the century; as one school lost its value to such parents because the day-boy fees became too expensive, or day-boys were discouraged or excluded altogether, so the 'sojourners' or 'squatters' moved on. The favoured centre in the late Victorian period was Bedford. In the late 1820s a number of Nelson's captains had begun to settle in Bedford, partly owing to the cheap education available at what was (until 1917) officially known as Bedford Grammar School. This process continued throughout the century, but "the extraordinary flow to Bedford of parents requiring education", noted in 1895 by the Bryce Commission,[111] was made up of a fresh great wave of newcomers in the 1880s and 1890s, which was to double the population of Bedford in twenty years.[112] Bedford's headmaster from 1874 to 1903, the Wykehamist and former Rugby master H. S. Phillpotts, raised the status of the school, and its numbers to over eight hundred—a large proportion of these being day-boys attracted by the fees which the subvention of the wealthy Harpur endowment and the conditions of the Charity Commissioners' scheme kept as low as £12 a year.[113]

The Harpur trust maintained several schools at different levels for boys and girls in Bedford. At another of these, the 'Commercial School', a former Rugby boy (under Temple) and Clifton housemaster, R. B. Poole, was appointed headmaster in 1877. His love of Rugby "amounted to almost an obsession"; by 1900 he had raised the status of "Bedford Modern School" (as it was now called) to that of "one of the best known public schools in the country"[114]—though this relative status was not maintained at quite that level under his successors. There was provision for boarders, but the majority were day-boys, paying £4 a year, who could stay till seventeen or eighteen. Boys came from South Africa, India, China, North and South America, Russia and France, as well as a large contingent who travelled in by train from the surrounding countryside and from as far away as Wolverton and Luton.[115]

4. The studies of a gentleman.

The degree of social-class consolidation *within* schools which we have noticed was matched by a process of consolidation by age. The expansion of provision of public schools was accompanied by a development until recently little researched,[116] the growth of a network of preparatory schools specifically designed for the education of boys going on to public schools. From perhaps only a score of such institutions existing by 1850 there grew to be some four hundred by 1900, and seven hundred by 1925.[117] In drawing attention to this remarkable phenomenon, Welldon of Harrow claimed that his school drew on one hundred and thirty-four such schools in 1890.[118] Preparation for entry to public schools had been available in the first half of the century by private tuition, typically at the hands of a clergyman who took a small number of boys in his own household, or, in the case of bigger establishments, by building on to the rectory a 'pupil room' to take about twenty boys.[119] Cheam School, and the school later known as Windlesham House, which had been started by Lt C. R. Malden at the instigation of Thomas Arnold,[120] were pioneers of the development which was to become general, whereby preparatory schools, from being a variety of domestic education, adapted themselves to the model of the public school and took on all the apparatus of prefects, games, fagging and numerous other rituals that were now becoming common, at the same time increasing their numbers to between fifty and eighty.

Whereas in the 1850s it was possible, but not common, for boys to be sent away to institutions of this kind before the age of ten,[121] in the period from 1870 onwards, as preparatory-school provision increased dramatically to match the expansion of the public-schools community, it became common for boys to go away to such schools at seven or eight. All this enabled the public schools to reduce their age range, and ultimately to exclude boys of five, six, seven and eight who were not unknown at Arnold's Rugby or Keate's Eton—with boys staying on to age twenty or twenty-one at the other end of the scale, so that it was not unheard-of for boys to have attended their public school for nine or ten years, and at least one Eton boy was there for sixteen years.[122] At Eton from around 1846 boys were inadmissible after the age of fifteen,[123] but many other public schools still admitted older boys for the rest of the century. The tendency was for the age of admission to the leading public schools to standardise. In the year 1856 the ages of boys who entered Marlborough ranged from nine to seventeen, at Lancing entrants were seven to fifteen, and at Rugby eleven to sixteen, though some boys of ten and some of seventeen were being admitted to Rugby in other years in the 1850s. By the year 1886 the ages of boys admitted to those three schools had narrowed, at Marlborough to ten–fifteen, at Lancing to ten–sixteen, and at Rugby twelve–fifteen.[124] Despite this tendency to a higher minimum age, there were still in the year 1874 boys of eight, nine and ten entering Lancing, some of whom, on leaving at eighteen, would have been a full eight–ten years in the school.[125] One boy in that year entered at seventeen and left aged twenty.[126] And twelve, thirteen or fourteen as the age of public-school entry was by no means standard at the end of the century. Marlborough's bursar in the period 1860–1897 adopted the attitude, doubtless beneficial to the numbers in his school, that boys should come "straight from their mother's knee",[127] but the school's governors in 1887 raised from nine to twelve the lower limit of age of admission.[128] The age ranges at the leading public schools by 1900 all reflect this higher age of admission, but a host of less eminent public schools still had boys entering at eight or nine at that date,[129] even if in the larger of these schools measures were introduced to segregate boys by age.

Thring pioneered the introduction of a more 'comprehensive' curriculum and range of activities, and most public schools by the end of the period possessed 'modern' or 'military' sides to cater for boys whom Arnold might ruthlessly have superannuated. Only in 1903–4 did some schools begin to standardise their entrance requirements by the adoption of a common entrance examination. The classics retained their central place in the curriculum, offering excellent mental pabulum to a small minority of able boys, but were generally taught less for the moral lessons afforded by ancient history, literature, and philosophy than for what Westcott implied was the "moral value of exact scholarship",[130] which in practice (outside the hands of a few brilliant teachers) was restricted to fussy linguistic commentary, training in versification within narrowly prescribed forms, and a heavy reliance on memory work. Curricular reform awaited not so much the new inclinations or efforts of the schoolmasters but the willingness of the universities (as Arnold had pointed out) to adjust their demands, and indeed their ability to send out men into the schools to teach new subjects, or old ones in new ways. Meanwhile, to able pupils, the classical training offered the surest rewards. To a talented St Paul's boy from a humble home who wanted to change to science because of its supposed utility for earning a living, Walker (headmaster 1877–1905) advised:

> My boy, you are making a great mistake. If you go in for science, your future is quite uncertain. If you stick to your classics properly, I will undertake to say that you will pay for your education in scholarships and be able to earn £400 a year within a reasonable time afterwards.[131]

A similar, if more peremptory, answer, was given by the head of Manchester Grammar School (the future Sir Samuel Dill) to the young Ernest Barker, who entered the school with a professed intention to study French and German in order to become a foreign correspondence clerk in a business-house:

> 'Don't be a little fool; go into the Upper Classical First, and stay there.' I did what I was told, and that determined the course of my life.[132]

These cases serve to show how the position of the classics, in public schools and in English education in general, was if anything more powerful at the end of the nineteenth century than it had been at the beginning. The 'spoils' system operated by the universities is, of course, only a small part of the answer. Oxford and Cambridge offered a series of rewards (fellowships, scholarships, degree examinations and prizes) not exclusively, but mainly, open to classicists—even Mathematical Wranglers had to show prior competence in Greek and Latin. It was the achievement of men like Butler of Shrewsbury, even more signally than Arnold of Rugby, to have exploited this system by devising what became something of a classical scholarship-factory for the ancient universities, in which the classics could be regarded as "no more than a graduated series of problems in ascending order of difficulty, posed in order that they might be solved—of course, by Salopians".[133] One of the greatest triumphs of this system had been achieved as early as 1831 when Thomas Brancker, while still a Shrewsbury sixth former, carried off the coveted Ireland scholarship at Oxford against such seasoned competitors as the third-year undergraduate, W. E. Gladstone.*

It would be a mistake, however, to dismiss the prevalence of classics by explanations which simply point to their entrenchment in the university system, the jobs they led to, and the vested interests that were thus at stake. The Victorians had a number of real reasons, as well as a number of rationalisations, for defending the classics as the staple in education. The theory of 'transfer of training', partly discredited in modern psychology, enabled them to believe, and certainly to maintain, that training in one subject would automatically lead to a facility in the learning of other subjects, by constituting a 'training of the mind': "the chief benefit is . . . that one learns how to learn".[135] A sounder claim was that they trained the memory, and examples of schoolboys able to recite up to 10,000 lines of some classical author, as they were encouraged to do at Winchester and some other schools, lent support to this view. The practice of those teachers who insisted first on exact translation and then on a rendering into elegant English was held to produce "fluency, the command of good language, readiness, and presence of mind".[136] For the majority who would never get this far, the very dullness of the subject-matter was held to have advantages, for to headmasters like Pears of Repton in 1865 there was merit only in those subjects which required hard work by the boys which could be checked and controlled by the masters, and classics constituted this kind of "grind" in his opinion, while science never could.[137] Dr Balston, headmaster of Eton, had implied a similar argument when he justified the primacy of classics in his school to the Clarendon Commissioners in 1862 on the grounds that Latin and Greek "are in themselves distasteful to boys, and only with great difficulty, and after much laborious perseverance . . . gain a hold upon them".[138]† Greek and Latin

* The examiners marked Gladstone's papers as "desultory, beyond belief", but he was *proxime accessit*.[134]

† *Cf.* Lord Berners' account of classics teaching at Eton in 1897: "no effort was spared to make them as uninteresting and as unprofitable as possible".[139]

primers which had grammatical rules stated in English, rather than the Latin which was common in the great schools for much of the nineteenth century, were a concession introduced by Dr Arnold at Rugby, of which he afterwards repented.[140]

Later apologists were to go further, and the products of a Victorian classical education who produced in 1923 the Report on the *Position of Classics in the Educational System* wrote of this study as providing "access to beauty" and "power of understanding" by means of "a remarkable combination of memory-training, imagination, aesthetic appreciation and scientific method."[141] In this they went much further than the newly-appointed professor at University College, London, in 1863—the famous J. R. Seeley—who defended classical syntax and grammar as the discipline necessary as a *foundation* for higher studies in philosophy and history: this linguistic content of classics was "eminently suited to drill the mind into method and accustom it to the satisfaction of certainty".[142]

But the notion that within the classics themselves—as opposed to philosophical or historical studies outside them—a complete aesthetic and historical frame of reference could be built up, as the authors of the 1923 Report seem to imply, was far nearer to the assumptions of most Victorian educationists than was Seeley's more limited defence. It is impossible to escape the conclusion that the Victorians valued classical studies because they looked for, and believed they found, in them a values-system which helped to explain their own situation, and thus acted as a guide in matters of taste, of politics, and of morals. For Sir Richard Livingstone, a product of Victorian Winchester and New College, "the influence of Christianity and of Hellenism" were *the only sources of values in Western civilization.*[143] Even the theologian F. J. A. Hort, when a fundamentalist undergraduate at Cambridge around 1850, had placed Plato next to the Bible as an influence.[144] "The tendency", noted by R. M. Ogilvie, "of educated Englishmen to view themselves and their country in the mirror of Ancient Athens" is seen in many instances: Empire-builders like Mountstuart Elphinstone, immersed in Thucydides ("The British in India", Mr Ogilvie tells us, "never travelled without a copy of Thucydides") and thinking of Indian problems in Attic terms;[145] or Lord Cromer, in Egypt and elsewhere, formulating in a book his explicit comparisons between "Ancient and Modern Imperialism"; or Curzon, lecturing his Cabinet colleagues on the dangers of retreat from the Dardanelles and quoting at length Thucydides' account of the disastrous Athenian retreat from Syracuse;[146] above all, a procession of British political leaders, from Canning through Lord Derby and Gladstone to H. H. Asquith, for all of whom, and pre-eminently for Asquith, the literature of the Ancient World was the predominant influence on their outlook. Defending this influence (at its widest), Sir Maurice Bowra would later assert that the comparison of "the endless differences between the ancients and ourselves" constituted the principal claim of classics to be "so fine an instrument of education";[147] but in saying this Bowra unwittingly identified its main defect, for one can only profitably compare two things when one understands them both, and certainly no systematic study of their own contemporary society was ever an essential part of the apparatus of the Victorian classical scholar. Many of the analogies which the Victorians sought, and sometimes acted upon, in politics, government, war, or the Empire, were inadequate, misleading or downright fallacious; ultimately, as Ogilvie himself admits,[148] "the fatal weakness of the British Empire" was exposed by those very problems—race, religion, and colour—to which the Athenian empire provided no parallels. Furthermore, two themes emphasised in the classical teaching of Victorian England—blind patriotism[149] and the glorification of death in battle[150]—may be said to have contributed materially to the disaster of World War I. Admittedly, against these must be counted the ideal of disinterested public service which classical literature undoubtedly helped to foster.

The "satisfaction of certainty" specified by Seeley had an enormous appeal; it was offered by a discipline whose subject-matter possessed set limits and, apart from textual and archaeological discoveries, was in most respects established for all time. Many of the great classical scholars in schools did not read at all in other subjects, and some did not feel the need to do so even in their own—for example, the brilliant Latin versifier Dames Longworth, sixth form master at Charterhouse, who rarely read a book in any subject.[151]

Probably the greatest single difference between the common rooms and high tables of public schools and Oxford and Cambridge colleges of the Victorian period and of today is the disappearance of that common culture, centred on the classics: a culture which offered intellectual security, good fellowship, and, not least, one readily applicable standard of appraisal of one's colleagues. An Oxford don, complaining in 1862 that "there are now so many things which a tolerably educated man ought to know", suggested to the Clarendon Commission that schoolboys could not be expected to master both Latin *and* Greek,[152] but academics, at any rate, could accommodate both with ease; indeed so limited in 1889 was the range of erudition expected of a Hellenist that at the age of only twenty-three Gilbert Murray could be described by a fellow classicist (Jebb) as "the most accomplished Greek scholar of the day".[153]

The extent of this common culture among the Victorian ruling classes made possible the exchanges in the House of Commons in which an epigram from a classical author quoted by one speaker might be capped by another from a speaker on the other side, or in which a false quantity was liable to be hissed. Lord Chandos reports an extraordinarily apposite quotation of one-and-a-half lines of Virgil with which Gladstone once commented on a financial deal with the Turks which rescued the British government from an unbalanced budget.[154] This was no longer possible in our own century when the products of a different educational system were represented in Parliament in large numbers, and when in any case the culture even of the ruling classes had become diluted and fragmented by the recognition of new subjects. When (Sir) Winston Churchill dazzled the House of Commons with some very appropriate lines of Homer (in translation), they turned out to have been drawn from Bartlett's *Popular Quotations*.[155] The 1930s saw the end of the use of classical allusions in the Commons, and when Sir John Anderson began a somewhat ponderous reference with "As Horace has it, 'If you drive out nature . . .' " the rest was drowned, we are told, "by ribald and Boeotian shouts of the Labour Party, 'Good old 'Orace!' "[156]

Thus, whilst it lasted, a classical education offered tangible advantages, in terms of intellectual self-confidence and access to a prestigious and aesthetically rewarding intellectual system. In addition, there was the elusive 'moral' component, illustrated by the exchange in 1862 between Moberly, headmaster of Winchester, and the Clarendon Commissioners, which asserted the unique *residual* value of a classical training long after all the subject-matter had been forgotten:

> All classical learning tells on a man's speech; it tells on a man's writing; it tells on a man's thoughts; and though the particular facts go, they leave behind a certain residuum of power; and precisely the one great problem educationists have to consider is how to constitute a system of education which will impart to the mind that power in the highest degree.[157]

The 'moral' content of that residuum was made explicit by a former master at Victorian Charterhouse and (with 'Ian Hay') at Fettes, who, when headmaster of an overseas public school after 1906, answered parents who queried the relevance of Latin to a commercial career: "If you want your son to be a bookkeeper, then by all means let him drop Latin and take bookkeeping: but if you want him to be a *good* bookkeeper he had better stick to Latin".[158]

More important than all these intellectual, aesthetic and moral considerations which contributed to the *mystique* which surrounded classical education was its connection with the idea of a gentleman. Back in the seventeenth century, John Locke in his *Thoughts on Education* had supported Latin (though not Greek) as necessary for a gentleman. In the *Rugby Magazine* for 1836 Arnold's pupil A. H. Clough was asserting the necessity for classical studies for the achievement of "the one great purpose for which boys are sent to Public Schools", namely, "to prepare themselves by study for the station of a gentleman".[159] And some eighteen years before H. H. Asquith entered the City of London School, the boys there were being told of the utility of the classics as enabling one "to maintain with comfort and respectability the station of a gentleman".[160] Because the classics were so strongly entrenched in those schools, which, in the first half of the century, catered for the upper classes, as well as in the universities frequented by those classes, the curriculum of the newer and competing schools*—in any case staffed by men with a similar training—inevitably had to be dominated by those subjects which were associated with the education of gentlemen.†

Because classics required a long training, they were a good excluder. And since a smattering of classical learning—the ability to make a classical allusion, if not actually a quotation—continued to be one of the hallmarks of a gentleman, some writers have tended to explain the prevalence of classics in British education by reference to the concept of 'conspicuous education' (by analogy with conspicous consumption): a form of education with great importance for purposes of display and the assertion of status, but of no intrinsic or utilitarian value. When Dr Gerald Rendall, headmaster of Charterhouse in 1897, began an address to a social evening of local villagers with the words "If you open your Euripides . . ."[163] he was not only displaying his naivety but also emphasising his social rank. In addition to the genuine classical learning of a proportion of the men who ruled India—and we may include a Secretary of State for India, Lord Kilbracken, who acknowledged a lifelong and profound interest in the ancient literatures to which he had been introduced at school[164]—there were thousands of lesser products of Victorian public schools who retained just enough Latin vocabulary to be able to enjoy the stories (whether true or not) that the men responsible for the conquest of Sind and the annexation of Oudh announced these acquisitions to their superiors with the terse messages "Peccavi" and "Vovi". Their enjoyment was enhanced by the satisfaction that it was available only to the initiated—in this case, largely members of their own status-group—and it underlined the truth of at least the first of two justifications for classical study put forward by the man who was Dean of Christ Church when "Tom Brown" (Thomas

*A good example is Wellington, founded to give weight to non-classical subjects, which soon fell back on a standard classical curriculum for many of its pupils.[161]

† And not necessarily because, as Prof. M. L. Clarke suggests,[162] the Victorian public schools were "better than anything else available": the excellence of the Dissenting Academies which flourished before the Victorian period, often with modern and even scientific curricula, had not caused this type of study to predominate.

Hughes) was up at Oxford—though Dr Gaisford was actually offering a defence of Greek when he claimed that it "not only elevates above the vulgar herd, but leads not infrequently to positions of considerable emolument".[165]

As we shall see, the 'conspicuous education' value of classics began to recede towards the end of the Victorian period as a new criterion of gentlemanly status became available. However, throughout the nineteenth century its importance for this purpose is indisputable, though recognition of this fact must not lead us to discount the extent to which genuine appreciation of classical culture shaped the whole lives of many of the Victorians. One consequence of the idea that a high level of classical education in gentlemanly surroundings, as exemplified by an honours degree in Greats at Oxford, "should fit a man to earn his living in most professions",[166] was the cult of the gentlemanly amateur and the suspicion of professionalism, training and expertise in the professions and, even more, in the business world. Another result was the disdain with which other school subjects were regarded. French, both because it was held to lack academic rigour and because it was the native language of people who could not be counted upon to be 'gentlemen', was openly derided by masters as a "tinpot" subject.[167] This attitude, compounded by the low status allowed to its teachers—Frenchmen or refugees from other Continental countries—meant that few pupils took the subject seriously and indiscipline was rife. At some schools, like Eton throughout the Victorian period and at Radley even up to about 1905, such provision was supplemented by lessons by ordinary form-masters who treated the subject as though it were a dead language.[168]

At the end of a varied career, from 1875 onwards, as officer and army educationist, Maj. Gen. Sir Edward May wrote: "I can remember that I have met Englishmen who could hardly carry on conversation with a French or German railway official being entrusted—pronunciation and all—with the instruction of these languages at a great public school".[169]

It was this sort of situation which enabled Gladstone's colleague Lord Granville, who had lived for some time in France, to say that "he knew of only three Englishmen in the whole of his life who could speak French so as to deceive a

Frenchman".[170] Not surprisingly, the Etonian Lord Curzon spoke French "with an English accent", and, as Foreign Secretary, served under a Prime Minister "who confessed that the only French he himself could understand was the Northumbrian variety spoken by Sir Edward Grey".[171] All this was reinforced by upper-class and jingoist prejudices which made it customary to pronounce Monsieur as *Mounseer*, "lest perchance the speaker should be dubbed Frenchified".[172] As a further example of the limits of the teaching of what was called "classical French" at Eton at the turn of the century, we may recall the story of the occasion when Father Ronald Knox, a brilliant classical linguist at Eton and Oxford, heard confessions while doing a locum in a French parish. Confronted with a female penitent who confessed to an impressive list of adulteries, all he could find to say in French was "oh, vooz avay, avay voo?"[173]*

Mathematics had been taught at Winchester from 1834[175] and at Eton from 1851,[176] but in general the status and rewards of the mathematics master in the Victorian public school were lower than those of his classical colleagues; at some schools he was, in the mid-Victorian period, not allowed to wear a gown or to have any part in the discipline of the school—though this was not true of Harrow, where the mathematician J. W. Colenso was a housemaster in 1839. The position of maths in the scale of values readily permitted the key teacher of the subject to be an ineffective disciplinarian (such a master at Radley in the 1880s once spent a whole teaching period under a desk),[177] and this was even more likely to occur with science masters. The second headmaster of Wellington, Dr Wickham, countered the governors' insistence that the teaching of science should be part of the curriculum by appointing "a middle-aged man from a school in the north midlands, who had no experience of public schoolboys and had a defect fatal in their eyes, that he was socially not out of the top drawer". To these handicaps Wickham added an impossible timetable, and disorder and in-

* W. W. Vaughan, a product of Rugby in the 1880s and later headmaster of Giggleswick, Wellington and Rugby, became an enthusiast for the teaching of French by the direct method, and even became President of the Modern Languages Association, despite his own French accent which gave rise to amusement.[174]

effectiveness followed, as, presumably, they were intended.[178] No science was taught at Radley in the early 1880s, and the laboratory was used for storing hampers; the first science specialist appointed to the staff, in 1883, was "no great disciplinarian".[179] Eton's senior science master, who joined the staff in 1885, was the Rev. Dr T. C. Porter, an amiable buffoon "generally considered as a paid charlatan who was employed to entertain the boys by his absurdities".[180] His general effectiveness, and his standing in the school at large, can be gauged from the comment of an Etonian who entered the school in 1898: "He preached once in Lower Chapel, but was so amusing that he never preached again".[181]

It was possible well into the twentieth century to encounter traces of the "old-fashioned view that the sciences were not a respectable occupation for anyone who regarded himself as a gentleman" and the supposition that a scientist was "a sort of mechanic".[182] Those who chose to specialise in science in later Victorian public schools had to brave this kind of attitude, but we must note that there were schools in which good science teaching was going on, often at the hands of men who were themselves distinguished in their fields (see below, Chapter 5). The botanist H. N. Ridley, who helped establish the rubber industry in Malaya, had found his interest in the biological sciences encouraged at Haileybury in the 1870s.[183] The scientific career of the chemist Frederick Soddy, joint formulator with Lord Rutherford of the influential theory of atomic disintegration, was initiated by his science master at Eastbourne in the 1890s, R. E. Hughes, with whom he published a scientific paper while still at school.[184] The scientific interests of the future Sir Henry Tizard, O.M., were well served at Westminster in the late 1890s, though a few years before this A.A. Milne's mathematical inclinations had been discouraged at the same school.[185] At later Victorian Eton, science was normally only available—apart from the army class—as an option for a minority of able boys after they had successfully completed their classical grounding: on this basis T. H. Huxley's grandson Julian found inspiration from one of the Rev. Dr Porter's abler colleagues, but it is true that at school he came to study his specialism, biology, almost by accident;[186] doubtless family background played its part. Despite contrary pressures we have noted at Manchester Grammar School, the inspiring teaching of chemistry at that school towards the end of the century produced some notable scientists.[187] There had been a time, in the late 1880s, when the discovery that it was comparatively easy to get scholarships at the ancient universities in science and mathematics furnished "an enormous temptation to a large class of schools to devote an almost exclusive attention to those subjects",[188] but against this temptation had to be set the relatively bleak employment prospects for such graduates, not to speak of the discouraging conditions in which scientists operated at those universities. Harrow's Modern Side was created in 1869 under Edward Bowen. In 1870 it contained a mere 7% of the boys, which had risen to only 12% by 1883.[189] At Rugby the newly established Modern Side in 1886 constituted 20% of the boys in the school; by 1906 the Modern and Army sides together constituted 40%. At Charterhouse in 1899 only 13% of the school were excused Greek.[190]

English, in many schools throughout the Victorian period, was not 'taught' as a separate subject but was expected to 'emerge' as a by-product of classical studies, with the additional stimulus of holiday tasks and prize-essays in English literature. A few schools were notable, however, as pioneers of imaginative and systematic teaching of English, among them the City of London School under Dr Abbott from around 1866[191] and Westward Ho! during Kipling's schooldays.[192] We can illustrate the general quality of the teaching of geography—other than the geography acquired in classical and biblical studies—by reference to the incident when a Cambridge don, a product of Victorian Rossall who had obtained the highest classical honours, received in 1901 a letter from the Archbishop of Canterbury offering him the Bishopric of Rangoon. He sped round to the rooms of his brother, also a Cambridge don, with the question "Where is Rangoon?". As his brother did not know either, they got out an atlas and began looking in Africa.[193]

5. An object of worship.

The community of a public school—"a world in itself, self-centred, self-satisfied"[194]—possessed in the institutions and activities which were to become characteristic by the late Victorian period, and not least in athleticism, powerful means of generating ideals, attitudes and emotions, and above all loyalty to the school itself. The elaboration of a house system, with games and other activities organised on a house basis, produced a more immediate and potent focus of sentiment, and attitudes towards house and school were sharpened by the intensity of communal life in schools which (except for a few expensive ones) provided little occasion for privacy. These sentiments found expression in rivalry with other public schools at games and other activities, and were cultivated by forms of ritual such as celebratory house suppers and, above all, in the singing by houses or by the whole school of school songs, which were expressions not of aesthetic strivings but of school or house *tribalism*.[195] The music-master John Farmer and the housemaster Edward Bowen provided Harrow with some splendid songs whose tunes were lifted and words amended by other public schools for their own benefit:

> When you hear [wrote an observer of Harrow] the great volume of fresh voices leap up like a lark from the ground, and rise and swell, and swell and rise, till the rafters seem to crack and shiver, then you seem to have discovered all the sources of emotion.[196]

And these were emotions in which Winston Churchill and many less distinguished Harrovians[197] constantly indulged in the course of their lives. H. M. Butler testified that the Harrow songs proved "of quite extraordinary value in promoting good fellowship among the boys and in forging links of love and loyalty between the passing generations of Harrow men".[198] Leo Amery, Conservative statesman and journalist, went even further in explaining their abiding significance: they were "an all-round education in themselves, the embodiment of a manly conception of personal life, of public duty and public policy.[199]

As headmaster of Sherborne, E. M. Young, former Harrow master, encouraged school songs in the 1880s and arranged for the publication of a series of these from 1881 onwards.[200] His successor revived these songs twenty years later, specifically in the hope of "bringing the school back into the sunlight" after the decline associated with Young's resignation•: "the men and

• For the circumstances, see below Chapter Five, Section 8.

boys of those days made the school almost a religion and the school songs their hymns."[201] An Eton master, William Johnson Cory, wrote the somewhat meretricious words—and an Old Etonian serving in India the irresistible tune—of the Eton Boating Song.[202] An Old Etonian prime minister (Rosebery) gave elaborate instructions, well in advance, for this song to be played on his death-bed, and these were faithfully carried out.[203] To a real Wykehamist, the mere sound of the tune of the Winchester song *Domum* "made him realise afresh his deep loyalty and love to his school"; groups of Wykehamist undergraduates at Oxford in the 1880s used to meet regularly for the specific purpose of singing Wykehamist songs, and Wykehamists were heard of in distant places who observed the school's festal day by singing *Domum* as a solo: "there was one who sang it at intervals in the Australian bush".[204] Lesser schools similarly equipped themselves with songs: Bedford Modern's was written by Poole,[205] and the Devon County School sang one written by Brereton whose words expressed the hope that the school might "with book, bat and pen, fit its sons to be men".[206]

Old-established schools like Harrow could reinforce the sentiments thus generated, by an emphasis on the past—the example of the great heroes of Harrow's history.[207] What was more remarkable was the ability of new public schools like Clifton to arouse the passionate loyalty observable in, for example, the poet Henry Newbolt. Powerful emotions thus generated within such communities took various forms. Charles Raven, who went to Uppingham in 1898, "fell in love first with Julius Caesar . . . and then for a little time with Hannibal; and then with Hector, the Hector of the great parting with Andromache . . ."[208] Others, like Arnold Wilson, fell in love with their school and carried away into an early manhood conditioned by the middle-class convention of prolonged celibacy a fixated attachment for (in his case) Clifton.[209] For others it was the intense friendships, the intense hatreds, the rewarding enthusiasms and ambitions of adolescence spent in such a community. Compared with these, the emotional tempo of the outside world to which they returned in the holidays, or on leaving school at eighteen, was an anti-climax. Alfred Lyttelton

had been one of the legendary figures at Eton, the

> acknowledged leader of the school in almost all fields. He was Captain of the XI, Keeper of the Field [*i.e.* Captain of Football], Keeper of fives and racquets, in Sixth Form, and President of Pop. He lived to be a leading Counsel and a Cabinet Minister, but he often said no position in after life began to accord the *réclame* or prestige which he enjoyed at Eton.[210]*

Ronald Knox's success at Eton removed from him any desire to grow up. Leaving school he saw as a tragedy and Oxford was always a poor second-best,[212] though for one former Eton Captain of Boats the change was a welcome relief: (Sir) L. E. Jones "was quite unprepared, on arriving at Oxford, for the surge of pleasure I felt at being a nobody again",[213] and his experience of authority at Eton cured him (he claimed) of any future wish for power.[214]

The reactions of their schoolfellows who did not enjoy such prestige at school, or who were in lesser schools where their triumphs had less "*réclame*", might be different. Winston Churchill was denied by Harrow's curriculum the measure of recognition which his non-classical literary gifts would otherwise have earned him, and his sole athletic distinction at school was that of champion fencer of 1892.[215] It is at least arguable that, whatever the effects on his emotional development of his relationships within his family, his lack of success at school helped to feed a sense of ambition which in his early career was almost obsessive.†

6. The rising tides.

The ability of a school to inspire such emotionalism was a function of the intensity of communality fostered by various characteristics of the developed model of the later Victorian public school. We can see these characteristics present in a number of schools prominent in what during the last three decades of the period (and not before) we can call the public-school *system.* Among factors which intensified the con-

* "Only forty-eight hours now between me and insignificance," said Lyttelton shortly before his last day at Eton.[211]

† Note Churchill's prep. school headmaster's perceptive comment in his school report: "*He has no ambition.*"[216]

sciousness of community were, as we have seen, athleticism, the development of a house system with strong house-loyalties, and school songs. The codification of 'bounds' and the consolidation of school buildings within a defined area rather than spread around the town (one aspect of what Thring called "The Almighty Wall") emphasised the idea of a self-contained, self-conscious school community. Services in the chapel—often designed on the 'collegiate' plan with seats facing each other—symbolised the community at prayer. The extension 'inwards' (as it were) of this idea of community by the development of house loyalties was parallelled by its extension 'outwards', in the form of the development of the idea of a community of Old Boys of a given public school and finally (as we shall see) a community of those who recognised each other as products of public schools generally.

A condition of such a feeling of community was the prevalence of boarding.[217] In the nine schools examined by the Clarendon Commission in 1861 (including, of course, the predominantly day-schools, St Paul's and Merchant Taylors') nearly 27% were day-boys. In 572 endowed schools examined by the Taunton Commission in 1868, nearly 75% were day-boys, and in proprietary schools examined in 1867 nearly 70% were day-boys.[218] This fairly high overall percentage of day-boys, in an age when the cost of boarding education represented a smaller proportion of the income of professional men than it has in the twentieth century, can be compared with the 7% of day-boys in the thirty-seven most expensive public schools in 1938.[219] In general, the nineteenth century was a period of steady growth in the size of schools. Numbers at Eton grew from 357 in 1800 to 568 in 1825, after which they fell off to 446 by 1835, apparently because of rebellions during the Keate régime.* Under Keate's successors numbers rose fairly steadily to top 900 in 1871 and a thousand in 1891, despite the Clarendon Commission's recommendation of an optimum maximum of 800.[221] Such large numbers put Eton in a class of its own, as we can see from the Clarendon Commission's figures for numbers at the top seven public schools in 1861: Eton 793, Rugby 465, Harrow

* They had fallen off even more dramatically during the period of rebellions against Dr Foster in the decade after 1765.[220]

464, Winchester 197, Westminster 136, Shrewsbury 132, Charterhouse 126.[222]* Insofar as the relative sizes of the schools reflect a similar picture (though with smaller totals) around 1800, we have a useful guide to which schools were most prone to rebellions during a couple of decades before and after that date. All these schools increased in numbers by between 20% and 400% in the next forty years, the most spectacular increase being Charterhouse's, after moving from London. However, the size of the 'typical' public school was still rather smaller in the late Victorian period than the 'typical' public school has been in recent years, and if our conception of a public school's size is built upon modern impressions, it is likely to be misleading. If we take the twenty-or-so schools which were leading public schools around 1900 and compare their size then with numbers at the same schools in the period 1960–70, it will be seen that the tendency is for all these schools (except one†) to show an increase of between 10–30%, with a few of them growing by even more: Repton, Rossall, Uppingham and Westminster have all become schools closer to 500 than 300, which was nearer their average size around 1900, and Glenalmond grew from a tiny school of around 130 boys to one of over 330, and Sherborne trebled its earlier numbers of only 200. Of the leading day public schools around 1900, St Paul's has increased from under 600 to over 700; Dulwich has nearly doubled to reach around 1300. Two leading day schools of lesser 'public school' status around 1900 have also grown considerably: Manchester Grammar School (from around 750, to become an enormous factory of about 1400) and King Edward's, Birmingham, from 450 to around 700. Apart from day schools like these and from the 'leading' public schools, the general picture of school size within the public-schools community is of the existence of numbers of very small schools, apparently viable in 1900, which have grown considerably in numbers by the 1960s and 1970s. There were schools of around 100 boys (or even

* When St Paul's and Merchant Taylors' were added, the total in the nine schools was around 2700 boys aged between eight and nineteen, "the average age being not far short of fifteen".[223]

† Cheltenham, whose numbers have remained fairly constant, assuming that earlier totals included the junior school.[224]

fewer), which, if they have survived into our own period, tend now to have numbers of between 240–450. Radley, Felsted, Shrewsbury, the Leys, Fettes and Dover have roughly doubled in size, Eastbourne has trebled, and St Edward's, Oxford, has quadrupled.[225]

The total picture, then, is one of a steady growth in the numbers involved in the public-school system in the Victorian period, a growth which was sustained into modern times. As we shall see in the following chapter four, the total numbers of schools recognised as public schools increased from about nine around 1860 to a figure between 64 and 104 (or even more) around 1902, and the schools which could claim to be public schools in the 1960s and 1970s may, on the widest definition, exceed two hundred. These schools were served by an infrastructure of preparatory schools whose spectacular growth between the 1850s and 1925 we have already noted. The total numbers of boys in each public school tended to increase within the Victorian period, despite a tendency, which in the leading schools was marked, to narrow the age range at admission, and so did the proportion of boarders—again, especially in the leading schools; these two forms of increase continued into the present century. However, two points should be noticed concerning the emotional hold which the schools undergoing these changes could exercise on their members. First, that hold was to operate, from the later Victorian period onwards, on pupils whose stay in the school was shorter than was common for many boys in the early Victorian public schools. Secondly, although the fact of boarding was an important ingredient of the conception of a school which exercised this kind of hold, there were several schools, including leading ones, which were members of the public-schools community by the end of the Victorian period which were not wholly or even substantially boarding schools.

Two other developments illustrate aspects of the conception of the school which was changing in the Victorian period. Both relate to the extent to which the school was originally regarded as the embodiment of the personality and teaching functions of an individual headmaster, as opposed to an organism of which one man represented only a part. The physical 'plant'[226] of schools showed one side of this change: the original plan, of a single 'schoolroom' in which the 'master' (headmaster) taught all the pupils together, or shared them with an usher operating by a contest of voices at the other end of the room, gave way to a series of individual classrooms, though often still grouped round a central 'schoolroom' which later did duty as an assembly hall. Two or even three masters teaching their classes in one long room had been common at larger schools, like Eton, in the first half of the century,[227] and towards the end of the century there were still traces of this system in some of the newer public schools, like Marlborough or Llandovery, whose 'plant' included purpose-built classrooms.[228] The other development involved the tendency for headmasters, on transferring from one school to another, to take a proportion of their pupils with them, thus advertising the boys' identification with the man rather than with the school. Holden had done this on removal from Uppingham to Durham in 1853, when he took a third of the boys with him, leaving Thring to take over a school of only twenty-five boys;[229] and Harper brought some thirty boys from Cowbridge Grammar School to join the meagre total of forty already at Sherborne in 1850.[230] On appointment to Cranbrook in 1866 the Rev. Dr Charles Crowden found a little school of forty boys whose numbers he raised in the next twenty-two years to one hundred and eighty; but on transferring to the headship of Eastbourne College in 1886 he took with him some ninety boys and several of the masters,[231] leaving his successors at Cranbrook to build up the numbers and fortunes of that school all over again.[232] When in 1935 a charismatic headmaster did this sort of thing he found himself in disgrace with the Headmasters' Conference, which is evidence of the wide extent to which the new conception of the school was established.[233] By the end of the Victorian period a school was to be judged not just by the calibre of its headmaster—though this was very important—but also by the quality of the whole staff, the characteristics of its clientele, by its buildings and playing-fields, its successes at work and play, its traditions, the loyalties of its Old Boys, and by those aspects of its moral collectivity which were known to the Victorians as 'tone''.

Thring's biographer places around 1873 an undated letter in which Thring notes that

> There is a very strong feeling growing up among the merchant class in England in favour of the public schools and hundreds go to schools now who thirty years ago would not have thought of doing so. The learning to be responsible and independent, to bear pain, to drop rank, and wealth, and home luxury, is a priceless boon. I think myself that it is this which has made the English such an adventurous race; and that with all their faults, and you know how decided my views are on this side, the public schools are the cause of this manliness. I think . . . that it is the fixed idea of every Englishman, in the lump, that it is the thing to send a boy to a public school, and the ordinary English gentleman would think he lost caste by not doing so. Then the boy world becomes a definite world by itself, and school world and its doings an important factor in the social world.[234]

Dr T. W. Bamford has shown[235] that in the first half of the nineteenth century the sons of gentry and aristocratic families were under-represented in public schools in proportion to their numbers in the total population. It was not until the second half of the century, and particularly the period from the 1870s onwards, that attendance at a public school became the common experience of the sons of the English upper classes. Just as it was a social handicap at Cambridge by the 1880s not to have been at a public school (at some colleges markedly so),[236] so too, prior attendance at a boarding preparatory school became sufficiently common for it to be a disadvantage for an entrant to a boarding public school not to have started out at a prep. school.[237] The system of entrance scholarships which "enormously extended among the public schools" in the last forty years of the century, to the point where by the decade 1885–1895 every leading school offered scholarships to lure able boys,[238] made attendance at a prep. school almost essential for those who wished to get public-school entrance scholarships, now no longer restricted to cases of financial need. Thus the prospect of sending one's sons away to boarding school from age eight to age eighteen began to figure in the expectations of every upper-class Englishman in the late nineteenth century, and to a large number of parents below that class who had aspirations to join or at least imitate him.

This phenomenon, involving as it did an important and eneral transfer of function from the parent to the school, is erhaps unique in modern history. All education, other than rictly domestic education of course, involves a transfer of function, but the completeness of the transfer to an alternative community—a distinctive emotional milieu capable of generating s own set of values—as the common practice of an influential ection of society, probably has no parallel among advanced ocieties.

How far was this process initiated and welcomed by the eadmasters themselves? We have seen the ambivalence of Dr rnold on this subject—his serious misgivings as to whether the hool-community as it operated in his own day could ever be roductive of good, and his keen interest in the formulation by is favourite pupil, Stanley, of a rationalisation of the potential f this developing institution. Arnold's successors accepted the otion of the school as a special kind of community with its own et of values and came to exult in the very intensity with which e school could implant those values in its pupils. Thus H. M. utler of Harrow glorified "public school esprit de corps" as a strong passion new in man's history",[239] whereas it is oteworthy that Arnold's only recorded use of the term *esprit de rps* is, significantly, in a reference to the Church.[240]

In some instances the headmasters recognised that there night be a conflict between, on the one hand, the values which ey themselves tried to propagate through the 'machinery' of e school—*i.e.* through the content of the teaching, the example of the masters, the chapel sermon, through religious observance generally, etc., and, on the other hand, the values hich were implicit in the operation of the system—the nachinery'—itself. Thus, for example, it was recognised by ome schoolmasters that the competitive ethos of community fe in a public school, with its emphasis on personal ambition in ork and play, conflicted with the Christian "sentiment of enerous goodwill"; and in the 1870s at Marlborough the Rev. . Llewellyn Davis preached in chapel on how this conflict could e reconciled if the "divinely ordained" elements, emulation nd competition, were kept in check.[241] Others might point out n the pulpit that public-school education was in practice "the rivilege of a caste" which separated the wealthy from their fellow-Christians: in opposition to this tendency they preache an ideal of social service which found expression in the es tablishment and maintenance of public-school 'missions' an 'settlements' in slum areas.[242]

But while there was this kind of recognition of a degree o conflict of values within the structure, headmasters never en visaged the values of the schools as being in serious conflict wit those of the home. Still less did they regard it as a specific func tion of the school to propagate values divergent from those o the home. Woodard, who did take that view, was untypical—bu after all, he was operating a system of schools very consciousl designed to take in social classes not already provided for (to an considerable extent) in the public schools of the mid-nineteent century. In a sense his aims involved a similar task of socia reclamation to that of the educators of pauper children, sphere in which the administrators (such as Kay-Shuttleworth quite explicitly conceived it as "the interest of society tha children should neither inherit the infamy, nor the vice, nor th misfortunes of their parents".[243]

In a pamphlet written in 1858, *Can we adapt the Public-Schoo System to the Middle Classes?*, a future headmaster of Bradfield an of Rugby (Hayman) asked the question:

> Is it possible to give a lower and less opulent class of societ the advantages which public schools afford to wealth parents, of placing their sons away from home in a larg society of boys?

The gist of his answer was that many advantages would accrue and not least the formation of a beneficial *esprit de corps* so feebl present in their existing day-schools. But there was one signifi cant snag—this concerned the holidays. Whereas these in an or dinary boarding public school are valuable for "the renovatin stimulus which they supply from home", in a lower-middle class public school there would be this difference:

> The effect of their holiday homes on the class of boys of whon we speak, would be partly, no doubt, to lower the standar which the school had been trying to raise, not necessarily b anything directly vicious, for of this there is perhaps les chance than in a more pampered social class, but by the mea

> habits and vulgar tricks which it would renew in them, the cockney or provincial slang which it would reinfuse into their speech, out of all of which they were being refined. I will venture, however, to say that there is little of that honourable love of truth, which distinguishes English public-school boys, to be found in the homes of the lower middling class. *The domestic reinforcement of school-life** must, then, be necessarily the weakest part of the system under these conditions . . .[244]

and he went on to propose that boys would have to be kept at school in the holidays.

It is true that it was not only at the lower end of the social scale that the "domestic reinforcement of school-life" was lacking: Arnold's suspicion of the aristocracy because of their habits of luxury and idleness would have been reflected in the attitude of any Victorian headmaster that it was one of the tasks of his school to save pupils with wealthy backgrounds from habits of dissipation picked up at home.[245] Thus, specific aspects of the home background might be deplored, but no headmaster of a conventional Victorian public school saw the values of the school as superseding, to any general extent, those of the home. On the contrary, the values of home and family were constantly held up before the pupils, in sermons and speech days, as values to be cherished.

This is true despite the completeness of the authority which the headmaster exerted over every aspect of the boys' lives, at least in term-time, and which manifested itself in the extension of the authority of the school, its rules and its officials, over the lives of day-boys outside school hours. Percival, first headmaster of Clifton, made a rule that parents of a day-boy were never to be both away from home at once during term-time, except by permission of the headmaster.[246] The authoritarian attitude of public-school headmasters led to friction with parents, and to frequent exasperation with over-solicitous ones: the troubles of Vaughan (of Harrow) with such mothers, among whom, he found, widows were worst, prompted him to declare he had been led to reconsider the objections to *suttee*, and at Marlborough Canon Bell is said to have been driven to pronounce that "parents are the last people who ought to be

* Author's emphasis.

allowed to have children".[247]

But such (understandable) expressions did not indicate any real belief that the headmasters intended the school to supplant the home in the formation of values or sentiments. We have seen how in 1868 Lord Fortescue echoed a speech of Vaughan's which suggested that home influences were deservedly more powerful than those of school. In 1857 Vaughan preached a sermon at Repton's Tercentenary celebrations which constitutes a classic expression of the conception of the mid-Victorian public school as a community. Of its organisation:

> What an admirable structure of parts! What a carefully constituted machinery!

—though it was liable, no doubt, to abuse, requiring watching and checking, and "the infusion of right principles, and the fearless enforcement of authority from above". Thus operated, it had inestimable potential for training in responsibility and in deference to others. But this institution must never appear to supplant the family, which is

> the institution which came most directly from the hand of God ... Never can that original bond be broken without fearful consequences, never should it even be modified without the gravest care and watchfulness. I call it "modified", when recourse is had to the schoolmaster for the discharge of any portion of the parental duties: I call it "broken" when a parent, committing his son to the schoolmaster, deems all done, resigns altogether the functions of instruction and discipline which God has committed to him.

The function of the school is seen by Vaughan "not as usurping, but as aiding, the office of the parent". "And in this capacity we claim for the institution the blessing, the very authorship of God".[248]

From other headmasters we get a similar, or even a more extreme, view. Tait, Headmaster of Rugby, preached that "God ordained the family relation before all others", and that "even bad parents will teach their children what is good".[249] Moberly of Winchester confided to his diary his concern at his son's reaction to boarding-school life: "Arthur is so confirmed a schoolboy that he seems to prefer school to home—a real ground for uneasiness".[250]

7. The expectations of parents.

A highly articulate conception of public schools as communities imparting a distinctive and valuable set of values partly generated by the 'machinery' of school life and partly infused by the headmaster and staff, was largely a rationalisation by Victorian schoolmasters of a development which had come about by its own growth rather than by their design. The transfer of function from parents to this institution which was involved in the expansion and widespread use of a public school *system* in the late Victorian period was similarly less the result of the initiative of headmasters than a response to the expectations of parents.

Yet the abandonment of the ideal of domestic education, the predominant educational ideal of the eighteenth and early nineteenth centuries,[251] and the consequent transfer of function to a separate educational community making powerful emotional demands and generating a separate loyalty, were caused partly by the ability of the schools to fulfil a function which was not in a strict sense academic. The first wave of new public schools in the 1840s and 1850s preceded the introduction of competitive examinations for the Indian Civil Service (from 1853) and for the Home Civil Service (from 1858),[252] and schools like Cheltenham and Clifton were being used to send boys into military careers for between one and three decades before the abolition of the purchase of army commissions in 1871. The principle of competitive examinations for almost every profession, by which between 1855 and 1875 "the old official world of patronage, purchase, nepotism and interest was turned upside down",[253] undoubtedly helped to popularise education at public schools, especially those which were tailoring their curricula to cater for these examinations, but it would be common practice till the end of our period that a boy would go to a public school before he went on to a "crammer" who would prepare him specifically, for example, for the army entrance examinations. In the 1860s the system was established whereby

Oxford and Cambridge awarded their scholarships as entrance awards to boys still in the sixth forms. In the school year 1886–7 a firm of 'crammers', Messrs Wren and Gurney, came fourth in the "scholarship success table", well above Winchester, Cheltenham, Harrow and the rest, and in the following year they actually came top.[254]

That public schools should be thus placed in comparison with "crammers" was to some headmasters (like Kynaston of Cheltenham) an "absurdity",[255] for they conceived the educational function of their own schools as quite different; and many parents valued public-school education for reasons which differed from those thought important by the headmasters. The greatest overall success in the scholarship examinations in the 1880s was gained, as the press was not slow to point out, by "the grammar schools or cheap day schools".[256] But what the parent clientele of the public schools wanted for their sons above all was not scholastic certification but status. This is what public schools, and especially boarding-schools, offered. Boarding was an important element because, with the right composition, it was a potent but subtle solvent of divergent social-class backgrounds, and a boarding community was seen to have the same advantages for a school which dons declared to derive from residential university colleges—"all that formation of character, resulting from the attrition of College life . . ."[257] It was this attitude towards 'residence' which led the United University Club around 1878 to withhold membership from non-collegiate students at Oxford,[258] and which was reflected in Caird's report to the Bryce Commission that employment prospects for non-collegiates were not as good as for products of residential colleges.[259] Boarding experience was to be, for many, the hallmark of the public school man. Even so, there were influential public-school headmasters who were not fully convinced of the advantages of boarding education over day-schooling. Percival's experience at Clifton "led him to the conclusion that the best education in English life was not to be had in the boarding school, but was obtained by the boy who lived in a good home and attended a good school near his home"; he was sufficiently convinced of the value of non-residential communities to consider in 1883 resigning the headship of an Oxford college to become Censor of non-collegiate students at

Oxford.[260] Brereton's argument for boarding public schools ultimately came to be one of economy—that "for all grades of society, good boarding schools can be found less costly to the parent than day schools and home living".[261]

Parents looked to the public schools to provide what the professions in the nineteenth century demanded—the 'education of a gentleman'. Yet among the most prestigious careers into which public-school men would be attracted, many offered little more than a bare living. Even after the establishment of competitive entry, the army remained a necessarily expensive occupation, except in India, and it was still difficult for an officer to live on his pay.[262] According to Sir Evelyn Wood in 1903, it was still a disadvantage in the army to have private means of only £50 a year or less.[263] The requirement of private means was even more the case for the diplomatic service[264] and for Parliament. But medicine, the law, the Church, the civil service (India and Home) would supply at least a modest competence, and, for a few, much more. What entrants to these professions would obtain was the maintenance of a status for which their public-school education had given the expectation, and to which it had bestowed or confirmed their right of entry.

8. The 'Old Boy' invented.

The school-communities to which parents consigned their sons had power to involve their emotions and fashion their values not just during school life, but far into the future. In the first half of the century the major boarding schools, with their historic associations and in some cases aristocratic clientele, had attracted the loyalty of their Old Boys, whose stay in the school might have extended over ten years or even more. Even so, Dr T. W. Bamford finds that, for example, fewer than 5% of Arnold's Old Boys sent their sons to Rugby; and at Winchester it was not until the last decades of the century that a good proportion of boys came from Wykehamist homes.[265] The 'Old Boy' phenomenon really dates from the second half of the century, especially from the 1870s onwards, when even the humblest would-be public school held an Old Boys' Dinner,[266] started an Old Boys' Association,[267] and published a Register; and a public school which by 1898 had not yet devised an Old Boys' tie might be under "loud and insistent" pressure from its Old Boys to remedy this lack.[268]

The earliest of these Associations generally had as their object the expression of loyalty to the old school, as well as some form of mutual help among the members.[269] The historian of Cranleigh noted within the first decades of its foundation one special feature

> which there has been a desire to cultivate, viz. *continuity*, and this has caused a close connection to be kept up between the boys, who have left, amongst each other and between them and the present School. Not a few boys have started life in positions obtained for them through School interest, and many evince their abiding affection for the School by constantly visiting it and corresponding with those who bear office in it; and this not only for a few years after leaving it, but Old Boys of all periods, from the very first, still keep up this connexion with the general body.[270]

It would probably be true to say that the membership of Old Boys' Associations has tended to be dominated by the extremes of age—by those who have newly left school and by the old who have leisure to indulge their sentimentality.* For the former, at least, the old school has formed a focus for games-playing, and the organisation of cricket, football and other games along public-school Old Boy lines has been one characteristic of British sport since Victorian times. By 1891, at least twenty public-school Old Boy cricket clubs were playing regular fixtures, and there was a similar number of football clubs. As well as Old Wykehamist, Old Etonian and Old Harrovian cricket there were even clubs formed from among Old Boys of individual prep. schools. Sherborne furnished not only an Old Shirburnian Football club but also a Cambridge Old Shirburnian Football club and an Oxford Old Shirburnian Football club. In 1898 it was a matter of resentment at Glasgow University that Old Boys of Fettes and Loretto preferred to play for school clubs rather than for the university.[271]

Boys who went up to Oxford or Cambridge from the

* A *reductio ad absurdum* of this kind of preoccupation among old men is pictured by William Trevor in his novel *The Old Boys* (1964).

better-known public schools found a ready-made circle of friends. From Eton (where he had gone in 1900) Ronald Knox went up to Balliol with a throng of friends who had known each other since the age of thirteen (and in many cases at eight, at prep. school): "most of [them] were content to live together undiluted for the whole of their Oxford lives".[272] The products of lesser schools with a smaller representation scattered throughout the colleges were brought together by an Old Boys' organisation specific to Oxford or Cambridge.

Public-school men who went out to India found a similar organisation: between twenty and fifty Etonians could be expected at each annual Old Etonian Dinner held in Simla in the last years of Victoria's reign; at Kabul in 1880 [Lord] Roberts dined with eleven "Eton Fellows" and helped them to storm a Harrovian mess,[273] and a good contingent of Old Marlburians in this period attended their annual dinner in Calcutta.[274] Products of Victorian St Paul's helped to found the Old Pauline Association of India and Burma in 1909, and there were around four hundred Old Paulines in India and Burma in the later 1920s.[275] Every year around 1900 Old Carthusians were celebrating their School's Founder's Day in India, Ceylon, Gibraltar, Malta and Africa, and in Britain the Old Carthusian Cricket and Football club had 3,000 members in 1904.[276]

The ability, noticed above, of Old Cranleighians to gain "positions obtained through school interest" was symptomatic of a whole new form of patronage, which was in our own century to be termed the "Old-Boy network". At its grandest level it found expression in the process described with candour by Baldwin in his speech to the Harrow Association in 1923:

> When the call came for me to form a government, one of my first thoughts was that it should be a government of which Harrow should not be ashamed. I remembered how in previous Governments there had been four, or perhaps five, Harrovians, and I determined to have six.[277]

The result, in Harold Laski's words, was "the largest number of Harrow men collected in a single cabinet".[278] More recently, we were reminded on Lord Attlee's death by one of his obituarists that during his first Labour government (1945–50) he contrived to find a post for an Old Boy of his own school (Haileybury).[279]* The large numbers of Etonians in Harold Macmillan's government—at one point in the 1960s all three ministers of Education were, like Macmillan himself, products of both Eton and Oxford—show that the prevalence of this mechanism was not limited to the Old Boys who attended public schools in the Victorian period†. It is an interesting question in any of these periods to see which schools seemed to have most power to promote the fortunes of their alumni in this way, and in what spheres. For the most famous schools the examples are numerous. At the other end of the spectrum, it cannot have been pure coincidence that the first three Principals of Durham University's College of Science after 1871 were all products of one London day public school—the City of London School.[282]

The unofficial freemasonry constituted by the "Old-Boy network" was also formalised by the establishment of individual public-school Masonic Lodges, the first of them by Highgate School in 1877.[283]

The interest taken by the formal Old Boy Associations in the fortunes of the 'old school' was bound to take a practical form. Where this involved exercising pressures on school policy, this was generally—and understandably—in a conservative direction, such as organising opposition to a proposed change-over from soccer to rugger as the school game,[284] or to a change of school site. Furious opposition by Old Boys to Moss's proposed transfer of Shrewsbury to new buildings at Kingsland in 1882 was frustrated, and the moving of the school was successfully carried out; in revenge, Old Boys sent their sons to other schools, and sons of Old Boys were rare in just the period when the Old Boys of the pre-1882 vintage would normally have been the school's chief source of supply.[285] Moss's successor found only one boy in the school whose father had been at Shrewsbury. This process, combined with the unexpected channelling away from Shrewsbury of good classical pupils

* As Deputy Prime Minister during the Second World War Attlee personally intervened to save his old school from evacuation to the Lake District by using his influence to reverse the War Office's requisitioning of Haileybury's buildings.[280]

† It was estimated that Eton and Harrow together contributed between 30% and 43% of Conservative M.P.s in the years 1905–38.[281]

"bribed"[286] by the institution of entrance scholarships at other schools, seriously affected the fortunes and the standing of Shrewsbury in the late Victorian period.[287] The basis for the Old Salopians' strong reaction is understandable; masters come and go, and a returning Old Boy cannot bank on finding anyone still on the staff who taught him, so what he depends on are buildings and playing-fields which are identifiable with the sentimentalised memories of boyhood.

'Old-Boy power' could be an invaluable weapon to a headmaster who was himself an Old Boy of the school he headed, as Ford was at Repton.[288] Old Boys were powerfully represented on governing bodies: that at Loretto, established to regularise the 'public school' status of the school at the beginning of this century, consists entirely of Old Lorettonians.[289] The Old Boys of a day-school, exercising their influence through the governing body, Old Boys' Association and games clubs, could "easily become a sort of resident mother-in-law".[290]

The cash value of Old Boy's Associations is of less questionable utility. Harrovians contributed substantially to the £130,000 raised by that school between 1829 and 1885,[291] and to the £420,000 raised between 1910 and 1926.[292] In the case of humbler schools, the benefactions of Old Boys have at critical times been decisive for the fortunes of the school.

9. Identification and dynasticism.

In being thus a community which could exercise an emotional hold not only during schooldays but for life, the public school became an alternative to the Victorian family as a reference group[293]—"an expression of shared perspectives, value systems, group norms, etc." used by those members who identified themselves with it "as a standard for self-evaluation and as a source for [their] own personal values and goals".[294] Within the reference group constituted by past and present members of the school-community, specially impressive headmasters or assistant masters had the power to act as referents, and in this role they may be seen as alternative parents, as the Victorian schoolmaster's phrase 'in loco parentis' suggests. The intensity of the loyalty some individual masters inspired produced extremes of identification and imitation in their pupils. We have seen how Arnold exercised this gift himself and also expected from his assistant masters qualities which would attract such sentiments. When the theological orthodoxy of Temple, headmaster of Rugby, was called in question because of his contribution to the controversial *Essays and Reviews*, a pupil wrote home that "if Temple turned Mahometan, all the school would turn Mahometan too".[295] Among Temple's Old Boys, none was more devoted than Hart, later headmaster (1879–1900) of Sedbergh, where

> Temple's portrait hung in his study where his eye might always rest on it; and, below the frame, Hart's own "Big Side" football cap, frayed and faded, like a votive offering at the shrine.[296]

Hart in his turn was to exercise a similar influence: for a former pupil weighed down by religious and moral perplexities, his old headmaster was the only one to whom he felt he could turn:

> If I could get hold of dear old Da he would understand, and I'd believe every single word he said.[297]

It was said of E. H. Bradby, headmaster of Haileybury (1868–83), that none of his former Haileybury pupils ever took an important decision in life without first consulting him;[298] of G. G. Bradley of Marlborough it was said that his former pupils when confronted in later life with an awkward situation would ask themselves "what would Bradley have said?"[299]

This individual form of identification reinforced the generalised loyalty inspired by the school, which could be a powerful influence in later life. An Eton housemaster was deeply moved to hear of the sentiments of two Old Etonians in a military hospital in the First World War, one of them horribly injured:

> He lay dying at Malta for 3 weeks and after the last fatal relapse wrote on a scrap of paper 'Anyhow floreat Etona' and passed it on Tufnell who simply added 'florebit'. Is one not proud of having the friendship or the education of such as that? or could any realschule or gymnasium in Europe nurse such loyalty?[300]

To a nation requiring the willing self-sacrifice of tens of

thousands of its sons in a possibly senseless war, the ability to call on such reserves of unquestioning loyalty has an obvious value. Old-Boy loyalty is one factor which helps to explain the immolation of enormous numbers of British officers—largely recruited from public schools—in World War I. The attitude of unreasoning conformity bred in the schools helps to explain the inhuman treatment of conscientious objectors in that war. That educational institutions ought to become, as since the Victorian period public schools have very self-consciously become, objects of sentimental attachment has been described by Prof. Bernard Williams as "a specifically English sort of assumption":

> Is it self-evident that it is a desirable feature of an educational system to engender a great emotional attachement to the educational institution itself? Might it not be that such devotion tended against certain aims of education, such as that of enabling people to recognize what is intellectually and culturally valuable wherever it shows itself?[301]

This criticism applies with some force to the Victorian public school, where loyalty was enforced by powerful sanctions. Disloyalty or disgrace in the school community could lead to expulsion—and this was not just a technical withdrawal such as was the case in public schools in the first half of the nineteenth century. For example, the boys expelled by Wilkinson for their part in the Marlborough 'rebellion' were given testimonials and later sent their own sons to the school. But expulsion in the later Victorian public school was a degradation which could mean being cut off from a life-long community, and it was a sanction which could even be imposed for actions after one had left. After the publication of his controversial novel *The Loom of Youth* (1917), Alec Waugh was called upon to resign from the Old Shirburnian Society, a sanction applied at the same time to his father,[302] Arthur Waugh, the publisher, an exceedingly loyal Old Boy whose lasting emotional involvement with Sherborne is indicated in his confession to his son Evelyn that "every night of his life he dreamed that he was back at Sherborne as a new boy".[303]*

* In later years the Sherborne Old Boys relented, and both the Waughs were restored to the pantheon of distinguished Old Shirburnians.

A further revealing aspect of the Old Boy phenomenon is the schools' ability to attract the devotion even of former pupils who had been desperately unhappy at school. Somerset Maugham hated his schooldays at King's School, Canterbury (1885–89), but later gave the school a fine library and thousands of valuable books, and on his death in 1965 his ashes were buried in the school precinct.[304] The same school had nurtured another future novelist, (Sir) Hugh Walpole (1896–98), who was also desperately unhappy there, but in 1935 he became a substantial benefactor to the school, where a house was named after him.[305] Public schools have always been ready to cultivate the successful and famous among their Old Boys and to hold up their achievements for emulation by the boys. Such blandishments may have smoothed the path for Maugham's and Walpole's return to the fold, but they do not explain away the phenomenon. Edward Lyttelton describes a contemporary of his at Eton in the 1870s, a misfit who was badly handled by boys and masters alike and who left the school early:

> Nonetheless, he looked on it later as a first charge on his attenuated income to send his sons to Eton. There lies the secret no one has quite explained.[306]*

The school's function as a reference group—acting thus even for its apparent outcasts—is a part of the explanation of the secret. Another part is the fact that the public school, as well as having the function of an alternative community to the family, also came to act in ways which expressed some of the functions of the family itself.

If the century since the middle of Queen Victoria's reign has witnessed a reduction of the social functions of the family (particularly the extended family), there is a sense in which identification by the members of a family with a particular school may be said to have represented an expression of certain of those social functions. Dynasticism could now be expressed by

* In fact, Lyttelton could have hit upon a more prestigious example from a quarter of a century earlier. The third Marquess of Salisbury, Conservative prime minister, had so hated his schoooldays at Eton that he could only bring himself on one single occasion to revisit the school in later life, despite his frequent official visits to the Queen at nearby Windsor.[307] Yet in due course he sent each of his five sons there.

the attendance of all male members of a family at a certain school, and though there were instances like the nine Rendall brothers in the 1870s spread around three major schools[308] there are even more instances of several generations within families being educated at one public school,[309] whether Eton or Malvern or Framlingham.

Continuity, in the form of sons succeeding father in attendance at a given school, was compromised by social mobility: when the product of a humbler public school became successful, he was tempted to send his sons to a more prestigious school whose status reflected the one he had gained. Thus Lionel Ford, one of seven brothers at Repton (all in the XI) sent his own sons to Eton or to Harrow, at which schools he was housemaster and headmaster respectively.[310] Albert Profumo, educated at the City of London School (1893–95), became a KC and sent his son John Profumo to Harrow (1928–33); Asquith, also at City of London, sent his sons to Winchester. On the other hand the tendency to express 'dynasticism' through one school was reinforced by the tendency for families attending a public school to intermarry*—there is, for example, a statistically demonstrable tendency, from the Victorian period on, for Old Wykehamists to marry the daughters or sisters of Old Wykehamists (as Arnold himself had done) and even to name Old Wykehamists as co-respondents.[311]

One of the functions of the new Scottish public schools in the later Victorian period was to offer a means of emphasising the Scottishness of families of Scottish descent who had settled outside the country. At Fettes (founded 1870), where the wearing of the kilt was encouraged, about a third of the entrants in 1880 and in 1890 came from England, Ireland, Africa, North and South America, France, etc.—many of them with Scottish surnames.[312] One of them, John Hay Beith (the writer Ian Hay), was the son of a Scottish cotton merchant prominent in the public life of Manchester, where the boy was brought up in a "passionately old-style Scottish background"[313] to which Fettes was a natural extension. (Among the entrants in 1929 was Iain

* Two of W. E. Gladstone's courtships, including the one that led to his marriage, were with sisters of his Eton friends.

Macleod, son of a Scottish doctor in Yorkshire. But when he became a Cabinet minister he sent his own son to Harrow).

For the nineteenth century, Prof. Harold Perkin reminds us, "the cost of acquiring a landed estate was at its highest in the mid-Victorian age. Competition for land was fierce, and many wealthy new men had to make do with more modest estates than previously, or even with country seats with little or no land attached".[314] For the landless and geographically mobile professional man, as well as the less wealthy 'new men', dissociation from birthplace or 'family seat', whose local church displayed the memorials of their ancestry, forced them to look elsewhere for an expression of family ties. The endowment of even a small prize or trophy in a Victorian public school could ensure the commemoration of a name. A chapel plaque or stained-glass window could perpetuate a memory where once a memorial in the 'family' church would have served. Such plaques in the cloisters at Eton testify to the self-sacrifice of several members of a single family in the Great War. As a result of the Boer War, Marlborough was faced with a crescendo of applications for memorial inscriptions in the chapel until space forced the governors in 1906 to limit inscriptions to cases of 'exceptional distinction'.[315] Those who, like the 'V.C.' from Victorian Framlingham,[316] left the insignia of their decorations to their old public school rather than to their descendants, were giving expression to a similar sentiment. Arnold had opened up the vaults of Rugby chapel for the burial of boys who died at the school[317] and was himself buried there. Similarly Percival, Bishop of Hereford, chose to be buried not in his birth place, nor in the cathedral of his bishopric, but in the crypt of Clifton College chapel "among the abiding monuments of his chief creative effort".[318]

Two public school men produced in the Victorian period chose a distinctive way of expressing 'dynasticism' through a school rather than a territorial connection. J. L. Maffey was the son of a Rugby draper who had sold shirts to the boys from the school and who had conceived the ambition (which he fulfilled) to send his own sons there. After an outstanding career as a Governor-General and head of the Colonial Office, Maffey was raised to the peerage and took as his title, not his own name nor that of his country seat in Bucks., but 'Lord Rugby', to emphasise his association with the school of which he had become governor and to which he bequeathed the insignia of his orders and decorations on his death in 1969.[319] (Sir) Godfrey Huggins was at Malvern in the 1890s but left without even sitting the matric. examination, and gained entry to medical school through a crammer's. His premiership of Southern Rhodesia and later of the Central African Federation gained him a peerage (1955), when he chose the title 'Viscount Malvern' in honour of his old school.[320]

These examples illustrate the emotional hold of the public-school community, whether as an alternative to the family—even as a release from the strains of Victorian family life and from Victorian family values[321]—or as a means to express certain historic forms of family consciousness which changes in Victorian society forced into this new channel. This hold helps to explain the fixation with his schooldays which is said to characterise every upper-class Englishman,[322] certainly in comparison with the products of day-schools[323] here and in other countries, and which has given to English literature a distinctive genre—the novel of boarding-school life—unique to England in its popularity. A hundred years ago this began to supplant in children's fiction (and even to infiltrate, in general fiction) the type characteristic in England in the first half of the nineteenth century (and characteristic of the French novel down to our own day)—the novel based on relationships within the family.[324]

Prof. J. A. Banks has shown[325] in his book *Prosperity and Parenthood* how in later Victorian England middle-class parents were consciously limiting the size of their families by various methods[326]* in order to achieve or preserve a style of life one of whose requirements was a public-school education for their children. T. H. Hollingsworth has documented some[328] of the implications of the adaptation by the English aristocracy to new roles forced upon them in the second half of the nineteenth century by their loss of political power. Public-school education became more necessary for them than it previously had been.

* *Cf.* Sir Oswald Mosley's account[327] of Margot Asquith's comments to the then Mrs Mosley soon after the latter's confinement: "Dear child, you look very pale and must not have another baby for a long time. Henry always withdrew in time, such a noble man." Late marriage, characteristic of the middle class, was one important factor.

These developments were both a cause and a reflection of that process involved in the development of the public schools in the later Victorian period which has been claimed in this chapter as a widespread and unprecedented transfer of function from the family to the school. That a transfer of this kind and scale should have taken place when it did is all the more remarkable in view of the self-confessed failure of the schools involved to deal with three serious problems: infectious diseases, sexual immorality, and cruelty.

10. In sickness and in health.

Epidemic diseases were so common in nineteenth century public schools as to have been almost endemic. Every school had its waves of infectious disease—scarlet fever, diphtheria, influenza, measles, whooping-cough, etc., and deaths of boys at school were a frequent occurrence. Cholera[329] had dispersed Rugby School in 1832, and there was another dispersal in 1841. Thring's evacuation of his whole school from Uppingham to Borth for a year, because of an outbreak of fever (variously described as diphtheria or enteric or typhus) caused by the town's defective sanitation, has became a legend.[330] Fettes was temporarily evacuated to Windermere in 1883 because of an outbreak of diphtheria,[331] and Wellington College was forced to migrate to Malvern by diphtheria in 1892*. Westminster enjoyed a bad health reputation after Dean Buckland's opening of the Westminster drains in the late 1840s,[333] and the school's fortunes for the rest of the century were injured by it. Lancing was struck by typhoid in 1886 after infected cream from a local dairy had been served at a match with the Old Boys.[334]

But the commonest scourge was scarlet fever, from which no school was free. The first school year at the new Rossall (1844) and at the new Cranleigh (1863) were marred by epidemics of it such as had led to the dispersal of boys from Winchester in 1843,[335] and two sons of the headmaster (Moberly) were to die of it at Winchester, in 1858 and 1871. Scarlet fever broke out while

* The repercussions of a decade of recurrent diphtheria, typhoid and other diseases at Wellington, publicised by the dismissed school doctor in the medical press (*e.g.* "The Wellington College Sore Throat", *Lancet*, 1892) are treated fully in the school's *History*.[332]

Gladstone was a boy at Eton in 1825, while the headmaster, Keate, himself caught typhus.[336] Parson Kilvert recorded in his *Diary* the deaths of Marlborough boys during a scarlet fever epidemic in 1870,[337] and the Rugby school doctor reported in the educational press in November 1888 that "during the last three weeks no fewer than eleven southern schools have broken up owing to . . . epidemics of scarlet fever".[338]

In the first three decades of the century, scarlet fever was "frequent, but mild . . . (and . . . not often fatal)"; by the 1830s it had become "the usual epidemic of schools" and, what was new, it was beginning to become a real killer:

> In 1840 scarlatina nearly doubled its mortality, and continued year after year for a whole generation to be the leading cause of death among the infectious maladies of childhood . . . The enormous numbers of deaths from scarlatina during some 30 or 40 years in the middle of the nineteenth century will appear in the [sic] history as one of the most remarkable things in our epidemiology.[339]

The years around 1860 were "the worst years for scarlatina" and also marked the return of diphtheria, to the bewilderment of most of the medical profession to whom it was a novelty:[340] indeed the disease came to be dreaded as much as polio has been in modern times.[341] The average annual *death* rate in England and Wales from scarlet fever (per 1000 persons living) rose to 0·83 in the decade 1851–60 and to a peak of 0·97 in 1861–70, falling off spectacularly in the 1880s and 1890s to 0·16 around 1900. In the present century mortality continued to fall until by 1930 it was negligible: although the prevalence of scarlatina remained high, it was no longer a killer disease.[342]

The years 1864, 1870 and 1874 were perhaps the worst years for scarlet fever; then there was the reappearance of diphtheria, and the great series of influenza epidemics of 1889 to 1893.[343] Yet it was precisely in this period, and especially in the years 1840–80 when the mortality of scarlet fever was at its most spectacular*,

* Even in 1896 scarlet fever was "a formidable disease . . . with a minimum of six weeks confinement" and could involve isolation in a room with a sheet steeped in carbolic over the door, and virtually no visitors. The victim in one such case, a Winchester boy, had contracted the disease at school twice in the same year.[344]

that there occurred the great expansion of public-school education and the beginnings of the domination of the public-school system in the education of the English upper and upper-middle classes. It is true, of course, that the mortality of some of these diseases, like scarlet fever, was at its worst among younger children, and that the home was no sure refuge from the scourge. At his deanery in Carlisle in 1856, Tait, former headmaster of Rugby, lost five daughters, all aged under eleven, in the space of five weeks: his wife's account of the tragedy* is so harrowing as to be virtually impossible to read.[346] The idea of contagion, and even to a lesser extent also of infection, was well enough understood among the better-informed section of the population.[347] Yet large numbers of such parents were prepared to expose their sons to the much increased risks which they must expect to prevail in boarding schools where the standards of care, hygiene, and—when necessary—isolation, could not possibly be maintained as they were for the individual boy in the home. The school authorities had limited facilities, if any, for coping with epidemics or any kind of grave illness;† in the early period their reaction was to send the boys home—even the infected boys as soon as they could be moved: as Glenalmond's headmaster put it in 1858, "I will *not* have boys die here.[349]

In due course the schools provided themselves with sanatoria and with resident doctors. In the early decades of the present century a schoolmaster could still notice that illness was common enough to be a major topic of boy conversation in public schools—"what epidemic sickness had plagued the school last year, or last term, and what was likely to plague this term".[350] Epidemics themselves were to become less common, and certainly less virulent‡, after development of chemotherapy (*e.g.* M & B) in 1936 and the antibiotics in the 1940s, leaving the almost empty school sanatoria[352] as huge white

* It was said that it was Queen Victoria's "maternal pity" for the Taits in this misfortune which led to his promotion to the Bishopric of London (1856), whence he went on to Canterbury (1868).[345]

† Pre-termly certificates of freedom from infection did not become common until the mid-1870s. The tubercle bacillus was not isolated until 1882.[348]

‡ In 1898, 13,000 people in England and Wales died of measles; in 1948 around 300.[351]

elephants to be adapted where possible in our own day as additional boarding houses.

11. Sex and the schoolmasters.

Immorality was a form of infection which was even more serious because its effects were so much more damaging—not only to the body but to the soul—than ordinary disease, and because a cure was so uncertain. What is more, the likelihood of exposure to contagion by attendance at a public school was to be most forthrightly acknowledged by the school authorities themselves precisely in the period when the public-school system was undergoing its greatest expansion—in the mid-nineteenth century, and particularly in the period from the 1860s to the 1880s.

We have seen how, for early Victorian headmasters such as Arnold, the words 'immorality', 'vice', 'sin' and so on, emphasised the wickedness of indiscipline (especially in a collective form) and drunkenness, rather than sexual impurity. Such an attitude also characterised the sermons of headmasters like Temple of Rugby (1857–1868), which reveal no trace of any obsession with sex: a sermon of "Secret Sins" (for example) is mostly about indolence and untruth, with only a passing and very inexplicit reference to anything that might be construed as sexuality.[353] But, for other headmasters, immorality with an increasingly explicitly sexual connotation was already becoming a frequent theme of sermons by 1860, and by the 1880s there were leading schools where 'morality' had narrowed down to one particular issue, and that one had become an "obsession".[354]

During and since the 1960s there have been a great number of studies which have documented the 'other side' of the Victorian 'front' of rectitude and prudery in sexual matters which, under the influence of evangelical morality, succeeded the more permissive attitudes and lax conduct of the upper classes earlier in the century. The middle-class expectation of a late age of marriage—at perhaps thirty or more—with no recognised or approved liaisons before then,[255] co-existed with the fact of an enormous prostitute population (including tens of thousands of juveniles)[356] in London and the major cities. The counterparts to the official standards of manners, speech and writing were the convention of indecent talk in after-dinner conversation among men,[357] the habit of swearing, and the existence of a significan market in pornographic literature and an interest in orienta erotica.

The tendency towards earlier onset of puberty, which Tanner and others have noted as a characteristic of Britain and certain other European countries for the period 1830–1960,[358] would *per se* imply for the Victorian public school an increasing problem of sexuality. But in this respect what was no less significant than the general 'secular' tendency to earlier puberty wa the *range of maturity* within a school at any one time. It is clear that this range must have been wider than it has been in this century in any school of the same age limits. There is plenty of evidence, certainly from the 1860s onwards, from memoirs and from team and house photographs at Clifton, Eton, Rugby Harrow, etc., that older boys were wearing side-whiskers or long moustaches;[359] probably the only time in his life that Edward Lyttelton wore a moustache was when he was Captain of the Eton XI in 1874.[360] Eton in the 1880s had a new boy aged twelve with a real bass voice while another boy in the school still had an unbroken voice at nineteen-and-a-half.[361] Earlier puberty, and the tendency towards consolidation of the age-range, simply meant an increase during the century in the proportions which sexually mature boys represented in the total of boys in any school. There will still have been many prefects and head-boys who looked (and sounded) ridiculously young alongside some of their subordinates, and this must even have been true of some of the young masters, fresh from the universities; as a schoolboy diarist recorded in 1854 of the first appearance at Marlborough of the new member of staff who was later to become its headmaster: "Mr Farrar, a *mere boy*, was in early Chapel this morning".[362]

In the first half of the century, when a wide range of sexual maturity in a given school was guaranteed by a very wide age-range, the schools showed a marked lack of concern over the opportunities for homosexual temptation which this presented. The practice of two or more boys sharing a bed was common even in the most expensive schools, including Eton and Rugby, at various times before 1850,[363] and separate beds were boasted as a special advantage by Harper of Sherborne in the 1850s,[364] and by the authorities at Framlingham in the 1860s.[365]* The concern over sexual immorality, when it first manifested itself in the Victorian public school, took the form of a concern not with homosexuality but with masturbation.

Dr Alex Comfort has chronicled[367] the extraordinary phenomenon of 'masturbational insanity' which, originating on the Continent in the eighteenth century, "reached England about 1829", and by 1852 had fixed upon medical orthodoxy for half a century (with traces even in the folklore of our own day) a direct connection between 'the habit of solitary vice' and debility of the brain, hysteria, asthma, epilepsy, melancholia, dyspepsia, mania, suicide, dementia, and general paralysis of the insane.

Of course, there had been strong traces of this theme in Continental Roman Catholic moral theology since the Middle Ages; what was new in Victorian England was the corroboration of powerful medical opinion, rendered more plausible and thus more influential by general medical advances in this period. The young Gladstone may have been ahead of his time in his deep feelings of guilt about masturbation[368] which coloured his strong conviction of sin, but soon theologians and, in their train, the public-school masters were adding to their hell-fire propaganda the cautionary legends of the doctors about the consequences of this specially dangerous form of 'sin'. From the pulpit, in his writings on moral theology, and even in the correspondence columns of the *Times*, Dr E. B. Pusey drew attention to the perils of "that sin" which "fifty years ago . . . was unknown at most of our public schools":

> Now, alas! it is the besetting sin of our boys; it is sapping the constitutions and injuring in many the fineness of intellect,[369]

and the terrifying part about it was the innocence of the victims:

> I must re-iterate this, that I never knew a case in which the evil

* Similar mention of single beds as a special feature was made in the prospectus of a private school at Radley Hall, Berks., in 1819, and by an advertisement for the boarding-house of the Royal Latin School, Buckingham, in 1874. At Dr Burney's famous (and rather expensive) private school in Greenwich (where George Henry Lewes had been a pupil) some boys slept two-in-a-bed in the 1830s.[366]

habit to which I alluded was begun with knowledge that it was sin. That knowledge uniformly came years afterwards, when the destructive habit was rooted.[370]*

The doyen of public-school doctors, Clement Dukes of Rugby, wrote prolifically in the 1880s on the causes and consequences of a habit which, he warned parents and schoolmasters, was a direct cause of adult promiscuity, prostitution, drunkenness (resorted to as a cover for shame), intellectual decay, insanity†, suicide, and murder.[371] The same theme dominates the writings on sex instruction by Edward Lyttelton, headmaster of Haileybury from 1890 and later Eton;[373] and Bishop Taylor-Smith, later to be Chaplain-General to the Forces in the Great War, sent his godson off to prep. school and public school with awful warnings on the subject:

> He was always talking to me about it, how semen was 40 times as valuable as blood, how if one lost it one got dark rings under the eyes and deteriorated mentally, how it stunted the growth even more than smoking.[374]

In the 1860s and 1870s most headmasters were still too squeamish to specify this evil, and the sermon literature is sprinkled with references to former pupils coming to a vaguely indicated "bad end" owing to character weaknesses leading to indulgence in activities vaguely specified as "corrupt" or "polluted".

Dean Farrar was a master of this style. In *St Winifred's or the World of School* (1862), he describes the changed appearance of Kenrick, formerly the hero's best friend but who in recent years has fallen among bad companions "who perverted his thoughts, and vitiated his habits":

> Something or other has left, in its traces upon his face, the history of two degenerate years . . . Within these two years he has lost—and his countenance betrays the fact in his ruined

* Mr A. R. K. Watkinson of Pembroke College, Cambridge, a specialist in Victorian church history, has evidence that under the influence of Dr Pusey, girls who were discovered to be practising masturbation were being referred to a London surgeon who performed clitoridectomy as a remedy.

† Such superstitions are not unknown among African tribesmen, *e.g.* in West Africa, who associate this habit with madness and sterility.[372]

> beauty—he has lost the true joys of youth, and known instead of them the troubles of the envious, the fears of the cowardly, the heaviness of the slothful, the shame of the unclean.[375]

In *Eric, or Little by Little*, his allusions are, if anything, even vaguer, and in his sermons as headmaster of Marlborough, he would first play on the guilt of his hearers ("a corrupt heart may lie under the smiling countenance"), then remind "insolent, guilty and polluted souls" of the watchfulness he expected of the prefects in classroom and dormitory, and finally strike terror into many by a histrionic device in which he seemed to be about to challenge the most corrupt boys in the school to stand up there and then in chapel and denounce themselves.[376]

Thring's sermons at Uppingham contained a similar catalogue of the symptoms and consequences of ill-defined "secret acts", "hidden pleasures", "hidden impurity":

> And so the poisonous breath of sin keeps tainting and corrupting all the freshness and purity of young life; and the corruption spreads, and gets into the very soul, destroying all its power to do true work, and win even earthly credit; and the face loses its frank and manly expression; and the poison begins to be seen outwardly; and after disappointing father, and mother, and family, and himself most of all, the wretched victim either sinks down to a lower level and lives on, or often finds an early grave, killed by his own foul passions.[377]

Nor was this limited just to the great schools. One of the first sermons to the boys of Brereton's Norfolk County School warned against the danger of a "bad habit" creeping in: "at first it is perhaps practised by one boy; but it spreads and spreads till more or less it leavens the whole school";[378] and the preface to the first issue of the new school's magazine promised that

> Just as the drains . . . will not be allowed to pollute the river where the boys will bathe and boat and fish, so vice and folly will not be allowed to poison the habits of a place to which many generations of wellbred boys may go to be educated.[379]

We must understand, therefore, that the measures which

were designed by the mid-Victorian public school to cope with 'immorality' as it was now understood were aimed primarily against boys' contracting, practising, and spreading a habit of 'self-abuse' which carried such dire consequences. They were thus only indirectly concerned with 'homosexuality'—insofar as they understood it at all: the activity was only more serious if engaged in with another boy because the fatal habit was thereby being passed on. Among the measures specifically devised to cope with immorality was the cubicle system adopted in several schools. Sewell, who founded St Columba's and Radley, intended the privacy fostered by his cubicle system and the strict enforcement of a rule of silence to give his dormitories " a sanctity second only to that of the Chapel".[380] But privacy was a mixed blessing, and to those boys whom the cubicle system failed to protect from 'bad habits' it afforded a greater cover from detection, as Benson discovered at Wellington in 1861.[381] Rugby's school doctor was astounded at some of the arrangements he saw in public and private schools he inspected, especially the provision of cubicles: "it seemed as though the constructors . . . had set themselves this question to solve: 'How to *foster* immorality in schools?' " and he argued for "large, open, *lighted* dormitories".[382] It is possible that considerations of this sort were behind the failure to provide opportunities of privacy in some schools. This privacy was not lacking in all, but at Marlborough, for example, one hundred and eighty boys not yet senior enough to have their own studies spent a large part of their day herded together in a large room called "Upper"—an institution which persisted until after World War II; and there was a similar situation at Charterhouse.

Thring argued that boys "should be protected by all their surroundings being framed so as to shut off temptation. The whole structure and system should act as an unseen friend".[383] One institution which it was obviously within the power of the authorities to control was the timing of meals. Among the worst schools for the prevalence of masturbation, argued Dr Dukes of Rugby, were "those where hearty meals were given at supper time". Meat, tarts, cheese, or beer at nine p.m. or later engendered physical conditions whereby "it is almost a physical impossibility for any boy of a certain age, with his bounding passions, to remain pure, however much he may desire it", and in addition he argued for fewer bed-clothes.[384]* Edward Lyttelton, in his manual of advice to mothers on the upbringing of their sons, warned "If you find that your son is having beer or meat from 9 p.m. or onwards, insist on both being stopped at once".[386]

Other heads relied on different safeguards. The founder of Bradfield argued that "rather than trust to mechanical arrangements, he depended on a high tone of opinion in his prefects, and if he could not do that he would shut the place up".[387] The watchfulness of masters was another factor. The saintly John Smith of Harrow made it his special business to waylay every new boy "in a secluded spot" to warn him of the special dangers of public-school life and to invite the new boy to make "certain promises, couched in carefully veiled language". It seems that new boys looked upon this experience "with dread", and opinion was divided whether he did more harm than good by this.[388]

Religion was looked to as the most important sanction against this evil, which was explicitly or implicitly the theme of endless sermons in chapel (and at Eton was to become "a particular obsession of visiting preachers").[389] With the schools' increasing acknowledgement of their failure to cope with the problem, the 'priestly' functions of the headmaster were seen as an essential weapon for "decency and morality"—"the secular arm is not strong enough and it requires the thunders of the Church"[390]—and this factor helped to sustain the preference for ordained headmasters in the closing decades of the century, even when such men represented a declining proportion of the able candidates available. The quality of chapel sermons and their relevance to school life (especially on the issue of morality)

* Dr Dukes added to the third edition of his influential book *Health at School* in 1894 a section advocating cold baths every morning but arguing strongly against hot baths at bedtime, a practice "capable of serious harm to many a boy by suggesting ideas and feelings which lead to practices that otherwise might never have originated". Naturally Dr Dukes favoured school games, adding with emphasis that they "always furnish *a topic for innocent conversation*, which is an inestimable boon". The Rugby doctor also emphasised the necessity for *daily natural relief*, and the adverse mental and physical consequences of not moving the bowels daily—preferably at the same hour each morning.[385]

undoubtedly improved in the course of the century, not least in the older schools where their general level of fatuity had become something of a scandal. Preparation for confirmation, a duty entrusted to housemasters or sometimes carried out by the headmaster himself, became an important vehicle for official teaching on morality. Indeed, it could be something of a two-way process: at Rugby in the 1880s, for example, it was commonly believed among the boys that masters looked upon preparation for confirmation as an opportunity "to obtain information about the shadier side of what went on in their houses".[391] Thring, who wanted boys to be confirmed by the age of fourteen, took to addressing the whole school each year in three groups—the confirmation candidates, the already confirmed, and 'the rest':

> And I plainly put before them the devil work of impurity, and [warned] them that I will pitilessly turn out anyone who after such warning is found guilty. So I am sure that no one who is not a new boy can be ignorant either of the sin or its consequences. Well, I found out four boys, and required their withdrawal."

This detection required "probing to the very end every bit of evidence I got, and following every clue". The nature of the "impurity" is not recorded, but two things are noteworthy. First, that the sixth form petitioned to have the expulsions reversed, and it required a further campaign by Thring to persuade "virtually the whole school" to pledge themselves as a body to put down all indecency. Secondly, that Thring's much-vaunted toleration (in contrast to Arnold) of the less able boy, who deserved to be educated no less than the brilliant, was not matched by any accommodation of boys who may well have learned their habits of "impurity" at Uppingham itself.

Thring looked to "the purifying influence of good women" as a force to counteract the evil,[392] but most schools made few concessions to feminine influence, and those with housemasterships reserved to bachelors maintained an almost monastic atmosphere.[393] Welldon, headmaster of Dulwich and Harrow (who believed that in boyhood "irreligion goes hand in hand with immorality")[394] warned the HMC in 1890 against preparatory schools headed by "lady principals": much immorality manifested at public schools (he claimed) originated in such preparatory schools, whose heads were by their very nature unqualified to give the right moral guidance.[395]

Dr Pusey reinforced his crusade against what he called the "besetting sin" of public school boys with a campaign in favour of sacramental confession in schools. This evil was, he asserted, "absolutely unknown" in schools where confession was habitually used. " 'My seminarists, said the Bishop of Countances to me in 1866, are as pure as angels.' " Pusey liked to quote an anonymous English public school (almost certainly Lancing, whose chaplain, Field, was in sympathy with Pusey) where "before confession, out of 100 boys, only 10 were innocent; after confession, 68: the more aggravated forms of sin fell from 66 to 4."[396] Woodard had boasted of the effects of voluntary confession at Lancing in 1857:

> A school of 100 boys, many of whom are nearly men, without the semblance of an act of gross immorality . . . is . . . unknown [elsewhere] in England.[397]

Pressing the case for sacramental confession in schools upon Tait, now Archbishop of Canterbury, Pusey in 1877 redefined his category of "more aggravated forms of sin" as indicating "boys who had sinned in some way with others"[398]—evidence which would justify an increasing concern in the schools by that time over less 'solitary' forms of vice.

Three developments in the later nineteenth century public school may be seen as functioning to assist the schools to cope with immorality: the principle of "mapping-out"—devising a number of activities, such as societies and hobbies, to occupy boys' out-of-class hours;[399] the triumph of athleticism, which to some housemasters embodied the idea 'Send the boys to bed tired, and you'll have no trouble';[400] and thirdly, the slow-moving diversification of the curriculum, which by bringing in subjects more obviously within the grasp of the average pupil raised the level of output of work which could reasonably be expected.[401]

It was a former Fettes housemaster, Cotterill, by 1890 headmaster of a successful preparatory school, who raised as urgent the question how far public-school life equipped the large numbers of Old Boys who would go into business to deal with the temptations attendant upon their leisure time in large cities. "Say it is five o'clock when he turns his back upon his office . . . he has six hours of vacant evening time before him in which to find himself occupation. He must have some means of getting rid of his pent-up vigour and energy." Has his school training, asked Cotterill, taught him to regard it as *wrong* not to take daily exercise, and trained him in enough other 'accomplishments' to occupy him on long dark winter evenings, and thus "ensure his moral safety"?[402] Almond of Loretto expressed a similar concern over the moral dangers of 'sedentary commercialism';[403] Charles Kingsley's writings on *Health and Education* had a similar message.[404] But by the end of the century this sort of propaganda merely served to nourish the idea that only by going to such public schools could boys destined for careers in business, in offices, etc. be trained by the experience of organised recreation in habits of healthy exercise which would save them from ruin in after life.

Sexual morality in school was the most obvious sphere in which we can see the schoolmasters resisting that transfer of parental functions to boarding schools whose generality has been described. Their appeal was always to family and home influences as a safeguard against misconduct and ruin. Theologians directed fathers to "save countless ills to their sons" by enjoining "this simple rule: Do nothing, when alone, which you would be afraid of your mother and my knowing".[405] Remembrance of home, and especially of mothers and sisters, was constantly on the lips of Victorian schoolmasters,[406]* a use of family members as a moral referent which chimed with popular sentiment as illustrated by Mary Sewell's enormously popular story, *Mother's Last Words*, in which two poor boys are kept from evil courses by the memory of their mother's dying words.[408] Announcing in the course of a sermon at Marlborough the death of a boy "who had been quite well the week before", Cotton was clearly proud to be able to reassure his hearers that "he died a Christian's death and uttered no one word in his delirium that his parents did not wish to hear",[409]

* *Cf.* for example, the recurrent theme of the sermons at Winchester of R. S. Barter (warden 1832–61), on the text "Son, remember", appealing "to the memories of home and parents as a talisman against temptation".[407]

and this sort of identification with home was a constant basis of moral teaching in schools throughout the rest of the period.[410]

But the willingness of parents to take positive steps over the responsibilities concerning their sons' moral development which the schools thrust back upon them was a different matter compared with just acting as a benign emotional influence. Not many parents followed the custom of Lord Lyttelton, as each of his eight sons went off to public school, of writing them a letter "fine and robust in tone", warning of the dangers they might face, holding up before them the memory of their beloved mother and the example of his own triumph over youthful sexual temptation, and advising them of the aids to rectitude supplied by "constant occupation of body and mind" and by the prospect of marriage. Yet even he finished his letter by saying "I do not wish you to acknowledge this letter or ever to say anything to me about having received it", which cannot have encouraged the sons to confront their "habitually reserved" father with any problem of advice or to ask for information about sex.[411]

Not many parents, either, would have shared the reluctance of Lord Salisbury (later premier) to send his sons away to school until after they had been confirmed.[412] The more typical Victorian parents—99% in fact, claimed the Rugby school doctor—sent their sons away to boarding school without any warning of the sexual danger to which they were bound to be exposed, and this parental reticence (said Dukes) was thus a direct cause of the prevalence of the "vice of masturbation" among boys in boarding schools to an extent involving 80–90% according to some authorities, but nearer 90–95% according to Dr Dukes himself.[413] Delegating the invidious task to the family doctor might be no less ineffective. The future Lord Pethick-Lawrence, examined by the family doctor before being sent off to Eton, was merely baffled by the mysterious warning against "bad habits".[414] It is also true, of course, that the home of the Victorian public-school boy did not automatically represent the fount of the kind of sexual information and attitudes of which the school authorites would have approved. A boy with venereal disease at Wellington in 1872 had contracted the infection when at home in the holidays—a circumstance which actually caused members of the school's governing body to attempt to overrule

Benson's decision to expel the offender.[415] There were attitudes like this among parents or even governors which the schools had to resist. In passing back to the family and home the ultimate responsibility for the morality of their charges, the schools were in a sense resisting the process whereby some parents were only too ready to abandon to the school the upbringing of the children which earlier in the century they would have abandoned to the nursery and the servants.

12. The blight of friendship.

The 1880s were significant for two things: the acknowledgement by the schools of their failure to cope with the problem of 'morality' was publicly, almost stridently, admitted, and became a matter openly discussed in the press; and an increasing suspicion of friendships between boys, because of their implications for 'morality', made more definite impact on the organisation of the schools.

In 1881 the Rev. J. M. Wilson (headmaster of Clifton) chose 'Morality in Public Schools' as the theme of his Presidential address to the Education Society.[416] What he said was nothing new. Implying by 'immorality' in schools any form of boyhood sexual activity, dangerous because it was the direct cause of promiscuity in adult life, he rehearsed the list of favourite remedies with which we are now familiar: "exercise abundant, carried on up to the point of fatigue"; occupations to "fill the thoughts, and break up those deadly blank times in which evil germs breed"; "mechanical arrangements" such as cubicles; the need for physiological information to be given at an early age, etc.;—and above all, the reliance on the religious spirit in a school.

Wilson's address, to an audience of whom three-quarters were women, was reprinted in full as a supplement to the *Journal of Education* and commented on extensively in that journal and given coverage in a section of the national press (especially the *Daily News* and the *Pall Mall Gazette*), thus giving rise to what was probably the first public discussion in Britain of the problems of sex education.[417] It had required no little courage, as the *Journal* pointed out, to break the silence of convention and to "lay bare the cancer of upper-class education;" the *Journal* went on to emphasise the duties of parents to provide elementary instruction and warnings against "vicious habits" whose medical consequences were fraught with such "terrible danger".[418] Nevertheless, it considered, such "monastic evils" were a necessary accompaniment of a system which removed boys at ten or eleven onwards from home influences and the society of women.

In the correspondence which ensued, the most interesting letter came from an Old Etonian ("Olim Etonensis"). He freely admitted the prevalence of immoral habits in schools—in his own schooldays, he said, they were rife—but argued that they were not a matter for alarm, since their results had been "ludicrously misrepresented":

> I have in my mind's eye a list—a long one, I regret to say—of those who at my school were unfortunately conspicuous (I mean only in this particular manner; I should have a different story to tell of those who were addicted to drinking, bad language, stealing, idleness, etc.) and what ought I to find was the case with them now to bear out Mr Wilson's views and those of other contributors to your pages? Why, of course I should have to point to mental and physical wrecks, men who have dragged hitherto a miserable existence, preys (not martyrs) to consumption and atrophy and insanity; or else to outcasts from all good society. Now, what do I find? That those very boys have become Cabinet Ministers, statesmen, officers, clergymen, country gentlemen, etc.; that they are nearly all of them fathers of thriving families, respected and prosperous, and the only invalids I can discover . . . can trace their complaints to a cause with which Mr Wilson's bugbear had nothing to do. The moral to be pointed is, that happily an evil so difficult to cure is not so disastrous in its results. How many boys, or rather men, can Mr Wilson point to who owe their ruin to the immorality which he talks of?[419]

Olim Etonensis was a lone voice•, and he got a good wigging

• Another 'Old Etonian', but of a later period (c. 1897), reported years later that one of the most depraved of the boys he knew at Eton, whose name was a by-word for scandal, "has since become a highly revered dignitary of the Church of England.[420]

from later correspondents for his "cynicism", though no one offered to answer his question about statistics of 'ruin'.

Public-school headmasters like H. M. Butler (Harrow) and Benson (Wellington, but by now Archbishop) were active in the foundation[421] of the Church of England Purity Society (1883; later the Church of England White Cross League)[422] to promote sexual morality in national life, partly through the publication (from 1885 onwards) of tracts giving physiological information for boys and young men.[423] Butler* headed a committee appointed by the Purity Society in 1888[424]† to promote its objects in public and preparatory schools—for it was recognised that in the latter the need for a campaign was probably even more urgent—though Wickham of Wellington told the HMC in 1890 that this committee was "in a state of quiescence, but might again be called into activity".[426]

These activities took place at the very time when Thring, for example, was first discussing publicly[427] his own efforts to grapple with the problem at Uppingham, and his conviction that many schools were "unable to cope with it at all".[428] This was the very time, too, when a Rugby housemaster, H. Lee Warner, was drawing to public attention, in the *Contemporary Review*, his misgivings as to whether boarding schools could ever overcome the problem. The only way in which *The* schoolmaster (and he was particularly concerned with preparatory schools) could, he argued, meet "the deadly danger" was by always keeping the boys employed or amused, which left no time for natural development and defeated the aims of education. His article ended with a strong argument for "a reversion to the family system"—by which he meant day schools, at least at preparatory level—"in the interests of both family life and school life".[429] In

* This preoccupation lends special significance to the words of the now famous hymn "Lift up your hearts! We lift them, Lord, to Thee", written by Butler originally for school confirmations. Above the level of the former years/The mire of sin, the slough of guilty fears,/The mist of doubt, the blight of love's decay. . . Above the swamps of subterfuge and shame,/The deeds, the thoughts, that honour may not name,/The halting tongue that dares not tell the whole. . .

† When the activities of the Purity Society in relation to public schools were discussed in 1884 by the HMC annual meeting, the headmasters went into private session and their deliberations were not recorded.[425]

some preparatory schools, headmasters saw the problem in a different light and set about organising boys into 'bands of purity', whose members were "under promise to keep themselves pure and to do all they [could] to promote purity in others", both at prep. school and at the public schools to which they would go on.[430]

This was also the period when a fear of schoolboy sexuality in a form other than that, primarily, of masturbation, came out into the open: the suspicion of school-boy friendships. The letter of "Olim Etonensis", partly quoted above, had gone on to ridicule suspicion of affairs between older and younger boys, and he even praised the benefits of such alliances:

> Every old public school boy knows what is meant by "spooning" (Mr Wilson, I suppose, would call the word a mere euphemism). It exists in all large schools, and I contend it would be wiser to regard the habit with contempt than with horror. A friend of mine—a peer, the Lord Lieutenant of his county, and the father of a public school boy—told me that when he was at school he was "taken up" (as it is called) by boys bigger than himself, and petted—he supposed because of his good looks; that before he received such notice he was an "untidy, slovenly little ruffian", and that he dated his conversion to gentlemanly habits and refined manners from the time when he was so patronised . . .[431]

That the school authorities were always aware of certain dangers in such alliances is obvious: Grignon, lately headmaster of Felsted, referred in the course of the same correspondence in the *Journal of Education* to an occasional expulsion for "spooning, carried to its worst possible extreme".[432] But a circular ('private and confidential') sent round to all Haileybury parents by the headmaster, Robertson, in 1884 and again in 1885, is significant in the distinction he made between "solitary vicious habits" and "any form of moral evil in which two are leagued together". Robertson urged strongly that specifically-worded warnings be given by parents (or by a doctor or clergyman arranged by them) against "talk, example, or impure solicitations" to which their sons might be exposed, at school or elsewhere,

> including emphatically such lover-like advances from older boys as often flatter first, but corrupt afterwards. (One minor point, but of real importance also, is the use of female nicknames. The more this practice can be got rid of the better.)[433]

and the school rules issued by Haileybury in March 1886, which ran to seventy-nine printed pages, contained the following: "At pastimes, the impersonation of females is, with certain rare and unobjectionable exceptions, to be avoided". (The rules also stated, "Bare legs are not to be exposed at games,"[434] a prohibition which was shortly to be introduced, in respect of football, by Percival at Rugby as part of his "moral reformation" of the school.)[435]

The increasing obsession[436] in schools with the problem of sex*, and now also the suspicion of spontaneous associations between boys as containing the seeds of contamination, had certain tangible effects. One was to give greater impetus to the attempt by schools, especially the greater schools, to exercise total control over the lives of day-boys, as they did over boarders. The conception of a uniform community engendering a strong *esprit de corps* made this desirable in any case, but now there was an additional motive. The prestige of the most famous schools made it easier to exact from parents the enforcement of school rules, attendance at matches, etc., out of school hours; at a rising school, Bedford, Phillpotts enforced 'lock-up' on day-boys and boarders alike in the late seventies, and even persuaded the governors to pay the expenses of a drill-sergeant to help enforcement: "Big boys were in the habit of going to small boys' houses, and would pull them out of their houses". This argument was effective with the Bedford parents

* But there were still pockets of innocence, among them schools which had not yet awakened to the dangers to which the doctors and theologians were struggling to alert them. As late as 1894 Dr Dukes of Rugby was impelled to add to the third edition of his book the cautionary tale of "one of our most important public schools" which, because it still operated a system of two-in-a-bed for some boys, caused a distressed little boy forcibly to undergo "heartrending misery for 13 weeks with an impure big boy". "Most emphatically I condemn this system, which is still unhappily in existence, as distinctly conducing, without the need of my entering into further details, to a flagrant species of immorality and depravation of character."[437]

and governors, and Phillpotts recommended the use of similar facts to his HMC colleagues to "show that you are not interfering with the parents, but even helping them to govern their boys."[438]

A second consequence was, by the end of the century, the *ascription* of friendship. Close associations between boys of different ages or in different houses were suspect: indeed, in some schools by 1900 if such boys were even seen speaking, "immorality would be taken for granted".[439] This was not yet true (for example) of Repton in the 1880s[440] but by 1900 it was the case at Clifton,[441] at Westminster, where it was an offence, punishable by caning, for scholars to associate with fellow-scholars more than one form senior or junior to themselves,[442] at Harrow,[443] at Eton,[444] at Charterhouse,[445] at Rugby,[446] and possibly at Fettes and other schools.[447] The consequences of such a situation at Wellington were described by (Sir) Harold Nicolson:

> The authorities in their desire to deprive us of all occasion for illicit intercourse, deprived us of all occasion for any intercourse at all. We were not allowed* to consort with boys not in our own house; a house consisted of thirty boys of whom ten at least were too old and ten too young for friendship; and thus during those four years my training in human relationships was confined to the ten boys who happened more or less to be my contemporaries. In addition, one was deprived of all initiative of action or occupation . . . We had thus no privacy and no leisure . . . I entered Wellington a puzzled boy and left it a puzzled child. And the vices which this system was supposed to repress flourished incessantly and universally, losing in their furtive squalor any educative value which they might otherwise have possessed.[449]

* Such prohibitions might be enforced—in the interests of house loyalty—more by the schoolboys' own code, backed unofficially by prefects and housemasters, than by any written school rule: so much so that in the 1930s Wellington's headmaster Malim (with a background of Marlborough, Sedbergh and Haileybury) denied all knowledge of any such convention. Similarly at Winchester, where it had been a "bad notion" (*i.e.* "not done") as early as 1883 for boys of different houses to go about together, Burge (headmaster 1901–1911) worked through his prefects to discourage the persistence of this "odious unwritten law".[448]

It was not long before the obsession spread to parents: at least it was easier for them to warn their sons against indiscriminate friendships than to specify the activities which such friendships were feared to imply. Thus Desmond MacCarthy's father, seeing him off as a new boy to Eton in the 1890s, made a special excursion in order to have an opportunity to "give him some good advice":

> He did not know exactly how to put what he wanted to say, so he left it very vague. But he did say, with an emphasis I thought rather odd, considering the comparative triviality of the matter, that I was on no account to go about with boys much older than myself. 'It is not,' he added with some embarrassment, 'good form. So look out'."

The young MacCarthy was not left in the dark for long. He has left us an account of the "perplexingly impressive" address with which Dr Warre—a huge, awesome man with a tremendous voice—greeted the assembled new boys, not all of them as innocent or as bewildered as MacCarthy himself:

> He bade us welcome—it was awful; he hoped we would avoid all conduct which would bring discredit on the school—it seemed impossible. We must learn now or we should never learn that we were among the fortunates of the nation and that also implied responsibilities; some of us would perhaps be called to high positions, we must make ourselves worthy now. Above all—we must keep clear of the evil thing, that which defiles, and shun the abomination in our midst. His voice rose to a tenor cry. 'Have none of it, don't touch it, stamp it out.' And he went on to describe how he had been sometimes forced to send boys away on that account, and how one father had said to him he would far rather he had been told his son was dead. This frightened me. My poor father, how agonised he would be if I should die, yet if I did something or other he would be still more miserable, and the horror of the situation was that I didn't even know for certain what it was.

However, enlightenment soon came, when the other new boys

in his house discussed the headmaster's address "with exuberant ribaldry" that evening[450]*

It is difficult to know whether the immorality which flourished despite these official attitudes and organisational changes was more, or less, widespread, or different in kind, from the 1880s onwards compared to the early period. Its prevalence in both periods must have varied from school to school—at Eton in the days of 'Olim Etonensis' and in the 1870s[453] it was more open—and within one school its incidence varied from generation to generation and from house to house.[454] Possibly the climate of opinion fostered in the late Victorian public school by the attitude of the authorities created expectations which 'corrupted' boys more effectively than the earlier attitude of laisser-faire.

13. Friendship and passion.

We can see strong reasons why Victorian schoolmasters should have moved from an attitude of comparative neutrality towards schoolboy friendships to an attitude of hostility and suspicion culminating in certain forms of taboo. But there is evidence that this process of changed attitude was more extensive even than that.

In 1854 a Marlborough schoolboy recorded in his diary:

> 12 Feb., Sunday. Septuagesima. Cotton preached an excellent sermon from Matt. 25. 45. Amongst other things he mentioned the practice of elder boys making great friends with others much younger than themselves. Went out with Smith as usual. Thomas gave us a blow-out of bread and butter and marmalade.[455]

What thunders, we would like to know, did Cotton let loose against the terrible dangers of such potentially sinful alliances? Unfortunately no copy of this sermon seems to have survived,

* Almost identical warnings were being given by the headmaster of Summer Fields, a leading and aristocratic preparatory school in Oxford.[451] Warre used also to interrupt his masters' lessons at Eton to deliver his homilies about "morality"—"the words were sometimes hard to understand, but the voice commanded".[452]

but among Cotton's published sermons is one dated three years later, which is given the title 'School Friendship'.

This sermon is too long to be quoted fully (as it deserves), but it constitutes a glorification of schoolboy friendships which forty or fifty years later would have seemed to a public-school housemaster to be dangerously naive, even actually subversive. Its text was John XIII. 23 (a reference to the disciple 'whom Jesus loved'); it spoke of the appropriateness of lasting and devoted friendships formed at school, and discussed at length the purpose and advantages of such friendships when properly conducted, "*especially between an older and a younger boy*" [Author's italics]; the principle of unselfish *love* which should inform such friendships, and, through their relationship, bring boys nearer to God. True, such 'peculiar friendships' could (he said) involve practical evils—principally "idleness and much time wasted in frivolity. They become so absorbing that instead of being helps they are hindrances to duty . . .", but Cotton was satisfied that such attendant evils did not exist at Marlborough "in greater force than elsewhere". At any rate not in the way pictured in the newly-published *Tom Brown's Schooldays* which some Marlborough boys had just been reading, where "the older friend has led the younger into positive wickedness, has taught him to be disobedient and idle, and to drink and to swear".[456]

This wholly different antecedent phase in the Victorian public-school masters' attitude to friendship was hinted at by Hughes in *Tom Brown's Schooldays*, in his representation of the friendship of his hero and a much younger boy (Arthur). Despite the older's leading the younger into wrong-doing, this relationship is presented as having the approval, even the encouragement, of Dr Arnold: "the Doctor . . . looked out the best of the new boys . . . and put the young boy into your study, in the hope that when you had somebody to lean on you, you would begin to stand a little steadier yourself, and get manliness and thoughtfulness . . ." The relationship was similarly fostered by the 'young master', who is made to observe to Tom about the young boy: "Nothing has given me greater pleasure . . . than your friendship for him, it has been the making of you both".[457]

Then we remember that Cotton was the original of the 'young master' in *Tom Brown's Schooldays*, so that despite the liberties Hughes took in describing the results of the influence the older boy exercised in leading the younger into scrapes, the idea of a master's encouraging such a friendship is completely authentic. The two volumes of the *Rugby Magazine* in Arnold's time contain several examples of the unaffected use of the word 'love' to describe feelings of friendship between boys, and there is one very touching passage which describes how the "love and trust of hearts" between school friends united by "strong feelings" are "tried and proved" by the loyalty and prayers of the one throughout the grave illness of the other.[458] Tom Brown when at Oxford is represented by Thomas Hughes as having been loved by a fellow-undergraduate, "as David loved Jonathan"; we judge Tom's reaction to this love when we learn that, in a moment of great emotion, Tom was tempted to kiss him. At the same time both of them are pictured as striving towards ideals of "true manliness and purity".[459] In the context of a predominantly day school, King Edward's, Birmingham, another of Arnold's former masters, Prince Lee, "undoubtedly encouraged intimate friendships among his pupils", which in some cases became life-long.[460]

Even Dean Farrar's novels, with their frequent, though veiled, admonitions about the dangers of "pollution", did not allow this to compromise the love which his 'good' schoolboys —even of different ages—declared to each other. "Of all earthly spectacles," Farrar wrote in *St Winifred's*, "few are more beautiful, and in some respects more touching, than a friendship between two boys . . ."; and he shows us the hero, Walter, befriending an unhappy younger new boy, visiting him across the dormitory at night to tuck him up in bed and hold his hand as comfort. Unselfconsciously Farrar describes the prefects and the older boys "angling" for the favours of the new boys, among whom the "pretty" ones become favourites, even "idols".[461] *St Winifred's* was based on Marlborough in the 1850s, and we know from other sources that his picture of the courtship by older boys of "pretty" younger boys as an accepted feature of public-school life which caused no alarm, except when leading to detectable sexual acts, was true for many schools, certainly for Marlborough at that period[462] and also for Winchester in the 1840s, where the Second Master (Charles Wordsworth) defended in a sermon his practice of having favourites or pets (boys whom, "if he loved [them], he would champion through grave misdemeanours") by reference to the example of the Patriarch who "loved Joseph more than all his children". (The result in the school was that "his protégés, *hitherto designated by a coarser name*, were known thenceforth as 'Joes' ".[463] Even Sewell, with his elaborate arrangements to protect the 'sanctity' of behaviour in the Radley dormitories, nevertheless urged that older boys should play with younger ones—"as with a younger brother"—and his main fears of 'sin' between them related to swearing, improper conversations, and the circulation of 'sinful' drawings.[464] In the 1860s at Lancing, where the chaplain, Field, kept a sharp eye on morality and reported back on it to Dr Pusey, we find that a seventeen-year-old prefect who was about to become Captain of the School chose for his regular companions boys who were two, three or even six years younger, and recorded in his diary quite unselfconsciously his feelings of special friendship with a boy two years younger who entered the school five years after he did.[465]

It is too easy to trace this attitude of what is now popularly known as 'Platonic love' to the Victorians' study of ancient Greek culture, for in fact the schoolmasters at least were very ambivalent about the moral content of classical literature. "Every pious parent must feel," declared one of the founders of Cheltenham (Francis Close), "that there is a great peril in putting into the hands of youth the abominable mythology of the ancients, tending as it [does] to warp their understandings and destroy their better feelings. It is painful to think that a classical education [can] not be acquired without the use of such works . . ."[466] Sewell's encouragement of friendships between older and younger boys was not inhibited by his awareness of the temptation that might come

> when you older boys sit before your classical books, mixed, as they are and must be, with so much that you must turn your eyes from with abhorrence . . .[467]•

• The expulsion of three boys from Wellington in 1872 after it was discovered that they had been seduced by a young servant girl at the home of one of them, caused a boy who was a prefect at the time to draw attention, when writing thirty-five years later, to the incongruity that they were expelled by "a Church of England dignitary" [*i.e.* Benson] "who only a few weeks previously had set the Classical sixth a grossly indecent play by Aristophanes", which had been found to be "strong meat" even by the prefects. He went on to

Certainly the influence of the great Plato scholar Benjamin Jowett was to operate against any glorification of idealised male friendships, though friendships which we would describe as in some sense 'homosexual' were a feature of the Oxford movement, both in Newman's relations with his closest disciples and among other Anglo-Catholics after Newman had left the movement.[469]

At least for the first half of the Victorian period—*i.e.* up to the late 1870s and 1880s—schoolboy friendships retained the presumption of innocence* despite the fear of 'moral' contamination with which medical opinion had, from the 1840s on, invested such relationships in boarding schools. But there were already warning signals. Dr Phyllis Crosskurth has revealed that C. J. Vaughan's resignation from his highly successful headship of Harrow in 1850 was forced upon him by a committee of parents and dons because he had sent a passionate love-letter to a pupil. Such conduct, however common among boys in public schools at the time, was obviously inappropriate in a headmaster, especially one who had recently instituted a campaign against certain relationships between boys which involved the use of female nicknames. The full details of the Vaughan affair and the attitudes adopted by the chief actors in the drama are not yet available;[472] the case was the best-kept secret of all the nineteenth-century educational scandals that we now know of,† but it is worthy of note that Vaughan was one of Cotton's closest

deprecate the study of classics in public schools: "A clean mind in a healthy body should be our ambition; but how can we hope to attain either when we place in the hands of boys, at the most critical period of their lives, a knowledge of languages which unlocks the door to about the lewdest literature in Western Europe. . .?"[468]

* *Cf.* Disraeli's famous passage in *Coningsby* (1844): "At school, friendship is a passion. It entrances the being, it tears the soul. All loves of after-life can never bring its rapture. . ."[470] Robert Blake records that in an earlier novel, *Contarini Fleming* (1832), Disraeli had described even more explicitly the passions, lovers' quarrels and embraces of his schoolboy hero with another boy, Musaeus.[471]

†Even G. G. Coulton, one of Vaughan's most devoted theological trainees, who had encountered Pretor (one of Vaughan's Harrow "favourites") at Cambridge, knew nothing whatever of the case, though he discusses Vaughan's character and career frequently in *Fourscore Years* (1943); moreover, Coulton was a medieval scholar with a nose for clerical scandal.

friends and that his chief accuser was a medical doctor. In considering what exactly Vaughan is said to have done—apart from being a monumental hypocrite by his effort to punish others for desires which he possibly feared might get out of hand in himself—it must be borne in mind that the surviving evidence against him is derived from a document of "passionately partisan propaganda".[473]

The circumstances of William Johnson Cory's peremptory dismissal from Eton in 1872, though never explained, leave no doubt in the mind of one modern writer[474] of the "gross character" of his activities, but at the time the causes of his departure were veiled in discretion. It was the Eton housemaster Oscar Browning's prurient and somewhat possessive interest in the 'morals' of boys in other houses* which led to his sacking in 1875, though to the outside world this was presented as the clash between a reforming master and an autocratic head.[476]

In none of these cases—insofar as they were generally known—did the overtones of what we would now call homosexuality serve to alarm the Victorians in the 1860s and '70s about the dangers of friendships between boy and master or between boy and boy. The fact is that Victorian public-school staffs, in common with Victorian society in general, contained many men whose inclinations would nowadays be regarded as homosexual. But homosexuality did not exist in the eyes of the mid-Victorians as an identifiable *condition*†. Schoolmasters recognised that there were dangers in boyhood which could involve the practice of sodomy, but this was hardly more dangerous in its medical consequences than solitary vice, and anyway its practice in boyhood was not seen as leading in later life to a preference for one's own sex which involved psychological maladjustment and social disabilities. Idealised friendships at school were, if anything, some guarantee that such debased activities would be less likely to occur. Percival of Clifton was aware of the "coarse and vicious habits"[478] which

* and, in particular, Dr Hornby's alleged suspicion that O. B. had been "'spooning' with that 'most superior person' who was to become. . .the most magnificent of Indian Viceroys" [*i.e.* the young Curzon].[475]

† According to Canon D. L. Edwards, the word itself was not coined until 1897.[477]

boys learned in boarding schools, and he "had an unerring eye for the unwholesome boy",[479] but he was (at least until the 1880s) utterly innocent on the subject of homosexuality, as J. A. Symonds discovered—and used to his own advantage.[480] We cannot ascribe the censorious attitude of Benson of Wellington towards even slight acts of 'indecency' among boys to the effects of the shock he must have felt when his old schoolfellow and Cambridge contemporary, Twells, fled his colonial bishopric in 1869 to escape a charge of sodomy[481]—circumstances well known in England despite his resignation on 'health' grounds.[482] For Benson's attitude had shown itself in an extreme form as far back as 1861.[483] Idealised friendships, such as Gladstone himself had had with a boy two years younger, Arthur Hallam,[484] in the 1820s, were not uncommon in Edward Lyttelton's circle in his Eton schooldays* in the 1870s—a period he describes as one of open barbarism and vice when public opinion was more definitely against drunkenness than against immorality.[486] And when he himself had become, at the end of the century, a leader of the campaign against 'immorality' in schools, Lyttelton's writings[487] on the subject show that his target was the evil of masturbation rather than the friendships which were now suspect in many schools.

What began to die in later Victorian England were attitudes and spontaneous expressions of love between males which were characteristic of the earlier period. For what could be more natural and delightful than the account by H. E. Luxmoore—acknowledged as an outstanding moral influence when an Eton housemaster—of his arrival as a freshman in Oxford in the 1860s:

> I was too poor to subscribe to many clubs or enter freely into University life. But my first Sunday in Chapel I picked out the most attractive-looking man there and determined to make him a friend: he was a senior man and very exclusive but with much painstaking I gained him and loved him . . ."[488]

* Since this was written, Kenneth Rose has published in his biography of Curzon a letter from Edward Lyttelton, then eighteen, to his much younger school-fellow Curzon, which can be seen as a discreetly-worded expression of Lyttelton's own romantic interest in the strikingly handsome, "milkmaid-complexioned" younger boy.[485]

With a similar lack of self-consciousness, Augustus Hare described his attachment to an undergraduate contemporary at Oxford.[489] Henry Hart's biography prints a beautiful letter sent to him in the 1860s by a dying schoolfellow at Rugby who plucked up courage to declare his love.[490] Schoolboys were not afraid to use the word 'love' to describe their feelings for their masters, nor undergraduates for their tutors,[491] nor were they ashamed to have these feelings.

Sewell, at Radley in the 1850s and 1860s, confessed he had found it hard to like boys;[492] but once his feelings were engaged, his affections were bestowed with an artlessness of expression which the boys seemed ready to return. He once thrashed "two large athletes" for cribbing:

> both of them . . . when they got up from their knees came to me and burst into tears and put their arms around my neck and kissed me—as a child would its father. They knew I had a great affection for them and that what I did was done for them.

On another occasion he summoned his head prefect and ordered him to kneel down to be caned:

> Then I flung away the cane . . . I think when I made that boy get up from his knees, and he put his arms round my neck, was the most exquisite moment of enjoyment I ever had.

This was not just his way with the boys; he made similar demonstrations to his colleagues, laying his head on the shoulder of one with whom he had quarrelled, or kneeling before him in his study—though in this case it was to the latter's "acute and miserable embarrassment".[493]•

One cause of change was the principle of control over the emotions inculcated by the later Victorian public school, the 'stiff-upper-lippery' which discouraged as 'unmanly' the spontaneous expression of feelings like affection or grief.[495] Other factors were the legislation concerning adult homosexuality in the Criminal Law Amendment Act (1885), and, ten years later, the most sensational prosecution under that Act: the trial of

• Effusive tears and kisses between masters and their pupils—whether eighteen-year-olds or much younger—were by no means an uncommon characteristic of scenes of great emotion in the 1860s and 1870s.[494]

Oscar Wilde*; and secondly the popularisation in England around 1900, at least among the educated, of the psychological ideas of Havelock Ellis and others and the propaganda of writers like Edward Carpenter.[497] The effects of these two factors upon anyone who thought about the problem were that male homosexuality became, in the first place, an *identifiable* condition; and in the second place, a *criminal* one. (The law did not cover lesbianism, and female friendships largely retained their presumption of innocence). All this powerfully reinforced the suspicions that were already becoming common in schools and which in some had already been embodied in the organisation of school life. In literature, apart from the works of a few proselytising homosexual authors,[498] there was a new self-consciousness about the expression of 'love' between males,[499] and this was of course true also of the literature of school life. An exception was the idealised picture of schoolboy friendship (at Harrow) in H. A. Vachell's *The Hill* (1905)—"You have been the best friend a man ever had; the only one I love as much as my own brother—and *even more.*" (Vachell's emphasis)[500]. The expression of such feelings was incongruous in the atmosphere of the public schools at the turn of the century, and it is significant that Vachell himself went to Harrow in 1876 and was only there for about five terms.[501] By 1900 intense friendship was regarded as insidious, and the emotions involved in such relationships should rather be *communalised*—directed into attachment to the school-community itself.†

From now on eyebrows would have been raised at anyone who, for example, imitated the endearing habit of the future

* As one indication of the effect of the Wilde case, it may be noted that in the same year (1895), in response to an allegation that he himself had participated at Sandhurst in "acts of gross immorality of the Oscar Wilde type", the twenty-year-old Winston Churchill sued a fellow officer's father for £20,000. (The case was shortly settled by a withdrawal, an apology, and token damages).[496]

† Another anachronism, doubtless disconcerting to public-school housemasters, was E. F. Benson's *David Blaize* (1916), a bold piece of propaganda for innocent but intense romantic friendships between older and younger boys, kept pure by sermons, schoolmasters' homilies, and the requirements of "good form".[502] (We must take note of the author's own possible homosexual inclinations.)[503] It must also be stressed that both Benson and Vachell had been pupils, but not masters, at public schools.

Bishop Gore in the 1870s and 1880s of enfolding his students in the "Cuddesdon cuddle" when out walking with them;[504] and in no public school after 1900 would 'public opinion' have failed to comment if their headmaster had re-introduced Dr Arnold's delightful custom of taking the younger boys on to his knee when examining a class;[505] still less would the manifestations of Sewell's emotional hold over his pupils have been tolerated.*

This was part of the price for the loss of innocence. Another part was paid, in some schools, in the suspicion of close relations between masters and individual boys—that relationship whose development had been at the very core of the mid-century transformation of certain public schools. Perhaps the extreme of this phenomenon is seen at Rossall just after the end of the Victorian period, when around 1910 a resolution was passed at a staff meeting that no master should have a boy alone in his room for longer than ten minutes, and that no master should ever allow a boy to be alone with him in his room with the door shut.[506]†

Such was the logic of the new obsession.

14. Vice unmasked.

It has been argued in the preceding section that in the course of the nineteenth century the terms vice, immorality, wickedness, corruption, evil and sin with which public-school headmasters promised that their schools would infect their pupils, together changed their connotation. In the first half of the century the emphasis was on 'rebelliousness'. Only by around 1860 did a mainly sexual connotation become common, and this reflected in the first instance fears about masturbation rather than about homosexuality, which were not to intrude until after about 1880, and whose dominance by the end of the century involved a complete reversal of the early Victorian attitude to schoolboy friendships. In confirmation of this interpretation of the first stage of the process, let it be noted that many others besides Thomas Arnold used 'evil', 'sin', and similar words in the same

* Another who would have been vulnerable in a more Freud-conscious age was the founder of Abbotsholme, Dr Cecil Reddie, a tortuously repressed homosexual who populated the school's gardens with nude Greek statues and forbade married staff.

† We know that at Rugby in the 1860s it had certainly been permissible for boys to lock themselves in their rooms.[507]

general sense of rebelliousness. When, writing in the 1830s of the monitorial schools founded or extended as a result of the work of Joseph Lancaster, a schoolmaster referred to his task of *controlling vice* among his pupils[508]—nearly all under twelve and indeed mostly aged six, seven or eight—he clearly meant dishonesty and indiscipline rather than anything sexual. The problem of subordination was a social as well as an individual one. The "flood of evil" which, in the view of a school inspector in the 1840s, only more widespread provision of education could contain, was the evil of crime and pauperism combined, with its implicit threat to the survival of the social order—all this a theme, and a terminology, very close to Arnold's own. By the same token, this school of educational and social thinkers could use the word 'moral' with the implication of social—as opposed to individual—improvement.[509]

The first three decades of the nineteenth century saw a recurrent and persistent spate of criticism of the public schools of the day, mainly in the periodical press, and *immorality* and *vice* were among the evils which the schools were held to produce. Yet, according to Dr E. C. Mack, it was not until the middle of the 1830s that an example can be found of any sexual connotation being attached to these terms—in this case the suggestion that the exchange of dirty talk in schools would lead to sexual acts.[510] Before that the main connotations of immorality and vice involved cruelty, barbarism, and indiscipline. It is in this sense, also, that we must interpret that passage we have already noted in Dr Arnold's famous sermon on public schools as "nurseries of vice", and also his promise that new boys in a public school like Rugby would inevitably be corrupted "within one short month" of arrival.[511] For that, it seems, is how most of his audience—both his hearers at the school and his readers outside—would have interpreted his meaning in that period, and the more readily so since the references to "corruption" and "evil" in this sermon specified lying, bullying, and other manifestations of the spirit of rebelliousness which haunted the school authorities.•

•An Eton housemaster wrote to Dr Pusey in 1846 claiming a great moral regeneration to have taken place at Eton over several years because of the decline he had witnessed, in his own house and other houses he visited, of swearing, "indecent or irreverent expressions", and cases of intoxication.[512]

Nor did this non-sexual connotation of these terms lose currency after Arnold: Dean Farrar in a school novel uses 'vice' in the sense of *defiance* in the 1850s,[513] in much the same way as, a few years before, the unfortunate Dr Wilkinson referred to 'immorality' at the time of the Marlborough rebellion. Writing to a clergyman whose nephew had been sent home for his part in the disturbances, Dr Wilkinson reassured the uncle that though the boy's expulsion was on the grounds of his immorality, it was not for "*gross immorality in a general sense*" (*i.e.* in the sense in which the term *gross* immorality was then generally used), but "for *heading a mutinous body in very grave acts of outrage*".[514]

15. The ritual of the flogging-block.

In addition to the factors of killer disease and 'immorality' which ought to have prevented the expansion of public-school education, there was a third factor which should also have caused parents to hesitate before committing their sons to such institutions: the incidence of various forms of cruelty, at the hands of both masters and fellow pupils.

The use of corporal punishment was part of the fabric of nineteenth-century English education, not just in public schools but in all types of school. Only when a particular example of its being taken to excess came before them did the public take notice—as when in 1832 Dr Arnold gave a boy eighteen strokes for alleged lying (whereas his predecessor's maximum had been twelve, and that only for the greater offence of rebellion); to complicate the case, the "liar" turned out after all to be innocent.[515] The birch was part of the standard equipment of the Victorian schoolmaster, as central to the work of teaching as is the textbook or the blackboard of today, and was used not just for naughtiness but also for faulty work—a wrong tense or even a false quantity. The headmaster of St Bees in the 1880s who might start off a lesson with a stroke of the cane all round the class—"to warm you up"[516]—was not necessarily distinguishable from his colleagues in elementary schools, except possibly for two factors. First, the punishments of heads of *boarding* schools were more remote from the scrutiny of parents; secondly, if the school was a public school or aped the institutions of the public schools, there was a second rung of caning power, in the hands of prefects, with a similar degree of protection from parental control. Corporal punishment at both levels of authority might be highly ritualised: it might also be informal and spontaneous. Moss* of Shrewsbury once gave a boy eighty-eight strokes at a flogging, but with deliberation (it is said) rather than with passion—and, amazingly, his governors upheld his action.[517] At Eton Warre "used the birch rather as a symbol of disgrace than an instrument of torture",[519] but he used it nevertheless and with "all the awfulness of ceremony".[520] When Warre decided on a birching, one of the duty prefects was informed, and he would enrol two fags—among whom the task was apparently a popular one—to act as official "holders-down". These officiants waited outside the headmaster's room while Warre interviewed the victim. Then the headmaster emerged, and, followed by the victim, two "holders-down", two prefects, and finally the headmasters's clerk, processed solemnly to the sixth form room, where the clerk gave a birch to one of the prefects, who gave it to the headmaster. "The victim then made the necessary adjustments to his clothes, the holders-down held down, and the ceremony was consummated".[521] Warre had the regrettable habit of administering a moral lecture afterwards, when the victim's intense desire was to be somewhere else. His Lower Master, the Rev. E. C. Austen-Leigh, nicknamed The Flea, was, by contrast, more straightforward in the execution of a duty which he gave every indication of enjoying:

> . . . at the appointed hour the Schoolyard, outside the Flea's operating chamber, was packed with a surging and expectant crowd, that must have resembled one of those at the old public hangings. After a brief interval, during which the Flea must have been squeaking out his accustomed formulas of "Breeng out the block!" "Hold him down!" "Leeft up his shirt!" the expected sounds began . . . And at each swish the whole audience outside intoned in grim unison "*One! Two! Three! . . .*"[522]

For preparatory school headmasters to fail to prepare boys for such established institutions of public school life would be

* Moss retired to the Herefordshire village of Much Birch.[518]

an obvious case of neglect, and we know that there were many prep. schools where the Eton treatment was imitated, with differences only of frequency or ferocity. At the well-known prep. school headed by the Rev. H. W. Sneyd-Kynnersley (a product of Temple's Rugby), which was attended by the young Winston Churchill, the two senior boys were, as Roger Fry afterwards recounted, bound *ex officio* to assist at the executions and hold down the culprit. The ritual was very precise and solemn—every Monday morning the whole school assembled in Hall and every boy's report was read aloud:

> After reading a bad report from a form-master Mr Sneyd-Kynnersley would stop and after a moment's awful silence say, "Harrison minor you will come up to my study afterwards". And so afterwards the culprits were led up by the two top boys. In the middle of the room was a large box draped in black cloth, and in austere tones the culprit was told to take down his trousers and kneel before the block over which I and the other head boy held him down. The swishing was given with the master's full strength and it took only two or three strokes for drops of blood to form everywhere and it continued for 15 or 20 strokes when the wretched boy's bottom was a mass of blood. Generally, of course, the boys endured it with fortitude but sometimes there were scenes of screaming, howling and struggling which made me sick with disgust.[523]

The situation was similar at the aristocratic prep. school at Wixenford for several decades from the 1860s onwards, where the second master, Mr Dunbar, made himself responsible for all beatings, which were savage and frequent despite his "genuine fondness" for the boys, among whom he made great favourites. The young Curzon, who was one of them, left this account:

> He executed all or nearly all the punishments whether by spanking on the bare buttocks or by caning on the palm of the hand or by swishing on the posterior. I remember well all three experiences. He was a master of spanking, though he used to say that it hurt him nearly as much as it did us. I remember that it was at about the 15th blow that it really

> began to hurt and from thence the pain increased in geometrical progression. At about the 28th blow one began to howl. The largest number of smacks I ever received was I think 42.[524]

Yet these rituals represented only a small part of a boy's liability to frequent corporal punishment, at least if he were at a public school, for the prefect system also normally involved a right of corporal punishment, sometimes, in fact, when this was denied to assistant masters, and certainly there were many schools where boys could expect more beatings from prefects than from masters. At Radley, for example, the form of prefectorial "canings" or "swishings" had settled by 1890 into four categories, with graduated refinements of severity and formality.[525] This type of power in the hands of schoolboys could, and obviously often did, lead to abuse, in which younger boys, and especially new boys, were most commonly the victims. Sir Charles Oman afterwards described his first two weeks as a newly-admitted Scholar of Winchester:

> In a very few days I realized that I had chanced into the middle of a perfect nightmare of thoughtless cruelty . . . This fortnight in the last days of October and the first of November 1872 has left on my memory the most perfect impression of long-continued terror that I have ever known.[526]

A. A. Milne, who entered Westminster as a Scholar twenty years after this, lived in dread of the "ever-present threat of tanning by prefects": it was virtually impossible to live through a school day without infringing some petty regulation, all this producing an atmosphere poisoned by the constant liability to corporal punishment—"not the actual pain, but the perpetual fear of it".[527]

From time to time some scandal involving the cruelty of masters or prefects would break over the Victorian public: C. J. Vaughan had to defend his Harrow prefects in 1853 in the face of an outcry over the "whopping" of the Earl of Galloway's son for his insubordination to a prefect on the football field,[528] and the "reign of terror" which the young Charles Oman experienced at Winchester was soon exposed when the "great tunding row'' broke out, after a boy of seventeen received from a prefect thirty cuts across his shoulders, in the course of which beating, five ground-ash sticks were broken. ''A deluge of angry letters'' for several weeks in the *Times* and the *Daily Telegraph* led to the exposure of numerous such cases, and Ridding was forced to take action to curb the excesses of prefectorial caning.[529] Periodically there were still worse cases in Victorian boarding schools, even involving on occasion the deaths of pupils,[530] and from time to time complaints against schoolmasters, sometimes leading to court cases, reminded the public of the brutality which seemed to be an inevitable feature in such institutions. One of the most valued members of the Marlborough staff, a pupil of Wilkinson and Cotton who returned to serve the school for nearly forty years, was nearing the end of his career when a doctor parent laid a formal complaint against him before the governors. Not only had he damaged this doctor's son's ear-drum by boxing his ears, but he was charged with being guilty of ''a long-continued course of personal violence on boys with whom he had been brought in contact during his mastership''. Fortunately the Rev. J. S. Thomas could counter the small quantity of evidence from former pupils or their parents with letters from over two hundred Old Marlburians ''testifying deep affection and respect'', and the incident was closed by his ''voluntarily pledging himself never to strike any boy again with his hands''—a resolve which must have been strengthened when the boy, who was apparently delicate, died a year later.[531]

Cases of this kind came to light because of palpable injury or the watchfulness of parents, but the latter was largely inoperative during term-time and certainly did not help the unfortunate new boy (a parson's son) at Winchester in 1872, for whom this was the first taste of any kind of schooling, after earlier education at home. His fourteen beatings in his first fortnight for his failure to cope with the orders of his fagmasters rendered his body ''a really dreadful criss-cross of blue and black weals''.[532] In general, the system of brutality in boarding schools was protected by the ''taboo which every boy would have died rather than break, akin to that which prevents even a mortally wounded gangster from informing on his killer'' (as an Etonian of the 1890s later put it).[533] Add to this the dislike of being thought a coward or a cry-baby, and the further fact that insofar as such terrors could be represented as an inevitable part of the system,[534] it was not very profitable to the individual to complain—then their persistence and their generality are easy enough to understand.

Such disincentives protected not just cruel masters and prefects but also the ordinary bullying schoolboy who tyrannised his weaker peers. The prevalence of bullying varied widely, but it was known to be a regular hazard of public-school life, and in some schools at some periods it was rife. This may to some extent have been a function of the closeness of boy-master relations: a vigilant house-tutor could soon spot and put down the excesses which the boys themselves would never normally report. At Charterhouse in the 1890s, for example, where the housemaster might have little contact with his boys beyond taking evening prayers, employed no junior colleague as house tutor to help him, and left all to his prefects, school rules laid down solemnly that every boy had the right to appeal to his housemaster, thus offering theoretical protection against prefects or lesser bullies. But this right was never exercised, and, says one observer, if it had been, "the final result would probably have been calamitous"; removal of the victim from the school was virtually the only remedy.[535] The future Lord Berners, who had seen no point in complaining to his parents against the excesses of a sadistic prep.-school headmaster (around 1892), because "my complaints would probably have been discredited at the time, and led to further punishment", reports that a powerful schoolboy code operated against the "sneaks" who reported cases of bullying by schoolfellows to the masters.[536]

When confronted with these forms of brutality, how far were the Victorians able to identify, as we post-Freudians can, the elements of sadism and eroticism in such institutionalised cruelty? For Victorian prep. schools and public schools must have been a paradise for sadistically-inclined masters and boys. The prep-school headmaster around 1900 whom C. S. Lewis represents as making a small boy bend down at one end of a schoolroom and then taking a run of a room's length at each stroke of a merciless thrashing, is exonerated by Lewis from any erotic impulse;[537] and Roger Fry attempts to acquit the odious Mr Sneyd-Kynnersley, who was "genuinely fond of boys and enjoyed their company", of being even "an unconscious Sodomite"[538]—presumably the nearest Fry could get to identifying such a man's motive as erotic. But without benefit of Freud and of course without identifying these impulses in their precise terminology, Etonians of the 1890s appeared to be able to recognise their Lower Master as what one of them could later describe as "a jolly old sadist, naked and unashamed", and the events in a number of Eton boarding houses as "a regular routine of sadistic orgies".[539] And although he could not have analysed it in these terms in the 1870s, Charles Oman some sixty years later correctly identified the "wave of Sadism" which had "swept over" the Winchester prefects of 1872 as being, in some of them, what he called megalomania, in others "that same pleasure in inflicting pain which inspired the too-celebrated Marquis de Sade in the reign of Louis XV".[540]

So regularly was recourse had to corporal punishment in Victorian schools, and so great the zeal which was expected of the performer, that its exercise must have accommodated a wide spectrum of motives and feelings. This will have included those who regarded the whole process with distaste or indifference; secondly, those who enjoyed the sensation of power or righteousness which it afforded—as was said of Benson of Wellington, "it was a treat to see the zealous satisfaction with which he chastised a boy caught out in a lie";[541] and thirdly, those who derived even conscious erotic stimulus from beating, some of whom doubtless contrived as many opportunities as they could for indulging their passions. The system provided a cloak of respectability to these second and third categories, when in our own age their obvious motivation would have discredited the system of punishment itself. The only time the cloak was thrust aside, and the system thrown into disrepute, was when the sadistic punishments were accompanied by overt erotic or indecent phenomena. Then, at least, the real nature of the punishment process was recognised for what it was. This was the case with, for example, the celebrated pioneer of the monitorial system, Joseph Lancaster, who earlier in the century had been removed from the control of the schools founded on his initiative, after complaints were proved against him that he used to flog his monitorial apprentices "for his amusement".[542] It was the evidence, not of the floggings themselves, but of the erotic activities which accompanied them, which convinced Lancaster's colleagues that he was a "damnable beast".[543]* Men with similar impulses later in the nineteenth century had only to act with greater discretion to be regarded as strong and successful disciplinarians. Among the consequences of the system were products like the poet Swinburne, whose experiences at Eton in the 1840s left him with a life-long obsession with masochistic fantasies, many of them centred around the flogging-block at his old school.[545] It was presumably the predilections of such products of English schools which helped to fasten upon sado-masochistic practices, at least across the Channel, the nickname *le vice anglais*.

16. The complaisant family.

Three factors, then, have been identified which ought to have deterred the Victorians from sending their sons away to the schools of the developing public-school system: the prevalence of killer epidemic diseases, the schools' own admissions concerning the probability of 'moral' contamination, and the recurrent exposures of the cruelty involved in public-school life. One of the reasons why parents were prepared to defy or overlook these deterrents has already emerged: the rewards, in terms of status, of public-school attendance. It remains to explore further reasons for this.

The facts of geography provide one uncomplicated explanation. The expansion of Britain meant that both in parts

* In the year that Thomas Arnold was appointed to Rugby, the London radical Francis Place set down his account of the sub-committee of enquiry set up thirteen years before by the Society which controlled the Lancasterian schools, to investigate "a considerable number of cases", ultimately proved "beyond all doubt": "It came out that Lancaster frequently flogged his [monitorial] apprentices with a rod when they displeased him, and he was very easily displeased when he wanted to flog the boys. At other times he flogged them when he was in good humour for his amusement. His practice was to hug and caress and kiss them to induce them to consent to be flogged. Sometimes one boy kissed another, sometimes he laid them down upon the Sopha [*sic*], and sometimes several of them stood before the fire with their trousers down and their shirts tucked up round their waists while Lancaster flogged them. The lads who were thus treated were from about 12 to 18 years of age."[544]

of the world coloured red on the map and in other areas such as Latin America and the Far East where Britons were creating an economic empire, there would be parents in need of boarding-school education for their sons. Thus every public school could count on a proportion of overseas pupils by 1900, and at some schools this representation was large. At Westward Ho!, for example, around 1880, some 75% of Kipling's schoolfellows had, like Kipling himself, been born outside England, mostly of Army fathers.[546] Within Britain, the geographical distribution of suitable secondary day schools was such that many middle-class parents were forced to send their sons away to board—if by 'suitable' we understand schools in which middle-class boys were present in sufficient numbers to predominate. Nevertheless, geography is not by itself an adequate explanation of so widespread a tendency. Furthermore, we know of numerous instances of pupils being sent as boarders to schools in the very towns in which their parents resided, or even of parents moving house to towns in which their sons were boarders.[547]

As has already been suggested, the examination of the process whose implications for schools this book claims to describe, namely the transfer of function from family to school in the Victorian period, is hindered by the lack of any authoritative analysis of the nineteenth-century middle-class family. Thus, some of the hypotheses here brought forward to explain this transfer will be tentative ones. But we might begin with the assumption that in the nineteenth century the concept of the 'family' was a changing one, just as this institution had undergone change in previous centuries. We need to note that the practice of sending children out of the family and into the households of strangers, from the age of ten or eleven—or even as early as eight or nine—was common in pre-industrial England, certainly in the sixteenth and seventeenth centuries among the lower classes; and in the case of boys this service—for that is what it involved—might last for up to twenty years, and normally until marriage.[548] While poor families thus boarded their children with less poor families, middle-class families put their children into other middle-class households for at least some period of service, in a process described by a modern social historian as "the traffic in children from the humbler to the more successful families".[549] Already in the late fifteenth century a foreign observer had commented upon the practice in England wereby parents put out their children "to hard service in the houses of other people" at the age of seven or nine, binding them to service possibly up to the age of eighteen. ". . . And during that time they perform all the most menial offices; and few are born who are exempted from this fate, for everyone, however rich he may be, sends away his children into the houses of others, whilst he, in return, receives those of strangers into his own". This practice, the English parents explained, was "in order that their children might learn better manners". Such practices, says the French social historian Ariès, were probably common in Western Europe during the Middle Ages; they affected all classes, and persisted, at least in England and France, into the sixteenth and seventeenth centuries, until, at any rate for the upper classes, the school took the place of this traditional method of out-apprenticeship.[550]

This form of traffic or exchange offers us some precedent for the process we are examining in Victorian England, though the analogy must not be pushed too far. In pre-industrial England and France, children were placed in an alternative family, partly in the hope of social betterment. What Victorian parents (again, partly in the hope of social betterment) looked to in the case of the public schools was placement not in an alternative family but in a powerful rival institution capable of generating alternative values, and itself capable of acting as a focus of intensive loyalties: none of this was implicit in the earlier tradition, or certainly not to the same degree. It is true that a few public-school apologists, like Sewell of Radley and H. B. Gray of Bradfield, attempted to rationalise this process by emphasising superficial analogies between the school and the family,[551] but these carried little conviction. What is more important to recognise is that this idea of the family as a corporate emotional unit, with a "family consciousness" powerful enough to predicate competition from the loyalties engendered by a school, is a comparatively new phenomenon anyway in the nineteenth century and would only have existed among the upper and middle classes. Both the lack of any strong "family consciousness" and the prolonged physical separation of children from their parents were probably characteristic of the mass of the population of Western Europe from the Middle Ages until perhaps the nineteenth century,[552] in marked contrast to the almost aggressive family cohesion and loyalty of the lower classes in Britain today. While it is theoretically possible that the social mobility which contributed to the development of the public-school system carried up into the upper classes a lower-class predisposition to a transfer of function at the expense of the family, against such tendencies must be set the powerful evangelical and middle-class ideology which now glorified and sentimentalised the family.

What we do know about the character of the middle-class family in the nineteenth century gives us some clues as to why they acquiesced in this transfer of function, despite these deterrents. It is a mistake to assume that propaganda, however powerful, can make parents love their children or even desire prolonged contact with them, as many a modern social worker will testify. The willingness of middle- and upper-class parents to delegate to the nursery and the servants the early upbringing of their children has already been referred to: the ubiquitous nanny, nurserymaid and governess were a standard element in the upbringing of young middle-class Victorians and Edwardians, sometimes decisive in the formative influence they exercised over their charges. At least in theory—and despite frequent evidence of unorthodox and 'unofficial cruelty' practised by them[553]—they operated under the control of parents and imparted approved values, even if the amount of time parents spent with their children might not make this control or approval effective. Of the parents of his contemporaries at prep. school and public school in the 1890s, Esmé Wingfield-Stratford wrote: "They wanted to have the responsibility for their children taken off their hands, and to be relieved of their presence except at bearable intervals".[554] Modern parents, typically with two or three children, will find such pressures less onerous, but social-class differentials in child mortality rates meant that households which patronised the Victorian public school might be swarming with children: as Professor Musgrove reminds us, "there can be little doubt that by the 1870s, middle-class children, by surviving in greater numbers, constituted a growing burden on their parents while they were growing up . . ."[555]—a burden, for many, in expense; a burden for all, perhaps, in keeping them occupied and amused. Half a century before, even Mrs Gladstone, the statesman's mother, with four sons and two daughters to bring up, was "always thankful when school resumed" and, though she loved all her children, was glad when she had packed all her sons off to school.[556]

It is also possible to see the Victorian period as marking the triumph of a new sex ethic impinging on family life: by this ethic upper-class Victorian women enforced upon their menfolk a stricter conception of marital chastity.[557] The triumph was, as we know, a hollow one, for it led to the notorious 'double standard' which tolerated the existence of a mass of unofficial sexual outlets for otherwise respectable Victorian males. A consequence of both the official code and the double standard was a new need for mothers to protect their sons from promiscuous sexual experience, either with girls of their own or of a lower class, or—what was an increasing preoccupation—with servants. This concern over promiscuity added new point to the process observable both in England and in France from the late eighteenth century onwards, by which the concept of the 'family' tended to be reduced to parents and children, excluding the clients, servants and friends whose presence in the middle- and upper-class household had been accommodated in earlier concepts of the 'family'.[558] Packing the young menfolk off to boarding school was an obvious way of reducing their contact with the temptations of servant girls, indeed of reducing their contact with servants generally—association with whom in hours of recreation was already a matter of concern to the upper classes in 1790[559] and would be of even greater concern to the *parvenu* classes of the nineteenth century, who would tend to be more conscious of their need to maintain 'social distance' from their servants. The public schools had, it is true, armies of male servants, but their duties, and their segregation from the organised games of the boys, had become carefully regulated by the middle of the Victorian period. The hordes of "cads", or lower-class spongers who had, earlier in the century, hung around Eton, Winchester and other such schools,[560] operating for the boys an illicit traffic in food, drink, bets, and probably sex, had similarly been dealt with by the school authorities by about the same date. Nor is it perhaps too far-fetched to suggest that the practice of fagging, of which further mention will be made later, served partly to symbolise independence from the contamination of servants.

Philippe Ariès sees the period from the 1780s onwards as one in which the French family, now tending towards a reduced scale of "family consciousness" which excluded all but parents and children, began to "organise itself around the child", drawing a new emotional identity—in sharper distinction from the society at large—from the greater value that could be placed upon individual children in a period when more could be expected to survive infancy.[561]

In Britain, on the other hand, our analysis suggests that the increasing "family consciousness" took a different form. Instead of guarding their sons to their bosoms, Victorian parents deliberately sent them off to boarding school, for a number of reasons, some of which have already become evident. Where families were using these schools as part of a process of upward social mobility, a measure of discontinuity between home and school was essential: claustration of their sons in institutions which must be as nearly 'total' as possible was a necessary guarantee of their losing the values, manners and speech-patterns of their home background and taking on those of the classes they were entering. While the nineteenth-century French family was organising itself around the child, in England the middle-class family can be seen as organising itself around the school and using the public schools to express certain forms of 'dynasticism'. Parents themselves could gain social prestige through the attendance of their sons at famous schools; the sons of *parvenus* could procure a substitute pedigree through attendance at an old-established school which placed their achievements in a long line of successes stretching back into history.* But probably all these were incidental benefits rather than real motives for organisation of the Victorian upper-middle-class family round the school, when the developing ideology of the family ought to have prompted too great a devotion to their children to allow them to risk exposing them to the hazards we have examined. The decisive factor was the

* Schools ambitious to assert their standing as public schools went to great lengths to emphasise their antiquity: the decades 1890–1910 were the great period for the writing of school histories.

emergence of a powerful new value in Victorian society which the family was itself powerless to generate: *manliness*.

The *machismo* which gripped the later Victorians embraced three interwoven strains: anti-effeminacy, stiff-upper-lippery, and physical hardness. The first two were erratic in their hold and imperfectly developed by the end of the century; the third was self-confident, consistent, and pervasive.

The suspicions of effeminacy which were involved in (for example) the attacks on ritualistic clergymen after 1850[562] co-existed with a persistent innocence which long tolerated (to take another example) all-male fancy-dress balls at Oxford colleges (notably the 'hearty' college, Brasenose) which gave free rein to the extravagant behaviour of transvestites, until indeed the goings-on became so obviously scandalous that this type of ball was stopped.[563] But the prejudice against anything held to smack of effeminacy was gaining strength. The young Curzon at Eton in 1872 had proudly decorated his study mantelpiece with a pink velvet bracket,[564] and Churchill in 1889 had tricked out his study at Harrow (shared with one other boy) with a pair of blue rugs, some vases given him by his nanny, and a number of decorative fans.[565] Yet R. St C. Talboys recounts how, at Wellington around 1904, a boy with an interest in gardening decorated his room with some rare and beautiful flowers until the Captain of the Dormitory XI spotted them, swept them on the floor and trampled them under foot—"There is no room for this rotten effeminate stuff here".[566] The Rugby School doctor had given support to this developing prejudice when in 1894 he introduced into the third edition of his manual *Health at School* a new section attacking "effeminacy" in the furnishing of studies in public-school boarding houses and declaring that the furniture, hangings, china and photographs in some of these "suggest an aesthetic lady recluse".[567] Another implication of this prejudice, when it had become established, was the prohibition against boys taking girls' parts in school plays (on the grounds that "no sound boy would want to take a cissy part") which a product of Victorian Sherborne found operating among some of his experienced housemaster colleagues after he returned as a master in 1911.[568]

We have already noted examples of the ready expression of the emotions among public-school masters in the 1850s and

1860s which warn us not to antedate the convention of the 'stiff upper lip'. Even great apostles of "Christian manliness" such as Charles Kingsley can be cited as marked exceptions to generalisations about the prevalence of this value (David Newsome represents Kingsley as "the very quintessence of Victorian emotionalism"),[569] and its diffusion among late Victorian public school products was very uneven. Lady Wootton records the scenes of uncontrolled grief of fathers at the memorial services for their sons killed in World War I;[570] nevertheless, the degree to which this convention had become accepted, at least by 1918, is implicit in her shocked reaction to such open emotionalism.

Yet if not all its elements were equally established, the general pervasiveness of the concept of *manliness* in later Victorian society is undoubted, and that of physical toughness is most obvious: the specifications for the award of the Rhodes Scholarships at Oxford, with a heavy premium on qualities of 'manliness', are a case in point*. And once this value had achieved this hold, it was obvious that the school was far better fitted than the family to foster it. Tender relations between parents and children were not a proper background to the toughening process: the parents could only provide for this vicariously, by delegation to an institution where the unpalatable aspects of the hardening process could be shielded from their affectionate gaze. Thomas Arnold had conceded his conviction that "the trials of school are useful to a boy's after character"; and as the conception of 'character' changed, with increasing emphasis on the three elements of 'manliness', so the family's need increased for a type of school whose institutions were seen to develop it. It was, again, Charles Kingsley who criticised the middle class in that its education had been lacking in that experience of pain and endurance necessary to bring out

* Cecil Rhodes's admiration for the products of English public schools led him, in founding the Rhodes Scholarships at Oxford, to specify as qualifications, not only "literary and scholastic achievements" but also "fondness for, and success in, manly outdoor sports such as cricket, football, and the like", other qualities such as "manhood", courage and devotion to duty, and qualities of "fellowship" and "leadership". Before he died, Rhodes supervised a 'trial-run' selection of a scholar from a leading South African 'public' school in 1901, in which the weighting of specifications was a mere 40% for scholarship, as against 20% each for athletics, "manhood", and "character and influence".[571]

the masculine qualities.[572] Now, as the cult of 'manliness' spread, parents demanded even earlier access for their sons to the institutions which fostered it—which helps to explain the proliferation after 1870 of preparatory schools.

This conception of the school as a forcing-house turning molly-coddled nurslings into *manly* young men is a vital clue to the problem of why parents defied the powerful deterrents of disease, immorality and cruelty in the Victorian public school, and set up a demand for an expansion of public-school education even before the 'status' benefits of the system had become as obvious as they were by around 1880 or 1890. Writing of the cruelty and hardship prevalent at a preparatory school in 1908, C. S. Lewis says, "If the parents in each generation always or often knew what really goes on at their sons' schools, the history of education would be very different".[573] This assumes that parents did not know or could not guess: whereas it can be claimed that a degree of cruelty and hardship were precisely what they were sending their sons away to such schools for, though of course they averted their eyes from the actual details and deplored such palpable excesses as came to their notice. As the *Times* commented in 1857, in a discussion of public-school education: "Parents may well abstain from looking too closely into the process, and content themselves with the result".[574]*

In the course of the exposures of prefectorial sadism in the "great tunding row" at Winchester in 1872, Charles Oman's parents' advice to him was to "grin and bear it", though of course they said they hoped that conditions would improve.[576] E. W. Benson, between his headmastership of Wellington and the Archbishopric of Canterbury, sent his eldest son Martin off to Winchester in 1874 in the wake of those same exposures of the misuse of the ground-ash; but when the fourteen-year-old boy's letters home reported that "tundings" with the ground-ash were still common, Benson's main concern was that the boy

* Thring, who had vivid recollections of the cruelty, suffering and "wild profligacy" of his Eton schooldays, educated at Uppingham the son of an Eton contemporary who claimed to have experienced worse things than he, and who furthermore believed that Eton was now [1863] in a worse state than in their time [c. 1840]. Yet this parent made clear he would have sent his son to Eton even under these worsened conditions, if he had been able to afford it.[575]

should avoid being beaten for "carelessness or anything in that line",[577] rather than that a practice so open to abuse should cease. The very ritual of a headmaster's thrashing at a prep. school in 1890 (as reported by Wingfield-Stratford, complete with capitals), contained a significantly phrased injunction: "Be a man! TAKE DOWN YOUR BREECHES LIKE A MAN!"[578] The old barbarism of the early nineteenth-century public school had cried out for reform, not because the system involved cruelty, but because this was unlicensed and uncontrolled. The reformed public school of Victorian times represented a measure of cruelty, operating towards the fashioning of a desired product, in conditions which were now largely under control.

The parents' willingness to expose their offspring to serious risks of killer diseases in these schools must be examined in the light both of changes in the concept and size of the Victorian family and of this 'hardening' function of the school. We must at least consider the possibility that the greater numbers of surviving children in middle-class families in the nineteenth century may have given rise to the notion that children were more expendable and facilitated their wilful exposure to such perils. Against this possibility must be set the increasing sentimentality towards childhood and towards individual children which we see emerging even before the period when declining child mortality rates, and a measure of birth-control practice, "made children worth taking seriously" (as one historian has put it).[579] More helpful to our understanding of this apparent callousness of parents is the ideology and practice to which Professor Musgrove has drawn attention, in accordance with which, in the eighteenth and early nineteenth centuries, individual children were subjected, especially in "the most enlightened and progressive" English households, to a régime of fresh air, cold baths and other "hardening" devices designed to fortify them against disease.[580]

It might perhaps be objected that in any case the large, many-servanted, upper-middle-class Victorian household was itself not free from disease and thus hardly safer from infection than the public boarding school. Even if this be conceded, it does not dispose of the fact that living conditions in Victorian public schools were glaringly inimical to even the most primitive notions of hygiene, *and that parents had every opportunity to become aware of this.* Radley, founded in 1847, was infested by "omnivorous rats" throughout its nineteenth-century existence and indeed well on into the present century.[581] Obviously not all schools were as bad as Wellington, a school with strong royal connections, where in some dormitories in the early 1900s nightly attacks by rats "caused consternation and even wounds":[582] but we remember that when Stalky and his friends placed a dead cat under the floorboards to score off an enemy housemaster, the stench was automatically assumed to come from a decomposing rat.[583] A Winchester colleger in 1883 found toadstools growing under his bed;[584] at Wellington the filth in one of the dormitories was actually exposed in the journal *Truth* in 1910 by a visitor who considered the cubicles were "not fit for human habitation" and expressed surprise that under these conditions epidemics could be avoided.[585]

The maintenance of the boys' personal hygiene was rendered doubly difficult in that, amidst such conditions of squalor, washing conditions were in many schools "meagre in the extreme". At Charterhouse, newly built on its Godalming site in 1872, the son of a Harrow housemaster who entered in 1899 records that no hot or cold baths were obtainable until his last year—1903: "it was expected that each boy should have had one on the last day of the holidays which should last him until he next returned home", normally some thirteen weeks later. So it was difficult for a boy to wash even after a hard game of football: the Charterhouse boys were not provided with the "toshes" available at some other schools—"small buckets where, with care, limited ablutions were possible". Yet house custom compelled every boy to take part in a form of football game for an hour a day before dinner, playing in his normal black suit and linen shirt with stiff cuffs and front. "By dinner time he was immersed in perspiration, and, after an afternoon change into football clothes, put on these wet clothes again for afternoon school": a practice plausibly identified as the cause of later ill-health.[586] At Winchester in the 1840s collegers washed their feet once a week in a "toe-pan" (footbath), the same hot water often serving more than one boy; apart from other occasions of washing hands and face, this was the only cleansing their bodies received, unless they went bathing in summer.[587]

Thirty years later the situation had hardly improved, despite the development by then of compulsory organised games. Prefects had cold baths every morning, juniors had a once-weekly immersion in hot water, either in a flat tin bath in the middle of the dormitory floor or in a "toe-pan". Other ablutions were performed in cold water at a row of stone washbasins.[588] Scholars at Westminster in the 1890s had no fixed baths, and there was no hot water at all until around 1900. Every boy's cubicle had a shallow tin bath "in which one could make cold splashing noises every morning".[589] Though similar conditions were common[590] at other public schools, it must also be conceded that our Victorian forebears would have been less shocked than we, though they might have been expected to have given some thought to the implications for their children's health of such extremes of neglect. Many of the homes from which these shoolboys were drawn, including country-houses and substantial parsonages, would not, even in the late Victorian period, have possessed a bathroom as such; and we remember that it was as late as 1912 that the venerable head of an Oxford college opposed "with some acerbity" a suggestion to instal bathrooms in the college, on the grounds that the young men were only up for eight weeks at a time.[591]

So the 'toughening' function of the public schools was apparent in other features besides corporal punishment and like forms of cruelty. At the great schools patronised by the rich, boy life was a mixture of austerity and luxury; at humbler schools the austerity was unmixed. Sometimes the privations resulted from a bursarial policy of extreme economy, sometimes from corruption, sometimes from incompetence.[592] The consequences were real suffering for the boys, especially from hunger and cold. At Charterhouse in the 1880s junior boys in each house, who "lived and moved and had the whole of their being in Long Room", enjoyed the benefit of a blazing fire there in winter, but studies were not heated in any way, and boys sat in their cold rooms clad in greatcoats.[593] The situation was exactly the same twenty years later, both for the dozen senior boys who had the "privilege" of studies and for the forty-odd others in the Long Room, and water would freeze in the washbasins on cold nights.[594] During a cold winter in the mid-90s the ink in one Radley classroom remained freezing until mid-day, four hours after the lighting of the fires and gas-lights.[595] Sir Francis Chichester, who entered Marlborough in 1915, has recorded his abiding memory of the extreme coldness of "Upper", the huge communal day-room which was no less formidable in Victorian times.[596] A survivor of the Charterhouse régime that has been described, commented seventy years later, "Yes, we certainly lived a hard life, *but it did us good rather than harm*".[597] Chichester's later exploits would have been taken by many as further confirmation of the value of this side of school life as a training for endurance. Colonel Richard Meinertzhagen, who entered Harrow in 1891, had harsh words to say about the poor diet and the total neglect of hygiene at what he called "a hard school, facing facts, and teaching realities", but he later waxed eloquent over the benefits he had derived from this kind of experience of "hard living, hard fare, and hard work" and claimed that contact with "faults, vices, and even cruelties" had quickened his judgment of character.[598]

Many boys at Winchester in the 1870s suffered from the official diet of inadequate food, repulsively served—a "starvation diet" which had to be eked out by supplies purchased with one's own pocket money.[599] Hunger was intensified by the practice of holding lessons before breakfast. In the 1840s this had meant that a boy who rose in decent time for 6·45 Chapel, followed by early school, would have been up and hungry for at least two hours before he was given breakfast at 8·30:[600] by the 1870s this wait had been cut by perhaps an hour.[601] But at both Winchester in the 1870s and Charterhouse in the 1880s this breakfast might consist only of tea, bread and butter: anything extra had to be paid for.[602] A. A. Milne, who entered Westminster in 1893, records the disgusting and inadequate diet he endured after the funds had run out with which he supplemented official rations:

> one was left with an inordinate craving for food. I lay awake every night thinking about food; I fell asleep and dreamt about food. In all my years at Westminster I never ceased to be hungry.[603]

The Cambridge historian F. A. Simpson went to Rossall in 1898, entering at the age of fourteen and leaving, a prefect at eighteen. During those years the boys at Rossall were "scandalously underfed". In his first year at university he put on some two stone in weight and increased in height by inches.[604] All these privations prevailed despite the constant solicitude of parents, especially mothers, over their sons' health and feeding arrangements, though parental concern stopped short at a barrier marked with slogans about "doing them good", "making men of them", etc. It is also true, of course, that the average public-school boy around 1900 was markedly taller than the average working-class boy,[605]* though statistics suggest that the average thirteen-year-old Marlborough boy of the 1960s was about four inches taller than his counterpart in the 1870s.[607]

These facts help us to see that cruelty and privation were part of an initiation process whose benefits in terms of a toughened end-product reconciled Victorian parents to those elements which whould otherwise have affronted thier own sentiments. And they were only parts of a complex double cycle of initiation which had other important elements. The double cycle began, typically, at age eight with a brutal transition from the affections of home to an institution where manifestations of affection were suppressed by the insensitivities of boy tribalism. Within the school there was a new vocabulary to be learned, a hierarchy to be climbed, a public opinion to be appeased. By various pressures of official teaching and boy-public opinion, in both cases capable of invoking some degree of physical cruelty, certain forms of childishness, of effeminacy, of self-assertiveness in the pupils, were suppressed. Boastfulness, or any form of what was considered "side", was subjected to the sanction of heavy ridicule. Hardly had the boy learned to manipulate this system, or at least come to terms with it, than he was plunged into a new abasement in the second cycle, at around age thirteen. Here was yet another school vocabulary to learn, by methods which might involve cruelty; sometimes there was a formal initiation ceremony symbolising his humiliation.

* Miss Marghanita Laski, the source for this, goes on to state that "the average height of working-class schoolboys was five inches below that of public schoolboys", but this statement needs elucidation, since the average age of public-school boys was several years greater than that of working-class schoolboys around 1900. It would also be significant, in view of the conclusions of Chapter 4 below, to know which schools rated as "public" schools to produce these figures.[606]

Typically he began this new stage of his school life as a fag. Some of the worst excesses of the early nineteenth-century fagging system had been remedied by the late Victorian period, and the Clarendon Commissioners, by refusing to interfere with this system,[608] helped to emphasise it as an essential ingredient of an authentic public-school education which new or emergent public schools hastened to imitate. Tuckwell described the essential function of the system at Winchester in the 1840s, and also the degree to which it was entrenched:

> . . . slavery is the only word which summed up the three years' experience of a college junior. Its details, whether cruel or grotesque, were all so contrived as to stamp upon the young boy's mind his grade of servile inferiority, and his dedication to the single virtue of abject unquestioning obedience. Nothing was more resented by the seniors than the faintest manifestation of independent feeling on the part of any fag. No maxim was oftener cited than the unwritten law that a boy was not allowed "to think" until he had twenty juniors. Anyone who showed tacit dislike of the degradations he endured, or even a desire to retain in spite of them some fragments of that refinement and self-respect which he brought from home, was designated "spree", and to be spree was to be a mark for spite and insult from every one senior to one's self. And yet so inscrutable is boy nature, so intense its natural conservatism, so passionately unreasoning its devotion to the thing which is, that I believe any attempt from without to annul these time-honoured abominations would have met with bitter opposition as well from the juniors who were their victims as from the seniors who inflicted them.[609]

Around this system the schools developed rationalisations which portrayed it as a training in service to others.[610]

Having survived this stage, the boy then began again to climb the ladder representing the internal hierarchy of the school, in its gradations representing academic ability, athletic prowess, and the structure of authority.[611] Dress and other privileges were tightly controlled in order to reflect a boy's position in these hierarchies at any one time—by whether he wore this or that school tie or cap,* left this or that button undone, carried his hand in or out of this or that pocket, or walked on this side or that of a certain part of the school. Yet these distinctions constituted important stimuli and rewards for the internalisation of approved values, as well as helping to delineate the structure.

Fighting his way up through the double cycle† of this system, learning to endure pain and to know his place, the boy was tested and re-tested in a process of prolonged and constantly renewed attrition by which a new type of social personality was formed. The beauty of the system was that the hierarchy was usable by the majority of boys, for there were sufficient avenues of success to offer some kinds of reward to a large proportion of those undergoing the process. Academic ability had an established *cursus honorum*; there were degrees of privilege tied to seniority alone, and athletic achievements earned the most elaborate and observable forms of privilege apart from those associated with positions of power in the prefect system at school or house level. Those who negotiated this hierarchy with any success were repaid for their earlier acceptance of humiliation by exaltation to an assured position of respect, advertised by the appropriate insignia and by the exercise of certain rights. All this generated in them an enormous self-confidence which was indeed to become the hallmark of the public-school product. There were those who rated public schools by their ability to foster these qualities of self-confidence and poise. Archbishop Benson's son Arthur, an Eton housemaster for many years until 1903, would commend the products of Repton or Wellington for their approximation to the "prefect aplomb" of the "best type of Eton boy",[614] or for displaying "a sort of

* In a modern history of Harrow a summary of the main refinements of sartorial privilege alone, mostly elaborated in the nineteenth century, takes about four pages to set out.[612] Mercifully the clothing shortages of two world wars curtailed their further elaboration and forced a reduction of distinctions of dress in most schools.

† A third cycle might be furnished by certain forms of military training which had a similar emphasis on the humiliation of the new recruit. Similar phenomena are seen in the 'hazing' and other traditional initiatory procedures for freshmen at some American and South African universities.[613]

quiet good manners that emulates (and surpasses very often) the Eton unembarrassment of which we are proud";[615] throughout the century this sort of self-confidence had been favourably commented on as one of the things public schools were for,[616] and it clearly had decisive value in situations such as interviews for jobs. Meanwhile happiness was in no way a necessary ingredient of the process itself. Many boys were extremely happy at school, but in general "the happiest days of one's life" was a phrase to be applied in retrospect, when the arduous process had been successfully completed, or to be likened to the intense pleasure which follows upon the exercise of knocking one's head against a wall. A man who was headmaster in turn of two public schools after 1903 was regarded as noteworthy for his aim to make it "an unwritten law that no boy might be unhappy".[617]

The parallels are striking between the process we have been describing and the initiation rites which are a characteristic of pre-literate societies, whereby the young are systematically inducted into full participation in adult life. The scholar W. J. Ong drew attention in 1959 to the extent to which the school study of the Latin language in the Renaissance period, because of the "hardening" procedures by which it was accompanied, and of other features comparable with tribal initiation processes, fulfilled some of the functions of a "puberty rite".[618] Ong makes an interesting case, but it is possible to extend his analogy to cover not just the curriculum and teaching methods but indeed the whole process of education in the Victorian public school. The Flemish anthropologist Arnold van Gannep is the foremost of a number of observers who have analysed various forms of what van Gennep called "rites de passage", among which he discerned three major phases of separation, transition and incorporation. These ritual processes are associated with what he calls "social puberty", which may have nothing to do with physiological puberty and in some cases takes place long before. His account of these rites among certain African tribes, for example, describes members of the young élite of the tribe gathered into fraternities to undergo ceremonial initiation over a period of up to six years. This involves their separation from their previous environment: they are put into seclusion and subjected to flagellation. The actual ceremonies of transition involve bodily mutilations and prolonged instruction, in the course of which they speak a special language. Among most pre-literate people, he finds, promotion of the young between age-groups is determined by physical prowess.[619] The general characteristics of such rites, as specified by van Gennep and others, include the creation of a special environment, distinct from home, for the initiates;* the elaboration of special forms of unlicenced and special taboos, and, by contrast, the specific relaxation of normal taboos (including sex taboos) for the period of claustration; the symbolic tearing-away of the initiate from mother and home, and from all womenfolk—activities and rituals involving pain, hardening and actual mutilation, which serve to emphasise entry into manly status; the teaching of 'indelible lessons' in tribal law, morality and custom, and initiation into new roles, under conditions of special tension and accompanied by the use of special forms of language which have to be learnt.[620]

We have noted—admittedly selectively, since primitive initiation rites have other aspects and other social functions also—those ingredients of such rites which appear to have counterparts in the process of education associated with the Victorian public-school system. The total analogy helps us to confirm that, so far from being a deterrent to parents, the aspects of cruelty, humiliation, fagging, and exposure to disease and privation which we have been examining fulfilled important functions in terms of a toughened end-product able to "stand on his own two feet", to "take hard knocks without flinching",[621]† and that other institutions in the schools similarly served to prepare pupils for new roles in adult life, for which family life was held to be an inappropriate preparation. We even have a hint as to why parents were prepared to expose their sons to

* literally *initiands*, but 'initiates' is less pedantic.

† Nearly fifty years after he had left school the successful general, Sir Ian Hamilton., wrote: "Wellington College taught me no learning, brought me no fame—that was my own fault. . .but Wellington taught me to smile whilst I was being thrashed, though the blood surged like hammer strokes through my temples; to eat whatever was chucked at me or go without; to admire without envy Athletes, Caps, the XI, and even, in a milder way, Prize-winners, and Prefects".[622]

'sin', 'vice', 'pollution', etc., in the founder of Radley's claim to have campaigned successfully against the theory which "certainly prevailed in connexion with public school life . . . that a schoolboy must needs go through a career of carelessness, irreligion, *acquaintance—familiarity rather*—with *sin and defilement*, in order to the *formation of a manly character*".[623]

What is slightly surprising is how little explicit were the Victorians, and especially those responsible for the development of public schools, in regard to the functions of all these characteristics of school life. The contempt for "coddling" about which the founder of the Woodard schools made no secret was afterwards held to justify primitive buildings, defective drains, public floggings and the tolerance of a measure of serious bullying,[624] though of course no Lancing or Hurstpierpoint prospectus ever advertised these methods or, explicitly, the end they served; and at Lancing, as at other public schools, the advance of the nineteenth century saw the progress of organised games take the place of the early compulsory fisticuffs which had contributed to this hardening process.[625] The terminology in use at some schools did make implicit reference to one of these functions: it was the custom of Winchester, for example, "to promote her sons to manhood on the day of their arrival, and the word 'boy' was seldom heard within her precincts"; new boys were "new men".[626]

Amazingly, despite the awareness of ancient history in these schools, the analogy of Sparta was seldom invoked by schoolmasters or other apologists of the system. Almond of Loretto was something of an exception to this, and at Loretto "*Spartam nactus es, hanc exorna*" was the school motto, as it had also been at Sedbergh, but the words of a school song changed this to "*Sedberghiam nactus es* . . ."[627] The awareness of anthropological analogies was of course less widespread, but even where it existed, few seemed concerned to point them out in ways which would help explain the system. R. R. Marett (born 1866), who became head of an Oxford college and who had himself attended a school which regarded itself as a public school, was a leading British anthropologist in his time. Explaining how he came to send his two sons off to a certain preparatory school around 1908, he wrote that he "thoroughly approved" of its headmaster "as one who had no use for mollycoddles, and could turn out a good scholar without neglecting Plato's rule that he must likewise learn to be manly". Marett not only knew van Gennep's work on *rites de passage*, which had appeared just before the elder son went off to school, but was a close personal friend of van Gennep's.[628] Yet the educational function to which he draw attention was illuminated by no anthropological parallel, only by a milder Athenian rather than even a Spartan one. One of the few references of any kind to be found, within the Victorian period itself, was, characteristically, by Leslie Stephen in the *Cornhill* in 1873, when he wrote:

> To be flogged in accordance with traditions handed down from hoar antiquity, and embodied in a special local jargon, is to have gone through a sacred initiatory rite.[629]

Nor, in a period which saw the publication of Darwin's *The Origin of Species* (1859) and the controversy to which it gave rise, were the arguments about public-school education laced with references to "the survival of the fittest".

This contrast between the stated functions of public schools and their latent ones is not unique to these institutions. Delicacy likewise veiled the status-conferring function of the school system, of which no headmaster or school governor boasted on prize day; instead headmasters firmly deprecated references to the market value of the Old School tie.[630] The brutal parting of sons from mothers and other womenfolk which was involved in the system—which, as we have seen, had anthropological parallels—conflicted sharply with the contemporary ideology of the family and with the presuppositions of moral educators, not least in public-school pulpits; to have acknowledged the important functions of this element in the *rite de passage* of a public-school education would have advertised the conflict of values, and the ambivalence of thinking, of those who ran these schools. While boys were encouraged to make it one of their aims in life "never to say or do anything that might cause [their] mother or sisters to blush",[631] the character of school life emphasised the separation from womenfolk. Teaching staffs in the Victorian public school were almost without exception monosexual, and in prep. schools were dominated by men; female servants and even matrons often came from the category of gorgons and harpies which tradition says were prescribed as bedmakers by the medieval statutes of Cambridge colleges, and in official school parlance were known as "hags".[632] And at schools like Rugby, for example, the wives and daughters of housemasters were expected to refer to the names of boys in their house, however small they might be, with the prefix "Mr".[633] In school the mystique of womenfolk was kept pure: in conversation, home—and particularly mothers and sisters—were taboo subjects,* and even the display of their photographs in boys' private rooms might be forbidden by school custom.[635] Similarly, by the end of the century, the use of Christian names among the boys, another reminder of home, had become largely taboo, in chilling contrast with the days of Tom Brown and Arthur.[636] "Milksop" and "molly-coddle", which we have already met in this chapter, were two frequent and significant terms of disapproval among the later Victorians: boys were sent to public schools where the rigours of the régime would stop them from being milksops and where they would be out of reach of the molly-coddling influence of women.[637]† This sort of attitude underlay the approach to the place in their curricula of aesthetic activities such as music, which was considered by some schoolmasters to be "not the sort of thing to appeal to nice manly Englishmen";[638] in any case, according to one headmaster, music "rotted the moral fibre".[639]

This whole process which, with its anthropological parallels, we have been discussing, was dedicated to the production of that entity so often on the lips of the Victorians, *character*. Yet the total end-product was more complex, involving a number of attributes besides toughness and independence—"standing on one's own feet". As has been suggested, self-confidence—especially in a social context—was

* This, too, would seem to have been a phenomenon which developed, along with the new cult of 'manliness', in the later Victorian period: back in the 1860s a new boy at Marlborough tended to be greeted with "What's your name?" and "Have you got a sister?"[634]

† The introduction of co-education in some leading public schools from the 1960s onwards represents, of course, a fundamental reversal of policy concerning what the Victorians regarded as one of the key functions of the schools.

also held to be cultivated by the system. A product of Victorian Sherborne later summed up the essentials of the system which he served, as a public-school housemaster, well into the twentieth century: "consideration for others, being at ease in any company, keeping your head in a crisis, treating servants well, courage, loyalty, respect for women, and modesty".[640] A surprisingly similar catalogue had been given by the radical journalist H. W. Nevinson (at Shrewsbury in the 1870s) when writing of the Boer War period, as being "the qualities that our family life and public school training aim at producing".[641] Consideration for others, and especially for one's subordinates, is at first sight an unlikely derivative from the sustained process of attrition to which, as has been described, boys were exposed, and which the Victorians implied by the term "knocking the rough edges off". It seems a strange assumption that a process in which boy-public opinion cruelly exposed and exploited every individual quirk and short-coming should be a fit preparation for a life-long attitude of sensitivity to other people's feelings—a perverse form of 'sensitivity training', in fact. But this is what the Victorians appear to have believed—and certainly in retrospect claimed—and they may of course have been right. Some apologists have argued that the system did not stifle individuality and have pointed to lists of war heroes, explorers, Everest climbers and other 'adventurers' who were produced by the generation of (say) Wykehamists who entered their prep. schools in the 1890s.[642] Others, more critical, have attacked the system as geared to a completely standardised product. A Wykehamist at school in the early 1920s wrote that "with the exception of a few eccentrics, [Winchester] produced a breed of almost compulsive conformists: brilliant yet safe men . . ."[643] This division of opinion may simply reflect the difference in the atmosphere of a school in the course of twenty years. Sir Francis Chichester is another witness to tendencies which may only have hardened after the end of the Victorian period. As a result of his schooldays at Marlborough (1915–1918) he would, until late in life, shake with fear at the prospect of speaking in public, "because the terror of doing or saying anything which would not be approved of by the mob was so deeply rooted in me".[644]

Yet conformity and conventionality of this degree may have been—or have become—an inevitable feature of the process.

Philippe Ariès has attributed to the English public schools the creation of the 'gentleman' as a new social type, "unknown before the nineteenth century";[645] and there is a sense in which he is right, for though the concept of the 'gentleman' was an important one long before the nineteenth century, the specifications were now changing significantly. It is possible to view the high Victorian period as one of tension between two contrasting sets of specifications of the 'gentleman'. In both, the 'gentleman' was the product of a fairly long and therefore relatively exclusive form of education. The first, and older, set, put a premium on intellectual success within a narrow range of studies; the new one's priorities were the production of 'character', self-confidence, etc. We can see an aspect of this tension operating, as late as the period around 1911, in the rift between Fletcher, headmaster of Charterhouse, and one of his chief classical masters, F. Dames Longworth. Both were first-class scholars and united in their love of classical learning. "But they differed utterly and from their roots in their conception of scholarship".[646] Fletcher, from a modest Mancunian background,[647] had been a scholarship boy at Rossall; Dames Longworth, from a gentry family, had himself been a boy at Charterhouse. "Fletcher loved learning because it was learning; Longworth loved it because it was something without which no gentleman was quite complete, a polite adjunct to the finished social article".[648] Born within a decade of one another, both regarded an intensive classical education as a necessary but not a sufficient attribute of gentlemanliness. For the older man, Longworth, it would needs be allied to birth and 'breeding'; for the younger, it would be allied to the fact of having come through the public-school system which he was to spend his whole career in serving.

Though much of our evidence[649] on the excessive conformity noticeable among public-school products relates to the post-Victorian schools, there may have been good reasons for an intensification of tendencies towards conformity from the late Victorian period onwards. Carving out an empire called for one set of values: administering it required attention to quite another set. 'Clubability' and respect for rigid social convention were equally important in all the social groupings whose heyday were in the Victorian and immediately post-Victorian period—the City boardroom and Club, the country house, the school or college Common Room, and—no less important—the regimental mess and Indian hill-station. A world which was becoming smaller, involving Englishmen in dealings with Continentals, Americans, orientals and suchlike, put a premium on shared values, predictable social and political behaviour, and, for these, public-school membership offered some means of ready identification. Back in the 1860s, criticism of the newly established system of recruitment to the Indian Civil Service, by open competitive examinations in place of patronage, gave a foretaste of the criteria which would come to be judged pre-eminent by the end of the century, and it also offers a commentary on the contrasting specifications of the 'gentleman' that have been postulated above.

The type of objection raised against the new system was that it recruited men who were "shy, retiring, and socially inept", lacking in social graces, and inconsiderate in their treatment of their subordinates, neither riding, shooting, dancing, nor playing cricket—at their worst, having the character of "milksops".[650] An examination syllabus which emphasised the classics failed to ensure the recruitment of men, who, together with "the ordinary education of a gentleman", had "the habits and principles of a gentleman"; it did not keep out "very clever fellows" who were "not up to the mark and manners in conversation"; in particular, it failed to keep out "well crammed youths from Irish universities or commercial schools".[651] Interestingly, the authorities' first remedy was to increase the classical content of the examination—adding more marks for Latin and Greek.[652] But soon they began to look at other criteria. In 1865 they had been seeking to recruit the "best cultivated", "well-educated" young men, without regard to the type of institution where these qualities had been imparted; by 1876 the ideal candidate was "the man who got a second or double third, rowed in the college boat, played in the cricket team and made his mark at the union".[653] And significantly, it was the Harrow housemaster Edward Bowen who in 1877 proposed for entrants to the Indian army and Civil Service an additional examination in physical fitness. This must not be (he argued) in those accomplishments in which boys could be specially coached, such as riding or shooting, but in general fitness

—"those physical excellencies which are natural and customary among all boys or all youths"—or rather, as he should have admitted, among all boys in the public schools, which were already being given over to the systematic pursuit of athleticism.[654] (Some of Bowen's proposals were in fact adopted.) Thus were laid down specifications to which both public schools and universities responded warmly, with consequences for the future character of the recruitment of British colonial administrators which were neatly summed up in the 1930s in the stated ambition of a Shrewsbury boy at Oxford—"I shall row myself into the Sudan, a country of Blacks ruled by Blues".[655]

A similar development had involved army recruitment. In the wake of the Crimean War, Britain's military academies were between 1855 and 1858 opened to competitive entry, on the basis of increasingly stiff examination requirements, and during the 1870s all officer entry began to be on a competitive basis, signalled by the abolition of the purchase of commissions in 1871. However, in 1869 the first Dufferin Commission Report noted that "some of the smartest and most capable officers of the army have been furnished direct from the public schools *without having exhibited any scholastic efficiency*";[656] and this emphasis on the qualities held to be produced in the public schools* persisted in the selection of officers, so that in the First World War, and to some extent in the Second, a commission was the expected rank of a public-school product. All that these reforms really achieved, at least within the Victorian period, was

* It might be imagined that of all public schools those designed to prepare boys for careers in the armed services would have been most open in their emphasis on 'toughening'. Indeed, at Wellington, "started by the Prince Consort as a semi-military academy" in 1859, and two-fifths of whose pupils of the first twenty years became army officers, the original plans had been for a severe training "to harden [boys] for the Service", as at "other institutions where the boys were supposed to be rendered impervious to pain—with a view to active service". But toughness in itself was not enough: future officers must also be gentlemen, and the efforts of the first two headmasters, Benson and Wickham, were directed to persuading the reluctant governors to allow the strengthening of the classical side, the attraction to the school of more fee-payers, and the fostering of all those activities and institutions which would enable the school to "develop entirely into *a public school like the others*".[657]

the certification of minimum academic competence. In fact, the introduction of competitive examinations for entry to the I.C.S., the army and (especially after 1870) the Home Civil Service, while appearing to give advantage to strict academic merit, served only to draw attention to schooling; and, as among the various kinds of schooling available, the system favoured that kind which was associated with the status of a gentleman.

As the contrast widened between the old specifications of the 'gentleman', based on classical learning leavened by Christianity, and the new gentlemanliness fashioned by games-playing and the other hardening processes of the public school, occasional voices were heard proclaiming the need to reconcile the two. Thus Dr Potts, headmaster of Fettes and a former Rugby master, declared:

> I should like my boys, and all boys, and all men, to be ever mindful, in the hottest scrimmage and at the most exciting period of the game, that they are not only football players but also Christian gentlemen.[658]

There were two essential features of this new development in the specifications of a 'gentleman'. First, the desired product was the result of an education whose essence was not the *content* but the *process*: not *what* was taught but the *manner* of the training. Addressing an Old Etonian dinner in 1916, General Plumer, soon to be a Field Marshal and a Viscount, looked back at the character of the education he had received at the school he had left forty years before: "We are often told that they taught us nothing at Eton. It may be so, but *I think they taught it very well*".[659] It was indeed this new emphasis on the process which was being undergone, in preference to the subject-matter imparted, which made possible the relaxation of the grip of the classics on the public schools' curriculum at the end of the Victorian period. Secondly, one of the key functions of the process was to produce an *identifiable élite*, a community of men who recognised in each other a similarity of outlook, values and code of honour because they shared a similar type of boyhood experience in what was becoming, in effect, a community of schools. Thus it fulfilled what by 1872 the founder of Radley had come to recognise, after twenty-five years of that school's existence, as "one of the many great uses of our public schools"—"to confer an aristocracy on boys who do not inherit it".[660]

17. A new aristocracy.

The growth of this community of schools and their products, and the elaboration of the marks of identification by which the new élite of 'gentlemen' could recognise one another, were a feature of the development of public-school education as a *system* in the later Victorian period, and the emergence thereby of a wider community than simply the products of individual schools: the community of 'public-school men', the entrée to which may be interpreted as the last stage, *incorporation*, of the whole *rite de passage*. This wider community came into being at the time when, as we have noted, Englishmen were being brought into ever closer contact with 'foreigners' of various kinds in situations which demanded scrutiny of each other's values and background; furthermore, within Britain itself, this was a time of accelerated social change which saw, among other things, the decline of English provincial society, much greater movement between social classes, and the decay of country-house society as a form of social organisation exercising important political, literary, and even religious and ideological influence.[661]

John Henry Newman had drawn attention[662] in 1854 to the influence available to the community of graduates of Oxford and Cambridge scattered all over the country. This community was institutionalised in the establishment around 1830 of London clubs such as the United University and the Oxford and Cambridge.[663] By the end of the century a public-school education provided a criterion for ready recognition of common values among a much wider section of society than just Oxford and Cambridge graduates. Public-school boys would give jobs not just to products of their own old schools but to the recognisable products of public schools generally. Already in the 1880s a young man could offer this in lieu of a graduate qualification for a post in a private school:

> Vicar's son wants junior mastership. Public School boy. Good athlete. County Football. First class references . . .[664]

and in the twentieth century men wanting any kind of job would offer the credential "public-school boy" to employment agencies and in advertisements for jobs*. Though a public-school education, generally following on attendance at a preparatory school, conventionally lasted four or five years, at Clifton (for example) in the first decade of this century there were boys entering at age sixteen, seventeen, or even eighteen, to stay for a few terms in the fourth or fifth forms before going off into army or business careers.[666] They thus became 'public-school men'. with all the attendant advantages in later life.

The term 'public-school' came to be a useful label of general social acceptability. A Public Schools Winter Sports Club was founded in 1905 (public-school masters, including some well-known headmasters, had been prominent in the passion for 'Alpinism' which began soon after the middle of the nineteenth century). The Club's objects were "to secure the presence at one or more Swiss resorts during the winter season of a congenial society of people interested in small winter sports . . . Ladies and gentlemen are eligible for membership". In fact, their criteria for election were very accommodating—a candidate had to be a "public school or university man" (schools unspecified) *or* should hold or have held a commission in the army or navy, *or* be the daughter, sister or wife of one of these categories; but in fact any person "of distinction" could be invited to be a member of the Club.[667]

Englishmen overseas found public-school membership a convenient credential when deciding with which of their compatriots they would choose to interact. As we have seen, there were reunions among the Old Boys of individual schools in India and elsewhere, but there was not always a big enough representation in one place to form a distinct organisation for each school. In Cape Colony they overcame the difficulty that only four or five men attended each local Old Etonian or Old

* It is significant that the registers of the Royal Military Academy, Woolwich (founded in 1741), began in 1900 to record the previous schooling of entrants,[665] and that in the year 1904 *Crockford's Clerical Directory* made its first (and only) attempt to indicate the schooling (in addition to the university and theological training) of Anglican clergy: such was the value of, and the interest in, this new credential.

Wellingtonian dinner by founding an "Old Public School Boys' Association" in 1898. But their main motive was not merely festive:

> The chief reason is as follows: a large number of Public School boys who had been failures at home, but really good fellows in the main, are sent out here to make a fresh start. Often and often [*sic*] these men fall into vice, being away from all home influences, and go from bad to worse, and become irreclaimable. It was felt that much could be done to give a helping hand to such as these before it was too late.

This task of moral reclamation was carried forward by the Association's committee whose president was the Archbishop of Cape Town, with an Old Cheltonian as secretary. Periodical meetings of the Association, keeping contact with the Old Schools, an annual festival, and support for a local good cause were all methods designed to "cement relations between Old Public School boys of the British Isles resident in South Africa".[668]

In England for perhaps a century now, the most important superficial index of social class has been speech. With a few exceptions (notably some forms of Scottish accent)[669] regional accents have carried certain social disabilities outside the regions concerned, ever since the emergence in the Victorian period of standard English pronunciation (the phoneticians' "RP")—itself the product of the public-school system.[670] It was common for eminent products of the public schools in the first half of the nineteenth century to retain regional accents, which also outlasted their university days. This was true of Sir Robert Peel (Harrow and Oxford), of the fourteenth Earl of Derby (Prime Minister; Eton and Oxford) and of the fifteenth Earl (Rugby under Arnold, and Cambridge),[671] who spoke, according to his colleague Disraeli, "a sort of Lancashire patois".[672] Gladstone's boyhood in Liverpool, in the days before 'scouse' had developed, lent to his speech a "Lancastrian burr" which survived Eton and Oxford and, together with other idiosyncratic forms, made his speaking voice very attractive.[673] Frederick Temple (Blundells and Oxford) had a "marked provincial accent"[674] which Rugby boys attempted to reproduce by "Bies, yer getting ruude: this must cease";[675] and among other public-school headmasters who retained strong regional accents after Oxford were Mitchinson of King's School, Canterbury, (a "harsh Durham accent"[676]) and Percival of Clifton and Rugby (a lingering Cumberland accent).[677]* At least two heads of Oxford colleges at the end of the century, Fowler and Warren, spoke with regional accents.[679] Sir Herbert Warren's much-quoted admiration for the well-born had not led him to abandon traces of his West-Country speech which had survived Clifton (in the 1860s) and Magdalen;[680] the Lincolnshire-born Fowler,† President of Corpus, had been a school-fellow of Dean Farrar at King William's, Isle of Man.

All this is not to deny that certain regional forms of speech had attracted some prejudice in the earlier period. The Yorkshire squire who in 1778 was seeking to recruit for his children a new tutor "who can correct their Yorkshire tone"[682] may have been more sensitive about local usage and intonation than about accent as such; and there have always been prejudices, on sheer aesthetic grounds, against certain regional accents compared to others. When Thomas Arnold brought a twelve-year-old boy back from the Midlands to his coaching establishment at Laleham in 1820, he commented that "the very sound of his Nottinghamshire accent is pleasant to my ears in this land of cockneys",[683] which merely tells us that Arnold liked one set of sounds and, in common with one of his successors at Rugby, disliked others.

The form of English pronunciation which earned widest acceptance as an index of social and educational background by 1900 was that standardised and transmitted by public schools, especially those in the south of England, in the later Victorian period. The Rev. J. L. Joynes, Eton master (1849–77) and the scourge of Swinburne, pronounced 'died' as 'doyed' and in sermons castigated the 'oidle',[684] but by the 1890s a new generation

* Percival's pupils noted that at on occasion this became very strong, as when he was angry, or as in his favourite exhortation "Dawn't live the life of a cabbage, maan!" and in his fulminations against "law tawn" (low tone).[678]

† In addition to his regional accent, Fowler never learned to control his aitches, as in his account of his first arrival in Greece: "I 'opped up the 'atchway, and said 'ail Hathens".[681]

of masters at the school would rebuke a Norfolk* boy for his 'loike' for 'like'—"Keep your eyes (i's) pure, Wodehouse!"[686]

But transmission of the approved accent was less a matter of conscious teaching than of assimilation from one's peers. At Bedford Modern School from the 1880s onwards local boys with a North Bedfordshire accent "were so mercilessly imitated and laughed at that, if they had any intelligence, they were soon able to speak standard English".[687] Yet it was not so much a matter of intelligence as of 'ear', which put a premium on early exposure to the right accent, and this emphasised the importance of the preparatory school and of course of boarding schools generally. Only those with a good 'ear' could hope to make the required adjustment in later life—at Oxford, for example, where by around 1900 it was virtually a condition of social equality among undergraduates that one must "speak the Queen's English with a specific accent and intonation".[688] When F. E. Smith arrived at Oxford from Birkenhead School in 1890 his Wadham contemporaries noticed he had an accent "that would rival Gracie Fields", but, discovering its disadvantages, he succeeded in curing himself of it "in about six weeks, and indeed developed a tendency to preciosity".[689] These 'disadvantages' were making themselves felt in many spheres by 1900†. Walker, High Master of St Paul's until 1905, used to talk of a pupil of his at Manchester Grammar School (where he had been head 1859–77) "who would have been a bishop if he could have learned to pronounce 'sugar' otherwise than to rhyme with 'lugger'."[692]‡

* Cf. George Borrow's reference to the people of Norfolk, who "speak the purest English".[685]

† In his autobiography, Sir Ernest Baker wrote of the humble circumstances of his boyhood: "I spoke the dialect of North-East Cheshire, which was much the same as that of Lancashire... It was not till I was 17 that I weaned myself from the use of dialect, and forced myself, even at home, to speak something that sounded like English. I lost many riches of vocabulary in the process..."[690] But *cf.* the account of Barker in 1919 by (Sir) Maurice Bowra: "He spoke with a strong Lancashire accent, but was thought to have learned it after he came as a scholar to Balliol from Manchester Grammar School. Anyhow he indulged it freely, and his remarks got much of their savour from it".[691]

‡ In modern times, it was not until 1959 that a suffragan bishop was appointed with a strong non-U (in fact, cockney) accent.

The declining prestige of local accents made a public-school education a necessity for ambitious parents who could not guarantee the right accent for their children at home and in the local school. The extension of secondary education in 1902 reinforced the demand for boarding public-school education among parents who might previously have been satisfied with the local school but to whom the new social mixture offered the danger that their children would "pick up an accent".[693] There was a similar reaction after 1944, and the replacement of grammar by comprehensive schools from the 1960s onwards has confronted yet more professional parents with a reason to desert the state system altogether.

Yet the function of public schools with regard to accent must not be exaggerated. Some public schools have always had a strong representation of boys and even some masters with marked regional accents—this was true of Rossall at the beginning of this century[694] and has been the case there ever since. Nevertheless we would expect to find the greatest concentration of public schools in the south of England, especially the southeast where variations between the local accent and 'standard English pronunciation' were less general and often less marked, so that any strong representation of local accents in a school would not be too noticeable.

When the pattern of pronunciation as standardised in the public schools was becoming the common medium of the educated, public-school boys developed a new device for recognising each other—the special language of 'public-school slang'. Every major school already had its special vocabulary requiring special induction courses for new boys: Winchester with its 'notions'[695]* (for example) and Christ's Hospital with the rich jargon of its comparative isolation in London were particularly extensive.[697] But the various forms had enough in common by the end of the period for it to be possible for any boy from the leading schools to get the drift of

* *Cf.* Martin Benson writing home as a new boy from Winchester in 1874: "I have been learning no end of slang. Guess what this means—'You brockster, to splice hollises at a man's duck. . .' " (you bully, to throw stones at a boy's face).[696]

'Twas Banco; and the keelie Hoips
Did snook and waffle in the pupe;
All puffy were the Ostiars,
And the home-bugs outgloope

—though difficulties could be resolved by recourse to J. S. Farmer's "Public School Word Book" (1900), from which the above verse was compiled by the *Public School Magazine*.[698]

The most widely diffused form of public-school slang was what came to be known to lexicographers as the "Oxford *-er*"—the abridgement of a word and the addition of the syllable -er, or -ers, which gave Oxford words like 'the Giler' for St Giles and 'Rudders' as the nickname of the examination in the Rudiments of Faith and Religion.[699] Its impact on Cambridge was less marked, though 'bedder' and 'cuppers' became general. This form "got itself generally into upper-middle-class speech",[700] and its influence in popular speech is seen in the adoption in common usage of rugger, soccer, header (dive head first), boater and topper; 'greaters' or 'congraters' (for congratulations) were common among those who wished to imitate the usage of Rugby[701] or Eton[702] schoolboys around 1900. Introduced at Oxford by about 1875, it was an established fashion in the university by 1883* and had appeared at Durham University by 1881. But in fact it seems to have been 'invented' at Harrow around 1870, and that school popularised what must surely have been the finest flower of the species—"wagger-pagger-bagger" for waste-paper basket.[703]

Public-school fiction popularised these forms of special language and made them available to those who cared to learn. The higher circles of polite society guarded against invasion by those who had mastered such more freely available forms of accent and usage by maintaining even finer peculiarities of both.

* The *Diary* (Oxford, 1969) for 1911–12 of Oxford undergraduate W. Elmhirst (Malvern and Worcester) uses the following forms throughout: fresher, brekker (breakfast), footer, bedder (bed*room*), leccer (lecture), colleccer (collection, *i.e.* college examination), togger (training practice), hence togger brekker; the Ugger for the Union. Personal names are similarly treated—Puggers for Pearson and Jaggers for Jesus (College). An Oxford don explained to the present writer in the 1960s that the vintage of Oxford men could be identified as before or after 1939 depending on whether they spoke of "the Giler" for St Giles.

At the turn of the century the Countess of Munster (born in 1830, a grand-daughter of King William IV), wrote her memoirs, in which she included a section which discussed some of the refinements which distinguished the true members of polite society:

> The pronunciation of the word 'girl' is . . . a test. The higher classes pronounce it as if it were spelt 'gairl' whereas the [vulgar] pronounce it as if it were spelt 'gurl' . . . Certain expressions . . . unmistakably proclaim themselves. For instance, a bridegroom who informs you that he is going to *get* married, instead of 'going to be married'. Then what is more grating to one's feelings than to hear of people 'riding in their carriages' instead of 'driving' . . .[704]

The distinctions of usage in our own time between 'U' and non-'U', identified by Prof. Alan Ross and popularised by Nancy Mitford since 1955,[705] remind us of the persistence of differences between those aspects of socially acceptable behaviour which are fairly readily assimilable and those which are a good index of social origins because they are so difficult to learn. Upper-class speech forms persisted beyond the end of the Victorian period to create distinctions even among members of the community of 'public-school men': the dropping of the final 'g' in 'ing'—a characteristic of both Hornby and Warre at Eton[706]* survived during this century among those who went huntin' and shootin'. The early nineteenth-century aristocratic habit of giving words like 'grass' a short A as in 'bat'[708] was evident in Lord Curzon, and archaisms like orficer (officer) and yaller (yellow), such as were natural to Gladstone,[709] survived the public-schools' standardisation of 'RP' to indicate real social quality. Only the very top public schools, frequented by those of the highest social class, could be expected to prepare boys to observe all these very fine kinds of distinction; attendance at one of the more aristocratic Oxford or Cambridge colleges, provided one gained admission to the right set, might also help achieve this.

* *E.g.* the homily from Warre around 1898, this time not about sexual morality, which sounded to the boys like "Dere's an evil elephant [*sc.* element] come into de school. Nobody saw it come in. It came in bit by bit. But we must stamp on it, and destroy it. It's de elephant of bettin' and gamblin'."[707]

We can see, therefore, that entry into the very highest positions was made easiest for those whose privileges of birth and familiarity with a range of refinements of speech over and above 'RP' blended with school experience to form the 'public-school manner' which some observers have claimed to identify as distinctive of the products of the most famous schools.[710] But at a lower level, for certain limited purposes of recognition and interaction, a common accent and certain forms or language were important criteria for identification among the community of 'public-school men'.

CHAPTER FOUR

The Public-Schools Community at the end of the Victorian Period

1

" 'Where were you at school?' was the first question asked . . . of applicants for salaried appointments," wrote Lord Ernle[1] of the period from *c.* 1870 onwards.* For answers to this question to have had any significance—and we know that they could be crucial—presupposed some kind of consensus or conventional knowledge about the comparative standing of schools in that period and, in particular, about the applicability of the term 'public school'. In the last chapter we noted the emergence, during the last three decades of the nineteenth century, of a generalised category of 'public-school men'. Accent, manner and speech forms were necessary but not sufficient credentials for acceptance as being in this category for purposes of any serious forms of interaction, and the development in this period of distinctive Old School ties would not in itself resolve, but only make more urgent the need for an answer to, the vital question *which schools would have counted as public schools?*

The same question is difficult enough to answer even today when we have a Headmasters' Conference, representation on which has come in the twentieth century to be accepted as definitive in some sense of a school's right to be considered a public school—though that criterion is a very blunt tool since it allows no distinction of status as between schools like Eton,

* This may still be the case today. A writer from All Souls College, Oxford, claimed recently that England is perhaps the only country in the world "where the first testing question, whether from prospective employer or potential mother-in-law, is more likely to be 'Where did he go to school?' than 'Where does he come from' or 'What did his father do?' "[2]

Battersea Grammar School, Marlborough and Leeds Modern School, all of which are or have been HMC schools in recent times, or even as between Eton and Manchester Grammar School. Indeed, the British sociologist Ian Weinberg, writing in 1967, stated baldly that "the schools on the HMC are not all public schools" and went on to say that in his judgement as a sociologist "there are 84 public schools".[3]*

In Tom Brown's day, and indeed up to about 1870, it was relatively simple. Only nine schools could, strictly speaking, claim the title of public school, though several other schools, founded in the 1840s to give a public-school education, would have been classed with them. The term in its loose sense was widely and indiscriminately applied in the nineteenth century: private and grammar schools, boarding and day, were included in a wide general category of public schools by various writers.[4] But purists, at any rate by 1861, were given an opportunity to hold that the strict sense of the term applied only to the nine schools studied by the Clarendon Commission in 1861–4—Charterhouse, Eton, Harrow, Merchant Taylors', Rugby, St Paul's, Shrewsbury, Westminster and Winchester.[5] Yet even the right of all these schools to be regarded as public schools was not invariably accepted. In 1818 a challenge to Westminster from Charterhouse to play them at cricket was "very properly refused, not only on account of [Charter-houses's] being such inferior players, but also because it was thought beneath Westminster to accept the challenge from a private school". A second refusal, couched in slightly less open terms, is dated 1829, but in 1850, by which time the headmaster of Westminster was a Carthusian, the match took place.[6] Harrow boys of the 1840s are reported as recognising as public schools only Eton, Harrow, Winchester, Westminster and Charterhouse; Rugby was admitted to the list only after Harrow's new headmaster, C. J. Vaughan (a Rugbeian), had made himself acceptable. Harrow boys enjoyed quoting a story that when Eton was challenged by Rugby to play a cricket match the Eton captain's reaction was "Rugby, Rugby . . . well, we'll think about it if you'll tell me where it is".[7]

* The HMC in 1967 numbered some 210 schools in the British Isles.

By 1860, however, the claims of Charterhouse, Eton, Harrow, Rugby, Westminster and Winchester were well established and were strengthened by regular cricket fixtures in the 1850s among Eton, Harrow and Winchester on the one hand and between Westminster and Charterhouse on the other. The right of those two of the Clarendon schools which were essentially day schools (St Paul's and Merchant Taylors') was always less secure, and Shrewsbury's right to inclusion was also less certain. *Bell's Life* for 24th March 1866 printed the exchange between the cricket captains of Shrewsbury and Westminster a few weeks earlier:[8]

The Schools, Shrewsbury.
February 27, 1866.

Dear Sir,

I write to ask if a match between Westminster and Shrewsbury can be arranged for this season? The most convenient date for us would be any day in the week beginning June 17. We shall be happy to play on any ground in London which you may select.

Yours, etc.,
J. Spencer Phillips, Capt.

To the Captain of the Westminster Eleven.

Westminster, March 5, 1866.

Sir,

The Captain of the Westminster Eleven is sorry to disappoint Shrewsbury, but Westminster plays no schools except Public Schools, and the general feeling in the school quite coincides with that of the Committee of the Public Schools Club, who issue this list of public schools—Charterhouse, Eton, Harrow, Rugby, Westminster and Winchester.

Yours truly,
E. Oliver, Capt.

To the Captain of the Shrewsbury Eleven.

together with Shrewsbury's icy riposte:

The Schools, Shrewsbury.
March 9, 1866.

Sir,

I cannot allow your answer to my first letter to pass unnoticed. I have only to say that a school, which we have Camden's authority for stating was the most important school in England at a time when Westminster was unknown, which Her Majesty has included in the list of public schools by the royal commission, and which, according to the report of the commissioners, is more distinctly public than any other school, cannot be deprived of its rights as a public school by the assertions of a Westminster boy, or by the dictum of the self-styled Public Schools Club. I regret to find from your letter that the Captain of the Westminster Eleven has yet to learn the first lesson of a true public school education, the behaviour due from one gentleman to another.

I am, Sir, your obedient Servant,
J. Spencer Phillips.

To the Captain of the Westminster Eleven.

The Public Schools Club referred to in that exchange was an attempt to found a club for members of those six schools only. In 1865 they had advertised in the *Times*:

> PUBLIC SCHOOLS CLUB: The committee will proceed to Elect, on or before 5th April, 50 additional Members. Gentlemen who have been educated at Charterhouse, Eton, Harrow, Westminster and Winchester are alone eligible. Apply to the Secretary, 17 St James's Place, SW.[9]

But the attempt proved abortive, and the Public Schools Club, in the sense of a residential club with its own premises (at 100 Piccadilly) was the creation of 1909.[10] Yet the query about Shrewsbury remained, and a speaker in a House of Commons debate in 1868 referred to Shrewsbury as "on the boundary line . . . between the public schools usually so called and the other endowed schools of the country".[11]

And it must be recognised that both the Clarendon Commissioners and some of their witnesses appeared to recognise the arbitrariness of the choice of the nine, for the Commissioners also took some note of newer types of public school and considered evidence concerning Marlborough, Cheltenham and Wellington, as well as evidence on two "great metropolitan" day schools, the City of London School and King's College School. Witnesses found it difficult to stick to the Commission's original distinction: some spoke or wrote as though they obviously regarded Marlborough as in the same category as the nine; another recognised a category of "schools in England of the class just below the large public schools", in which category he appeared to place Merchant Taylors', despite that school's inclusion in the nine. Yet another, in evidence to the Commission, submitted a list of data on "the various public schools" which considered not only the nine but also King Edward's Birmingham, Bromsgrove, Cheltenham, Christ's Hospital, City of London, King's College School, Repton and Rossall.[12]

The publication of the Commissioners' Report (which foreshadowed legislation on seven of the nine schools—the Public Schools Act of 1868) furnished abundant material for Howard Staunton's compilation on the *Great Schools of England* (1865). But he too departed from the Commission's brief by including Christ's Hospital to make up the ten "Great Endowed Schools of England" and then adding a short account of Cheltenham, Marlborough, Rossall, Wellington, and the newly-reorganised Dulwich.[13]

The recognition even by the Commissioners of the existence of other public schools became more general over the next thirty years, during which the "charmed circle" of the Clarendon schools was "very considerably enlarged", to deny which, an Harrovian of this period conceded, "would be affectation and impertinence".[14] The schools most obviously qualified for admission to this circle were the foundations of 1841 onwards; as examples of which, by 1880, the writer T. H. S. Escott nominated Marlborough, Cheltenham, Leamington, Brighton, Bath, Malvern, and Clifton as being among "a host of new claimants, throughout the country, for the honours and prestige which the nine public schools used to divide among them".[15]

The "host of new claimants" for public-school status by the end of the Victorian period comprised a wide variety of schools of a type whose establishment or transformation has been referred to—they included the expensive proprietary boarding schools such as Escott named; cheaper, 'middle-class' boarding schools such as those founded by J. L. Brereton and the County School movement, and by the Anglo-Catholic Woodard; endowed 'grammar' schools, whether country boarding schools or big city day schools, which had been transformed on the initiative of an outstanding headmaster or as a result of reorganisation by the Endowed Schools Commissioners and their successors; and some 'middle-class' urban day schools. Beyond these there were some private schools educating boys up to eighteen years of age which by the end of the century, despite their 'private enterprise' character, had come to be regarded in some sense as public schools. Sending some of its pupils up to the universities might give a school a claim to be a public school in the very loosest sense, but the only essential common characteristic of the many categories of schools competing for the status of 'public school' around 1900 was that they were all boys' schools.

In 1897 there were nearly 2,000 boys' secondary schools in *England*, but this figure includes a very large number of private schools, including preparatory schools.[16] The much narrower category of *boys'* schools *having some pupils aged eighteen and over* contains 253 schools of an endowed or proprietary character, 7 local authority schools and 177 private schools, a total of 437 schools.[17] In Wales and Monmouthshire, Scotland, Ireland, the Channel Islands and the Isle of Man, for which comparable statistics are not available but where the proportion of such schools may have been smaller than in England, the number of boys' secondary schools might increase the total to around 600 schools or more.

Which, out of this total of possibly 600 schools, were to be regarded as 'public schools' by the end of the Victorian period? This was a question which the Victorians themselves had not answered by 1900. Some kind of answer became more necessary after the turn of the century when the wider community of public-school Old Boys became more established and it became necessary to scrutinise the antecedents of those educated—especially before 1900—in them, and who claimed membership of that community.

Those six Clarendon schools whose public-school status would have been unchallenged by, say, 1870 may be described as a 'short-list' of public schools; the mass of schools to whom this term was much more loosely applied may be described as a 'long-list'. In classifying public schools, the characteristic of a short-list is that its members' claims to inclusion are more or less equal, whereas a long-list contains schools whose claims to inclusion are grossly unequal. By this definition it is possible to have a short-list of schools of more or less equal claim to inclusion, extended by the addition of many further short-lists of schools more or less equal to each other, until all the groups together constitute a long-list in which the schools of the first constituent group are grossly unequal to those of the last. It is thus feasible to conceive of the nine Clarendon schools as comprising around 1870 an extended short-list (6 + 3) and the mass of all schools with any claim to public-school status as a long-list. In any classification of twentieth-century public schools, Eton, Harrow, Marlborough and Clifton would be on almost any short-list (though only two of them on the shortest) whereas Manchester Grammar School, Strathallan, City of London School, and Solihull School would be on some classifiers' extended short-lists and not on many others, but might feature in a large number of long-lists, at least in the 1970s.

The terms short-list and long-list are an essential tool in our present consideration of the limits of the public-school community as it was seen by the late Victorians and as it has been seen by social and political historians since then. This chapter examines a number of criteria by which schools might have claimed to be included in either short-lists or long-lists of public schools in a period which, as will be shown, is crucial for the study of twentieth-century British élites.

2

One possible determinant of 'public-school' status (at least in a general sense) for the Victorians was academic success as measured by examination results.

In the 1880s and 1890s newspapers like the *Pall Mall Gazette* and the *Daily News* examined what they called the "Public School Record" and tabulated the examination successes of the various schools whose pupils won entrance scholarships to Oxford and Cambridge or had scored the most successes in the Higher Certificate examination of the Oxford and Cambridge Board (whose results were regularly tabulated in the *Guardian* in the 1890s) and in the army entrance examinations.

In *Table 1*, an Oxford and Cambridge scholarship 'success table' is set out, indicating the twenty-two most successful

Table 1. Top 77 Schools by Oxford and Cambridge Scholarship Success 1885–92

A 22 Schools 20–100 Scholarships	B 39 Schools 10–19 Scholarships	C 16 Schools 6–9 Scholarships
d St. Paul's•	Bristol GS•, Oundle	Boston
d Merchant Taylors'•	Cheltenham, Durham	Brecon (Christ)
Clifton	Repton, Llandovery	Lancing
d Manchester GS	•Uppingham, Haileybury	Bromsgrove
Marlborough	•Blundell's, Derby	Berkhamsted
Eton•, Winchester•	Sherborne, Bradfield	Newcastle HS (Staffs)
d Dulwich	Highgate, Hereford	KWC (Isle of Man)
Westminster•	King's CS, St Peter's (Yk)	Newton (Abbot) C
Christ's Hospital	Aldenham, Oxford HS	Fettes
Charterhouse, Rugby	Kingswood, Worcester KS•	Giggleswick
d City of London	St. Bees, Tonbridge	Merchants Ts' (Crosby)
d Bradford GS	Blackheath, Weymouth	Wyggeston
Bath, Rossall	Felsted, Radley, Wellington	Epsom
d KES Birmingham	Portsmouth GS, Magd. CS Oxford	Eastbourne
Shrewsbury	St J. Leatherhd, Leys,	Exeter
Harrow	Liverpool C, Sedbergh	Nottingham HS
d Bedford	Leeds GS, Wakefield GS•	
d St Olave's•	Leamington, Ipswich	
Malvern	Canterbury KS, Carlisle GS	

Schools are arranged in rough order of merit, schools with most scholarships at the top of each column.
d indicates those of the leading 22 scholarship-producing schools which were specified by the *Pall Mall Gazette* as 'mainly day' schools.
• indicates those schools whose totals contained a proportion of *closed* awards.
(Compiled from the annual 'scholarship success tables' in the *Pall Mall Gazette*, 1885–92).

schools, with twenty scholarships or more in six years in the period 1885–92, and including St Paul's with one-hundred awards; thirty-nine schools with between ten and nineteen awards; and sixteen schools with six to nine awards in that period. Among these seventy-seven schools the Clarendon nine are creditably represented, even if in many cases the awards were 'closed'.[18] But the new foundations did well too, particularly Clifton, Marlborough and Bath College. In 1887–8 Bath, a school of only one hundred boys, gained more scholarships than Eton, a school then of over nine hundred.[19] Another feature of these lists that the press was at pains to emphasise was the success of day schools—of the top twenty-two scholarship-winning schools, nine (including St Paul's) were "mainly day schools".

There is plenty of evidence that headmasters took these results tables seriously, though the impression they made on parents was less marked. If academic results had been *their* main criterion, the *Pall Mall Gazette* pointed out, "the biggest schools should be those who win the most scholarships: in fact, it is rather the other way . . . Take two West Country schools, and see whether failure to win scholarships has emptied the one, or success filled the other.[20]

The Oxford and Cambridge Higher Certificate examination was established in 1874 partly as a result of pressures from the Headmasters' Conference,[21] and this was the Board whose examinations featured in the discussions of later Conferences. These certificates had the advantage that they could exempt their holders from important preliminary examinations at Oxford, Cambridge, the Inns of Court and similar professional institutions. The identities of the main schools regularly presenting candidates for this Higher Certificate in the six years 1892–1897 are indicated by symbols used to mark schools in *Tables 4* and *5* below, and some other schools whose pupils were similarly entered are included in *Table 6*. The schools thus identified include nearly all[22] the schools which are leading public schools by other criteria (see *Table 4*), and the presentation of candidates for the Oxford and Cambridge Higher Certificate thus offered lesser schools an opportunity to compete academically with the major public schools even if they could not rival them in winning university scholarships.

The thirty schools which were most successful in presenting candidates direct for army entrance examinations (Sandhurst and Woolwich) in four years between 1892 and 1898 are indicated by a symbol in *Table 4* (twenty-nine schools) and *Table 5* (one school). All these three types of examination—university scholarships, the Higher Certificate, and army entrance—were ones in which public schools characteristically competed, and the participation in all three by schools which are leading schools by other criteria is evident in *Table 4*. In addition, *Tables 4* and *5* identify twenty-six schools singled out for mention by Mr S. M. Leathes of the Civil Service Commission, in his evidence to the MacDonnell Commission on the Civil Service in 1912, as having contributed between them a third of the successful candidates in Class I competition for the Civil Service (including ICS) in the five years 1906–10.[23] Nearly all these post-university candidates can be assumed to have been at their public schools before 1902. (twenty-five of the twenty-six schools named by Leathes are leading public schools by other criteria.)

3

In the twentieth century, as we have already noted, the criterion for being regarded as at least a long-list public school has been the school's representation, through its headmaster, on the Headmasters' Conference. The Conference was founded in 1869 on the initiative of Thring and others in order to form a "defensive phalanx"[24] among headmasters of endowed schools against clauses originally in the Endowed Schools (No. 2) Bill which would have had the effect of limiting the independence of headmasters, particularly in such matters as their choice of assistant masters. The schools represented at the first meeting of the Conference in the Schoolroom at Uppingham on 21st December 1869 were Bromsgrove, Bury St Edmunds, King's School Canterbury, Felsted, Lancing, Liverpool College, Norwich, Oakham, Repton, Richmond (Yorks), Sherborne, Tonbridge, and Uppingham. Out of the total of thirty-seven "leading schools of England" whom Thring had invited, nine others besides these thirteen had expressed willingness to join: City of London, Christ's Hospital, Dulwich, Durham, Ipswich, Highgate, Marlborough, Magdalen College School Oxford, and St Peter's York.

Pears of Repton, Butler of Liverpool and Welldon of Tonbridge urged upon the Conference the necessity of getting "the great schools" in, and of inducing the headmaster of Eton if possible to come to the next meeting, though other heads were more doubtful of the implications of association with these "great schools". At the 1870 Conference thirty-four schools were represented, including ten of the original thirteen. Among the thirty-four were Cheltenham, Clifton, Shrewsbury and Winchester; Harrow, Marlborough and Wellington were among an additional fourteen who sent apologies.

The first committee, elected in the same year, consisted of the headmasters of Winchester (chairman), Eton, Cheltenham, City of London, Harrow, Clifton, Sherborne, Repton, and Uppingham, and illustrates a dominance of the larger public schools in the committee of the HMC which lasted throughout the Victorian period and well into the twentieth century. Some headmasters, such as Howson of Holt, were in the post-Victorian period to make this dominance a matter of complaint; others such as Flecker of Dean Close School (in 1915) openly expressed satisfaction at being led by, and thus in a sense identified with, the more "celebrated" headmasters.[25]

But if the HMC had soon settled the character of its leadership, it had not yet fixed the qualifications of its membership. In its early years there were those like Ridding of Winchester who saw its role as a "club for schoolmasters"[26]—and in its very first few years assistant masters did attend. Other heads were much more concerned to use the Conference in a campaign for the defence of those endowed schools whose public-school character was threatened by state activity in the immediate form of the Endowed Schools and Charity Commissioners. This campaign would combine the weight of numbers of the threatened schools with the prestige and influence of the established public schools. The 1871 conference resolved, at the instigation of Thring, to establish "an annual meeting of the headmasters of the Highest Schools to discuss all questions affecting schools and education", the headmasters of "all schools of the First Grade, whether they be called Public Schools, Endowed Schools, Proprietary Schools or Colleges to be *ex officio* members of the Conference".[27]

Following the failure of the Endowed Schools Commission to produce their expected definition of the term 'First Grade' which had been devised by the Taunton Commissioners in their report in 1868, the Conference had by 1877 reconciled itself to leaving each case for admission to the judgment of the committee as to the character of the school and the status of its headmaster.[28] The criteria they tended to apply to new applicants were the numbers of boys in the school, the number of undergraduates from the school at the universities, and the constitution of the governing body,[29] but these principles were not enshrined in a formal constitution by the HMC until 1906.[30]

The membership of the HMC grew from fifty schools in 1871 to seventy-nine in 1886. In 1902 there were just over one hundred schools on the Conference and between 1914 and 1937 membership was limited to one-hundred and fifty, with some 'associate members' after 1930; in 1937 it was increased to two hundred.[31] The 1971 HMC list, according to *Whitaker* 1971, had two hundred and fourteen schools other than overseas schools. Whereas in 1876 Harper could identify the HMC schools as "doing the bulk of the work of middle-class education in England",[32] by 1901 the Headmasters' Association (founded 1890; later the IAHM) which represented a wider spectrum of secondary schools, especially schools of a 'second-grade' type, had five times as many members as the HMC, though from 1895 overlap in membership between the two bodies was permitted.[33]

If we take the year 1902 as an appropriate date to mark that short period (1901–3) which saw the end of Victoria's reign, the passing of an Education Act which initiated a great expansion of English secondary education, and the establishment by the HMC of a Common Entrance examination, we can say that by 1902 there existed what could be called a 'long-list' of public schools in the form of a list of headmasters who were members of the HMC. We also know that it was beginning to be so regarded: when an association of (English) public-school Old Boys was founded in Cape Colony in 1898, "great difficulty was found in defining what was a Public School. In the end it was decided that only those schools represented at or recognised by the Headmasters' Conference should be placed upon our list".[34]

4

Unfortunately, if such a long-list existed, it was not readily available. The HMC did not publish a list every year, and no list for 1902 seems to have survived, even at the secretariat of the HMC, though a hypothetical list has been compiled from other sources and checked against the list of headmasters who actually *attended*[35] the Conference in the six years 1898–1903.

By 1914 the *Public Schools Yearbook* and *Whitaker's Almanack* were giving reasonably reliable lists of HMC schools, but this was not true of the Victorian period.

Public Schools Yearbook. This directory has been published, annually or biennially since 1889, adding "Preparatory Schools" to its title in the course of the twentieth century. Pleading costs as the excuse for limiting the coverage to thirty schools, the three anonymous editors in 1889, "representatives of Eton, Harrow and Winchester", claimed to have selected schools which they regarded "as belonging to the same genus as our own".[36]

The 1891–2 edition added without explanation ten schools, and the preface to the 1893 edition announced the addition of a further twenty, though in fact they only added nineteen. The composition of the original thirty and of the twenty-nine added in 1891–2 and 1893 indicates that whereas most schools among the original thirty (except St Paul's and Merchant Taylors') had a strong boarding element, respect was now paid to the 'scholarship success table' (see *Table 1*), and successful grammar schools like Oundle (before Sanderson) and large urban day schools like City of London and Nottingham High School were admitted to this 'extended short-list'. The academic standing of these added schools had already, of course, been recognised by their admission to the much longer list of HMC schools. One original *PSYB* school which could not be on the HMC was Loretto—then still (and indeed until the twentieth century) a privately-owned school.

In 1897 the preface to the *PSYB* promised that the next edition would treat of all the schools on the HMC list. In fact it was to give eighty-seven schools, explaining that not all eligible schools had furnished details. But by 1903 it was offering what purported to be a complete list of schools which "with a few exceptions" were "connected with the HMC".[37] Whatever discrepancies there were in this list, its circulation offered one readily available long-list of public schools around 1902. After 1912 the *PSYB* was recognised as authoritative for certain purposes by the HMC, to prevent publishers from offering alternative lists in which non-HMC schools had paid to be included,[38] but there has always been a slight element of discrepancy in the *PSYB's* list of schools. In the *PSYB* 1902–3 list the element of discrepancy could have misled as to the HMC status of a number of schools including Birkenhead, Buxton, Chatham House (Ramsgate), and possibly Holt (Gresham's), Kendal, Woodbridge and some others.

Whitaker's Almanack. Before 1898 *Whitaker's* had for many years published an extensive annual list of the principal boys' schools. Their edition for that year purported to indicate by the use of an asterisk which schools were on the HMC, but their list was unreliable and omitted a small number of schools whose headmasters are well-known from other sources to have been members (*e.g.* Westminster) and it wrongly credited other schools with membership. Their 1902 list was less inaccurate. Not till 1929 onwards did *Whitaker* produce a tabulated list of HMC schools allowing convenient comparison of number of boys, date of foundation, and boarding/day fees.

Schoolmasters' Yearbook and Directory. The *SMYB*, published annually or biennially between 1903 and 1933, normally contained a list of HMC schools. Their first list in 1903, purporting to indicate the HMC schools of 1902, is also not totally reliable (*e.g.* it omits Sherborne). But the lists in these three sources—*Whitaker, PSYB*, and *SMYB*—checked by the list of actual attendances of headmasters 1898–1903, combine to offer to *us* (though not necessarily to the Victorians) an approximate long-list of public schools at the end of the Victorian period as indicated by their representation on the HMC.

The HMC list was already by 1902 a fluctuating list, growing year by year, but also dropping out not only schools which expired, like Isleworth International College and Godolphin School, but schools which had fallen below its specifications, like Beaumaris, Richmond, and Oswestry. Its criteria of membership were heavily academic, and many of its schools were only 'public' in the sense of not being run for the private profit of the headmaster or owners. Furthermore, the exclusion of private schools disqualified a few important schools (like Loretto and Blair Lodge) which by 1902 would have been, and indeed were, admitted even to exclusive short-lists of public schools based on other criteria.

The approximately one hundred and four[39] schools of the HMC in 1902 included many whom the universally recognised public schools would not have accepted as being public schools in anything other than the most vestigial sense—the generalised sense in which, in the mid-nineteenth century, academically successful schools were described. It was claimed in the previous chapter that later Victorian England saw the emergence of a community of 'public-school men' who derived a certain status, enjoyed certain privileges in their later careers, and interacted in certain ways, because they had a public-school education in common. Such an education may have been available in up to 100–105 schools by 1902; which of the schools on the HMC list (with its long tail of largely day-schools, academically successful but otherwise very unlike the 'great schools' in character)—or indeed, which schools out of all the 2,000-odd boys' secondary schools (in England alone)—would in fact have been accepted for this purpose?

5

Having examined the serious limitations of other criteria of classification available either to the Victorians or at least to historians, this chapter now offers the argument that the most useful criterion for the classification of schools whose pupils would have accepted each other as members of the 'public-schools community' before 1902 is a consideration of which schools interacted with one another. Interaction, in the marginal sense of academic competition, has already been indicated by the extent to which schools which had any pretensions to be public schools competed for university scholarships, for Oxford and Cambridge Higher School Certificates, and for the army examinations, all of which would tend to make the most successful competing schools aware of one another. Much more significant occasions of interaction were provided by the fact that certain schools played games with each other and that specifically 'public school' competitions were instituted which provided opportunities for much larger numbers of schools to compete—at rifle shooting, rowing, athletics, fencing, gymnastics, etc.; and corps camps and field-days brought representatives of public schools together in a competitive atmosphere. This criterion of public-school status—who played whom—parallels the now rather dated 'Ivy League' classification of American universities, originally a group of East Coast colleges who played each other at football. In addition to interaction at games, etc., the publication for four-and-a-half years (1898–1902) of a 'Public School Magazine' helped, by popularising these occasions and by giving special attention to certain schools, to confirm the limits of the public-school community.

Table 2: Interaction: Summary summarises details[40] of the representation of various public schools in certain Public School Rowing events in the 1880s and 1890s, in the Public School Gymnastics competitions held at Aldershot, the Public Schools Athletics Championships organised by the London Athletic Club, in shooting for the Ashburton Shield (Public Schools Rifle Shooting), in activities connected with cadet corps (including the Public Schools Battalion), and in exchanges between schools at cricket, football (rugby, soccer, etc.), fencing and racquets.

1. *Public Schools Rowing*: The schools taking part in 'Public School' Rowing events before 1902, such as the Public Schools IVs at Henley and afterwards at Marlow in the 1880s and 1890s, are listed in column 1 and in the notes to *Table 2*.

2. *Public Schools Gymnastics Competition*: The figures in column 2 summarise the participation of forty-six schools in the Public Schools Gymnastics Competition held (in conjunction with public-schools boxing and fencing events) at Aldershot in the

Table 2

	1 rowing	2 gymnastics	3 athletics	4 rifle-shooting	5 Ashburton	6 corps	7 uniforms	8 cricket	9 Lords/MCC	10 football	11 fencing	12 racquets	13 P.S. XI	
Aldenham		2	4											4
Ardingly									x	A				4
Bath	x					–	U		x					3
Bedford (Gr)	x	4	2	5	8	x	U	2	x	R	x			1
Bedford Modern	x		1					3	x	+				3
Berkhamsted		3		17	5	x	U							3
Blair Lodge				9	5		U	4		S				2
Blundell's		3						5		+				3
Bradfield		4		2	8	x	U	3		A	x		x	1
Brighton			1				U	2	x	A				3
Cambridge, Leys						‡			x	R			x	3
Canterbury, K.S.	x	3	2					3		+			x	3
Charterhouse				1	8	x	U	2	x	A	x	x	x	1
Chigwell			1			x								4
Cheltenham	x	5	3	12	8	x	U	2	x	R		x	x	1
City of London			1			L	L	5						4
Clifton		5	1	3	8	x	U	2		R		x	x	1
Cranleigh		5				x		5	x		x			3
Derby	x			23	0									4
Dover		1								+				4
Dulwich		4		14	8	x	U	2	x	R			x	1
Eastbourne		1	2	24	4	x	U	3	x					2
Edinburgh Acad.								4		S				3
Epsom		3	2			x	U		x		x			3
Eton	x			7	8	x	U	1	x	*		x	x	1
Felsted		3		n	4	x	U	5	x	A				2
Fettes								4		S				3
Forest		3	3			x	U	3	x					3
Framlingham		1	3											4
Glenalmond		1		15	8		U	4		S				1
Haileybury		5	1	16	8	x	U	2	x	R		x	x	1
Harrow		5		4	8	x	U	1	x	*	x	x	x	1

1. *Public School Rowing Events before 1902.* From 5 sources, schools marked 'x' appear to have been the main schools participating before 1902. In respect of *other* schools who also participated, some kind of rough (and very fallible) kind of weighting of Public School Rowing events has been made to try to take into account factors such as dates,

Table 2 (cont'd.)

	1	2	3	4–5		6–7		8	9	10	11	12	13	
Highgate		3	1	21	5	x	U		x				x	2
Hurstpierpoint		2		28	5	x	U	3	x	A				2
I.O.M., K. William's		1	1											4
King's Coll. S.						L	L	5						4
Lancing		3	3			x	U	3	x	A	x			2
Leatherhead, St. J.		2	1					3	x					3
Loretto								4		S				3
Malvern		2		26	7		U	2		A		x	x	1
Marlborough		5		8	8	x	U	2	x	R		x	x	1
Merch. Taylors'	x	2	4			L	U	3	x	R				2
Merchiston							U	4		S			x	3
Oundle	x	3	1											4
Radley	x	3						3	x	A		x		2
Reading		3	1			x	U		x					3
Repton			3	n	1			2		A			x	1
Rossall		3		19	8	x	U	3	x	A			x	1
Rugby		5		11	8	x	U	2	x	R		x	x	1
St Paul's	x	3	4	22	6	x	U	2		R			x	1
SEC (St Lawrence)			1	–	(1)									4
St Edward's, Oxford	x	1												4
Sherborne		4	3	27	4	x	U	2	x	R			x	1
Shrewsbury	x	1						3		A			x	3
Tonbridge	x	5	2	18	5	x	U	2	x	R	x	x	x	1
Univ. Coll. S.		2		30	2	L	L	5	x				x	3
USC, Westward Ho!		2	1							+				4
Uppingham				6	7	x	U	2		R			x	1
Warwick			1			x	U			+				4
Wellington		5		10	8	x	U	2	x	R		x	x	1
Westminster		1						2	x	A			x	1
Weymouth		4		25	5	x	U	5						3
Whitgift			1	20	6	x	U	3						3
Winchester	x			13	4	x	U	1	x	•		x	x	1
	rowing	gymnastics	athletics	rifle-shooting	Ashburton	corps	uniforms	cricket	Lords/MCC	football	fencing	racquets	P.S. XI	

amount of interaction with the leading schools and placings in these and similar prestigious events (*e.g.* with Eton in Ladies Plate).

This seems to offer two residual groups, (1) Durham, Hereford, Magdalen C.S. Oxford, Abingdon, Christ's Hospital, Monmouth, Worcester K.S., and St Mark's Wind-

Notes to Table 2 (Interaction: Summary) cont'd.

sor (see *Table 5*); (2) Westminster (rowing abolished 1884), Monkton Combe, Beaumont, and International C. Isleworth (before 1890), which, apart from Westminster, are in Table 6.

2. *Public Schools Gymnastics Competition*. Aldershot, 1889, 1890, 1898, 1899 and 1900. The figure in col. 2 indicates the number of times the school entered competitors. In addition to those listed, these schools competed this number of times: Bury St Edmunds 1, Cranbrook 3, Elizabeth C. Guernsey 3, Ipswich 4.

3. *Public Schools Athletics Championships*, 1898–1901. In addition to those listed, these schools competed this number of times: Gt Yarmouth Gr S. 3, Milton Abbas 2, and these once each: Birmingham K.E.S., Ely K.S., Mercers', Mill Hill, Oakham, Perse, Sutton Valence, Stonyhurst, Tavistock, Woodbridge, Worcester K.S.

4, 5. *Public Schools Rifle Shooting*, 1861–1901. Col. 4 is the order of merit of schools competing in the Ashburton Shield from 1861 to *c.* 1896, based on a table in the *P. S. Mag.* Late-comers Repton and Felsted not included in the order. Add: Oxford Military C. *31:0* and Portsmouth Gr S. *29:2*. Column 5 summarises the participation of 31 schools in 8 years 1889–91 and 1897–1901 in the Ashburton Shield. S.E.C. Ramsgate is recorded as having participated in the Cadets Challenge Trophy competition.

6. *Public School Corps Camps* (Public Schools Provisional Battalion, etc.) at Aldershot, and Field Days at Camberley, Hertford, etc. 1898–1901. ‡ Leys School participated as part of Cambridge University R. V. at P. S. Field Day, Hertford, 1901. L: schools participating as part of London Rifle Brigade.

7. Schools whose Corps Badges and Uniforms were described, illustrated, etc. in two articles on Badges and Uniforms of Public School Corps in *P. S. Mag.* 1901. L: see note 6, above. Thirty-five Commanding Officers of P. S. Corps met in London on 13th March, 1898: 29 of these replied to a questionnaire which was used as the basis of a Report to the HMC on School Cadet Corps. All 29 named feature in this column.

8, 9, 13. *Public Schools Cricket*. Figures 1 to 5 in column 8 indicate cricket interaction of 46 schools as classified by *Wisden* ("Public Schools Cricket") 1898–1903, *Encyclopaedia of Sport* 1898, etc. 1 = 3 schools (Eton, Harrow, Winchester) who play each other only; 2 = 17 schools; 3 = 13 schools, of whom 12 are listed (the other is Wellingborough Gr S.); 4 = 6 Scottish schools; 5 = 7 schools. Column 9 lists 33 schools who either played vs. MCC and Ground, or played each other at Lords; in 1902, Bedford County School, Leamington, Mill Hill, Stonyhurst and Wellingborough Gr S. did too. Col. 13 lists 26 schools represented in first seven years of the 'official' Public School XI from 1903–9, offered as confirmation of short-list Public School status of these schools immediately after 1902.

10. *Public Schools Football*, 1898–1902 (based mainly on articles on P. S. football in *Encyclopaedia of Sport* (1898) and in *P. S. Mag.* 1898–1902). • = 3 schools (Eton, Harrow, Winchester) with distinctive football games; R = schools who play one or more other 'R' schools at rugby, 'A' ditto soccer (*n.b.* some schools play both types); S = Scottish schools who played each other regularly (individual Scottish schools also played Giggleswick, Sedbergh, Leeds Gr S., Durham); + = Schools in other groups or pairs acknowledged to play each other regularly at Rugby Football.

11. *Public Schools Fencing* 1899–1901. Finalists in the Public Schools Fencing Championships at Aldershot in these three years are listed. (Charterhouse, Harrow and Tonbridge were finalists in all 3 years).

12. *Public Schools Racquets*. Thirteen schools competing in the Public Schools Racquets Championships in the 3 years 1899–1901 are listed. These schools competed regularly throughout the 1890s except for Tonbridge, competing only from 1898 (See *Table 3*).

five years 1889, 1890, and 1898 to 1900. The entry of thirty-four schools in 1898 (each offering two competitors) was described at the time as a record.[41] Though Eton stood aside from this competition in those years, Harrow competed regularly. Cranleigh won the Public Schools Gymnastics Shield for four years running between 1893 and 1896, and in 1897 tied with Harrow for first place: this must have been of advantage for Cranleigh's standing as a public school. Details for the boxing and fencing competitions are not so readily available for these years, but at boxing St Paul's had a formidable reputation. For fencing finalists, see below, column 11.

3. *Public Schools Athletics Championships*: Column 3 indicates the participation of certain schools in the London Athletics Club's "Public Schools Championships" at Stamford Bridge, London, an established annual event in the 1890s but already in decline by 1900. The notes to this table list a fairly large number of other schools—a motley collection—who also participated. The decline of this fixture and the varied character of the contestant schools were not unconnected. The *Public School Magazine* noted in 1898 that the LAC "had been the subject of some controversy" and referred to the journal *Truth*: there were suspicions that the event was made the occasion of betting; furthermore, there were headmasters who "preferred that their boys should not enter into the world of popular athletics as long as they were schoolboys".[42]

The "popular" character of this fixture, and above all the concern that this event was organised by a body outside their control, led the headmasters at their Conference in 1900 to pass a resolution against the organisation of sport by outside bodies. This disapproval had already been reflected in attendances, particularly by the better-known schools, before it turned to outright censure—a censure which, in the words of the *Public School Magazine*, "hastened the inevitable doom of this annual meeting";[43] its correspondent went on to point out the irony of the situation in which a

> Public Schools Challenge Cup for the 440 yards race, which had been held in previous years by Haileybury,

> Charterhouse, Marlborough, UCS, Rossall, St Paul's, and Merchant Taylors', was competed for by only three schools—Great Yarmouth Grammar School, USC, Westward Ho! and Woodbridge: the title "Public School" for these competitions is a misnomer.

This comment suggests that for that writer at least, Haileybury and the other six schools named were in a short-list of public schools in 1901, whereas the three lesser schools would only be on a long-list, if at all (*cf.* the entries for these schools on *Table 2, "Interaction: Summary"* and in *Tables* 5 and 6, below).

4, 5. *Rifle Shooting*: The Ashburton Shield for rifle shooting was presented by the 3rd Baron Ashburton in 1861, the year after the foundation of the National Rifle Association. It was open to all "schools having unenrolled Volunteer Corps". The Spencer Cup, given by Earl Spencer for an individual marksman event held at the same competition, was also first shot for in 1861. Throughout the 1860s and 1870s five schools dominated these two competitions—Eton, Harrow, Winchester, Rugby and Cheltenham, but the names of the winners of these two competitions from 1873 to the end of the century form a useful guide to the expansion of the public-school community in later Victorian England. After 1873 teams from Marlborough, Charterhouse, Clifton, Dulwich and Bradfield won the Ashburton Shield, and in the period after 1874 Glenalmond and Tonbridge were among the schools carrying off the Spencer Cup; Whitgift won it in 1881 and again in 1891, and a Blair Lodge cadet won it in 1898. In the case of Bradfield, the Shooting VIII's performance in the Ashburton from 1886 onwards was a decisive factor in the establishment by H. B. Gray of the fortunes of that little-known school, which had nearly collapsed around 1880.[44] Column 5 in the table summarises the participation of thirty schools in the eight years 1889–1891 and 1897–1901. Column 4 gives an average order of merit of competitors in the first twenty-five years of the Ashburton.

These schools, and occasionally one or two others, also competed in the Public Schools Veterans Cup which was first shot for in 1874, and in the Cadets Challenge Competition, which came later. Bisley, as the competition came to be called in the 1890s after it had moved from Wimbledon, attracted to itself the character of an important social occasion.[45] Some aspects of the conduct of the competition could be handled by the organisers; others were (as we shall see) to be made the subject of discussion by the HMC at the turn of the century.

The schools who shot at Bisley also shot in individual matches against each other. Thus in 1898 each of the twenty-six competing schools at Bisley[46] had matches with about six of the others—Blair Lodge, for example, shooting against Eton, Marlborough, Bedford, Harrow and several others[47]—thus consolidating and rendering more personal the contacts between members of the rifle-shooting public-schools community formed at Bisley.

6, 7. *Public Schools Cadet Corps Activities*: Most public schools which had cadet corps by 1902 had established them in or after 1860. The various 'Public Schools' rifle-shooting events from 1861 onwards at Wimbledon and later at Bisley such as the Ashburton Shield (for teams of eight), the Spencer Cup (for individual competitors representing their schools), and, by the 1890s, the Public Schools Veterans Match for teams of public-school Old Boys serving in the army, and the Public Schools Cadet Corps Competition, all gave the schools opportunities to compete with each other.

Occasions of interaction which were no less important to the boys themselves (though they received less coverage in the press) were the camps and field days which were characteristic corps activities and ones in which different schools took part. We also know from many sources that these occasions affected the reputation of the schools by advertising the smartness, military efficiency or even just the general demeanour of the boys—in 1898 Haileybury, for example, "had a reputation for smartness among Public Schools Corps second to none".[48]

Column 6 of *Table 2* summarises the interaction of thirty-seven schools[49] in corps camps and field days in the four years 1898 to 1901. Column 7 summarises the selection of forty-one schools (including those which formed part of the London Rifle Brigade) made by the *Public School Magazine* in 1901 to document its articles on the badges and the uniforms of public schools cadet corps. Such a list has less of the character of a short-list of public schools corps than the list in column 6, since it does not claim that these schools' corps interact with each other, but at the very least it has the character of a long-list.

8, 9, 13. *Public Schools Cricket*: Throughout this period, the cricket XIs of Eton, Harrow and Winchester still played no schools except each other.[50] Schools which played each other at Lords in 1870 were: Eton-Harrow: Eton-Winchester; Charterhouse-Westminster (from 1850); Marlborough-Cheltenham (from 1856) and Marlborough-Rugby (from 1855). A Harrow-Winchester fixture (from 1825) was discontinued in the 1850s. The Charterhouse-Westminster fixture was later in the century played elsewhere than at Lords. Other cricket fixtures which began in the Victorian period on the schools' own grounds were: Uppingham-Repton (1864); Uppingham-Haileybury (1868); Malvern-Repton (1871); Clifton-Cheltenham (1872); Dulwich-Tonbridge (1874); Cheltenham-Haileybury (1893) and Repton-Shrewsbury (1901).

Between 1870 and *c.* 1902 the interaction of schools at cricket expanded to the extent where an influential commentator on public schools cricket in 1898 could informally classify schools in four groups—the first comprising only Eton, Harrow and Winchester. (These groups are set out in column 8 and details are given in the notes to *Table 2*.) The groups cannot be called 'leagues' because each school played not all the other schools in the group, but only a few;[51] indeed it could be argued that the criterion for highest status as a cricketing public school was not how *many* other schools a given school played, but how *few*—provided they were the right schools. Six Scottish schools who did constitute a league, and who all played each other, comprise *Wisden's* fourth group, and a fifth group has been established which is composed of schools who are known from other sources to have had regular matches with schools in groups 2 and 3.

Thirty-seven schools are mentioned in *Wisden* as having played against "MCC and ground" in the 1902 cricket season. Six schools played each other in pairs at Lords in 1902: Eton-Harrow; Rugby-Marlborough and Cheltenham-Haileybury. Five of these were among the thirty-seven: the grand total of thirty-eight schools thus associated with Lords are listed in column 9 (MCC) of the table, or (in the case of five) in the notes to that table.

The institution of a formal "Public Schools XI" dates from 1903,[52] though *ad hoc* "Public Schools" teams had played before that. The annual fixture which pitted "The Lords (or Southern) Schools *vs* the Rest" was not established until 1913. The twenty-six schools which were represented in the Public Schools XI in the seven years 1903 to 1909 are offered in column 13 as further confirmation of the short-list 'public-school' status of these schools in the immediate post-Victorian period.

10. *Football*: Whereas cricket was a game in which all boys' schools were equipped to compete, the extent to which they could play each other at football was limited by the variety of forms of the game which existed in the public schools even in the late Victorian period—a period in which Rugby and Association had only just emerged in anything like their twentieth-century form. Eton with its "wall game" and "field game" could not play outsiders, other than Old Boys, though the school did develop soccer. Harrow and Winchester also had distinctive forms of football which could not be played with outsiders. These three schools are included in the list of schools who interact at rugger and soccer simply to emphasise that in their cases the failure to play other schools did not in any way diminish their standing as public schools.[53] Schools which are listed as playing each other at rugger (or in a few places both games) and schools which played each other at soccer, in accounts[54] of Public Schools Football in the period 1898 to 1902, are set out in column 10. The high-status criterion observed above in the case of cricket, by which certain schools showed extreme restrictedness as to whom they allowed to play them, was also evident in football; among schools which did play other schools at all, Westminster played (apart from its Old Boys) only Charterhouse: Clifton only played Marlborough.[55]

11. *Public Schools Fencing 1899 to 1901*: Along with the Gymnastics Competitions at Aldershot each year there took place the Public Schools Fencing Championships. Details of competing schools are not readily available—the event was given far less coverage in the reports, and this distinctly minority activity among schoolboys cannot have earned competing schools the same prestige as other forms of sport. However, the eight schools which reached the finals in the three years 1899–1901

are listed in column 8. Charterhouse, Tonbridge, and Harrow (whose champion fencer, Winston Churchill, had carried off the Public Schools championship trophy in 1892) were finalists in all three years. It can only have benefited the standing of schools like Cranleigh, founded in 1865 as a 'middle-class' school for farmers' sons, to have reached the finals with schools like these.

12. *Public Schools Racquets*: The Public Schools Racquets Championship was instituted in 1868. Until 1886 it was played at the Old Prince's Club (Hans Place); then after being played in the year 1887 at Lord's it moved to Queen's Club.

Harrow was the first of the public schools to take to racquets—around 1823—and dominated the restricted world of racquets in the nineteenth century; in 1868 Harrow had only three rivals in the championship. The growth from these original four to a public-schools racquets-playing community of thirteen by 1898 and fifteen by 1908 is documented in *Table 3*: the thirteen who competed in the Championship in the three years 1899 to 1901 are listed in column 12.

Table 3. Public Schools Racquets Competition

Thirteen schools competed in the Public Schools Racquets Championships in the three years 1899 to 1901. The schools began competing in this competition as follows:

1868	Charterhouse	1873	Winchester, Marlborough
	Cheltenham		
	Eton		
	Harrow	1883	Malvern
1869	Rugby	1886	Clifton
1870	Haileybury	1887	Radley
1871	Wellington	1898	Tonbridge

(In 1904 Rossall competed, and from 1908 Westminster.)

6

The thirteen columns of *Table 2*: *Interaction: Summary* enable us to observe the amount of interaction at the close of the Victorian period among sixty-four schools in two or more of a wide range of activities which by then had come to be regarded as characteristic of public schools. Not all of these activities would have been regarded as of equal weight: one at least (competing in the Public Schools Athletics Championships) was at the turn of the century very suspect, and any exact appraisal of the relative importance for public-school status of participation in each of these would be impossible. Also, note must be taken when reading this table that rifle shooting, cadet camp and similar activities are given two columns each in the summary, which gives a special disadvantage to schools not thus represented. Probably cricket, football, rifle shooting, and corps activities were the most prestigious. All schools could play each other at cricket and most of them at football: roughly half of these schools had corps, and slightly fewer than half regularly sent to Bisley.[56] However, absence from, or low rating at, one of these activities could perhaps be compensated for by participation in a number of others.

It is now suggested that the total amount of interaction, assessed in accordance with the weighting in favour of the four activities specified above, seems to offer a division of the sixty-four schools into groups, which are listed as groups I to IV on *Table 4*.

That the first two groups combined should conveniently total the round figure of thirty, and the first three together fifty, is a coincidence not foreseen by the compiler. It would be possible to rearrange the grouping differently, but it seems difficult to believe that the overall picture, in the sense of an extended short-list with Eton and Harrow at one end and Dover, Framlingham and Warwick at the other, would be substantially different. Indeed, additional evidence exists for the validity of at least two of the groupings.[57]

Taking aside group I, the schools in groups II, III and IV present a spectrum within which almost any one of group II might be in group I and those in group IV shade into the long

Table 4. Sixty-four Public Schools "By Interaction" c. 1880–1902 (see Tabl 2)

GROUP I— (22 schools)		
Bedford (Grammar)[1,2,3]	Glenalmond[3]	St Paul's[1,2,3]
Bradfield[1,2,3,4]	Haileybury[1,3,4]	Sherborne[1,2,4]
Charterhouse[1,3,4]	Harrow[1,2,3,4]	Tonbridge[1,2,3,4]
Cheltenham[1,2,3,4]	Malvern[1,2,3,4]	Uppingham[1,2,3,4]
Clifton[1,2,3,4]	Marlborough[1,2,3,4]	Wellington[1,2,3,4]
Dulwich[1,3]	Repton[1,3,4]	Westminster[1,2]
Eton[1,2,3,4]	Rossall[1,2,4]	Winchester[1,2,3,4]
	Rugby[1,2,3,4]	
GROUP II— (8 schools)		
•*Blair Lodge*	Highgate[1,2]	Lancing[1,2]
Eastbourne[1,2]	•Hurstpierpoint[2]	Merchant Taylors'[1]
Felsted[1,2,3,4]		Radley[1,2,3,4]
GROUP III— (20 schools)		
Bath[1,2,3,4]	•Cranleigh	•Loretto
•*Bedford Modern*[3]	Edinburgh Academy[3]	Merchiston
Berkhamsted[1,2,4]	Epsom[1,2]	Reading[2]
Blundell's[1,2,3,4]	Fettes[1,2,3]	Shrewsbury[1,4]
Brighton[2]	•*Forest*[2]	University C.S.[2]
Cambridge, Leys[1,2]	Leatherhead, St. John's[1,2]	*Weymouth*[1,2]
Canterbury, K. S.[1,2,4]		•Whitgift
GROUP IV— (14 schools)		
Aldenham[1,4]	Dover[2,3]	St Edward's (Oxford)[2]
•*Ardingly*	•Framlingham	SEC (St Lawrence), Ramsgate
Chigwell	I.O.M. King Wm's[1,2,3]	•*Utd. Services C., Westward Ho!*[3]
City of London[1]	King's Coll. S.[1]	Warwick
Derby[1]	Oundle[1,2]	

Schools in *italics* are omitted from one or more (or, in the majority of cases, *all*) HMC/PSYB lists since 1927 (and esp. 1927–52) used as bases of long-list classification of public schools by analysts of élites. (See *Table 9* and notes to *Table 7*).

•not on any known HMC list, 1898–1902.

[1]one of top 77 schools by Oxford and Cambridge scholarship successes, 1885–92 (see *Table 1*).

[2]one of 68 schools regularly presenting successful candidates for Oxford and Cambridge Higher Cert. Exams. 1890–7.

[3]one of top 30 schools for army entrance exams in 6 years 1892–8.

[4]one of 26 schools around 1902 other than Metropolitan Day Schools, identified by S. M. Leathes of Civil Service Comm. as producing 33% of future C.S. entrants.

list of public schools established by other criteria (see below, *Public School Magazine* and *Table* 5.) Of the eight schools in group II Eastbourne's claim is compromised by being in the "third division" at cricket and by not being significant at football; Felsted's case may be stronger and Merchant Taylors' stronger still, apart from the latter's absence from Bisley and its less secure status as a corps school. Radley, with similar disabilities, would almost certainly have the edge on Merchant Taylors' and Felsted in virtue of its participation in Public Schools Racquets which, together with a rowing reputation which rivalled Eton's, may be held to argue strongly for Radley's inclusion in group I. Radley had been one of the first schools (1860) to institute a corps, but this had been sabotaged by the hostility of a group of fractious masters, and was not revived until nearly fifty years later, by which time (1909) "most schools of Radley's standing" had one.[58] Whereas most of the Scottish schools (interacting almost exclusively, but frequently, with each other) are in group III, Blair Lodge's prestige at Bisley and interaction with individual rifle-shooting public schools such as Eton gave it a distinct position despite its being, like Loretto, still a private school and not on the HMC. Glenalmond, with an even wider range of interaction, and without the disability of private-school status, appears to qualify for group I. If Blair Lodge had survived as a school, it would have been (on its showing by 1902) well placed to rationalise its formal status (as Loretto was to do) and thus confirm its position as a leading public school; among the clientele which it attracted was the future Lord Cherwell, whose parents had an income of £20,000 a year.* The position achieved by Lancing (in group II) and, even more significantly, by Hurstpierpoint, is noteworthy, since they had both been intended by their founder, Woodard, to cater for a broader spectrum of the middle classes than the old

* In 1874, one of Almond's Loretto masters, J. Cooke-Gray, had bought an almost defunct private school at Polmont, Blair Lodge, and built it up within fifteen years into a successful school of some three hundred boys. By the 1890s the policy of active participation in inter-school sports with leading schools had raised the school to a high reputation. But Blair Lodge, which became a limited company in 1901, did not long survive Gray's death in 1902.[59]

public schools, and Hurstpierpoint was in fact a 'second-grade' school in Woodard's system.

Participation in 'public school' extra-mural activities, especially the playing of games (like cricket and football) with other individual schools or joining up with other public schools for field-days, do not *in themselves* provide a means of measuring interaction: plenty of schools, for example, played cricket on occasion—or even more frequently—with other listed schools yet do not themselves figure in the cricket columns of our lists. The criterion is that schools be recognised by each other as regular opponents and reported by observers who have some claim to authority for their assessment. For this reason, the sources for the relevant tables have included works such as the *Encyclopedia of Sport* (in which the lists which schools provide of their games opponents can be checked against each other, to see if both sides acknowledge the fixture) and *Wisden*, which had a special authority among its public-school readership[60] and among the cricket community which gave support to the schools whose matches it chose to describe as 'public-school' matches.[61] Another valuable, if in one respect less reliable, source is the *Public School Magazine*.

7

The *Public School Magazine* began publication at the beginning of 1898 and ceased nearly four-and-a-half years later. Its monthly issues contained a wealth of material on a wide range of schools: over one hundred and forty are mentioned in its nine volumes. Understandably, in the interests of a wide circulation, the editor adopted an 'all-comers' policy and printed material on any school which was sent to him, some of it in school magazines. But even when these are discounted the number of schools given significant mention is fairly large, if by significant mention we mean inclusion in accounts of public schools playing each other at cricket or football etc.; or the regular submission by a school of its athletics record to be tabulated and compared with other schools' athletics records; or special feature articles on individual schools; or descriptions of the traditions and customs of individual schools or of Old Boy activities. This sort of news, description and comment formed the bulk of the material of the magazine: a very small proportion of space was allocated to biographical information about leading headmasters (*e.g.* the newly-appointed headmaster of Harrow in 1899) or to more general items such as stories of school life; P. G. Wodehouse contributed a few humorous items as well as serious articles on public-schools' football.

The 'all-comers' policy adopted by the *Public School Magazine* from its inception soon provoked criticism. Before the end of its first year of life a reader who signed himself "E. H. A." wrote to refer to what he conceived to be the object of the magazine—"to chronicle the news of the various public schools in such a manner as to promote feelings of mutual interest and companionship among the boys of those schools". This object, he suggested, had failed, because "it is quite clear that mutual interests cannot exist between all the schools mentioned in your pages, but only between some . . .; many of the schools whose names appear cannot be called public schools". He went on to admit the difficulties which beset the "delicate" task of arriving at a list of "public schools proper", but the basis of selection of such a list which he put forward is significant: he suggested the list, published in an earlier issue, of schools which had taken part in the Public Schools Rifle Shooting at Bisley, and which competed throughout the school year among themselves. "Certain of these names are doubtful, but their places might be filled by others not mentioned".[62] (Twenty-six schools had competed that year:[63] of these three had a largely day-school character—St Paul's, Dulwich, and Bedford; Blair Lodge was a private school; any one of Weymouth, Eastbourne, Hurstpierpoint, Berkhamsted, or Felsted might have been questioned for one reason or another. The 1898 Bisley list omitted three Clarendon schools—Merchant Taylors', Shrewsbury and Westminster.)

Another correspondent pressed home the same charge: "if the *Public School Magazine* is to keep its name and serve its purpose, it ought to cease to become a private school magazine". The editor's reply to this sort of criticism was to return to the difficulty of definition. Rejecting size or antiquity as inapplicable criteria, "that which constitutes a public school", he

Table 5. Forty "Long-list" Public Schools "By Interaction" etc., by 1902

Abingdon	Giggleswick[1]	•†Magdalen C.S. Oxford[12]
•*Bedford County S.*	Guernsey, Elizabeth C.[2]	Plymouth[2,3]
Birmingham, K.E.S.[1,2]	Hereford Cathedral S.[1]	*Pocklington*
Blackheath[1,2]	Ipswich[1]	Portsmouth Gr S.[1]
Brecon, Christ C.[1,2]	Jersey, Victoria C.[2]	St Olave's[1]
Bromsgrove[1,2]	*Leamington*[1]	Sedbergh[1,4]
•*Bury St Edmunds*	Leeds Gr S.[1,2]	Stonyhurst
Cambridge, Perse	Liverpool C.[1,2]	Sutton Valence[2]
Carlisle Gr S[1]	Llandovery C.[1,2]	Wakefield, Q.E. Gr S.[1]
Christ's Hospital[1,2]	Manchester Gr S.[1,2]	• Wellingborough Gr S.
•Cranbrook	Merchant Taylors', Crosby[1]	•†*Windsor, St Mark's*
•Denstone[2]	Mill Hill[2]	Worcester, King's S.[1,2]
Durham[1,2]	Monmouth	York, St Peter's[1]
	•*Newton (Abbot) C.*[1,2]	

Schools in *italics* are omitted from one or more (or, in the majority of cases, *all*) HMC/PSYB lists since 1927, as in *Table 4*.
•not on any known HMC list 1898–1902, except two schools also marked †which appeared *only* in the PSYB 1903 (as if HMC 1902).
[1,2,3,4] as in *Table 4*.

claimed, "is a certain spirit. You may call it *esprit de corps*, or you may call it chivalry, or you may say that there is no word for it. Where that spirit exists, there is a public school. Our desire is to foster that spirit—to show that there is no English gentleman who lacks it. That spirit unites in one comradeship the dull and the brilliant, the junior and the senior boys in one school. Why should it not unite schools in the same way?"[64]

The explicit aim of the *Magazine*, therefore, was to give expression to a community of public schools which already existed and to try to extend it. It continued to notice a wide range of schools, but in tracing the schools mentioned it has been found possible to distinguish those given significant mention in the sense defined above, of a special article, or an indication of at least limited interaction with other schools already known to be interacting as public schools in *Table 4*. This list of schools compiled from nine volumes of the *Public School Magazine* has been added to those lists of schools whose cricket results were listed by *Wisden* (under the heading of "Public Schools") for the seasons 1898, 1901 and 1902, or who played vs. "MCC and ground" in 1902. From this list, sixty-four schools already classified in groups I to IV are subtracted and the residual category of some thirty are treated as long-list public schools and figure in *Table 5*. In addition, a count has been made of three volumes in the *Public School Magazine*—two early, one late—and a rough check made of the remaining volumes, to establish a further list of schools of which some kind of news is given (excepting those whose magazines only are mentioned).

Of these forty-three schools, thirty-six figure in *Table 6*, 17 of them being identified as having no claim to public-school status beyond the fact that readers of the *Public School Magazine* may be said to have heard of them. The remaining seven belong to that category of schools whose participation with schools of groups I to IV in *one only* of the "public schools" activities listed in *Table 4* (other than the suspect Public Schools Athletics)[65] earns them a mention in the notes of *Table 3*; and this, together with their mention in the *Public School Magazine*, causes them to be put in *Table 5*. *Table 6* also contains twenty-three schools which are identified as owing their slight (if any) claim to public school status exclusively to some 'academic' criterion, in some cases a very slender one.

By this analysis, the public-schools community by 1902 is seen as consisting of four groups, in an extended short-list totalling sixty-four schools (*Table 4*) the last of these groups shading into a residual long-list which at its most generous added a further forty schools (*Table 5*) whose claims, in some cases very marginal, might have been admitted (especially by readers of *Wisden* and the *Public School Magazine*): plus an outside category of schools (*Table 6*) which may only have represented either the *Public School Magazine's* attempt to extend the bounds of that public-schools community, or an 'academic' criterion such as putative membership of the HMC, or participation in the Oxford and Cambridge Higher Certificate. The really 'fringe' character of that outside category is illustrated by the fact that whereas King's School, Ely, gets a mention in a volume of the *Public School Magazine*, another issue carries an article on the town of Ely which contains no mention of the school.

One hundred and four to one hundred and sixty-four schools must therefore represent the most generous estimate

Table 6. Sixty Possible "Fringe" Public Schools by c. 1902

†*Ackworth*	Exeter Gr S.	Norwich S.
†*Alleyn's*	x*Gloucester, Crypt S.*	Nottingham H.S.
x*Armagh, Royal S.*	x*Godolphin S.*	xOakham S.
†*Bernard Castle*	*Heversham Gr S.*	*Oswestry S.*
†Beaumont	xGresham's, Holt	x*Oxford H.S.*
Birkenhead	Hymer's C., Hull	*Ramsgate, Chatham Hse S.*
x*Boston Gr S.*	x*Kendal Gr S.*	*Ripon (Gr) S.*
Bradford Gr S.	†*Kidderminster S.*	xSt Bees
xBristol Gr S.	*International C., Isleworth*	†St Columba's
x*Bury (Lancs) Gr S.*	Kingswood C.	†*Sandwich SR Manwood's*
Buxton	Lancaster (R) Gr S.	x*Silcoate's*
Canterbury, St Edmund's	x*Latymer Upper S.*	†*Stratford, Trinity S.*
Dean Close S., Cheltenham	x*Leicester, Wyggeston Gr S.*	†*Taunton, King's C.*
xChester, King's S.	x*Lincoln S.*	†*Tavistock (Gr) S.*
x*Coventry, KHs*	x*Liverpool, Royal Instn.*	xTrent C.
x*Doncaster Gr S.*	†*Mercer's S.*	x*Wallingford Gr S.*
†*Dublin H.S.*	†*Milton Abbas*	xWolverhampton Gr S.
†Edinburgh, G. Watson's	Monkton Combe	*Woodbridge*
†Ellesmere	Newcastle (Staffs) H.S.	†Worksop
Ely, King's S.	x*Newport/Salop (Adams) Gr S.*	†*Gt Yarmouth Gr S.*

Schools in *italics*—see *Tables 4* and 5.

† indicates schools included *solely* in virtue of "mention" in *Public School Magazine*; this slender claim to public school standing before 1902 could justify their omission from public-school classifications used by later analysts.

x indicates schools included by virtue of having *one or more* of the following characteristics, which are here considered as 'academic' criteria:

(a) authenticated membership of HMC in 1886 and/or 1892.
(b) one of top 77 schools by Oxford and Cambridge scholarship successes, 1885–92.
(c) one of 68 schools regularly presenting successful candidates for Oxford and Cambridge Higher Cert. exams. 1890–7.
(d) on first list offered in Whitaker 1899 as being HMC 1898.
(e) school whose HM actually *attended* HMC in any one year 1898–1903 inclusive.
(f) in PSYB 1903 as if HMC 1902.
(g) in Whitaker as HMC 1902.
(h) in SMYB 1903 as HMC 1902.

(For some schools this argues a very slender claim indeed, *e.g.* Bury's inclusion is for (b) only; Gresham's for (f) only; in the case of 4 schools (Crypt S., Gloucester; Latymer Upper; Silcoate's; Wallingford Gr S.) inclusion is solely for (g), almost certainly a misprint in all 4 cases.)

Schools not prefixed † or x enjoy a combination of above two criteria, *i.e. P.S. Mag.* "mention", and 'academic' standing represented by one or more of (a) to (h). (In the case of the International College, Isleworth, its HMC membership (1886) is complemented by its interaction in early P. S. Rowing events before 1890.) Seven schools in this category are *italicised* as not figuring in key HMC lists after 1927 used by analysts; so are 13 schools marked † (and 16 marked x).

Compare the public-school standing before 1902 of these 7–36 schools with that of the schools in *Table 7*.

that can be given of schools which had any sort of claim whatever the public school status before 1902. At its outer limits the value of the list is less for the identities of the schools it includes than for those it omits, so that any twentieth-century classification of nineteenth-century public schools which goes outside those limits is liable to be wrong. Insofar as any of the forty schools in *Table 5* or the sixty in *Table 6* owe their place to the amount of notice given them by the *Public School Magazine*, this group could probably be expected to show a weighting towards the schools which were on the HMC—an editor in pursuit of an 'all-comers' policy would at least give respect to the HMC criterion even if ordinary public-school boys did not. Even so, when the putative list of around one hundred and four HMC schools in 1902 is compared with the one hundred and four schools on *Tables 4* and 5, the HMC list is seen to include several schools who would not yet have been considered part of the public-schools community—certainly a good number are outside groups I to IV. Among these are schools with a high scholarship record—Boston Grammar School, Oxford High School and Wyggeston School (Leicester), and other schools like Coventry (King Henry VIII School), Newport (Salop, Adams) Grammar School and Gresham's School (Holt), the latter still at an early stage of its transformation by Howson after 1900: none of these seem to have any very significant claim to inclusion in the public-schools community. Other HMC schools of a largely day-school character may have rated passing mention in the *Public School Magazine*, but their HMC status really derived from their scholarship record—*e.g.* Bradford Grammar School, Exeter Grammar School, Newcastle (Staffs.) High School and Nottingham High School. The *PSYB* for 1902 specified yet more schools which were for the time being outside the real public-schools community, such as Buxton, and Chatham House (Ramsgate)—the school which was to educate Mr Edward Heath. Among schools in *Table 5* which were omitted by the HMC list in 1902 were Bedford County School, Bury St Edmunds (a public school in decline) Cranbrook, Denstone and Wellingborough Grammar School—the latter prominent in public-schools cricket around 1902; Ardingly, Framlingham, and USC, Westward Ho!, whose interaction with other public schools puts them in Group IV; Bedford Modern, Cranleigh,

Forest, Weymouth and Loretto[66] in Group III, Blair Lodge and Hurstpierpoint in Group II. The total number of omissions and additions in the HMC list, compared with the one hundred and four of *Tables 4* and 5, is something of the order of 20%, though some of these—in particular omissions of schools in groups II to IV—are very important.

That the HMC list and the public-schools community were not co-extensive around 1902 is vividly illustrated by the discussions among the headmasters in Conference in 1904, when it was agreed that there should be a truce concerning the practice which had grown up among some rifle-shooting schools of sending their teams to practise at Bisley several days in advance of the Ashburton. But this gentlemen's agreement had one signal disadvantage compared with the changes in the rules which the organisers of the competition had power to effect. The headmaster of Glenalmond, which had been represented at Bisley since 1878, complained to his HMC colleagues that certain Scottish schools who competed there would not be bound by the truce as they were not represented at the Conference.[67]

Yet the claim made in this chapter that at the very end of the century membership of the HMC was beginning to become relevant as one criterion (if not a very readily discernible one) of public-school status is supported by a remark in the *Journal of Education* in 1900. In describing an incident at an unnamed leading public school, the *Journal* defined the school's status as follows:

> "Z College" is one of the elect. It was "founded to supply a liberal education". It sends its team to Aldershot and its headmaster to the Headmasters' Conference.[68]

The order of priority of these two criteria deserves to be noted.

By 1926, the admission to the HMC of the headmaster of a long-established (1880) private school, Wrekin, could justify the grant of a triumphal half-holiday to the boys, but even then it needed to be explained publicly that HMC membership gave the school a status among "officially recognised public schools".[69]

8

To summarise, we can say that by the late Victorian period the term 'public school' may most properly be used to reflect a community of schools who interacted with or recognised each other in varying degrees represented by short-lists of twenty-two or fewer schools extending to thirty, fifty or sixty-four schools, or by a long-list of up to one hundred and four schools, with an appendix or fringe of up to sixty schools all of highly questionable public-school standing.

In comparison, the HMC list by 1902 showed a significant margin of inaccuracy as an index of that community; the list was not readily available, its published forms were not yet authoritative and they showed some discrepancies. Nevertheless, since it contained *nearly* all the *leading* public schools, and above all because there was no other list, it was at the turn of the century beginning to be looked to as some kind of authority concerning the limits of a community of public schools which was becoming more self-conscious about itself and which the expansion of Secondary Education after 1902 would make even more self-conscious.

The elucidation of the sixty-four to one hundred and four schools, offered here as a more accurate guide to the public-schools community by 1902 than the HMC list, is in itself of some historical and sociological interest. If any doubts remained as to whether that would justify the tedious industry of its compilation, attention should be given to the uses to which the classification 'public school' for the period before 1902 has been put.

The connection between education at a public school and entry into various forms of privileged position in after life in the late nineteenth and twentieth centuries has become a commonplace: more specifically, sociologists and social and political historians have studied a number of élites in British society in such a way as to show parentage, education, etc., as factors in recruitment to those élites. The best-known of these studies so far were published in the period 1928 to 1963, though there have been several more since then. Many of them analyse the school education of élite members by means of a classification of short-lists and long-lists of public schools based on membership of the HMC, and most of those who use the HMC list make use of a list adjacent to the time of writing—*i.e.* within the period 1927 to (say) 1963, even in respect of élite members whose schooling would have taken place forty or even eighty or more years before.

Such a basis of classification would be a defective guide to the pre-1902 public-school community in proportion as the discrepancies between the 1902 HMC list and the public school community represented by the schools of *Tables 4* and *5* were perpetuated in the particular HMC list after 1902 used by the analysts of élites.

But the HMC list changed considerably after 1902. Some of the schools it took in were schools which had in fact been part of the public-schools community before 1902; but it also enlarged to take in a great number of schools which had not been. As the twentieth century proceeded the disparities between the schools represented on the increasing HMC list and those which before 1902 had been in the public-schools community became more marked (*Tables 7* and *8*).

Even in the nineteenth century the HMC had been a fluctuating category in which some schools dropped out and a greater number were added. We have already seen how, of the 'originals' for the first few years of the Conference, some schools had dropped out before 1902 and others closed their doors—as yet more would do after 1902, most notably Bath College and Blackheath. The HMC lists also demonstrate the effect after 1902 of changes in the status of schools in the changed situation in English secondary education produced by 'state' intervention in that sector. The membership of the Conference doubled between the outbreak of the Boer War and the end of World War II. *Table 7* gives an indication of this great expansion; it also illustrates the impracticality of using the HMC list for years before or after World War II as a criterion of the 'public-school' education of samples of the population educated at the beginning of the century or even before.

Yet this is in fact what has been done. Ever since the late 1920s, from the days of Harold Laski and R. H. Tawney, analyses have been made, at the London School of Economics and elsewhere, of the educational backgrounds (among other

Table 7. Eighty-one Schools Existing Before 1902 Treated as Public Schools by Recent Classifications

The following 81 schools existing before 1902 figure in one or more (and in the majority of cases *all*) identifiable HMC lists used as classifications of 'public school' since 1927 (see *Table 9*), most notably the following:

(1) 1927 HMC list used by Tawney (1931) (Tawney used English schools only).
(2) 1932 HMC in SMYB 1932–3, the basis of Jenkins and Jones (1950); see also Coats (1970).
(3) 1937 HMC list, the basis of Clements (1958).
(4) 1939 HMC list, the basis of Kelsall (1958); see also Edwards and Jeeves (1943); Guttsman (1963); Morgan (1963–4).
(5) 1944 HMC schools as used in Bereday's long-list (1947).
(6) 1947 HMC (PSYB) contributing to Banks' List R (1954).
(7) 1952 HMC used by Acton Society (1956); see also Copeman (1955); Thomas (1958).

Allhallows	Emanuel	Rydal
Ampleforth	Glasgow Academy	St Alban's
Arnold S., Blackpool	Grays, Palmer's S.	St Dunstan's, Catford
Bablake	Haberdasher's (Hmpstd)	Salisbury, Bp Wordsworth
Bancroft's	Haberdasher's (Hatcham)	Sebright
Belfast, Campbell C.	Harpenden, St George's	Sevenoaks
Belfast, R. Acad. I.	Harrow, J. Lyon Lower S.	Solihull
Bishop's Stortford	Haverfordwest (Gr) S.	Southampton KE6
Blackburn (QE) Gr S.	High Wycombe R. Gr S.	Stafford KE6
Bloxham	Kelly C.	Stamford
Bolton	Leighton Park S.	Stourbridge KE6
Bootham	Macclesfield, K. S.	Stockport Gr S.
Brentwood	Maidstone Gr S.	Taunton
Bridlington	Manchester, Wm Hulme's	Truro
Bruton, King's S.	Mount St Mary's	Wallasey Gr S.
Cambridgeshire H.S.	Newcastle/Tyne, R. Gr S.	Walsall, Q. Mary S.
Caterham	Newcastle/Tyne, D. Allan's	Watford Gr S.
Cheltenham Gr S.	Newport H. S. (Mon.)	Wellington S., Somt
Chesterfield (Gr) S.	Northampton Gr S.	Whitgift Middle/Trinity
Clayesmore	Oldham, Hulme Gr S.	Winchester, P. Symonds
Cooper's	Owen's	Woodhouse Grove
Culford	Pontypool, W. Mon. S.	Worcester R. Gr S.
Dauntsey's	Portora Royal S.	Worcester, Blind C.
Dorchester, Hardye's	Ratcliffe S.	Wrekin
Douai	Redcar/Coatham, Turner's	Wrexham, Grove Pk S.
Downside	Rochester, K.S.	Wycliffe
Eltham	Royal Masonic, Bushey	York, Abp Holgate's

Note: The above 81 schools had *no* identifiable claim to public-school status before 1902 by *any* of the following 12 criteria of academic standing or of interaction etc. with the main public-schools community:

Table 7 (contd.)

(a)—(h) Eight 'academic' criteria, including real or hypothetical HMC membership between 1886 and 1902–3, or scholarship or Higher Certificate record, as set out in *Table 6*, notes (a) to (h).

(i) inclusion in top 30 schools for army entrance exams in 6 years 1892–8 (see *Table 4*).

(j) citation as leading producer of future Civil Service entrants *c.* 1902 (see *Table 4*).

(k) regular interaction with any one of 64 public schools in any one of approx. 9 games or corps or similar 'public school' activities (see *Table 2*, columns 1–13 and notes).

(l) mention even in non-selective *P. S. Mag.* 1898–1902.

Table 8. Twenty-five Schools Existing pre-1902 which Appear in HMC Lists 1965 and/or 1971

Abbotsholme	Hutcheson's Gr S., Glasgow	Prior Park C.
Ashville C.	Kelvinside Academy	Queen's C., Taunton
Battersea Gr S.	Kent College, Canterbury	Reed's S., Cobham
Cardiff H.S.	Kimbolton S.	R. Gordon's, Aberdeen
Daniel Stewart's, Edinburgh	King Edward's, Bath	Tettenhall C.
Edinburgh Royal H.S.	Kingston (Thames) Gr S.	Weybridge, St George's
George Heriot's, Edinburgh	Leeds Modern S.	West Buckland S.
Hampton Gr S.	Loughborough Gr S.	William Ellis S.
	Oratory S., Reading	

things) of British cabinet ministers, diplomats, MPs, samples of 'top people' from *Who's Who,* Cambridge graduates, managers, higher civil servants, members of Royal Commissions, authors, Anglican bishops, army officers, economists—hardly a year passes but a new study appears, giving exactly the same treatment to the educational origins of some new 'élite' or professional group.[70] *Table 9* shows the basis on which a whole host of such authors classify schools as public schools, which in nearly all cases relates to HMC membership at some point between 1927 and the 1960s: the subjects whose education is being thus classified, however, include a proportion, varying between a handful and 100%, who were at their 'public schools' before 1902. It will readily be seen that if one studies a sample of those who were 'top people' in (say), 1944, it is likely that one's archbishops, viceroys or field marshals will typically be in their sixties or seventies, which means they entered their 'public schools' (at age thirteen) before 1898, sometimes before 1888. A classification which reflects the public-schools community of 1944 rather than that of 1898 (or 1888) may therefore be a seriously misleading one, and this sort of thing will make nonsense of the impressively precise percentages of 'public-school' representation such as bolster Laski's conclusions about the élite character of British government, or Tawney's conclusions about the relative inaccessibility of élite positions in the 1920s to those outside the "closed educational system" of the public schools.[71] Such arithmetic has been used to illustrate the "democratization of the ruling class" in the twentieth century;[72] to show that (in a study of managers in the 1950s) public-school boys have ten times the average chance of becoming managers, although a third of the sample studied may have been at their 'public schools' before 1902;[73] and to "ascertain *more or less exactly the percentage* of members of the liberal professions educated in the public schools"[74] on the basis of 1940s assumptions about the public schools applied to a sample of whom 40% entered upon secondary schooling before 1902.[75]

No less fallible are those researchers who have attempted to devise short-lists to measure the predominance in élites of the products of 'leading', as opposed to 'lesser', public schools. This activity is simple enough if you stick to Eton and Harrow, but the sociologists H. Jenkins and D. Caradog Jones come unstuck when they offer to identify the top twenty-three public schools for purposes of classifying the previous schooling of men who were at Cambridge in the period 1751 to 1899.[76] *Table 10* compares Jenkins' and Jones' top twenty-three public schools with the twenty-three schools (group I plus Radley from group II) suggested in this chapter as the leading public schools "by interaction" in the late Victorian period.

By the time schools like Haileybury and Clifton (but not, mysteriously, Wellington) had begun to figure in Jenkins' and Jones' totals, neither Sedbergh Grammar School nor Oundle had claims to anything like the status of a leading public school, and certainly neither had more claim than Bedford. What rights the products of Loretto (the small private school from around 1823 and for most of the nineteenth century until transformed by H. H. Almond) had to a classification which distinguishes them right throughout the century from other private-school pupils, is nowhere explained. Only Loretto's products of the last quarter of the nineteenth century would have enjoyed the benefits of the school's public-school status, and that not a

Table 9

Author	Elite or Professional Group Studied	Earliest Approx. Date for Sec. Schooling of Some of Group	Basis of Short-list Classification as "Public School"	Basis of Long-list Classification as "Public School"
1. Laski (a) 1928 (b) 1928	Br. Cabinet Ministers 1801–1924	*c.* 1770	(a) Eton, Harrow and 9 un-named 'great public schools'; (b) Eton, Harrow and 11 un-named 'great public schools'.	
2. Greaves, 1929	Br. MPs in 1900, '05, '09, '28	*c.* 1850	Eton and Harrow	10 named schools
3. Nightingale, 1930	Br. Diplomats 1851–1929	*c.* 1840	"11 most exclusive" (named)	HMC in (PSYB) *c.* 1930
4. Tawney, 1931	691 top Churchmen, Lawyers, Civil Servants, Colonial Governors, Bankers, etc. in 1927	*c.* 1870 (Tawney, p. 73)	"The 14 principal schools (un-named) (Appendix I) or "The most celebrated schools" (Tawney, p. 73)	135 *English* HMC schools, 1927 (Whitaker, 1927)
5. Edwards and Jeeves (W.E.A.), 1943	830 top Churchmen, Civil Servants, Judges, Bankers, etc. (cf. Tawney) in 1939–40	*c.* 1860	(a) Eton, Winchester, Rugby, Harrow, Marlborough; (b) 9 other un-named (HMC 1939); (c) 20 other un-named (HMC *c.* 1939)	(HMC 1939)
6. Bereda, 1947	750–1,000 prominent members of Professions (cf. Tawney) in *c.* 1945	*c.* 1890	GBA *independent* schools in England, 1944 (87 schools)	Rest of GBA + HMC schools (England) as in Fleming Report, 1944
7. Ross, 1948	MPs elected 1918–35	*c.* 1880	—	HMC n.d. (*c.* 1939)
8. Hans, 1950	2,500 writers, representing liberal professions 1948	1881	(a) 9 Clarendon Schools; (b) 51 other named 'public independent schools'	—
9. Jenkins and Jones, 1950	Cambridge Alumni 1751–1899	*c.* 1740	23 named schools (= "J. and J. 23")	HMC 1932 (SMYB 1932–3)
10. Banks, 1954	—	—	—	7 Clarendon schools + certain named schools (PSYB 1947)
11. Copeman, 1955	'Leaders of British Industry'	*c.* 1890–1900	—	HMC *c.* 1952
12. Acton Society, 1956	3,300 + Managers	*c.* 1902	28 'Major Public' = 23 (J. and J.) plus 5 named (incl. Dartmouth)	HMC 1952 (PSYB)

13. Thomas, 1958	MPs elected 1906, 1910	*c.* 1860	9 Clarendon Schools	'Other public schools' (un-named) = HMC *c.* 1952?
14. Clements, 1958	Managers	*c.* 1902	26 'Major Public' = 23 (J. and J.) plus 3 named	HMC 1937 (PSYB)
15. Kelsall, 1958	Higher Civil Servants since *c.* 1890	*c.* 1880	(1) Top 20 boarding (J. and J. minus 3 day) (2) HMC boarding (fees £140+) 1939 (3) HMC boarding (fees to £139) 1939 (4) HMC day 1939	HMC 1939
16. Williams, 1960	350 Br. writers 1480–1930, incl. 53 1830–80 and 53 1880–1930	pre-1850	—	"national grammar schools" treated as public schools
17. Altick, 1962	1100 Br. and Irish writers b. 1750–1909	1763	—	9 Clarendon schools
18. Guttsman, 1963	Cabinet Ministers 1868–1955; Parly. Under-secs. 1868–1945; Royal Commissioners 1944–; Rebel Tory MPs 1930s etc. ("Political Elite")	*c.* 1840–1900	(1) 7 Clarendon boarding (2) Top 20 as Kelsall (= 23 J. and J. minus 3 day schools)	"Other public" or "Other public and boarding", unspecified. (Possibly HMC 1939–, as in Kelsall, Ross, etc.)
19. Morgan, 1963–4	*c.* 200 Anglican diocesan bishops 1860–1960	1794	Several categories based on Kelsall and J. and J. disting. between fees above/below £140 in 1939 and boarding/day character, 1939	HMC 1939
20. Otley, 1965	300 top British army officers 1870–1959	*c.* 1830	major/minor public schools following 1939 boarding fees (cf. Kelsall)	HMC (PSYB) "at any time" (no details)
21. Laurenson, 1966	*c.* 125 Br. male writers born or died 1860–1910	*c.* 1830	—	HMC (*c.* 1965?)
22. Butler and Freeman, 1968	*c.* 1150 Br. government Ministers 1900–67	1841	—	HMC *c.* 1965
23. Compton, 1968	Entrants to Indian Civil Service *c.* 1850–74	*c.* 1845	9 "major" (i.e. Clarendon)	These plus 18 named "newer" schools
24. Coats and Coats, 1970	British "economists" 1890–1915	*c.* 1850	"the 23 schools in the J. and J. category"	HMC 1932?

Table 10

Comparison of Jenkins' and Jones' influential short-list of top Public Schools used for the classification of the education of members of élites for periods including latter part of the nineteenth century, with a short-list of 23 leading public schools 'by interaction' *c.* 1880–1902 (see *Tables 2* and *4*: Group I [22 schools] plus Radley).

Jenkins and Jones	Interaction
—	Bedford
—	Bradfield
CHARTERHOUSE	CHARTERHOUSE
CHELTENHAM	CHELTENHAM
CLIFTON	CLIFTON
—	Dulwich
ETON	ETON
Fettes	—
—	Glenalmond
HAILEYBURY	HAILEYBURY
HARROW	Harrow
Loretto	—
MALVERN	MALVERN
MARLBOROUGH	MARLBOROUGH
Merchant Taylors'	—
Oundle	—
RADLEY	(RADLEY)
REPTON	REPTON
ROSSALL	ROSSALL
RUGBY	RUGBY
ST PAUL'S	ST PAUL'S
Sedbergh	—
SHERBORNE	SHERBORNE
Shrewsbury	—
—	Tonbridge
UPPINGHAM	UPPINGHAM
—	Wellington
WESTMINSTER	WESTMINSTER
WINCHESTER	WINCHESTER

status related to the HMC—which (at least in its 1932 version) is the list used by Jenkins and Jones as the basis of their classification of long-list ('lesser') public schools. Up to a quarter of Jenkins' and Jones' whole basis of classification of the top twenty-three public schools before 1899 is open to question in comparison with the list of the top twenty-three by interaction; it can also be shown that the discrepancies between their top twenty-three and both the top twenty-three scholarship-winning schools 1885–1892 and the twenty-three most expensive public schools in 1902 are even greater.[77] These considerations support the supposition that the formulation of Jenkins' and Jones' short-list as applicable in the eighteenth and nineteenth centuries is arbitrary or even idiosyncratic, reflecting perhaps those authors' own impressions about the relative standing of schools in a much later period or illustrating the still more subtle danger of assuming that schools which are successful in projecting their pupils into élites must therefore be élite schools.

Unfortunately, Jenkins' and Jones' very questionable short-list has been made the basis of the classification of "leading public schools" used in analyses made by several other authors.[78] Perhaps the most notable of these is the study in 1963 of the British political élite, in which W. L. Guttsman uses, in different places, two short-lists of public schools, the seven Clarendon schools, and twenty of Jenkins' and Jones' top twenty-three (dropping the "predominantly day schools" Westminster, St Paul's and Merchant Taylors'). Guttsman appears to treat the second short-list as an extended version of the first, though of course his second now excludes Westminster, present among the Clarendon seven. These bases of classification support various computations of, and conclusions about, the contribution of public schools to the "political élite" throughout the entire period 1868–1955, and he considers attendance at one of the seven Clarendon 'boarding' schools (including, we remember, Shrewsbury) to be one of three criteria indicating membership of 'the traditional ruling strata and upper-class families', as opposed to the 'new men', throughout that period.[79]

Any activity of analysis or classification must allow for a certain margin of error, and some readers may enjoy spotting such slips as may have crept into the lists compiled for this chapter. But special hazards attend the kind of exercise of which we have noted some examples, for they require more than a smattering of conventional knowledge about the comparative standing of certain schools, and among the many pitfalls are the confusions which can arise over mere names. That the Surrey County School is also Cranleigh is not obvious to the authors of at least one of these many studies—why should it be?—and that Blundell's was also Tiverton escaped another; one would want to be reassured that when Jenkins and Jones encountered "Marlborough" throughout almost the first two-thirds of the period for which they analysed their Cambridge men, they realised that this was the Grammar School and not the College, and that they noted a similar distinction between 'Haileybury' the East India Company college and 'Haileybury' the public school. There have been at various times at least three Wellingtons, and several schools of King Edward's foundation in Birmingham could be confused with the famous one: similarly Whitgift/Whitgift Middle, Milton Abbas/Abbey, etc. These confusions can even be encouraged by public figures who appear in *Who's Who* and similar directories: there are identifiable cases of (*e.g.*) Bedford Modern products allowing themselves to be represented as from Bedford, and there was a recent Tory MP who used to like to appear as from a more prestigious Wellington than he actually attended. Similar confusions, whether actual or contrived, can involve Westminster/Westminter City, Liverpool College/Collegiate, the various Haberdashers', Latymer and Merchant Taylors' schools, and several more. Numbers of people in their directory entries suppress details of their schooling altogether—there are many of these even in the current *Who's Who*. That, as Guttsman rightly suggests,[80] the majority of these probably did not attend public schools is a factor of which some authors of élite studies take little or no account.[81] All these kinds of pitfall simply increase the proportion of error in twentieth-century analyses of élites educated before 1902—a proportion which, if the argument of this chapter be accepted, can become very substantial both for short-lists and for long-lists.

9

The interaction of schools in games and similar activities characteristic of public schools has been taken as definitive of a school's claim to public-school status, indeed as indicative of the school's probable rank within four categories in that community of schools, by 1902. Influential though this 'interaction' classification may have been, however, we ought not to rule out other factors from having possibly affected the standing of a school and therefore that of its Old Boys. We have already noticed that Radley's limited interaction, and in particular its non-participation in corps and rifle-shooting throughout the period studied, give that school a lower classification (group II) than its general standing in other respects—indicated, for example, by its expensiveness, and its academic and social attractiveness to pupils and indeed staff,[82] which otherwise suggest its inclusion in group I. Shrewsbury was a similar case: its limited interaction in these activities in the period studied, combined with factors in the same period such as the hostility of Old Boys towards its headmaster and their sending of their sons elsewhere, must be set against the school's long-established reputation for outstanding classical scholarship,[83] which must to some extent have mitigated the low 'interaction' rating of the school and perhaps given the school's products a standing slightly higher than that attaching to the pupils of a group III school. The position of Sedbergh, outside even group IV, is surprising, though that school was likewise exluded from a list of thirty-four "great public schools" listed by *Harmsworth's Encyclopaedia* in 1905.[84] Here, too, we may suggest that the school's low 'interaction' rating may to some extent have been counteracted by other factors, in view of such evidence as the citation of Sedbergh by Mr S. M. Leathes (see above, *Tables 4* and 5) and the popularity of the school in the later Victorian period with at least one northern preparatory school whose other pupils commonly went on to such schools as Rugby (group I) or Eastbourne (group III).[85]

These three instances allow us to modify a school's status by 'interaction' alone, to the extent of considering that school for inclusion in the group next above (thus, Radley in group I,

Shrewsbury in group II, Sedbergh in group IV), but none of them indicates any radical flaw in the general pattern, or alteration in the suggested limits, of the public-schools community by 1902 as outlined above.

Having made that qualification, we may summarise the argument of this chapter by saying that the public schools had developed as a self-conscious community by the late nineteenth century; the limits of that community (but not necessarily the *precise* status of any one school within it) are identifiable by the examination of various forms of interaction between schools in the period *c.* 1880–1902, but the classification of public schools based on this examination is valid only for the late Victorian period, and almost certainly not much before 1880. The degree of self-consciousness is perhaps measurable by classification in extending short-lists of 22–64 schools, while an outer community which existed in a less effective sense may have included some forty more schools before it tailed off in a border zone of schools of really dubious standing. If for purposes of examination of the character of the 'inner' and 'outer' community we arbitrarily place the fourteen schools of group IV with the forty in *Table* 5 we can see two classes of schools, Class A (Groups I, II, III, totalling fifty schools) and Class B (Group IV and *Table* 5) totalling fifty-four schools—the two classes together comprising what might be called the effective public-schools community at its widest, by about 1902.

What were the most notable characteristics of the main community of public schools, as manifested by the fifty schools of Class A? First, it was a pre-eminently Anglican community: all the twenty-two schools in group I were Anglican in character; furthermore Marlborough and Rossall, and to an extent also Haileybury, had a strong clerical connection. The Woodard schools Lancing and Hurst in Group II were strongly Anglo-Catholic and Bradfield and Radley had High Church connections, and St John's Leatherhead was a foundation for the sons of clergy. If most of the small category of Scottish public schools were 'undenominational' or Anglican-Presbyterian, the only one of them to find its way into group I was the strongly Anglican Glenalmond. In England University College School was the only professedly non-denominational school included. Of schools with a strong evangelical connection only Weymouth is in Class A; other such evangelical schools find their way into Class B—King William's College (IOM), South Eastern College Ramsgate (St Lawrence)—along with the Anglo-Catholic schools Ardingly, St Edward's Oxford, and Denstone, also in that class.

The sole nonconformist school in Class A is The Leys, a mainly Methodist foundation. Mill Hill is the only nonconformist school in the residual long-list in Class B. (It is in this context that we must interpret a reported reaction from Harrow to a request from Mill Hill for a games match in the 1870s—a postcard bearing the reply "Eton we know, and Rugby we know, but who are ye?".)[86] No Roman Catholic school was included in Class A, and Stonyhurst is the only one in Class B, though with Beaumont in 1902 perhaps not far behind.[87]

The second characteristic was that the fifty leading schools were not all exclusively, or even largely, boarding schools: some entirely or substantially day schools like Whitgift, Merchant Taylors', UCS, Bedford, St Paul's, Dulwich and Bedford Modern are included. Thirdly, some schools which had been founded as specifically 'middle-class' schools after 1850 had arrived at an established place in the public-schools community by 1902, including Lancing and Hurst in group II, Bedford Modern and Cranleigh in group III. Class B shows Ardingly and Framlingham in group IV and Bedford County School in the *Table* 5 long-list.

These latter aspects give Class A its fourth characteristic—the schools were by no means equally 'exclusive' in the sense of having high fees. Many of the schools, especially in group I, were very expensive, but even here the fees varied greatly according to the particular boarding-house chosen; day-boys paid much less, and at schools like Bedford, St Pauls', Dulwich, Merchant Taylors' and Bedford Modern a day-school education was relatively cheap (with average day fees among the five schools of £16 p.a.)—certainly compared with day-boy fees at Cheltenham or Westminster (around £34 p.a.). A proportion, even if only a small one, in most of the expensive schools had scholarships which paid from a fraction to nearly all of their expenses. At Marlborough, for example, one-eighth of the school had (as sons of clergy) foundation scholarships which could give them a top public-school education at the cost of a day boy's fees at Westminster or Cheltenham, and at least twelve other schools in Class A offered reductions for sons of clergy and/or military/naval officers or (in the case of Epsom) doctors, and at least one leading school in Bedford educated day-boys for £4 a year or less. Fettes had valuable foundationerships for very poor boys.[88] While the boarding schools were virtually closed to the sons of manual workers and the day schools listed could only have contained a tiny representation of exceptional boys of that class, on the other hand the leading fifty schools were not, *as a group*, the exclusive preserve of the rich. Even less exclusive as a group was Class B, with its proportion of schools with relatively cheap day-boys' fees, its 'middle-class' boarding schools, and also the 'charity' school, Christ's Hospital, before 1902 still based in London and interacting little with the main public schools.

Fifthly, the geographical distribution of schools in Class A shows that apart from six in Scotland they were all in England itself: two Anglican public schools in Wales were in Class B together with three schools in the Channel Islands and the Isle of Man, but none from Ireland. A high proportion of the fifty schools were in the south, and especially the south-east, of England—which facilitated interaction, though it did not of course determine it: far-flung schools were prepared to send boys long distances to play matches or participate in corps events if the occasion was appropriate to the participants' membership of the public-schools community. Shrewsbury, which has already been commented on, may perhaps have suffered from its comparative remoteness—a writer in the *Public School Magazine* in 1898 deplored the false impression current that the school was an *Ultima Thule* and difficult to get to and from anywhere.[89] Geographical remoteness must also have limited the opportunities for interaction open to Sedbergh, though we must recognise that there were other schools which overcame similar handicaps because they conceived interaction to be important, even if much of it was limited to schools in their own region, as was the case with Blundell's, in the south-west of England.

After 1902 the public-schools community grew in two ways: first in the increase in numbers of boys in the schools which were already a part of that community in the Victorian period[90] (except for a few which closed), and secondly in the extension of the boundaries of that community to take in more schools. Most of these were schools which had existed within the Victorian period but were still outside the community by 1902—Woodard schools like Worksop and Bloxham; schools of the 'county school' movement; private schools like Wycliffe and Wrekin, etc.; endowed local schools whose transformation (as by Howson at Gresham's School Holt, after 1900, and several others) was not complete until the twentieth century. By far the biggest category of schools were the nonconformist and Roman Catholic schools, so sparsely represented in Classes A or B by 1902, yet by 1939 constituting among the most expensive of the schools on the HMC and completely accepted as public schools by all other twentieth-century criteria, including games interaction. The massive non-Anglican breakthrough into the public-schools community was presaged by the first appearance at the very end of the nineteenth century of Downside and six other Roman Catholic schools competing for the first time in the largely public-school world of the Oxford and Cambridge Higher Certificate examination. The changes in the character and status of schools such as these between the Victorian period and our own are a significant commentary on the sociology of Roman Catholicism* and of Protestant nonconformity† in England in the last hundred years.

* An historian of Roman Catholic education in England, Dr Jack Kitching, tells me that the foundation of the Conference of Catholic Colleges in 1896 which foreshadowed the entry of candidates from numbers of RC secondary schools for the Oxford and Cambridge HSC examinations represented a conscious attempt by RCs to break into the public-schools community. Leading Catholic laity wanted a public-school education capable of competing with the top schools, attendance at which the RC bishops always deplored. George Scott's book *The RCs* (1967) mentions the transformation of Ampleforth in the first half of the twentieth century into a great public school "so that Catholics should no longer need to carry with them a sense of social inferiority as well as the 'impediment' of their religion"... Ampleforth was made what it is today because Catholic parents were sending their sons to Eton, Harrow and Winchester. The only way to ensure that their children would have a Catholic education was to put Ampleforth on a par with other schools. "...An old boy of Stonyhurst... told me 'I think of myself first as a public schoolboy and second as a Catholic public schoolboy' and recalled a remark from his headmaster's address to leavers: 'Remember,

Other schools which feature in this expansion were new boarding schools established after 1902—some of them very expensive—including Bryanston, Canford, Stowe, and Gordonstoun, which early achieved recognition in the public-school community. Others which achieved only the inconclusive recognition of representation on the HMC were some of the newly established LEA secondary day schools after 1902 (though the inclusion of these new schools, expensive or 'state', in classifications of public schools made by analysts of élites 1929–1971 would not compromise those classifications because they had of course no pupils before 1902). Some overseas schools came to be acknowledged as public schools and at last two Irish boarding schools gained such acceptance. Within Britain the significance of geographical remoteness came to be greatly lessened. The extent of fluctuation in the classification 'public school' since 1902 is further illustrated by *Table 8* and by the list of schools considered by the (Newsom) Public Schools Commission in 1968,[93] which contains the following (not all of them, of course, existing before 1902): Rendcomb, Rishworth, Langley, Lord Wandsworth, Grenville, Colston's, Carmel, Pangbourne, and Strathallan. Other (post-1902) schools to appear in recent HMC lists, like Hemel Hempstead (1931), Milton Abbey (1954) and the comprehensive successor (1967) to the old Banbury Grammar School, confirm the fluctuating character of this classification.

It is this sort of expansion, and particularly the taking into the HMC list of schools which had a nineteenth-century character as sectarian or private or local grammar schools but were then outside the public-schools community, which has bedevilled the procedures of classifying schools by their

---

when you leave here, you take with you the good name of Stonyhurst and Catholicism in England. You must remember what you have been taught here. If, for instance, you are invited to a house for the weekend, you must always clean the bath.' "[91]

† For example, the 'arrival' as quite prominent public schools in the twentieth century of Quaker schools like Leighton Park and Bootham, which would certainly not have had any such status in the nineteenth century, is clearly related to the transformation (largely achieved by the 1890s) of Quakerism from the religion, speech, dress, and group endogamy of a 'Peculiar People', and their emergence into general social and political life.[92]

twentieth-century status. This chapter in no sense seeks to overturn the general argument that there has existed for a century at least a connection between education at a public school and entry into élites. But to attempt to *measure* this connection by the devices which have been scrutinized in the above pages has serious weaknesses. First, the short-lists and long-lists used show a margin of disagreement with those put forward in this argument, which render those measurements invalid in proportion as the classification now put forward is accepted as more truly representing the public-schools community before 1902. Secondly, the attempt to demonstrate that successful candidates for entry to élites were mostly educated at schools which are then treated as élite schools obscures the extent to which the schools themselves acted as agencies for recruitment to the more privileged classes from the less privileged. Failure to recognise this is implicit in (*e.g.*) Guttsman's use of his preconceived categories of élite public schools to illustrate the claim[94] that "education is in many ways a better criterion of social class than membership of titled families or economic background". Thus Guttsman puts Fettes, for example, into the category of twenty élite schools which contributed most of the Cabinet in the period 1868–1955: but the Fettesian Cabinet Minister who in that period confirms his classification of Fettes (Sir John, later Viscount, Simon) was the son of a humble nonconformist minister and he went to that school on a scholarship which made his Fettes education almost free. Being at Fettes was not in itself an adequate criterion of his social class, which it only affected when it enabled him to win an open scholarship to Oxford and begin a political career in the Union there.[95]

Another Cabinet Minister who attended a public school by Guttsman's long-list classification was H. H. Asquith, since the City of London School has been on the HMC from the start. Yet the City of London School was, as a 'group IV school by interaction' and a day school, on the edge of the main public-schools community, and its significance to Asquith was[96] as a comparatively cheap school whose magnificent classical teaching launched the boy from a humble background by means of a Balliol scholarship into the political élite—to which he became so completely assimilated that he becomes, for one recent British sociologist, a scholar "educated in the conventional upper class manner".[97] That school achieved the same in the Victorian period for many boys from a distinctly lower-middle-class background who entered élites.[98] F. E. Smith attended a day school, Birkenhead, whose headmaster sat on the HMC from 1901 onwards though the school was outside the public-schools community and not even acknowledged as HMC by the *PSYB* in 1902. Its *later* HMC status guarantees its classification by Guttsman and others as a 'public school' for the Victorian period, yet its significance for F. E. Smith's career clearly lies not as an indication of his public-school background or even (as Guttsman would have it) as an index of his social class[99] but as the institution which equipped him by its teaching for a distinguished career at Oxford and thence in law and politics. Sir Ernest Barker, whose projection into the élite of professors and heads of colleges would be related by such studies to his 'public-school education', was in fact the son of a manual worker and went from an elementary school to Manchester Grammar School, and thence to Balliol in 1892.[100]

These four examples entered élites via universities (all, as it happens, Oxford).[101] It is much more interesting to consider the power of certain schools to facilitate the élite membership of their Old Boys *without* attendance at prestige universities. This is widely held to be the case with Eton, say, and Harrow, whose Old Boys are seen to dominate élite positions, irrespective of university education.[102] But how many schools, from the Victorian period on, have been able to profit from this 'Old-Boy net'? How extensive is the community of public-school Old Boys who give preference in certain important ways such as jobs, admission to clubs, etc., to Old Boys of their own school or to members of a wider class of what they acknowledge as 'public-school men' because in their own schooldays they interacted with each other, or read about each other in a 'public-school' context? Answers to these questions can only be given, for each different period in which 'public-school education' is thought to have afforded special privileges in after life, by an examination of the forms of interaction and recognition in which schools which had claims to be 'public schools' engaged—this chapter suggests the possible extent of that community for boys being educated up to 1902 at the stage of consolidation after the great expansion of the public-school system out of the original

Clarendon schools. It does not suggest that, in thus constituting some kind of community and according each other certain forms of recognition or preference, the pupils or former pupils of (say) 64–104 schools would come to regard each other as *equal* because they had public-school education in common. The Etonian was divided from the boy from Bedford or Hurstpierpoint by a social chasm which could be widened not bridged by a confrontation at Bisley in which the latter showed bad manners, say, or even bad marksmanship. But the fact of common participation in such events led to a form of recognition which to be significant needs only to have manifested itself when boy from a Bisley school came up before an Etonian for consideration for a commission in the Army, or a job in the City, and the other candidates were from schools of which the Etonian had never heard. Attendance at Oxford or Cambridge was still, in many spheres, more valuable as a passport than public-school education, but a large proportion of public-school boys would never go to any university—and we must note that besides the great schools with their army classes and modern sides by the 1890s, Class A contains schools like Hurstpierpoint and Bedford Modern which were in essence 'second-grade' schools whose pupils left mostly at sixteen or seventeen. And in its effects on opportunities in after life (in business, industry, the services etc.) for all these boys, membership of a self-conscious 'public-schools community' may have been decisive.

Any analysis of the relationship between attendance at specific schools and chances in after life which either fails to observe this kind of sociological mechanism or wrongly classifies the groups of schools among which it operated is bound to be defective. We may take some examples. Kingswood School (Bath) was in the course of the first half of the twentieth century to become an acknowledged member of the public-school community in every sense, a school where sons of Midlands industrialists (say) would be paying fees comparable with those at Haileybury, Marlborough and Wellington. But Kingswood throughout the nineteenth century provided free education, board, and even clothing exclusively for the sons of Wesleyan ministers whose stipends, often less than £100 p.a., could hardly have classified them as a privileged élite; the school was outside the interacting community of public schools right up to 1902. Yet when Kingswood's nineteenth-century Old Boys turn up in studies of twentieth-century élites they are classified by Kingswood's twentieth-century character and expensiveness, so that quite false assumptions are made about the élite origins of—or the advantages of public-school Old Boy status of—the Fellows of Trinity, FRS's, professors, eminent jurists, doctors and public-school headmasters produced in two Victorian decades alone by that school.[103]

King's School Canterbury would probably be placed in any list of the 'top twenty' public schools drawn up since World War II, a status reflecting the enormous advances made by that school following the appointment of an outstandingly successful headmaster (Canon Shirley) in 1935.[104] But its Victorian status as a public school was very different. On 'interaction' criteria for the 1890s King's School Canterbury is only a group III public school. Somerset Maugham in his semi-autobiographical novel, *Of Human Bondage*, which reflects his own schooldays there around 1890, compares the education of his hero, Philip, at that school with that of Watson, a fellow articled-clerk in a chartered accountant's office, who had been at Winchester: when he discovered the details of Philip's education Watson "became more patronizing still. 'Of course, if one doesn't go to a public school those sort of schools are the best, aren't they?' "[105]

Leighton Park and Gresham's have already been referred to briefly. Although Leighton Park School was founded in 1890 as a result of a growing awareness in the 1880s of the need to provide a public-school-type education for the sons of wealthy Quakers and thereby to break in to the circle of largely Anglican public schools, that school had certainly not by 1902 achieved public-school status, with its numbers of around forty and with very limited interaction with any other schools—let alone distinguished ones.[106] Though the school's place in HMC lists dates from 1922 with the then headmaster's election to that body, Leighton Park was still little known in 1928 outside the Society of Friends and the locality of Reading:[107] its firm public-school standing of today results from its progress in the 1930s and 1940s, and not before. Gresham's School, Holt, reached a similar firm status rather earlier, as a result of the headmastership of G. W. S. Howson, who took over in 1900 "a little-known grammar school in a remote corner of Norfolk";[108] its "entrance into the arena" of the public schools really dates from after 1903 when the governors facilitated Howson's transformation by spending what was then a very large sum on new buildings.[109] We can gauge the relative standing as late as the second decade of the present century of two other schools by the reported reaction of pupils in the schools to which their headmasters were being promoted. Giggleswick, in Yorkshire, had achieved representation on the HMC by 1886, and its limited interaction with schools of the main public-schools community around 1900 helps to place it among the forty schools of *Table* 5. When its headmaster, W. W. Vaughan, was appointed to Wellington in 1910, the Wellington boys "were at first horrified" at receiving someone from "a small and rather inferior school in foreign parts".[110] Bristol Grammar School was in "low water" for more than twenty years before 1906, despite its good record of open scholarships during those years; it was not even on the HMC at that time. The transformation of the school was at the hands of its "greatest headmaster", (Sir) Cyril Norwood (1906–16), by means which included Norwood's personal and energetic command of the revived cadet corps.[111] When this successful reign brought about Norwood's promotion to the headship of Marlborough in 1916, the specific fact of his having been appointed "from some minor grammar school" caused him [it is said] to be booed by the Marlborough boys on his first entrance in the hall of his new school.[112]

Beaumont's history illustrates a crucial aspect of the argument of this chapter, since that school's clientele during the later Victorian period contained a "small sprinkling" of sons of English peers and gentry and even some members of the Spanish aristocracy and royal family; in that sense the school could be described by 1891 as being the Catholic Eton. But this does not tell us that when Beaumont's Old Boys turn up in élites they could definitely associate their success with being public-school boys, for its Victorian products probably owed more in life to naked merit, or to family background. It was not until 1901, with the appointment of a new headmaster who "advertised widely, entertained magnificently and exhibited ruthlessly"[113]—and, no less significantly, fostered contacts at rowing, boxing, cricket and cadet corps activities with leading non-Catholic as well as Catholic public schools—that Beaumont's products can definitely be said to have benefitted from public schoolboy status.

We have already noted the case of Loretto. That which justifies the inclusion of Loretto (on a short-list, but not among the top twenty) in a public-school classification for the late Victorian period is not an HMC criterion (it was not yet on) nor its expensiveness (though it was very costly, there were other private schools charging nearly double) but its position in a category of esteem based on that school's interaction with other schools. An attempt to elucidate this category of esteem, and Loretto's place in it, suggests that the ranking of Loretto on some short-lists used for the Victorian period (and even earlier) is one of many faults in a basically mis-conceived classification. These are only a few out of many instances of schools figuring in short-lists or long-lists used for classification which are examples of the attribution of twentieth-century status to schools which had a quite different character in the nineteenth century. Though there is a sense in which some pupils of a given school might benefit from the rise in status of the school they had left decades before, this would only apply to a small proportion; in any case it is in the years immediately after leaving school that the job-gaining advantages of the school's status as a 'public school' have probably been most crucial. Such defects as these cast doubt on the conclusions reached by such studies of élites: in particular, figures in them which are used to support the arguments about the 'democratisation' or otherwise of élites since 1902 may in fact only illustrate the extent of the 'democratisation' or otherwise of the schools studied, or of the 'public-schools community' in general.

Whatever the accuracy of their methods, the exercise of tracing the representation of public-school men in élites is likely to continue to fascinate researchers. One modern effort which deserves a special mention—indeed deserves a prize, perhaps—is that of an eminent, if recent, Old Whitgiftian, Professor Liam Hudson, who together with a colleague devoted some time to the study of eminent members of the British medical profession in 1969 who were born between 1900 and 1925. The key distinction for educational background was between HMC schools (explicitly treated as "public schools") and grammar schools, though they offered no date for their HMC basis—presumably a 1969 list was used to classify those entering the schools 1913–38. The resulting margin of error would not be as gross in this case as it would have been for the Victorian period, but some of the quaint deductions yielded by this analysis deserve to be noticed, and not only because they achieved the distinction of inclusion in the "This England" feature of the *New Statesman.* Among the various kinds of British doctor studied, they found that *specialists* who had been to *English* public schools

> were more likely than others to work on living bodies rather than on dead bodies, on the head rather than on the lower trunk, on male bodies rather than on female bodies, and on the body's surface rather than its inside.[114]

CHAPTER FIVE

"Scholars and Gentlemen"

The profession of public-school assistant master is essentially the creation of the Victorian period. Any account of the development of the Victorian public shool, its characteristic institutions and the sociological roles of the system, is incomplete if it does not include in its scope the role of individual men, as teachers or headmasters, in the schools. As Bishop Westcott wrote in his tribute to his old headmaster:

> . . . appliances, methods of instruction, machinery, are capable of almost indefinite improvement and make no real impression; it is the teacher who is the spring of life in a school, and *is* the school for the highest purposes of education.[1]

This chapter is concerned with a few of the most important characteristics of this influential sector of the academic profession as it developed in the Victorian period.

We have noted the fairly exacting specifications of assistant masters looked for by Arnold. The Report of the Clarendon Commission shows us how much was being paid by the greater schools in the 1860s to recruit men of that calibre. (See *Table 11*)

As set out in the *Table 11*, these figures reveal a distinction between the large boarding schools (Eton, Harrow, Rugby) on the one hand, and the smaller boarding schools and the London (mainly) day schools on the other. They illustrate how the large salaries of headmasters and assistants derived from the total numbers in the school and especially from the profits of keeping boarding-houses. At the three largest schools in 1861 boarding fees could be very expensive, and within a school like Harrow

Table 11. Salaries of Public-School Headmasters and Assistants in Nine "Clarendon" Schools in the Early 1860s

	Numbers	Max. no. of Boys in division	Head-master (£)	Assistant Masters (£)
Eton	806	48	6,000*	to 1,845*
Harrow	481	37	10,000* 6,288	c. 450 – 2000*
Rugby	463	42	3,000*	340 – 1600*
M. Taylors'	262	32	c. 1,000	200 – 525
Winchester	200	41	3,000*	200 –(1500*)
St Paul's	146	40	c. 1,000*	300*– (400*)
Westminster	136	30	1,170*	210 – 290
Shrewsbury	131	40	2,000*	225 – (560)
Charterhouse	116	20	1,100	200 – (700)

* = residential perquisites.
Salaries in right-hand column are for *Classical* assistant masters, and the higher figure indicates stipends which may only be available to housemasters; those in brackets were only available to the Second Master. The Harrow HM's salary is given at both the 'gross' and the 'net' figure after 'various charges and deductions', and the Commissioners were prepared to accept that the HM's real income was in practice less even than the lower figure (PSC, I 209).
Figures derived from: Clarendon Commission Report ("PSC") 1864, Vol. I, part 2, *passim*.

there were variations between houses, the most expensive houses being very costly indeed. Such variations persisted, and basic fees ranged between £143 and £188 at Harrow around 1900, and between £85–£105 at Marlborough and £80–£114 at Haileybury.

The house system itself had grown up at Harrow in order to augment the stipends of assistant masters. At newer schools like Marlborough, as we saw in Chapter Three, out-college houses were grafted on to the original 'hostel' system from the 1860s onwards precisely in order to give opportunities for profit which would attract and retain men of ability. At Uppingham, Thring, who had no margin in the endowment to expand his school, guaranteed his masters to supply them with boys if they would build (for perhaps £8000) boarding-houses as private profit-making ventures.

The relationship between salaries, numbers, and boarding profits is well illustrated in the case of Harrow, where Longley (later Archbishop of Canterbury) is reputed[2] to have saved £30,000 in his seven years as headmaster (1829–36): under his successor, Christopher Wordsworth, numbers fell drastically and were a mere sixty-nine when C. J. Vaughan was appointed nine years later. He raised them to four hundred and sixty in fourteen years. The case of one Harrow housemaster from the early period is interesting as it exemplifies a variety of avenues of earning a living which were available to a competent academic in Holy Orders in the Victorian period—school and university teaching, parochial work and private pupils, authorship, and finally eccelesiastical preferment. Longley had appointed to his staff a young fellow of St John's, Cambridge, (2nd Wrangler in 1836) John William Colenso, who had fought his way up from an impoverished home in Cornwall. The cost of taking on and fitting up two Harrow boarding-houses in turn (the first was destroyed by fire) left Colenso £5,000 in debt,[3] after six years in the school, and he returned to St John's as a tutor. As luck would have it, his return coincided with a cut in the dividend of the college fellows,[4] and he moved to a Norfolk living (worth £500 a year) and took private pupils, charging them perhaps two-hundred guineas a year each.[5] But the debt was finally only settled by the sale to his publisher of the rights of his famous *Arithmetic for Schools* (1843). This text-book made Colenso a household name long before he ever set foot in the diocese of Natal, to which he was appointed bishop in 1853, or demonstrated the mathematical impossibility of the account in Leviticus (8 : 14) of the whole assembly of Israel (600,000 men) being gathered at the door of the tabernacle (1692 sq. yds).[6] Yet if Colenso had been able to stick it out three more years at Harrow he would have seen the tide of prosperity of the school and its masters turn, and he could have made more money than ever he made at St John's, or in his Norfolk living, or as bishop.

Another assistant master in Wordsworth's last years at Harrow was the classical scholar Richard Shilleto, then debarred from a college fellowship by marriage. He did not stay more than a year (presumably because he could not afford to) and returned to Cambridge as a coach.

Harrow and Rugby were schools where maths masters enjoyed a proper status and, as we have seen with Colenso, were allowed to become housemasters. At Eton this was not so: mathematics was only established in 1851, and for the better part of the century the maths masters were not allowed to wear gowns and had no part in the discipline of the school,[7] with consequent depression of their status and authority. Disparities in salary between teachers of different subjects were not as marked at Rugby in 1861 as at some other Clarendon schools. The *average* emoluments[8] of Rugby's thirteen classical assistants were £966, of the three mathematics masters £877, and of the modern language masters £755, but this latter figure reflected the senior French master's receipts of over £1,200—his junior colleague got between £100–250, a figure far more typical of French masters in public schools generally.

Where (as in most schools) the system of capitations related the headmaster's total earnings to the number of boys in the school, there was a temptation to keep down the numbers of teaching staff among whom such profits would have to be shared, with effects on class size which can be seen from the second column of *Table 11*. Keate, headmaster of Eton 1808–34, had at one stage a form of nearly two hundred boys, and forms of eighty or ninety were not uncommon in the great schools until late in the Victorian period. Trollope in 1865 complained that there were too few masters because those that were in office were unwilling to share their incomes with newcomers:

> Who is going to give up his wife's carriage or his own bottle of claret, because somebody else thinks the world might be improved by such sacrifices?[9]

But the fact remains that the tendency of the period was for headmasters to limit class size by appointing extra staff, and some headmasters consciously limited numbers of entrants in accordance with notions of an ideal size of a school-community.

Of the three top schools, Rugby was pre-eminent as a coloniser, in the sense of its assistant masters going off as headmasters[10] to other schools, but then its salaries were the lowest of the three, and in addition, from Temple's time onwards, its masters taxed themselves collectively by a total of as much as

£500 a year to pay for certain desirable objects, such as entrance scholarships to the school and the salary of a school Marshal. (At Rugby's 'daughter' schools, Clifton and Wellington, the rather lower stipends were a further incentive to seek headships elsewhere, at which the staffs of both schools were very successful in this period.) Harrow masters did go off as heads,[11] but normally only very considerable schools could lure away a highly-paid housemaster. Indeed the traffic was the other way: Sankey, headmaster of Bury St Edmund's school for eleven years, became a Harrow housemaster (1891–1905); even a professor at King's College, London, (Moriarty), could be recruited to teach the Army Class at Harrow in 1899. By a similar process T. E. Brown went on from the headmastership of the old endowed Crypt School, Gloucester, to be a housemaster—a memorable one—at Clifton under Percival.[12] There was also recruitment to assistant masterships at the three leading schools from the public schools next below them—Farrar (for example) from Marlborough to Harrow.

Eton presented a picture of greater staff stability throughout the century: earnings were such that after one had become a housemaster the only temptation to seek a headship elsewhere lay in the greater exercise of creative power, or in the value of a headship as a stepping-stone to ecclesiastical promotion. This stability and continuity were useful for the operation of Eton's 'tutorial' system; they were reinforced by the expectation, effective until 1905, that the headship of the school would be an internal promotion.

Moberly, headmaster of Winchester (1835–66), reckoned on an income of £3,000 a year. Under the new statutes of the 1870s the headmastership there was "financially a splendid appointment",[13] with a salary and perquisites probably worth well in excess of £3,500.[14] The headmastership of Repton, including the profits on the boarding-house, was reckoned by the *Journal of Education* to be "worth about £4,000 a year in 1900".[15] In the second half of the Victorian period an Eton housemaster might receive £3,000 or more: Oscar Browning claimed[16] that his dismissal from the Eton staff in 1875 caused a drop in his income from £3,000 to £300 (the basic pay of a fellow of King's, which itself dropped to half or less than half at the turn of the century; as an Eton master, Browning had been accustomed to spend

£300 a year on books alone). A classical assistant master at Winchester in this period earned £350–450,[17] and housemasters perhaps three times as much: Ridding told the young men whom he commissioned to build new boarding-houses that on a total outlay of £7,000 they could expect an income of £1,000.[18]

The salary of Marlborough headmasters was £2,000 plus free house and garden from 1858 to the end of this period, though G. G. Bradley was voted a special rise of £500 a year in his ninth successful year.[19] It is therefore not difficult to accept the statement of Dean Farrar's son that after Farrar's Harrow housemastership, each successive promotion involved a drop in salary:

> The headmastership of Marlborough [*sc.* £2,000] was far less lucrative than the command of a large house at Harrow, and the position involved a large expenditure in hospitality. His preferment [*sc.* to a Westminster canonry] was, again, less lucrative than Marlborough; while acceptance of the deanery of Canterbury involved a very heavy sacrifice of income.[20]

[*Whitaker* (1897) says that the deanery of Canterbury, nominally worth £1,400, was actually worth less because of the effect of agricultural depression on incomes based on property.][21]

These totals illustrate the situation for heads and assistants in the 'great schools'—the Clarendon boarding schools and the other boarding schools nearest in kind to them. The situation in the wide range of other schools which had claims to be 'public schools' might be very different. Here the headmaster's salary was generally compounded, as in some of the 'great schools' already discussed, of a fixed stipend plus capitation fees plus boarding-house profits, but the scale of all of these was a pale reflection of theirs. The endowment of the grammar schools, some of which were undergoing transformation as public schools, typically provided for a stipend of £100–200 for the headmaster. When Samuel Butler went to Shrewsbury in 1798 his stipend was £120, but the rewards of a successful headmastership of thirty-eight years made him "a comparatively wealthy man".[22] The headmastership of Sedbergh in 1900 was based on a fixed stipend of £200, but the 'head money' on two hundred and ten pupils and the profits and perquisites of the head's boarding-house for forty boys gave him a salary of about

£1,450 in addition to residence.[23] At Bedford Modern School in the same year the headship carried a basic stipend of £100, together with the profits of a small boarding-house, and a capitation allowance which when the school had four hundred boys would bring his total emoluments up to about £850.[24] Framlingham began with a fixed salary of £300 (plus house) for the headmaster in 1864 (and there were one hundred and fifty applicants for the post),[25] but the capitation principle directly linking the headmaster's income to the prosperity of the school was much commoner: at the Devon County School he received £500 when the school had one hundred and fifty boys, but between £290 and £390 when numbers dropped to ninety.[26] One of the implications of this connection with numbers of boys was the form of 'poaching' by which heads on moving to a new school took a number of pupils from the old school with them, which we have already noticed in the cases of Holden of Uppingham and Durham, Harper of Cowbridge and Sherborne, and others.

Numbers must therefore be a constant and real preoccupation of any headmaster: the success of many of these men was related to their qualities as businessmen. We can see this in the career of the Rev. (later Canon) W. R. Dawson, who at twenty-six took over King's School, Grantham, in the 1890s and built it up so successfully that he was called in to rescue the fortunes of Brighton College, which by 1900 was in debt to the Phoenix Insurance Company to the tune of £50,000.[27] Dawson soon built up numbers to over six hundred, including a large contingent of foreigners—Spanish, Argentinian, French and Italian boys—though they seldom stayed long in the school:

> I take them on my own terms [he explained to a confidant], two years fees in advance as surety for their good behaviour. They're all highly sexed, and it's only a matter of months till they sleep with a housemaid. Then out they go.[28]

2

The expansion of public-school education and of secondary education generally after mid-century created a new demand for the services of assistant masters, but while men who achieved headships in this expanded market got at least reasonable rewards, assistants were less fortunate. Harper of Sherborne drew the attention of his colleagues on the HMC in 1876 to the low average salaries of assistants in the schools next below the 'great' schools in standing, and there were many expressions of agreement there with his vehement delaration that "many masters of schools, from the top to the bottom, are villainously paid".[29] He had conducted a survey of salaries in eight schools—four endowed schools with over two hundred and fifty boys each, four "more modern colleges" with over five hundred boys each. The average basic salary in the eight schools was £250; only five masters in all had earnings which, with extra tuition and boarding profits, totalled £1,000 a year, and there were not ten who grossed £400 a year. By his reckoning, not two-fifths of the total staffs of assistant masters in eight schools could keep a house in which to support comfortably a wife and family.[30]

It was thus only a handful of schools—half a dozen at the most—that Welldon of Harrow can have had in mind when in 1888 he was quoted as saying that "the *average* salary of the junior public-school master of ability is £400–500 a year" and that "a housmaster would ordinarily receive £1,500–2,000 a year".[31] If these were the *average* for Harrow, Welldon must have known that in his previous school, Dulwich, the average salary for all except one assistant master a decade before had been £200.[32] In 1895 evidence on salaries in secondary schools was given by the Association of Assistant Masters to the Bryce Commission. Their figures showed that "while in 10 out of the best schools the average salary is £242.77, the average in 190 others is £105.19".[33] This latter figure took in a great number of 'second-grade' schools, only a few of which would have been considered 'public' schools by that date. To a correspondent quoted in the *Journal of Education* in 1900 it was "evident that there are about a hundred secondary schools of the type called 'public', and no others". He was prepared to accept that in these schools the figure of £200–300 would apply to most salaries and, referring to those who had boarding houses, there were "the 'licensed victuallers' plums for the few".[34]

In an article on "Salaries in Secondary Schools" in the

Contemporary Review in 1900, W. H. D. Rouse, Rugby master and later headmaster of the Perse School, pointed out that in the well-known schools like Cheltenham, Clifton, and Marlborough, there were no regular salary scales—"each man fights for himself", as an ill-paid Bedford School assistant master put it.[35] In these schools, as indeed in most, the starting salary and any annual rise were at the discretion of the headmaster and governors.

3

The emergence of public-schoolmastering as a distinct profession would involve a degree of severance from the two other professions to which it was regarded for much of the period as a kind of subsidiary activity: university teaching and Holy Orders.

Until the relaxation of the obligation of celibacy for the majority of college fellows at Oxford and Cambridge in the early 1880s, the desire to marry sent into the schools a supply of gifted academics. In 1835 Charles Wordsworth, one of the most brilliant men of his generation, was tutor and Greek praelector at Christ Church and set for an outstanding academic career at Oxford. Unfortunately a meeting in the Louvre with an English girl with whom he fell in love "at first sight" forced him to look around for a position in which he could marry. It was no strong pastoral conception of schoolmastering which caused him to apply for the Second Mastership of Winchester, then happily vacant:

> The appointment, worth [then] some £1,000 p.a., with a house, and other perquisites, was a most desirable one; in some respects, indeed, more desirable than the headmastership, as it did not involve the taking of boarders, or any but the slightest personal superintendence outside of school hours; and, upon the whole, I doubt if there was any educational position in England which possessed so many recommendations and so few drawbacks.[36]

Wordsworth became the first headmaster of Glenalmond, a new public school in Scotland, and in 1853 (after an election in which he had voted for himelf) Bishop of St Andrews. At Glenalmond his idea of the proper distance and respect between masters and boys was affronted by the "absence . . . of anything like awe" with which Scottish (as opposed to English) schoolboys treated their teachers:

> One day when a lesson I had been hearing had just ended, and I was still in the class-room in all my dignity of cap and gown, a boy came up, and without any consciousness of rudeness or impropriety, asked me: 'Please sir, can you tell me where I can find some good worms? I am going out fishing.'[37]

B. F. Westcott was one of "an unusually brilliant" generation at Cambridge in the late 1840s, but his prospects of a university career were blighted by the attachment he had formed during his schooldays to the sister of one of his schoolfellows at King Edward's, Birmingham: marriage would mean resignation of his Trinity fellowship. He became a master at Harrow in 1852. Here his influence was slow to make itself felt: he was regarded, until he had been there for a dozen years, as something of a dreamer and a recluse—"he was too good to be a schoolmaster"[38]—though his impact on a small number of intimate pupils and colleagues, and his effectiveness in the pulpit, were more marked.[39] His impatience with the trivial details of school life was shown by his habit of bringing books into masters' meetings to read, his prestige as a scholar shielding him from the headmaster's rebuke.[40] Schoolmastering was not his real métier, and it was the fruits of his theological studies pursued privately at Harrow which led ultimately to his return to Cambridge as Divinity professor,* whence he became a bishop.

The Rev. William Haig-Brown was another who was driven by marriage from a college fellowship—he had been Dean of Pembroke College, Cambridge—into school work, in 1855.[41] He, at least, was demonstrably more successful at it, moving on from the headmastership of Kensington Proprietary School to become 'second founder' of Charterhouse: he organised the removal of the school from London to the country in 1872 and its transformation into a large boarding public school.

A different category of dons *manqué* were those who taught in public schools while awaiting a chance to begin a university

*With some help from an 'Old Boy network'—the influence of certain of his former schoolfellows at King Edward's, Birmingham.

teaching career. Such a man was J. E. B. Mayor, who taught at Marlborough in the dark days under Wilkinson. He kept the boys' noses so close to the grindstone that he was spared some of the more usual phenomena of indiscipline; his hours out of the classroom were spent preparing his edition of Juvenal which paved the way for his return to a college post at Cambridge, where he became university librarian and then Latin professor (1870–1910). A philologist and antiquarian of vast learning, "keenly interested in lexicography, the Old Catholics, vegetarianism, and Esperanto",[42] his eccentricities and his bizarre conceptions of scholarship and teaching became legendary in Cambridge.[43] John Wordsworth, later Bishop of Salisbury, taught ineffectively at Harrow and with slightly more success at Wellington while competing for fellowships at Oxford. A procession of failures in fellowship examinations had reconciled him to the prospect of a career in schoolmastering when an opportune vacancy led to his election at Brasenose, where, again, he proved a good scholar but an abysmal teacher.[44]

The traffic between school and university teaching—and it was a traffic in both directions—continued even after the relaxation of the celibacy rule for college fellows, but those who found their way back into university posts after a start in the schools now did so as a result of chance factors rather than as a premeditated stage in the development of their careers. J. F. Bright, a Rugbeian who was one of Cotton's able recruits to the Marlborough staff, later joined Cotton's successor Bradley at University College, Oxford, and went on to succeed Bradley as Master of that college. G. F. Browne, an able university administrator and later a bishop, was brought back to Cambridge after some five years' successful teaching at Glenalmond.[45] Both J. R. Seeley (Regius Professor of Modern History at Cambridge) and H. Nettleship (Latin Professor at Oxford) began their careers as public-school masters. The Dulwich staffroom in the last two decades of the century contained at least two men who went on to successful careers as university teachers—G. G. Coulton, and A. C. Pearson (Regius Professor of Greek at Cambridge 1921–28), and a third master, the future Sir W. M. Ackworth, who after ten years on the staff left to become a specialist in railway transport economics and ultimately a railway tycoon himself and "the greatest expert in the world on the relationship between railways and governments".[46] The career of G. G. Coulton was exceptional. After redeeming a Cambridge *aegrotat* (1881) by study in France and Germany to increase his qualifications in languages, Coulton became an ordained schoolmaster in preparatory and public schools—including Sherborne, Sedbergh and Dulwich—then an army 'crammer', University Extension lecturer, and finally Cambridge University lecturer and research fellow of St John's. En route he abandoned his Orders but not his religious convictions.[47]

Moves from university posts direct to headmasterships, which had been common in the earlier period, continued to the end of the century (and indeed thereafter), but would be less common. Harrow took a risk in 1859 in choosing H. M. Butler, a Cambridge don of twenty-six, in preference to Alfred Barry (later primate of Australia) with similar academic credentials but also solid school experience. On appointment to Merchant Taylors' in 1900, J. A. Nairn was at the time the youngest public-school headmaster in the kingdom, bringing with him "the reputation of being the most brilliant scholar that Cambridge has produced since Jebb",[48] but his headmastership was not a great success, and in any case the new conception of the headmaster's role placed less premium on the possession of specialised academic gifts of that order. Oxford and Cambridge colleges had used their rights—in some cases absolute—to nominate to the headmasterships of particular endowed schools as an avenue of patronage for their fellows. The exercise by Corpus Christi College, Oxford, of this right gave Manchester Grammar School some of its ablest headmasters in the nineteenth century, most notably F. W. Walker, later of St Paul's. Their fellowships of St John's (Cambridge) fitted B. H. Kennedy and H. W. Moss for the headmastership of Shrewsbury in 1836 and 1866, the latter at age twenty-four. Changes in governing bodies which were among the reforms of endowed schools after 1869 replaced these actual or virtual rights of nomination by mere representation, but this still helped alumni of colleges with such representation on governing bodies to get headships—the Johnian Henry Hart at Sedbergh in 1879, and H. A. P. Sawyer of Queen's (Oxford) from a strong field of candidates in 1903 at St Bees, which he transformed into a public school.[49]

4

The laicisation of the profession of university teacher was largely achieved when the obligation to take Anglican Orders was relaxed for most Oxford and Cambridge fellowships between the 1850s and the 1870s. Public-school mastering, too, became a substantially lay profession during the last thirty years of the century. At Winchester only a quarter of the assistant masters were in Orders in 1887: at the pointedly High Anglican Radley in 1870, 80% of the staff had been clergymen, but by 1895 the proportion had fallen to 40%.[50] Statistics of the staffs of "ten great schools", both boarding and day, which were quoted at the HMC in 1907, illustrate this process:[51]

1870 – 54% ordained
1880 – 40.3% ,,
1889 – 28.7% ,,
1906 – 13.3% ,,

Even early in this period the 'great schools' had laymen who were among their most notable teachers: Edward Bowen and R. Bosworth Smith at Harrow, the formidable Robert Whitelaw at Rugby, William Johnson Cory and Oscar Browning at Eton. Indeed, by 1891, nineteen of the twenty-one housemasters at Eton were laymen, as were seven out of ten at Harrow, five out of nine at Winchester, and six out of eleven at Charterhouse.[52]

Yet few of these men were appointed to headmasterships in the Victorian period. In 1888 Welldon of Harrow was quoted as saying that "as a general rule it is not especially valuable for a headmaster to be in holy orders", but a writer in the educational press hastened to point out that Welldon would never have qualified, if he had not himself been in Orders,[53] for the lucrative headmastership he then held—to which the first layman would not be appointed until 1926. Referring to the reform of the governing bodies of public schools and endowed schools after 1869, Mr Gladstone in laying the foundation of an extension at Glenalmond in 1891 claimed:

> There is not one of the public schools of England of which the headmaster is not now chosen by large and free election, and by election I think in every case by a board on which the lay element largely predominates . . . and yet the headmasters

> chosen by these boards for the great public schools, for conducting the arduous part of the work of education for the young—every one of the headmasters of [the] great schools of England is at this moment a clergyman (Cheers).

T. E. Page of Charterhouse, layman, housemaster, classical scholar and editor of high repute, was one of many who wrote, in the correspondence in the press which followed the reports of Gladstone's speech, to point out the "public disgrace" in this situation. Parliament, he claimed, had given laymen a definite right, which many governing bodies were in practice denying. "The injustice done to schoolmasters is grave: the injury done to general education is greater."[54]

That laymen, who predominated among assistant masters and housemasters in the leading schools, were passed over for public-school headships in favour of clergymen, and felt this as an "injustice", points to a situation which deserves closer examination. In point of fact, over a quarter of the headmasters belonging to the HMC in 1886 were laymen; the numbers of lay heads on the HMC, and indeed their proportion to the total of HMC headmasters, were to increase steadily in the next decade: by 1903 nearly 40% of the HMC[55] were laymen. Yet Page was voicing a widespread resentment among lay public-school masters against what was felt to be a bottleneck in promotions. The apparent paradox is explained by understanding what was meant by 'public schools'. Gladstone's reference to all the "great schools of England" having ordained heads in 1891 cannot have referred to the Clarendon schools (one of these, St Paul's, had a lay head from 1877 onwards): he was speaking at Glenalmond and his audience must have assumed he was including them (and their ordained headmaster) in an undefined category of 'public schools' which must have been very different from the HMC schools with their 30% or so of laymen even by 1891. He was referring, in fact, to certain of the schools prominent in the 'public-schools community' at that date: to be precise, to the boarding schools of what in Chapter IV has been termed Group I*.

* The reference also fitted all the schools of Group II except one non-Anglican Scottish school.

The year 1903, which saw the lay Rugby housemaster Frank Fletcher's appointment as head of the strongly clerical Marlborough, was regarded as a turning point. The *Times* echoed the general surprise at the appointment, in a cautiously favourable leading article.[56] If we look at those public schools which from the 1870s onwards were appointing laymen as heads we can see the nature of the "injustice" suffered before 1903. Chief among these were St Paul's (1877 Walker), Dulwich (1885 Gilkes, ordained only on his retirement), University College School (1876 Eve, 1898 Paton), City of London School (1890 Pollard), Bedford (1874 Pillpotts), Manchester Grammar School (1859 Walker, 1877 Dill, 1888 Glazebrook, 1890 King), Blundell's (1875 Francis), Oundle (1872 Sanderson), Sedbergh (1879 Hart), Merchiston (1898 Smith), Perse (1902 Rouse), Bromsgrove (1873 Millington, 1901 Hendy), King Edward's, Birmingham (1900 Gilson). Thus, among those schools which interacted with, or recognised, each other as members of a public-schools community before 1903 it was only in those of the leading schools which were predominantly *day* schools, or in the smaller and less prestigious boarding schools, that lay headmasters were tolerated before that year.

Those lay masters at the great boarding schools who were prepared, for the sake of 'promotion', to relinquish lucrative housemasterships in this period found a restricted field of headmasterships open to them. From Rugby, Potts went to establish the non-denominational Fettes in Scotland in 1870, Kitchener went to Newcastle (Staffs.) High School in 1874, and Phillpotts went to Bedford (Grammar) School in the same year, though his "promotion in power and status" meant leaving a "much less anxious and far more assured" position.[57] J. M. Wilson was a layman throughout his twenty years as mathematics and science master at Rugby* and was actually refused ordination towards the end of that time, but was ordained after his appointment as headmaster of Clifton in 1879.[59] M. G. Glazebrook taught for ten years at Harrow as a layman before he was appointed to the headmastership of Manchester Grammar School in 1888, but he

* *Cf.* the reaction of a new boy at Wilson's house at Rugby in 1865, expressed in a letter home: "I like Mr Wilson what I have seen of him there is one blessing he is not a parson."[58]

took Orders on translation to Clifton two years later. There was some bewilderment among the Harrow staff in 1879 when they heard the announcement of Henry Hart's appointment to an almost unknown school of under a hundred boys at Sedbergh,[60] but in fact outside a few schools like Bedford and Manchester a layman like Hart could have little hope of serious consideration for his candidature. Though Millington of Bromsgrove had been short-listed for Cheltenham in 1898, it became an 'open secret' that he was not elected because "he did not happen to be in holy orders".[61] When the headship of a large day school, King Edward's, Birmingham, came up in 1900 there was a strong field of lay candidates. The final choice was between the Harrow housemaster Gilson and the Rugby housemaster Rouse (who was secretary of the A.M.A.);[62] the latter, unsuccessful on this occasion, was appointed to the Perse School soon afterwards. Among other laymen candidates for Birmingham were King, of Manchester, and Gow, of Nottingham High School. King was appointed to Bedford in 1903 in (again) a strong field of laymen,[63] including Spenser (later headmaster of U.C.S.), W. W. Vaughan (later headmaster of Giggleswick, Wellington and Rugby) and Fletcher (later headmaster of Marlborough and Charterhouse), but it was not until 1910 that King, still a layman, could be appointed to his own old school, Clifton. Dr Gow, a Cambridge Third Classic (1875) who had been called to the bar, was a layman throughout the sixteen years of his Nottingham High School headmastership, but after his disappointment at Birmingham he took Orders on his appointment to Westminster School in 1902. Gerald Rendall, layman as Principal of University College, Liverpool, was ordained on appointment to the headmastership of Charterhouse in 1897. H. M. Burge, fellow and dean of University College, Oxford, took Orders at the age of thirty-five just when his name was being mentioned for public-school headmasterships: he landed Repton in 1900, and, after two terms there, Winchester; ten years later he was a bishop.[64]

Nevertheless the connection between the schoolmaster and clergyman roles was not so well-established that it went without question even by bishops. Arnold's personal acceptance of this connection was symbolised by his proceeding to priest's Orders, after many years as deacon, when appointed to Rugby; the future Dean Bradley did the same on becoming headmaster of Marlborough, and H. D. Harper was still a deacon throughout his first headship and was not priested until he had been at Sherborne for four years and was about to take over the chaplaincy.[65] Yet though S. Rhodes James was ordained deacon in 1883 as an Eton master, Bishop Mackarness of Oxford declined to ordain him priest on his school title alone and without parochial work, and James remained deacon until a more obliging bishop priested him on appointment as headmaster of Malvern in 1897.[66] Nor did all bishops even agree that schools should be allowed to have their own chapels.[67] In 1907 Rhodes James put a motion to the HMC asking the Archbishops and Bishops to standardise their regulations for the ordination of public-school assistant masters so as to end the anomalies among attitudes still apparent among some on the Bench.[68]

As late as 1903 H. A. James, headmaster of Rugby, was prophesying to a junior member of his staff (Frank Fletcher) that none of the "great boarding schools" would accept a lay headmaster[69] during the latter's lifetime—and Fletcher was to live until 1954! It was in 1903 that Marlborough's advertisement for the headmastership specifically invited applications from laymen.

The initiative here came from one of the lay members of the governing body, R. Bosworth Smith, the former Harrow housemaster.[70] Though Percival (by now Bishop) gave it as his opinion that this specification was only a gesture,[71] Fletcher was appointed. Whereas his successor at Marlborough in 1911 was again a cleric, several boarding schools of what in Chapter Four have been called Group I by now had lay heads.* Even at Woodard's Anglo-Catholic Lancing (suggested as a Group II school) a layman was called in as head in 1902, on the initiative of the Old Boys, to save the school, at a time of crisis, from further serious decline.[72]

* The predominantly boarding schools of Group I appointed their first lay headmasters in modern times in the following years: Bradfield 1928, Charterhouse 1911, Cheltenham 1919, Clifton 1910, Eton 1933, Glenalmond 1938, Haileybury 1912, Harrow 1926, Malvern 1914, Marlborough 1903, Repton 1932, Sherborne 1909, Tonbridge 1907, Uppingham 1934, Wellington 1910, Westminster 1937, Winchester 1935.

Thus the grievance (in 1891) that "the highest positions in the scholastic profession are open to less than a quarter of those who should be able to compete for them"[73] reflected the blockage, which would continue for another decade, in the promotion of laymen to the headships of those of the leading twenty-two to thirty public schools which were predominantly *boarding* schools. Clerical rule was perpetuated because the special problems of boarding-school communities were thought to call for the exercise of functions which could only be looked for in a clergyman. Foremost of these functions were preaching in chapel (for, claimed Welldon, only an ordained headmaster could fully utilise the chapel),[74] preparation for confirmation, and religious teaching generally.

Among the more bizarre of many unsupported statements in a recent contribution to the literature on the English public school is Mr Rupert Wilkinson's assertion that "neither Chapel nor 'Divinity' were ever the main vehicles of moral education in the public-school system as a whole".[75] In fact, the preaching function of the headmaster was regarded as one of his two most important duties, and the key weapon in the armoury with which the school equipped the boys to cope with moral evil. It is true that Eton did not have a single able preacher as headmaster in the Victorian period[76] (indeed until 1905), but throughout the community of boarding public schools the performance of the headmaster in the pulpit was an important measure of his abilities. The sermons of Vaughan at Harrow, of Farrar and Cotton at Marlborough, of Benson at Wellington, created an indelible impression on generations of their pupils who discussed them in letters home, in their diaries, and later in their memoirs,[77] and sometimes pressed the headmaster to publish them—"published at the request of the Sixth form". In the desperate days of the unsuccessful first headmaster of Marlborough, the governors asked Wilkinson to publish his sermons in the hope that this might bring clients to the school.[78]

Vaughan's sole doubt about the fitness of his twenty-six-year-old former pupil H. M. Butler to succeed him at Harrow was his ignorance of Butler's abilities in the pulpit: he asked him to send him a sample sermon.[79] Welldon, when at Dulwich, established his chances of succeeding Butler at Harrow in 1885 by an impressive sermon he had delivered as a visiting preacher in Harrow chapel.[80]*

Even those lay headmasters who had resisted the temptation to become what the *Pall Mall Gazette* called "*clergymen de convenance*"[82] were expected to sustain the preaching function of the headmaster—a duty they tended to discharge especially conscientiously and sometimes with distinction, reinforcing the conception of the headmaster's pulpit role which lies behind the provisons in the 1944 Education Act for a daily act of worship in state schools. Lay housemasters in public schools had early accepted the obligation to prepare confirmation candidates and to teach 'divinity': it made it all the more unfair that Holy Orders were regarded, in the headmaster of a major boarding school, as an essential safeguard for the moral and religious content of education in the school, while laymen were widely considered fit for the hardly less pastoral and religious roles of housemaster.[83] The library of St John's College, Cambridge, preserves an interesting correspondence (1898–99) between Henry Hart of Sedbergh and one of his able assistants, H. W. Fowler, in which Fowler resisted, on grounds of conscience, the obligation to prepare boys for confirmation which Hart, imitating the practice in leading public schools,[84] insisted on as a condition of Fowler's becoming a housemaster. On this issue of principle Fowler resigned and left the school to live on his small private means and to write books on English usage which, when a classical education was ceasing to be the basis of the common culture of the English governing classes, popularised a public-school master's standards of correct language among the educated.[85]

5

Besides his preaching, the other essential quality looked for in a headmaster was as a teacher—his own standards of scholar-

* (Bishop) Hensley Henson, more perceptive and more demanding than Harrow schoolboys (and masters), was also more critical of Welldon as a preacher. "His style is simple, his manner slow and monotonous, his matter scarcely ever original—platitudes put forth with extraordinary appearance of sincerity."[81]

ship, his ability to impart these to the Sixth and, by conducting regular examinations, to authenticate standards through the whole school. As headmasters of Harrow, four Cambridge Senior Classics in turn spanned nearly the whole Victorian period—Christopher Wordsworth, Vaughan, Butler, and Welldon. Butler, at least, insisted on a first class degree in his classical assistants; to the one exception, a man who had been top of the second class, Butler made clear the man must not expect promotion to a housemastership and encouraged him to go off, as so many public-school masters did in the last three decades of the century, to found a preparatory school.[86] Warre of Eton, though he had a first, was not a good teacher or preacher, even if he compensated in part by his magnificent 'presence';[87] Ford of Repton (and later Harrow) was a good enough scholar but not an outstanding teacher.[88] Pollock of Wellington was both an able scholar and an outstanding teacher.* Fletcher's appointment at Marlborough in 1903 was largely due to the reputation for scholarship successes he had built up with the Rugby Sixth.[90] When F. B. Malim was being considered for the headmastership of Sedbergh in 1907, the governors were very impressed by the fact that a pupil of his in the *lower* Sixth at Marlborough had recently won an entrance award at Oxford. Because only Oxford and Cambridge degrees were thought to represent the highest standards of scholarship, only graduates of those two universities would normally have been considered for the headship of a leading public school in the Victorian period. In 1864 Woodard wrote to his chief lieutenant about the undesirability of appointing to the staffs of their schools graduates of other universities:

> we may get some queer characters from London University; and it might happen that hereafter an M.A. of that university might be elected Provost—an event not to be desired.[91]

On the appointment of Dr Robinson, a graduate of Trinity College, Dublin, to the headmastership of Glenalmond in 1873,

* At a crucial moment when Pollock was being considered for the headmastership of Wellington in 1893, the Master of Trinity's slight doubts about his classical scholarship were resolved when an Old Marlburian pupil of Pollock's at Cambridge was awarded the Porson Prize for Greek verse.[89]

fears were expressed that the selection of one who was not a graduate of Oxford or Cambridge must mean that the governors intended "to change and lower the educational status of the College".[92] F. W. Sanderson had a Durham degree, but this he had dignified by becoming a wrangler and mathematical prizeman at Cambridge, otherwise he would never have overcome his other handicaps of being a layman and a scientist to get the headship even of the then humble Oundle in 1892.[93]

Men with qualifications in other subjects than classics did get headmasterships in leading schools, though rarely did they get them on the strength of their non-classical specialism. Temple's "mathematical gifts were of a high and unusual order", but he taught mainly classical subjects at Rugby.[94] Mitchinson of King's School, Canterbury, had three firsts—Classical Mods., Greats, and Natural Science,[95] but his pupils' learning of science was mostly unofficial and informal. On the other hand, Wilson of Clifton was a mathematician and a pioneer of science teaching, and he had on his staff three men who became Fellows of the Royal Society—(Sir) William Tilden, A. M. Worthington, and W. A. Shenstone, but it is significant that after his appointment to the headmastership Wilson bravely set himself to teach the top boys in Latin and Greek, despite his own rustiness (and consequent howlers) in those subjects.[96] Harrow had three F.R.S.s on its staff (including Farrar) in the 1860s, and Marlborough's science master Meyrick, a distinguished lepidopterist, was later to be elected F.R.S., but of all of these only Farrar, elected a Fellow for his philological researches, ever became a head.

French in public schools was still, as we have seen, a cinderella subject, typically taught by a Frenchman who could not keep order, but the 1880s saw the beginnings of an improvement[97] as it began to pass into the hands of Englishmen, though the newly established Tripos at Cambridge was slow to produce an adequate supply of qualified specialists. More commonly the schools relied on men who had followed up a degree—in whatever subject—by a period of study on the Continent,[98] as G. G. Coulton had done. But public-school modern linguists, along with historians and scientists, had to wait until the twentieth century before they could expect to compete on fair terms with classicists for such headmasterships. The comparative standing of other subjects such as music and art can be inferred from the fact that at Marlborough (as at many schools) even in the early years of the present century "neither the Music nor the Drawing Master was a member of the Masters' Common Room".[99] Serious music, as represented by regular concerts and systematic training in instrumental (as opposed to vocal) music, was, with some notable exceptions,[100] a rare activity pursued "almost clandestinely" in the "musically benighted"[101] Victorian public school. The appointment of trained professional musicians as Directors of Music did not become common until the twentieth century, when, after a period of conflict with the "pretty deeply philistine"[102] attitude in many schools, the work of such men helped to produce one of the most significant differences between the Victorian and the present-day public school—the numbers of boys involved in, and the amount of time spent at, musical and other artistically creative activities.[103]

The combination of specifications that we have noted—high academic qualifications and impressive 'public personality' (not least in the pulpit), matched by high rewards and an impressive scope of personal power—attracted into the schools men of great stature whose gifts—and sometimes eccentricities—made them seem larger than life. But the roles of the headmaster were already undergoing modifications even before laicisation touched the great schools in 1903. The emphasis on the head's function as the foremost classical teacher in the school was the first to go. At Winchester in 1901 Fearon, who had had four firsts and was a magnificent teacher, was succeeded by Burge, with a second in Greats.[104] In 1900 it was rumoured (falsely) that Warre of Eton was to be appointed to the Deanery of Exeter; an educational journal commented that among those tipped to succeed him, the suggestion of either Lyttelton or Walker was "inept", since it was against all recent precedent to choose either a second class man or a layman.[105] Yet when Warre did retire in 1905, Lyttelton, a former captain of the Cambridge XI, was indeed chosen, despite his second class in the Tripos in 1878[106] and his serious limitations[107] as a teacher of very able boys. The emergence of the 'Sixth Form Master'—an assistant who took the top boys while the headmaster administered the school—was a late Victorian development: an attempt by a headmaster to establish such an institution at Cheltenham in 1861 had provoked a crisis with staff and governors.[108] Yet the great F. W. Walker—"unsurpassed as a schoolmaster"[109] and a considerable scholar—gave up teaching the top forms at St Paul's, confining himself to rudimentary teaching and to administration,[110] as many twentieth-century headmasters, even with far greater bursarial and secretarial assistance, have been forced to do. For most of his forty-two years as headmaster of Shrewsbury (1866–1908), H. W. Moss took all the sixth form classical teaching, ran a boarding-house with only nominal assistance from a house tutor, took daily chapel and preached every Sunday, took his turn at call-over and detentions, as well as doing a mass of administrative and bursarial duties without a secretary or even a typewriter. By the 1930s there were *nine full-time* staff doing the work Moss had done alone.[111]

6

Whatever priority each individual headmaster may have given to the roles of teaching, preaching, and administration (not to speak of 'public relations', civic affairs, or just running a boarding house), the underlying conception of his role owed much to the view of the job which Arthur Butler, first headmaster of Haileybury, conveyed to his successor: "I must be everywhere and I am to do everything".[112] The scope of the headmaster's power was expressed by Almond: "My idea of a school is that it should be the harmonious embodiment of the thought of one person, who is necessarily the headmaster".[113] In the view of the educational historian A. F. Leach in 1913:

> ... there is probably no position in English civic life where a single individual exercises such uncontrolled power as does the headmaster of a successful Public School[114]

and so much was this the case that for some of these men, removal from such authority (on, say, retirement into parish work) could involve a painful period of mental adjustment.[115]

In the first half of the Victorian period the prospects and rewards of such power attracted into the leading schools men who were among the most brilliant of their generation—men like Vaughan, Temple and Benson. Among men who showed early promise of a career in public life by becoming President of the Union at Oxford or Cambridge, and who became headmasters of public schools, were Butler of Haileybury, Fearon of Winchester, Awdry of Hurstpierpoint, Cruttwell of Malvern, H. A. James of Rossall, Cheltenham, Rugby; Ford of Repton and Harrow, Butler and Welldon of Harrow. It is not surprising to learn that in 1898 a recent president of the Oxford Union and newly-elected Fellow of All Souls, John Simon, should have been offered a public-school headmastership (Merchiston), nor is it surprising that he should have considered the offer seriously;[116] Alington, later headmaster of Shrewsbury and Eton, became a Fellow of All Souls early in his service as assistant master at Marlborough (1896). But already by 1898 public schools were ceasing to attract to their service the same proportions of outstanding men as they had done earlier in the period: a wider variety of alternative careers—expanded university provision in Britain and abroad, the civil service, the Indian and colonial services—offered obvious outlets to men of ambition.

The Victorian period saw both the rise, and the beginnings of the decline, of the notion of the schoolmaster-bishop as "the acknowledged type of ecclesiastical ruler".[117] The appointment of public-school headmasters as bishops was a new phenomenon since Elizabethan times. Samuel Butler of Shrewsbury was made Bishop of Lichfield in 1836 when he was in his sixties after nearly forty years as headmaster; in the same year Longley of Harrow began his ascent, via the bishoprics of Ripon and Durham, to Lambeth. There was some tendency for headmasters of major public schools to end up as deans, bishops or archbishops,[118] and a stronger tendency for assistant masters in major schools, and headmasters of lesser schools, to become missionary or colonial bishops.[119] It is true that of the eight Archbishops of Canterbury appointed in the one hundred years after 1860, six had previously been public-school headmasters[120] and four of these had Rugby associations.[121] But just over a hundred men were appointed as English diocesans in Victoria's reign, and fewer than a dozen of these had been public-school headmasters, and of those several were not appointed to the Bench straight from the headmaster's study.[122] In the present century the narrow stream slowed down to a trickle,[123] and in our own day only the odd suffragan testifies to the connexion between what, in Victorian times at least, were recognised as two great spheres of action for men of the highest gifts. Nevertheless, though a comparatively small proportion numerically in the nineteenth century, the headmaster-bishops represented one of the most forceful and valuable elements whose loss to post-Victorian Church and nation was to be deplored by Mr Asquith. Writing in 1913 to Archbishop Davidson, Asquith sent him a list of thirteen bishops in 1895 as "an *aperçu* of how things stood about twenty years ago":

> Without any wish to disparage the scholarship of the present bench, it is to be observed that the whole of these [in 1895] . . . were headmasters, professors, or dons.[124]

His list included Benson, Temple, Ridding and Percival, as well as two men who had taught in public schools but owed their elevation to their later eminence as "professors or dons", Westcott and John Wordsworth.

Success as headmaster did not, of course, guarantee success as a bishop—as Prince Lee and Percival both found;[125] happily Christopher Wordsworth was more successful as a bishop than he had been as headmaster. Nor was the idea of the headmaster-bishop entirely accepted even in the later Victorian period. In 1881 the *Journal of Education* commented on the appointment of the Rev. W. Inge (father of the future Dean Inge) as Provost of Worcester College, Oxford, that it seemed to be "as absurd to promote a country vicar to the Mastership of a College as to make a headmaster a Bishop".[126] Men like Farrar, who ended a dean, and Bell of Marlborough (a canon) are said to have been desperately disappointed not to have been made bishops;[127] Welldon of Harrow, who made no secret of his ecclesiastical ambitions, caused surprise by his acceptance in 1898 of a 'colonial' bishopric (Calcutta) normally held to be of lower status than an English see;[128] he later returned to England but although preferred to a lucrative and prestigious deanery he never achieved the House of Lords. Other headmasters actually refused to become bishops. During his third public-school headmastership (Rugby), H. A. James declined by return of post an offer from the premier, Balfour, of the see of Llandaff, and another from Bishop Knox of Manchester to be a suffragan in his diocese. James had had a short spell as Dean of St Asaph in between the headmasterships of Rossall and Cheltenham, but what he saw there of "ecclesiastical routine" decided him against such work.[129]

A headmastership of a major school could also lead to the Mastership of an Oxford or Cambridge college, and indeed for the lay headmaster of the twentieth century this would become, with the alternative of a Vice-Chancellorship, almost the only form of advancement he could expect. Arnold was thought likely to be appointed by the Whigs to the Wardenship of the new Durham University in 1834—to the consternation of Bishop Van Mildert;[130] fellows of Trinity, Cambridge, spoke "with horror" of the possibility that C. J. Vaughan would be set over them as Master.[131] But it is significant that Percival went *from* the Presidency of Trinity (Oxford) to the headmastership of Rugby;* and though his successor in that school, H. A. James, was in due course (1909) preferred to the Presidency of St John's College, Oxford, he did not consider it much of an advance. In his unpublished memoirs he wrote:

> I do not propose to enlarge upon my work at St John's. I have felt throughout that a considerable part of it could have been done by an intelligent secretary or clerk.[133]

It was perhaps fortunate for Harrow that H.M. Butler after twenty-five years as head was prepared to accept the substantial drop in salary involved in becoming firstly Dean of Gloucester and then Master of Trinity, otherwise he might have completed his half-century at Harrow, if, like Warre of Eton and Haig-Brown of Charterhouse,[134] he had continued as headmaster well into his seventies.

Laicisation, when it came, was to present the problem of devising honours to correspond with those available to ordained

* Twice defeated before for this headmastership—by Hayman in 1869 and Jex-Blake in 1874—Percival was appointed, this time on the invitation of the Rugby governors, in 1886. (Two years before, he had stood for Eton, when Warre was elected.) One of his Oxford colleagues now wrote to him: "The position of Head of Rugby is probably one of the most important [positions] in England", and the *Times* celebrated his appointment with a leading article.[132]

headmasters in the form of at least prebends and canonries, if not actually deaneries, archdeaconries and bishoprics. A token and arbitrary sprinkling of knighthoods and C.B.E.s around prominent members of the HMC has been the twentieth-century solution; T. E. Page, assistant at Charterhouse, was later made a C.H., and the same honour was bestowed on the Rev. H. A. James during his Presidency of St John's ("to tell the truth," he later confessed, "I had never heard of this distinguished order").[135]

More urgently, laicisation demanded the provision of pensions for both headmasters and assistants, who were no longer qualified to retire to quiet country livings. Well-paid headmasters of larger schools might hope to save something which would enable them to live without hardship, though certainly not at their former standard; it was also common even in the 1890s for endowed grammar school headmasters to be superannuated without pension.[136] In 1900 about one hundred and fifty schools, including Bedford, Dulwich, St Bees, Barnard Castle, Berkhamsted, Tonbridge and Whitgift, were involved in schemes to amend the regulations of their Foundations as reformed under the Endowed Schools Acts of 1869, 1873 and 1874 in such a way as to make provision for pensions for their headmasters.[137] There was now less need for a man who had resisted ordination throughout his teaching career to embrace it as a means of subsistence in retirement. Among the 'great' schools, Rugby's assistant masters had some form of pension provision as early as the 1820s, but this seems to have fallen away, because when he took over the headship in 1886, Percival's first resolve was to introduce a pension scheme for masters, but "so great was the rush of unexpected problems" that in his nine years there this scheme was "never even outlined".[138] Enquiries by the Cheltenham governors seem to have found only three of the leading schools with pension schemes in 1885:[139] Marlborough (whose provision dated from 1874),[140] Haileybury, and Westminster. Cheltenham itself did not establish its pensions scheme until 1905,[141] and well into the present century there were leading public schools which still had no proper provision for pensions for assistants or even headmasters.[142]

An increasing consciousness of professionalism among

public-school masters was accompanied by some awareness, at least, of the need for "systematic training in the theory and practice of education", such as Rendall of Charterhouse and Bell of Marlborough urged at the HMC in 1900.[143] In fact, at regular intervals from 1873 onwards the HMC discussed the subject of training assistant masters, and time after time passed resolutions affirming "in the strongest and most emphatic manner" their approval of this principle.[144] Yet when it came to taking action, again and again they refused to carry those affirmations to their practical end.[145] Not all headmasters even supported the principle, especially if it meant doses of educational theory and the watching of demonstration lessons; rather, said the headmaster of Lancing in 1873:

> give me the man who is a gentleman, who has tact, who has what I call a much more valuable qualification, *moral qualification* and sympathy, and he . . . would learn how to deal with his form.[146]

This view was supported by the Harrow housemaster Edward Bowen, who claimed that, as far as public schools were concerned,

> The art of teaching seems to me so much a matter of personal power and experience, and of various *social and moral gifts*, that I cannot conceive a good person made a good master by merely seeing a class of boys taught . . .

"Mere pedagogy," he went on to suggest, "could be taught in a fortnight"; the only valid kind of training, he implied, was that of experience, which in any case would only work if the right kind of man had been selected, "because a bad man teaching history well is a far worse thing than a good man teaching history badly".[147] Here, again, we confront the Victorian public-school assumption that value derived from who you were rather than what you knew: that in teaching and learning, the *process*, and its participants, were more significant than the body of knowledge imparted.

Certainly appointments such as that of the young Fellow of Trinity, Nairn, without any school experience, to the headmastership of Merchant Taylors' in 1900 gave the lie to the HMC's recurrent but empty protestations—as the *Journal of*

Education exclaimed with heavy irony: "What need we further evidence of the vanity of training? *Magister nascitur, non fit.*"[148] And in 1909 a young man fresh from Oxford with a good games record was being interviewed for an assistant mastership at Rossall:

> I was asked if I had taken a diploma in education. Rather shame-facedly I had to admit that I hadn't. The headmaster's brow cleared. "If you had, I shouldn't have had you. We want no theorists here. There's only one Theory of Education. Keep order. You start with an advantage. Boys always respect a Blue. Keep a tight hand. No fraternizing."[149]

Such attitudes were very persistent. After J. H. Simpson joined the Rugby staff in 1913 a friend of his consulted a well-known headmaster on whether to stay for a fourth year at the university to take a diploma in education. "It can do you no harm" was the reply, "and, after all, you need not *tell* people that you have been trained".[150]

Individual headmasters like Temple, Percival and Lyttelton took seriously the task of instructing new young masters. Both Cambridge and Oxford instituted vacation courses in the 1880s and 1890s which were used by some public-school masters,[151] and diploma courses for more systematic full-time training for secondary teaching came in the 1890s.[152] The duty of the Victorian headmaster to examine the work of the whole school, which some, like Warre, took further by actually inspecting lessons, imposed some kind of check on standards. Many who became successful, even outstanding, teachers—including Cotton, Rendall of Winchester, Bowen, and Sanderson of Oundle—made a decidedly shaky start as disciplinarians. Some men were discouraged by early difficulties, like W. R. Inge who was ragged at Eton[153] and went off to be a don at Oxford;[154]* the tragedy was for those who soldiered on unhappily without much hope or help. Some of the most succcessful teacher-headmasters were strong supporters of training—among them Dr E. A. Abbott, headmaster (1865) of the City of London School at the age of twenty-seven, who once

* Even so, Inge had serious qualms about having "surrendered a career which would certainly have been lucrative. . ."[155]

confessed that it was at the expense of a whole generation of schoolboys that he had learnt his business.[156]

7

"If a Headmaster can't teach and can't preach and can't organise, he ought to be either a scholar or a gentleman", jibed the Rugby masters in the course of their bitter and ultimately (1874) successful campaign to rid themselves of their headmaster, Henry Hayman.[157] "It was to be the mark of Eton for a century and a half," wrote a historian of Eton concerning the period from about 1700–1850, "that its boys were taught by persons of notably lower social origins than themselves. It was not till the middle of the nineteenth century that any general custom of appointing gentlemen to be school-masters came in".[158] Soon after 1903 Frank Fletcher was showing round Marlborough the headmaster of an aristocratic Austrian school, who expressed amazement at the equality of social relations of the English headmaster and his staff, and its implications for the social standing of the masters—"I could not ask *my* masters to dinner!"[159]

Arnold's principle of *identification*, paralleled even in his own day by the demand of a writer in the *Quarterly Journal of Education* that boys should be subjected to the inspiration and example of masters who "shall be a proper model for imitation",[160] depended on the ability of the schools to recruit men of a social standing within the range of that of their pupils, and we know something of the financial rewards which helped to ensure the supply of such men. It needs to be recognised that, to an extent, Victorian public-schoolmastering was itself a 'career open to talents' and that many men of social origins markedly humbler than those of their pupils chose this profession and were successful in it. Thomas Field was the son of a bankrupt linen draper, yet he went in 1886 from a Harrow housemastership to the headship of King's, Canterbury, and then to the faintly aristocratic Radley.[161] Another Harrow housemaster, who joined the staff in 1888, was a baronet; yet another, John Farmer, the brilliant creator of communal music at Harrow, made his impact despite his markedly humble social origins. The new head of Harrow in 1898 had risen to Oxford from Manchester Grammar School,[162] as indeed his successor at Harrow in 1942 would originate from Wolverhampton Grammar School.

In 1895 a Rugby master asked a colleague about the newly-appointed headmaster: "Tell me, is James a gentleman? Understand me, I don't mean, Does he speak the Queen's English? but—had he a grandfather?"[163] Whatever answer he was given, in fact H. A. James was the second of three successive Rugby headmasters (1887–1921) who had themselves attended grammar schools—Percival at Appleby, James at Abergavenny, and David at Exeter. And despite many kinship ties,[164] Victorian headmasters were never a closed circle. Fletcher's Marlborough staff, whose social standing inspired a foreigner's admiration, included one housemaster, Malim, later to be headmaster of three public schools in turn, who was one of the numerous children of a south-east London shoemaker. It is significant that the 'star' pupils of two groups of 'middle-class' public schools in the Victorian period, Stallard of Woodard's second-grade Hurstpierpoint and Stradling of Brereton's Devon County School (the son of a dairyman), both took up public-schoolmastering after graduating respectively from Oxford and Cambridge.

What we must not overlook is that lowly social orgins only became an insuperable obstacle to success as a public-school master if they were allied to some other unacceptable or unpopular characteristic. By themselves they could be tolerated, even regarded as a mark of extra merit in that they had been overcome—provided they *had* been overcome, in the sense that the master concerned had adapted himself successfully to the stereotype of the public-school man, particularly in matters like manners and accent. If he had not, then only exceptional qualities would carry him through. The immediate cause of the great rebellion at Winchester in 1818 had been the boys' resentment at the "ungentlemanlike conduct" and "very coarse manners" of a Commoner Tutor;[165] a key factor contributing to the Marlborough rebellion of 1851 was resentment against an unpopular assistant master who was rumoured to be the son of a fishmonger.[166] A Cheltenham housemaster who had joined the staff in 1895 suffered the stigma that he was "socially not quite right" because, despite all his scholarly achievements at Cambridge, he had himself attended the local grammar school and had no special merits in his pupils' eyes to atone for this[167]—a rugger blue might have been different. Even Thomas Field, whose career we have noticed, encountered resentment for "not being a gentleman", perhaps because he compounded this offence by being a Gladstonian liberal. The too-candid portrait of him—published in 1915 by his former pupil Somerset Maugham—which emphasised these two characteristics, may have helped prevent his ever achieving the expected deanery or bishopric.[168]

Social-class background was only one of many inextricably interwoven strands in the case of Hayman at Rugby which has already been alluded to, but which deserves fuller treatment because of the variety of issues which this unfortunate episode illustrates.

When in 1869 Gladstone promoted Frederick Temple from the headmastership of Rugby to the bishopric of Exeter, the school's governing body—the Trustees—viewed his departure with mixed feelings. Temple's liberal views in theology and politics, and more particularly his association with the publication in 1860 of the theologically controversial *Essays and Reviews*, had caused some of them a degree of pain similar to that which Arnold's political writings had given their predecessors. The Trustees were a self-electing body of "twelve noblemen and gentlemen of country pursuits";[169] confronted by a field of distinctly first-class men which included Percival (headmaster of Clifton), Arnold's own pupil Theodore Walrond, and Abbott of the City of London School (whose pupil H. H. Asquith had just carried off that scholastic blue riband, the Balliol scholarship), the Trustees chose Henry Hayman. Hayman's experience had been as an assistant at Charterhouse, then as headmaster in turn of what were then three quite undistinguished schools—St Olave's, Cheltenham Grammar School, and Bradfield. Moreover, he had taken only a second class degree at Oxford. But to the Trustees his decisive qualification must have been that he was a sound conservative in churchmanship and, so far as was known, in politics too. None of this, of course, commended him to the outgoing headmaster, whose prejudices were strongly reinforced by the impression he carried away from his first interview with Hayman, and it is clear that at an early stage Temple vowed to make Hayman's position untenable.

Hayman's enemies were soon armed with a weapon furnished by the new headmaster himself. As was customary throughout most of the Victorian period, each of the candidates had provided the Trustees with a batch of printed copies of all his testimonials. Percival had sent in forty-two, each referring specifically to his fitness for the Rugby post: the same was true of the twenty-eight sent in by Walrond. But a closer inspection of Hayman's thirty-seven printed testimonials showed that only two—or at most three—had been intended by their authors to commend him for Rugby: the rest had been obtained for use in his earlier applications for other headships. When this became known, the Rugby Trustees showed less concern than did the school staff at what these masters—and with them a number of leading headmasters—thought to be sharp practice. Within weeks of the appointment Benson was writing from Wellington to his friend Lightfoot:

> The masters at Rugby telegraphed for me to consult with them, and I have been hard at work ever since. Fourteen headmasters, including Eton, Winchester, Harrow, have . . . signed protests against the mode of Hayman's election—upsetting all testimonials as it did, and electing, merely on grounds of *supposed* conservatism, a vulgar low-souled person who has failed at three schools consecutively, [and who] steams fresh from a rebellion at Bradfield in which 35 boys left, and the rest *got their way*.

What specially stung Hayman's critics was his resort to half-truths, as in his mention in his application that Jebb, the noted Cambridge classical scholar, had been his pupil at Charterhouse, when it turned out (according to Benson) that Jebb "was apparently two months under him at the age of 13". Only a month after the appointment was announced, the masters, already smarting at these revelations, were staggered to receive a memorandum from the Trustees expressing their confidence in Hayman and refusing to see either the masters themselves or their representatives. Benson found the staff "a hapless body . . . old friends looking so pale and haggard", as they contemplated the sacrifices involved in immediate retirement, or, if they stayed, the "pure ruin" that must result from Hayman's administration, "with his vulgarity and his coarseness and its too plain results".[170]

Twenty out of the twenty-one Rugby masters had been associated with the original protest to the Trustees against the appointment, and in the first two years of Hayman's rule, the campaign to get him out was pursued by individual masters, some of them in correspondence with Temple at Exeter; and the disputes between the head and his staff were paraded back and forth before the Trustees. At the school itself the boys took sides: slogans appeared on the walls, and firecrackers were thrown down the headmaster's chimney while he entertained at dinner. But soon Temple could re-enter the ring in person. The Public Schools Act of 1868 had created a new governing body for Rugby (as from the end of 1871) which would contain university representatives from Oxford, Cambridge and London. Temple got himself made a representative of London, and two other opponents of Hayman were chosen for Oxford and Cambridge. From now on the quarrels between Hayman and his staff were brought before a governing body on which his enemies sat in strength, though not yet in a majority. Moreover, from its earliest stages the Hayman affair had been ventilated in both the local and the national press, with leader-writers and letter-writers taking sides and discussing personalities with that frankness which characterised Victorian controversy; so that, on and off for more than four years until Hayman's ultimate departure, the British reading public were regaled with the details of an educational scandal whose effect on the fortunes of Rugby school—not least in the numbers of entrants—was almost disastrous.

Eventually Hayman's weakness for half-truths caught up with him. The chairman of the governing body, the Bishop of Worcester, had been a consistent supporter of Hayman. When a dispute over the allocation of housemasterships was referred to the governors, Hayman armed himself with a particular piece of evidence, a letter which offered decisive support for his side of the dispute, but he foolishly contrived not to mention a second letter from the same source which corrected and virtually retracted the first. A copy of that second letter came before the

Bishop of Worcester, and its import made Hayman's loyal supporter into an embittered opponent. In December 1873 Hayman was dismissed, in time for the school's fortunes to be retrieved by his abler successors. Hayman took his case to court, and though he received much sympathy from the judge—and Temple's part in the whole affair was severely criticised—the dismissal stood.

Numerous facets of Victorian public schools and headmasters are pointed up by this episode. Headmasters could be political figures, actively engaged in, and openly identified with, the party politics of their period, in ways which only became impossible when, in our own century, British politics effectively polarised into two sides, one of which came to stand for the very abolition of the public-school system. Though the clientele—certainly the pupils, if not invariably the parents—of the leading public schools would mostly have identified themselves with conservative rather than liberal political principles, Temple was only one of many headmasters and indeed also assistant masters in public schools who were outspoken and active in both local and national political discussion, several of them on the liberal side.* This identification with politics could be rewarded in the conventional way, as Temple's ecclesiastical career shows. So also with Percival, whose politics no less than his churchmanship—or his standing as an educationist—led to his appointment to a bishopric in 1895 and would certainly have led to an archbishopric if a vacancy had occurred at the right time.[172] On the other side, it was Disraeli who stepped in to console the dismissed Dr Hayman in 1874 with the offer of a fat country living, ostensibly in recognition of his services to Homeric scholarship.

The opposition to Hayman has been represented as being due to his being "unknown", and an outsider, resented for presuming to intrude on the "headmasterly cliques of the nineteenth century".[173] His politics, which it soon became clear were the main grounds for his appointment, were not by any

* Headmasters who were known liberals included Arnold himself, Young of Sherborne, Wickham of Wellington, Thompson of Radley. The Harrow housemaster Edward Bowen actually stood for Parliament as a liberal.[171]

means the main grounds for his unacceptability to the Rugby staff and to the numerous other headmasters who objected to his appointment—certainly not a uniformly anti-conservative collection of men! Nor was he even "unknown", for those schoolmasters who like Temple had been at Oxford in the 1840s would have known, or known of, Hayman, who had made a name for himself in the Oxford Union and in the university generally,[174] though it was a name even then tainted by a particular brand of churchmanship and by his identification with a college (St John's) described by Mark Pattison as "corroded with ecclesiasticism".[175] It was not so much his social orgins as his rough manners and unhappy mannerisms which put people off him—even though people said the same things about Temple: as one letter in the local Rugby press pointed out, Temple wasn't such a gent himself.[176] Objections to the range and quality of his school experience were not pure snobbery, for they reflected the degree of success as a schoolmaster that he had enjoyed so far, though they incidentally also indicate the comparative standing of Bradfield in the 1860s, which was far below the Group I status to which it would be raised by the work of H. B. Gray from the 1880s onwards. The year of Hayman's appointment also chanced to be the year of the beginnings of the Headmasters' Conference, and not until this had got under way and begun to furnish an arena where headmasters could size up their colleagues, could one usefully speak of "headmasterly cliques".

All in all, it is what was *known* about him, not what was unknown, that made Hayman unacceptable. He had no recognised gifts as a preacher, and the worst fears about his effectiveness in the pulpit were soon realised.[177] Yet, politics apart, the decisive grounds for electing Hayman rather than his nearest rival, Walrond, may have been that Walrond was not in Orders: indeed one normally well-informed contemporary who was close to these events states categorically that this was the reason.[178] Because of Hayman's second class degree, it was pointedly observed that the majority of his staff were better qualified than he,[179] and the quality of his Greek scholarship had early exposed him to further opprobrium. One of Hayman's peculiarities was that he refused to recognise the 'rule for the final cretic', by then an accepted convention in Greek verse composition,* identified by Porson in 1797.[180] This foible alone meant that Hayman's verses were liable to contain what were regarded as howlers. One of his critics got hold of a set of iambics which Hayman had composed as a 'fair copy' for his Rugby Sixth, and showed it to Moss, headmaster of Shrewsbury and hitherto a supporter of Hayman, allowing Moss to assume it was a set of verses by a sixth-former:

> I listened to [Moss's] comments: "wrong accent—not attic—good line that—awkward—hullo, final cretic—*how old is the boy?*"

When Moss heard it was Hayman's fair copy for the Rugby Sixth he "utterly collapsed",[182] as did also (presumably) his previous conviction that Hayman was the innocent victim of a conspiracy. Twentieth-century headmasters can comfort themselves that their own command of their specialist teaching areas is not open to such universal and such searching scrutiny.

It may reasonably be asked whether the masters were right at the time in first expressing, and then persisting in, their opposition to Hayman's appointment. It was suggested in the *Times* that the staff should buckle to and "make the best of an indifferent appointment"; there was the feeling among some, at least, of the boys, that the staff were not giving the new man a fair chance.[183] The kind of opposition which—however understandable, according to their standards—the masters put up, shows how reasonable was the claim of some Victorian headmasters on taking up appointment to the right to dismiss all their predecessors' staff, an indispensible weapon for a reforming headmaster which might cause only small-scale tragedy in the typical small school but would have involved a major holocaust in a school like Rugby. It also shows the comparative resilience and durability of what were still at this period the few great schools: lesser schools, without a core of established and faithful clientele, could certainly not have survived five years of such torment and scandal.

* "Porson's law of the final cretic is even now familiar to every schoolboy," wrote a classical tutor of Balliol in—believe it or not—*1964*. Since then Mr R. M. Ogilvie has become headmaster of a public school, and is in a better position to judge the generality of this kind of knowledge, even within the confines of a leading classical school.[181]

One of the immediate repercussions of the Hayman affair was a tightening-up of the procedure covering testimonials. Just over a year after Hayman's appointment, the Marlborough governors, meeting to choose a successor to Bradley, were confronted with testimonials for one candidate which, it transpired, had originally been given in respect of a different headship. Despite the candidate's explanation his testimonials were rejected and another man (Farrar) elected.[184] In 1874 Rugby's appointment of Jex-Blake to succeed Hayman involved the scrutiny of ninty-four testimonials for Jex-Blake in a booklet of eighty-six printed pages; but by 1895, when H. A. James was appointed, the governors' advertisement for the post stipulated that the names of five referees be supplied and that "no testimonials would be required or received",[185] a recognition of their limited value and surely also of the validity of the assumption that by now, nearly thirty years after Hayman's appointment and the establishment of the HMC, any likely candidate would be sure to be known, or known about, within the smallish world of public schools and Oxford and Cambridge colleges.

8

"How easily one may find oneself sitting on a volcano!" wrote the Rev. James Robertson to a friend shortly after he had taken over the headmastership of Haileybury in 1884.[186] Robertson was a brilliant young Rugby master who had been sacked by Hayman in 1871; he had then been invited to teach at Harrow. His exclamation comes (in a letter to Bell at Marlborough) in a passage referring to "news from elsewhere" which suggests trouble brewing in another school.[187] Soon Robertson was to have serious troubles of his own which added point to his observation. In 1887 there was a spate of thefts from Haileybury studies; eventually a trap was laid, a marked coin was taken which was then found in the desk of a boy, Henry Hutt, against whom there was other circumstantial evidence. Robertson published a notice to the school that Hutt had been expelled for theft, whereupon he was sued in 1888 for damages for wrongly expelling, and for libelling and slandering, the boy. The court found that Hutt did not steal the money, though his headmaster and housemaster had reasonable grounds for suspecting him, and thus their libels and slanders were uttered in good faith: Hutt was awarded £100 without costs.

The Hutt case shows several similarities with that of Terence Rattigan's "Winslow Boy"—Archer-Shee, a cadet at the Royal Naval College, Osborne, who was vindicated by a lawsuit in 1910 after expulsion on a charge of theft.[188] But though Robertson's conduct in the Hutt case had attracted little discredit, the effect on entries to Haileybury in 1889 of even slightly adverse publicity in the press caused Robertson to retire to a country living—an occupation in which he was followed by his expelled pupil, for Hutt went up to Cambridge, took Orders and ended up a rural dean.[189]

An even more serious blow to the fortunes of a school—and the career of a headmaster—fell upon Sherborne in the reign of the Rev. E. M. Young. A gifted scholar and a brilliant teacher, Young went to Sherborne in succession to H. D. Harper in 1877; one of his testimonials was from Matthew Arnold, whose sons he had taught at Harrow. In 1888 he clashed with one of his staff—a giant rowing blue and British Israelite with an ungovernable temper, whom Young had appointed as his own house tutor in School House. The dispute split the staff down the middle, and when the dismissed master sued Young for libel both the local community and the wider body of Old Boys took sides with violent partisanship. Young had made enemies both by individual acts of policy and, in general, by ill-judged political activities as a liberal in a predominantly Tory fox-hunting neighbourhood. During the libel suit a large proportion of the staff were away in London giving evidence, their absence leaving behind at the school a disciplinary situation which, in that atmosphere of inter-staff recriminations, can be imagined; so, too, can the effect on the public of the innuendos which got around when it was judged necessary for part of the case to be heard *in camera*. The dismissed house tutor, who had claimed damages of £10,000 from Young, was awarded one shilling on each of two counts. But his supporters—on the staff, in the town, and among a section of the Old Boys—scored a more obvious victory in their campaign to ruin the school in order to bring the headmaster to his knees, a campaign designed to ensure that, as one of them boasted, "there won't be fifty boys in Sherborne School this time next year".[190] Here was the Old School tie shown up in its worst aspect. In 1890, the year following the court case, numbers fell to about half—one hundred and forty boys instead of two hundred and eighty. Despite a gallant campaign by the headmaster, the governors, loyal parents and Old Boys, the school could only be saved by a change of headmaster, and Young was eventually obliged by the governors to resign in 1892.

All these three cases—Rugby, Haileybury, and Sherborne—underline the truth of Robertson's prescient remark, suggesting that the headship of a Victorian public school could be very much of a 'hot seat', and that the enormous power was balanced by an element of insecurity if things did not go well, though it was an insecurity against which, as we shall see, he was well cushioned, as compared with the assistant master. The Hutt case also illustrates, incidentally, the lengths to which a pupil (or a father on his behalf) might have to go to try to clear his name if he had been expelled from a public school yet wished to pursue a professional career or even just to enter Oxford or Cambridge, for, as we have seen, this was just the period when the public-school community was establishing itself in its form of a widely extending universe in which disgrace could normally only be expiated in some distant colony.*

9

On the whole, public-school masters played a comparatively small part in the secondary-schoolmasters' struggles over salaries, security of tenure, registration, superannuation and professional standards—struggles which gained momentum in the 1890s with the establishment of the Assistant Masters'

* By the end of the Victorian period, special private schools existed to receive boys expelled from the public schools, and, by a training in agriculture etc., to process them for export to the colonies.[191]

Association (incorporated in 1901). As we have noted, security of tenure was a serious issue for headmasters and even more, for assistants. In 1888 Young dismissed six of his Sherborne staff, including three who were Old Boys.[192] Walker of Manchester Grammar School once dismissed nine masters for disloyalty at a single stroke.[193] At one point in his headmastership of Blackheath (1876–1887) E. W. South sacked four long-serving senior masters,[194] including men who despite Oxford or Cambridge firsts were too old to expect good jobs at other schools. In 1876 Grignon of Felsted was, like Hayman of Rugby, dismissed from his headship without redress, and in circumstances which were commented on "by every journal in Great Britain"—including *Punch,* which had a field-day—and were debated in the House of Lords.[195] In 1894 F. H. Browne was dismissed from the headmastership of Ipswich School after a dispute with the governors.[196] The demand for greater security of tenure was another sign of the increasing professionalism of schoolmasters, and it was those in lesser schools, including day schools, who had chosen teaching not just as a stepping-stone to ecclesiastical preferment or to a boarding-house,[197] who fought the battles against the assertion by newly-appointed headmasters of a disputed right to dismiss all their predecessors' assistants, a campaign which culminated in the passing of the Endowed Schools (Masters) Act of 1908 which regularised their tenure.

The contribution of the masters in the leading public schools to the making of the profession was rather in the example and influence of individuals, among them outstanding men, whose service as assistants lent lustre to the social status of the English secondary-schoolmaster generally and helped to create an alternative 'image' to that of the lowly usher. As we have seen, ex-presidents of the Oxford and Cambridge Unions became headmasters: they also became, and seemed content to remain, assistants—and not only men like Bowen and Bosworth-Smith in the plum housemasterships Harrow could offer, but in less well-paid posts in less celebrated schools, like Gould, Asquith's rival in the Oxford Union, who taught at Marlborough for thirty-five years, or John Sargeaunt, who taught at Felsted and Westminster for a similar span. A playing member of the M.C.C., an actor, orator, fisherman, botanist, gardener, archer, chess-player, antiquarian and scholar, Sargeaunt,[198] who was accorded a place in the D.N.B., was one of many virtuosi whose gifts found an outlet in the life and work of an assistant master or housemaster in a Victorian public school. And the schools drew on distinction in other spheres. T. E. Brown brought to the service of Clifton, as housemaster, the genius of a poet: the standing of his chosen occupation is indicated by the fact that it was one which a prime minister's brother (W. W. Asquith) rejoiced to share.

Even among the leading 30–50 schools by 1902 there was a wide range in rewards and styles of life available from school to school and also within one school—between the comfortably-off housemasters and those who toiled away on a couple of hundred pounds a year waiting to succeed to a housemastership before they could embark on marriage[199]—if indeed marriage was feasible for a housemaster in a particular school. At the 'great' schools the ownership of their houses gave the housemasters an exceptional degree of independence of the headmaster,[200] so that if they chose to act in concert, like feudal barons their power could be considerable. An Eton housemaster might write his reports to parents on Athenaeum notepaper[201] and maintain a very substantial household, while in a lesser school even a housemaster might never earn an income which would enable him to send his own sons as boarders to the school where he taught. The quality of social life for masters at some schools suffered because there was no common room,[202] and at others because they had one, but one which was dominated by the pettiness and faction sometimes prevalent in enclosed communities to which a certain type of person has a psychological need to belong. Hugh Walpole's experiences as a master at Epsom College early this century went into the writing of *Mr Perrin and Mr Traill*; and Glenalmond, in its "monastic isolation",[203] was the scene around 1860 of a duel between two members of staff, a German master and a future bishop.[204]

For an assistant master, the prospect of marrying might, independently of financial circumstances, be influenced by more arbitrary factors such as a headmaster's policy on the marriage of his staff. An assistant master at Victorian Marlborough who petitioned the head for an increase in salary on the grounds that he was about to be married, received the reply that he ought rather to expect a reduction, on the grounds of his reduced usefulness to the school.[205] On the other hand Lyttelton at Eton after 1905 actually circularised the bachelors on his staff (at least the younger and 'more eligible' ones) encouraging them to get married.[206] It is possible to see a new kind of prejudice at work here.

When the Clifton governors, interviewing Percival for the headmastership in 1862, remarked on his bachelorhood, it was by way of drawing attention to his youth and inexperience, and to a factor which might be a disadvantage in arranging the supervision of a boarding house with seventy boys, and nineteen servants, and a dairy farm and laundry four miles distant. "You are very young, Mr Percival," observed one of the governors. "And unmarried," added another. "A few years will correct the former," replied the candidate, "and a few weeks the latter."[207] The lady concerned was to be of enormous help to him during his two headmasterships, and there were many other Victorian headmasters—and housemasters—whose wives were a similar asset. Equally certainly there were men whose careers were prejudiced, even men whose headships were cut short, by the character or conduct of their wives.*

The case of one headmaster's wife illuminates important aspects of their role. Wickham, Benson's successor at Wellington, married the Prime Minister's daughter, Helen Gladstone. The tensions which had early become apparent between Wickham and his staff were accentuated by the indifference which the Wickhams showed to all social relationships with these men and their families. As an observer wrote after they had been at Wellington for nearly twenty years:

> It was not merely that many of the masters who had been there for years had never been invited into the headmaster's house, or that Mrs Wickham had never called on or made the

* This would seem to have been true of *e.g.* the Rev. H. A. Dalton, headmaster of Felsted 1890–1906, and the Rev. R. S. de C. Laffan, headmaster of Cheltenham College 1895–1899. The death of the Rev. R. Middlemist in 1877, after thirty years as a crusty bachelor housemaster at Harrow, caused a sensation when it revealed that for many years he had kept a wife and children secretly in a south-coast town. The reason for the concealment is obscure.[208]

> acquaintance of the wives of some of the married masters, but even when parents came to visit the school their entertainment had to be provided by the masters of houses and dormitories. I never came across people so utterly oblivious to the fact that those in a certain position in life have laid upon them certain social duties.[209]

The Victorians had no kind of prejudice against bachelor headmasters as such. Bachelorhood was no disadvantage to Welldon in the fierce competition for the headmastership of Harrow in 1885, or to H. A. James for his three headships in 1875, 1889 and 1895, or to Temple at Rugby or Pollock at Wellington, both of whom postponed marriage until after they became bishops. Only after 1900 do we see some kind of suspicion of the bachelor state: in Lyttelton's circular to his Eton masters, which we have noted, and in F. B. Malim's report that he was conscious of a prejudice against him as a bachelor when he was competing for headmasterships around 1905, which was shortly afterwards removed by his marriage.[210] It is at least reasonable to speculate whether there was any connexion between this new prejudice and the extension of fears concerning sex, which, as we have seen, began to be evident in just this period. Even so, these tendencies still had to compete with the kinds of economic consideration which in 1871 had caused bachelors to be declared more useful to Marlborough than married men: when new salary scales were introduced at Radley in 1911, staff were told explicitly that the governors did not encourage matrimony.[211]

10

The other distinct service rendered to the teaching profession generally by the men in this particular community of schools lay in their contribution to the development of a professional ethic. In this respect it was not just the men of outstanding personality or gifts who were most obviously involved.

Writing in the 1930s about the Eton he had left in 1870, Sir David Hunter-Blair said:

> If asked what is the great and vital difference between the Eton of sixty years ago and to-day, I should give an odd answer. The masters—housemasters and form masters—are human beings to-day. In my day they were not: they were (almost without exception) *freaks*.[212]

The exception Hunter-Blair might have made, if he had had the good fortune to come within his charmed circle, was William Johnson Cory, who worked to establish a new kind of schoolmaster role by which his successors transformed the quality of education at that school. It was only partly that a different kind of man was being recruited for the schools; more importantly, these men found in the Victorian public school new expectations of the life and work of the schoolmaster which emphasised his pastoral as well as his instructional role. The evolution of this new conception was a gradual and chequered process: the role (for example) of the housemaster, or of the house tutor—in such cases where the post existed—and the degree of supervision they ought to exercise over boys in the house, had certainly not assumed any uniform pattern within the Victorian period.[213]

Rather were there evolving ideals of self-dedication and general pastoral concern which were formulated and communicated among masters, not in the big meetings of professional associations, but in the informal groups like the "U.U." (United Ushers) from around 1870 onwards,[214] a small number of masters (mostly laymen) from the leading schools who dined together several times a year, or the "Thirteen",[215] a group which flourished in the 1880s, or "Dons and Beaks", an annual meeting of college tutors and of masters at preparatory and public schools, founded in 1886, which in its early years took the form of a gruelling religious retreat.[216] These ideals strengthened such men to face the drudgery and what Vaughan used to call "the healthy little humiliations" of a schoolmaster's life.[217]* Outside the pulpit, many of the values of the

* A headmaster, too, faced drudgery: *cf.* E. W. Benson's complaint, in a letter to Westcott after eighteen years in schools, eleven as a headmaster, about the preoccupations which made it "impossible to do more than two or three hours a week at literature or divinity"; ". . . I shall grow less and less capable of its exceeding wear and tear, and the multifariousness of one's petty

Victorian public school were seldom voiced explicitly: we remember the account in *Stalky and Co.* of the speech of the visiting politician which extols and coarsens the ambitions and values which the boys themselves have but which lie too deep for words.[220] These values were rather to be conveyed by the example of the masters than in any formal expression in chapel or classroom—"the schoolmaster's best sermon," wrote a member of the 'Thirteen', "is his life";[221] though the headmaster (Potts) of Fettes, dying of over-exertion, combined example and precept when he dictated his death-bed message to be read out by the head prefect to the assembled school:

> I wish to offer to all the boys at Fettes College, particularly to those who have been here any time, my grateful acknowledgment of their loyalty, affection and generous appreciation of me. I wish, as a dying man, to record that loving-kindness and mercy have followed me all the days of my life; that faith in God is the sole firm stay in mortal life; that all other ideas than Christ are illusory; and that duty is the one and sole thing worth living for.[222]

It was this gospel of duty which inspired the "men of little showing" praised by Kipling in his dedicatory verses in *Stalky*—men who submerged their own ambitions in their love for the school and their service to its members, and often in service to the local community also. It was this model, popularised even in eccentric stereotype by Mr Chips (based partly on Balgarnie of the Leys School)[223] whom James Hilton's novel of 1935 represented as being in mid-career in 1898, which, like the Victorian headmasters' concept of the school itself, has spilled over into national education at every point—though the implications for the teacher's and headmaster's roles of the changed circumstances of modern large, socially heterogeneous

---

business as a headmaster distracts and enfeebles one's mind".[218] But there were compensations, about which, when he laid down his headmastership, Benson waxed nostalgic: "Nothing can ever be more congenial to me than living with boys and talking to them morning noon and night of scholarship and its applications. It is with them that I feel really alive and on fire, and I much fear that life and heat will sink down when I part from them."[219]

state schools have never been properly thought out.[224] Just as the Oxford Movement was an important element in renewing the pastoral vocation of the Anglican clergy,[225] so also it can be claimed that the concept, as it evolved in the Victorian public school, of the teacher—laicised, ill-paid perhaps, but of secure social status, closely involved in the work, the leisure, indeed the whole life of his pupils in a community whose ties were life-long—helped to foster in England a vision of the separate, special and powerful vocation of the schoolmaster.

Notes

Principal abbreviations used in the Notes

BCAP	Brotherton Collection, Arnold Papers (Leeds)
DNB	*Dictionary of National Biography*
HCBP	Homerton College (Cambridge), Brereton Papers
HM	Headmaster
HMC	Headmasters' Conference
PSC	(Clarendon) Public Schools Comm.
P.S.Mag.	*Public School Magazine*
PSYB	*Public Schools Yearbook*
SERM	Arnold's published *Sermons*
SIC	Schools' Inquiry Commission (Taunton Commission)
SL	Stanley's *Life* of Arnold
SMYB	*Schoolmasters' Yearbook*

Introduction: The Irresistible Tides

1. Winston S. Churchill, *My Early Life* (1930), 1947 edn., p. 9.
2. Lord Ernle, *Whippingham to Westminster* (1938), p. 30. See also G. R. Parkin, *Life of Edward Thring* (1898), Vol. I, p. 66.
3. Sir A. Quiller-Couch, *et al., T. E. Brown, A Memorial Volume* (Cambridge, 1930), *passim.*
4. C. S. Lewis, *Surprised by Joy* (1955), Fontana edn., 1959, p. 82.
5. Emile Durkheim, *L'Education Morale* (Paris, 1925), translated as "Moral Education, a study of the theory and application of the sociology of education" by Wilson and Schnurer (Glencoe, U.S.A., 1961), pp. 232, 241.

Chapter One: Arnold and the First New Victorian Public Schools

References:

SL refers to citations of the 11th edition (London, 1880, 2 vols.) of A. P. Stanley's *Life and Correspondence of Dr Arnold* (1844).

SERM refers to citations of the *Sermons of Dr Arnold*, published in a collected edition (1878, 6 vols.), edited by his daughter, Jane.

BCAP refers to citations of manuscript materials in the Brotherton Collection (Arnold Papers) in the University of Leeds, consisting of a number of Arnold and Penrose family papers deposited by descendants, notably Mrs Mary Moorman. Other Arnold letters are in (a) the Temple Reading Room, Rugby School and (b) the Warwickshire Record Office (letters to Lord Denbigh).

1. For the nature and volume of criticism of the public schools in this period, see E. C. Mack (1938), Chapter IV and *passim*.
2. G. G. Coulton (1923), p. 14.
3. *Cf.* the views of H. H. Almond, headmaster of Loretto, in *Journal of Education* (Sept. 1900), pp. 563–4.
4. SL I 88, 292.
5. Arnold to Hawkins, 10.3.1833 (SL I 303).
6. SL I 89.
7. SL II 113.
8. This very marked difference is apparent in Arnold's own letters (BCAP).
9. SL I 58.
10. Letter from Arnold to Rev. G. Cornish, 23 Feb. 1820 (BCAP). Passage omitted from SL I 58 reads in part:
    "I shall receive little or nothing with my wife. When therefore I find the school most irksome to me, I think that this it is which enables me to think of marrying at five and twenty, without a penny of private fortune, and that at once puts me in the receipt of an income, instead of having to fight an up hill way to obtain one . . ."
11. SL I 58, 74, 320; II 182, etc. He viewed the prospect of a return to Oxford with mixed feelings; as late as March 1841 he doubted whether he could face the evil of Oxford, yet in December 1841 he wrote of how he always wanted to go. SL II 236, 214.

12. T. W. Bamford (1960), pp. 30, 67, 103.
13. Mary Arnold to her sisters, 4 June 1840 (BCAP); T. W. Bamford (1960), pp. 146, 222; SL II 186.
14. SL I 73–4.
15. SL II 170.
16. SL II 168, 273.
17. SL I 251, 338; II 41, 48, 383, 390.
18. Thomas Arnold, *Miscellaneous Works* (1845), p. 128, p. 236 ("Reform and its future consequences"); SL I 250, 252, 257; II 86.
19. SL I 43.
20. *The Englishman's Register.*
21. SL I 259.
22. SL I 77, 196–8; T. Arnold, *Principles of Church Reform* (1833).
23. *The British Magazine* XXVII (1845): long review of "the opinions of the late Dr Arnold", by "a layman"; SL II 15–16.
24. SL I 202.
25. SL 86–9, 95; SERM V 41.
26. SERM I v.
27. SERM II No. 6.
28. SERM V 49–50.
29. V. Ogilvie (1957), p. 111.
30. S. G. Checkland, *The Gladstones, A Family Biography* (Cambridge, 1971), p. 132.
31. W. R. W. Stephens, *Memoir of Lord Hatherley* (1883), Vol. I, pp. 11–14.
32. Arnold, *op. cit.*, pp. 371, 378 (On the Discipline of Public Schools, 1835); SL I 163.
33. SL I 34. This is in fact Arnold to Hawkins, 18 Jan. 1827 (BCAP), not ascribed by Stanley, I 34. See also SERM VI 232.
34. D. Newsome (1961), pp. 40–2.
35. L. Strachey, *Eminent Victorians* (1918), new edn. 1967, p. 184.
36. *Recollections of Dean Fremantle (1921)*, p. 11.
37. Arnold to Lord Denbigh, 21.9.1829 (original in Warwickshire Record Office).
38. Arnold to A. P. Stanley, 17.1.1836 (original in Temple Reading Room, Rugby School), On the "narrowness of view" of Dissenters and its connection with the lack of classical culture, see also SL II 161 (Arnold in 1840).
39. SL I 120.
40. SL I 96, 334.
41. SL I 94.
42. SL II 150.
43. SL I 91.

44. *Rugby School Register* (ed. Sollas) (1935), p. xxvi.
45. SL I 103.
46. SL I 103–4.
47. SL I 107.
48. SL I 104; *Miscellaneous Works*, p. 371.
49. H. H. Almond in *Journal of Education* (Sept. 1900), pp. 563–4.
50. Arnold to T. Penrose, 4 Feb. 1839 (MS letter, BCAP).
51. "Memories of Arnold and Rugby Sixty Years Ago, by a member of the school in 1835–36–37 [*sc.* I. W. Gover]", article in *Parents Review* (1895–96), p. 833.
52. C. P. F. Berkeley. See *Rugby School Register* (1935).
53. *Gladstone's Diairies* (ed. M. R. D. Foot, 1968), *e.g.* Vol. II, p. 150: 25 Jan. 1835, "read Arnold aloud"; and 22 June 1835, "Arnold's sermons—one aloud—". Gladstone also read up the *Principles of Church Reform* and the controversy it provoked (*Diary*: 8 Sept. 1833 and Vol. II, p. 48, List of Books Read 1832–33). For Queen Victoria's use of Arnold's sermons see L. Strachey, *op. cit.*, p. 187.
54. Gover, *art. cit.*
55. Reported in *Letters of the Hon. Mrs Edward Twisleton 1852–1862* (1928), p. 270, letter of 30 April 1855.
56. A. K. Cook, *About Winchester College* (1917), p. 63.
57. SL II 37–8.
58. Arnold to Lord Denbigh, 27.10.1832 (original in Warwickshire Record Office).
59. SL I 334.
60. H. C. Maxwell Lyte, *History of Eton College* (new edn., 1889), p. 360.
61. SERM II (1828–31), pp. 166–7. On 'emulation' as a mid-Victorian public-school headmaster's catch-phrase, see *e.g.* Moberly's evidence to the Clarendon Commission, PSC III, 344, §500.
62. Note, for example, an article by "T.C.A." in the *Rugby Magazine* II, 6 Dec. 1836), pp. 122*ff*, which discusses the advantages and disadvantages of emulation in work and play. Other indications to Arnold's own attitude to emulation are in SL II 314, 356; SERM III 237.
63. From A. H. Clough, "The Latest Decalogue".
64. SL I 116; R. E. Prothero and G. G. Bradley, *Life of Dean Stanley* (1894), Vol. I, pp. 65, 69, 74.
65. T. W. Bamford (1960), Chapter 12, *passim.*
66. G. H. Wilson, *History of Windlesham House School 1837–1937* (n.d.) and M. E. Sadler, *Preparatory Schools* (Board of Education Special Reports on Educational Subjects, 1900).
67. SL I 34.

68. Mary Arnold to her sisters, 19 Nov. 1839 (MS letter, BCAP).
69. *Cf.* SL I 127.
70. Prothero and Bradley, *op. cit.,* p. 63.
71. SL I 152, 160, 295.
72. *Rugby Magazine* I, 2 (October 1835), pp. 96–9.
73. SERM IV 67.
74. *Rugby Magazine* I, 101.
75. *Ibid.*, pp. 102–3.
76. A later article in the *Rugby Magazine* (II, 6 Dec. 1836, p. 124 "Sketches of School Character", signed "T.C.A.") adds the qualification to Stanley's view of the school as a little world that the masters are, in the last resort, the guarantors of morality.
77. S. Hawtrey, *Reminiscences of a French Eton* (1867), *passim.*
78. *Ibid.*, pp. 59–60.
79. Copy of letter, Matthew Arnold to S. Hawtrey, 18 Oct. 1863, in MS black note-book of miscellanea begun by Arnold 2 Dec. 1841, continued by members of the family (BCAP).
80. Matthew Arnold, *A French Eton* (1864), 1892 edn., pp. 63–4.
81. SERM II 34–5.
82. SERM II 59; for the intensification of this tendency in the late Victorian public school, see below, Chapter Three, Section 16.
83. SL I 109.
84. SL I 358.
85. T. Arnold to T. Penrose, 4 Feb. 1839 (BCAP).
86. T. Arnold to T. Penrose, 17 May 1830 (unposted, found by Mary Arnold in the 1850s; original in BCAP).
87. SL I 358.
88. SL I 70.
89. SL I 268.
90. SERM IV 68.
91. SERM V 44–5.
92. Mary Arnold to her sisters, 29 Dec. 1838 (BCAP).
93. Prothero and Bradley, *op. cit.,* I 320, 67–8 and Chapter IV *passim*; Rev. B. O. Jones, quoted in S. Selfe, *Chapters from the History of Rugby School,* with notes on the characters in *Tom Brown's Schooldays* (Rugby, 1890), pp. 157–8.
94. Selfe, *op. cit.,* pp. 62*ff.*
95. See especially T. W. Bamford, *art*: "Discipline at Rugby under Arnold" in *Educational Review* X, I (Birmingham, Nov. 1957), pp. 18–28. For the experiences of a pupil (Brereton) late in Arnold's reign, see below, Chapter Two.
96. H. W. Ord, *The Adventures of a Schoolmaster* (1936), pp. 55, 57 and Chapter III *passim.*
97. SERM V 51.

98. SERM VI 231. See also SERM IV 130, 132; SERM III 236.
99. SERM VI 139; V 60.
100. SERM V 110; II 247.
101. SERM V131*ff*; see also *e.g.* SERM V 42–3.
102. SERM VI 230*ff*.
103. SL II 294, Appendix A.
104. SERM II 128.
105. N. Wymer, *Dr Arnold of Rugby* (1953), pp. 12, 19.
106. *Spectator* (June 18, 1892), "Dr Arnold after fifty years".
107. Arnold to A. P. Stanley, 8 March 1841 (MS letter in Temple Reading Room, Rugby School), references to Lake and to Highton which are omitted by Stanley from SL II 214.
108. *Rugby School Register*, Vol. I: 1675–1857 (revised edn., 1933).
109. H. E. M. Icely (1953), p. 62.
110. DNB, entry for 15th Earl of Derby.
111. A. B. Gourlay (1951), pp. 100–1.
112. B. W. T. Handford, *Lancing 1848–1930* (Oxford, 1933), pp. 96–8.
113. A. F. Lace, *A Goodly Heritage* (Bath, 1968), pp. 27, 30, 40, 42–3, 46 and Chapter 6 *passim*.
114. T. W. Bamford (1960), Chapter 12.
115. M. Craze, *History of Felsted School* (Ipswich, 1955), p. 158 and Chapter 15 *passim*.
116. T. W. Hutton, *King Edward's School, Birmingham 1552–1952* (Oxford, 1952), p. 137.
117. D. Newsome (1961), p. 102.
118. T. W. Hutton, *op. cit.*, p. 86.
119. D. Newsome (1961), p. 96.
120. *Ibid.*, pp. 104–8 and Chapter II *passim*.
121. E. W. Benson to Lightfoot, Dec. 1869 (Benson papers, Trinity College, Cambridge, volume for 1869–72).
122. A. T. Brown, *Some Account of the Royal Institution School, Liverpool* (2nd edn., Liverpool, 1927), pp. 28–38, 53–65.
123. H. E. M. Icely (1953), pp. 81, 94.
124. A. F. Leach, *History of Warwick School* (1906), esp. Chapters 11 and 14. Grundy went on to be a successful HM of Malvern.
125. Notably H. H. Vaughan, Lake, Stanley, Congreve, W. Bright, Shirley, Conington, Hart.
126. On "Arnoldians" at Oxford, see W. R. Ward, *Victorian Oxford* (1965), esp. p. 130 and Chapters 3, 5, 6 and 7.
127. Cheltenham Proprietary College, Directors' Minutes, Book I: minutes for 9, 10 and 21 November 1840.
128. Report of Rev. F. Close, Inaugural meeting, 29 June 1841 (cutting in Cheltenham Prop. Coll. Directors' Minute Book, probably from local newspaper—*Chronicle*?).

129. Report of inaugural public meeting, 29 July 1841.
130. M. C. Morgan (1968), p. 24.
131. *Ibid.*, p. 23.
132. *Ibid.*, p. 31.
133. *Ibid.*, p. 35.
134. Highton, speech on 26 April 1862, reported in Cheltenham *Times and Record* (cutting preserved in Cheltenham College archives). (My italics—Author.)
135. Incomplete MS memorandum (of which only first four pages survive among Marlborough College archives), in response to circular of 11 Jan. 1842.
136. Typescript copy of letter (original lost) from G. E. L. Cotton to Bowers (Marlborough College archives).
137. Marlborough College: Council Minutes 13 May 1846.
138. *Ibid.*, 8 April 1848; 13 August 1846; 21 October 1847.
139. C. Norwood, *The English Tradition of Education* (1929), p. 63. The school *Register* records only one new boy aged eight years in 1850 who was alive to tell this story to Norwood in 1921: W. C. Rokeby.
140. Surveyor's Report to Council, Marlborough College Council Minutes, Jan. 1851.
141. Minutes of Council meeting, Marlborough College, for December 1850.
142. Early correspondence, bursar's file, M. C. archives: letters of R. Tweed, 28 Dec. 1850, and Rev. M. Wilkinson, 3 Feb. 1851; Wilkinson to Rev. W. C. Sharpe (second master), August 1850.
143. Rev. M. Wilkinson to Bishop of Salisbury, 31 May 1850 (M.C. archives).
144. Rev. M. Wilkinson to Rev. W. Howard, 30 Oct. 1849 (copy in M.C. archives). (My italics—Author.)
145. *e.g.* V. Ogilvie (1957), p. 152. For a highly-coloured and often demonstrably inaccurate account of the rebellion, see G. F. Lamb, *The Happiest Days* (1959), Chapter IV.
146. A. G. Bradley *et al.* (1923), Chapter XIII.
147. Canon W. Gildea, *Recollections of Schooldays at Marlborough College, 1848–1851* (privately printed, 1918).
148. MS diary of Boscawen Somerset for 1851–52 (M. C. archives). L. Warwick James, editor of the Marlborough College *Register* (9th edn., 1952), has produced a pamphlet (M. C. archives) giving an account of the 1851 rebellion, based on contemporary sources and showing the exaggerations of some later accounts.
149. Carbon book of Rev. M. Wilkinson's letters: 22 Oct.–20 Nov. 1851 (M. C. archives).
150. *Loc. cit.*: M. Wilkinson to Rev. G. Simpson, re his nephew

Twyford, 8.11.1851. For a fuller comparison with Arnold's interpretation of 'evil' and 'immorality' as rebelliousness, see below, Chapter Three, Section 15.

151. M. Wilkinson to Bishop of Salisbury, 21.2.1852 (M. C. archives).
152. St Vincent Beechey, *Rise and Progress of Rossall School* (1894), Chapter I.
153. Beechey to Bowers, 5 June 1844 (M. C. archives).
154. Dr Woolley's Rules, 1844 or 1845 (file "Rossalliana", Rossall School Library).
155. Quoted in Beechey, *op. cit.* (1894), p. 25.
156. (ed.) W. Furness (1946), Chapter II.

Chapter Two: Woodard and Brereton

References:

HCBP refers to citations of materials in the collection of Brereton Papers at Homerton College, Cambridge. In 1953 Brereton's son, the late Canon Philip Lloyd Brereton, deposited in the library of Homerton (the college which succeeded to Cavendish College's buildings) a mass of materials relating to J. L. Brereton's educational work. These have been arranged by Mr T. H. Simms and formed the basis of his unpublished typescript monograph on Cavendish which is kept with the Brereton Papers. Among the most valuable of these materials is Canon Brereton's transcription of what must have been virtually all the letters received by J. L. Brereton from the early 1860s to his death in 1901.

F to JLB indicates a letter from Fortescue to J. L. Brereton (in the HCBP).

W. B. D. Heeney's thesis cited is "The Established Church and the Education of the Victorian Middle Classes: a study of the Woodard Schools 1847–1891" (D. Phil., Oxford, 1962). This thesis was the basis of Professor Heeney's later book, *Mission to the Middle Classes* (1969).

1. T. Mozley, *Reminiscences . . . of Oriel etc.* (1882), Vol. II, p. 22.
2. On Monro, see W. B. D. Heeney: Edward Monro of Harrow, articles in *Canadian Journal of Theology,* XIII (1967), p, 4, and XIV (1968), p. 1.

3. W. Rogers, *Reminiscences*, comp. R. H. Hadden (1888), pp. 61, 157, 160, 164. For the work of Hale at the City of London School, see A. E. Douglas-Smith (1965), esp. Chapter IX.
4. VCH Middlesex (1969), Vol. I: M. E. Bryant, *art*: "Private education from the 16th century", pp. 262–3.
5. *e.g.* Jewish Middle Class School, Red Lion Sq., 1845; Cooper's Co. Middle Class School, Stepney, 1878; in 1864 the Ealing Deanery Middle Class School; St Pancras Middle Class School, etc., and after 1883 the schools of the Church Schools Company.
6. *Dulwich College Register*, 1619–1926 (ed. Ormiston), p. 681.
7. Rogers/Hadden, *op. cit.*, p. 197.
8. W. B. D. Heeney, "The Established Church and the Education of the Victorian Middle Classes" (D. Phil., Oxford, 1962), p. 16.
9. K. E. Kirk, *Story of the Woodard Schools* (1937), p. 28.
10. Heeney, (thesis), p. 11.
11. SIC I, Appendix II, 12, quoted in Heeney, (thesis), pp. 17*ff*.
12. Heeney, (thesis), p. 45.
13. On the early character of Lancing as a 'teaching order', see *Lancing Register* (1913), p. xvi.
14. Heeney, (thesis), p. 57.
15. *Plea*, p. 4, quoted in Heeney, (thesis), p. 16.
16. Sanderson to Woodard in 1871, quoted in Heeney, (thesis), p. 58.
17. See *Lancing Register, 1848–1912* (1913).
18. *Ibid.*, p. xxix.
19. Heeney, (thesis), p. 58.
20. *Ibid.*
21. *Ibid.*, p. 60.
22. Kirk, *op. cit.,* p. 152.
23. Heeney, (thesis), pp. 68–9; see also Bryce Commission Report (1895), Vol. VI, p. 222.
24. Kirk, *op. cit.*, pp. 131–2.
25. Kirk, *op. cit.*, p. 158; R. D. Hill, *History of St Edward's School* (Altrincham, 1962), pp. 186*ff*.
26. Estimate based on Heeney, (thesis), pp. 72, 393N.152.
27. Heeney, (thesis), p. 90.
28. Kirk, *op. cit.*, pp. 30–1.
29. *Plea*, quoted in *Lancing Register* (1913), p. xiv.
30. *Public Schools for the Middle Classes*, pp. 17–19, quoted in Heeney, (thesis), pp. 163–4.
31. *Loc. cit.* See also below, Chapter Three, Section 11.
32. *Lancing Register* (1913), p. xxiii.
33. See the calculation made by Arnold's pupil J. D. Collis, at Worcester College 1834–38, in the Oxford Comm. Report (*PP.* 1852. Vol. XXII, Evidence, p. 23).

34. N. Woodard in 1871, quoted in Heeney, (thesis), p. 117.
35. *Public Schools for the Middle Classes*, quoted in Heeney, (thesis), p. 117.
36. Heeney, (thesis), p. 164.
37. *Lancing Register* (1913), p. xvi.
38. For a brief treatment of this "now almost forgotten" man, as he calls him, see J. Roach, *Public Examinations in England 1850–1900* (Cambridge, 1971), pp. 42, 50–4.
39. J. L. Brereton, *County Education* (1874), pp. 64–5.
40. J. L. Brereton, Sermon: "Rugby and Elmham", preached at Norfolk County School, 1883. "Printed by request". (Norwich City library).
41. J. L. Brereton, "Dr Arnold of Rugby", a lecture delivered in the Church of England Young Men's Society Hall, King's Lynn, 4 November 1895. Reprinted from King's Lynn *Advertiser* (9.xi.1895).
42. *Loc. cit.*
43. Fortescue had gone up to Trinity College, Cambridge, and had begun reading for honours when his father, then Lord Lieutenant of Ireland, took him away to act as his private secretary in Dublin Castle. (Fortescue, *Public Schools for the Middle Classes*, 1864, p. 19N).
44. MS letter, Arnold to Hawkins, from Rugby, 10.xi.1841 (BCAP): ". . . My letter was answered by Lord Ebrington, expressing Lord Melbourne's pleasure at my accepting the office, but begging me to reconsider what I had said about the salary. . . ."
45. Arnold MSS: Little black book of miscellanea begun by Arnold 2.xii.1841 and continued by members of the family: letter from Lord Ebrington to A. P. Stanley, 9.vi.1844, copied in by Arnold's widow (BCAP).
46. J. L. Brereton, King's Lynn lecture.
47. Fortescue, *op. cit.*, pp. 6–7. See also J. L. Brereton, *County Education* (1861 pamphlet), addressed to the Earl of Devon.
48. J. L. Brereton, *County Education* (1856), addressed to Lord Fortescue, p. 75; J. L. Brereton, *County Education* (1861), addressed to the Early of Devon, p. 136.
49. J. L. Brereton, *County Education* (1874), pp. 1, 8–9.
50. *Ibid.*, Chapter IV *passim.*
51. J. L. Brereton, *Principles and Plan of a Farm and County School* (1858), pp. 118–19.
52. J. L. Brereton, King's Lynn lecture.
53. J. L. Brereton, preface to printed sermon "Rugby and Elmham" (1883).
54. J. L. Brereton, *Letter to S. T. Kekewich, M.P., on the Cost of the Devon*

County School (1862), pp. 157–8.
55. J. L. Brereton, *County Education* (1874), p. 11.
56. J. L. Brereton, *Cost of the Devon County School* (1862), p. 156.
57. Hugh Gawthrop, HM of Mount View Academy: letter in North Devon *Journal* (23.12.1858). (Cutting preserved in West Buckland School archives.)
58. Fortescue, report of speech at D.C.S. Speech Day, 2.10.1867 (WBSA).
59. J. Booth, *Framlingham College, the First Sixty Years* (1925), pp. 23, 62.
60. Heeney, (thesis), p. 327.
61. *Sketch of the History of the Surrey County School* (n.d., *sc.* 1888, Guildford) and *Surrey County School Register 1866–93*, p. 3 (Cranleigh School library).
62. G. Cubitt, quoted in *Sketch of the History of Surrey County School*, p. 22.
63. Reported in *Sketch of the History etc.*, p. 9.
64. Mr (later, Sir Henry) Peek, M.P., speech at luncheon (Dedication of Chapel), quoted in *Sketch of the History etc.*
65. Articles on Surrey County School in *Globe* (21.10.1875).
66. *Ibid.*
67. SIC XIV 516.
68. Fortescue to J. L. Brereton, 28.11.1873.
69. Heeney, (thesis), pp. 248–320.
70. SIC XIV 516.
71. Sir John Walrond, Bradfield, Cullompton, to JLB, 17.1.1886; and to F, 2.2.1886 (HCBP).
72. SIC XIV 471.
73. Private information (1969) from then headmaster.
74. F to JLB, 29.6.1866 and 1.3.1871.
75. SIC V 294.
76. F to JLB, 10.3.1874.
77. See references to the school and its headmasters in L. R. Conisbee, *Bedfordshire Bibliography* (1960).
78. F to JLB, 1.9.1875.
79. J. L. Brereton, King's Lynn lecture (1895).
80. ". . . one or other, County School or pupils, you *must* give up, for I am sure your health cannot stand both." F to JLB, 1.12.1861.
81. This was, in fact, the term used of Brereton by Fortescue in his correspondence (HCBP).
82. F to JLB, 6.12.1861.
83. F to JLB, 25.6.1870.
84. F to JLB, 29.6.1866 and 4.7.1866.
85. F to JLB, 21.1.1872. In 1890 the proprietor of a private school in

Wellington (Salop) which was later to be known as Wrekin School announced the opening the following May of a second venture, the "Shrewsbury County School", but on May 16, 1891, the local press carried an announcement that the proposal had been abandoned. (B.C.W. Johnson, *Wrekin College 1880–1964*, n.d., Shrewsbury, p. 13.)

86. F to JLB, 20.3.1872.
87. F to JLB, 24.8.1871.
88. F to JLB, 31.12.1869 and 26.1.1870.
89. F to JLB, 26.1.1870.
90. F to JLB, 2.2.1872.
91. F to JLB, 29.6.1866.
92. F to JLB, 2.2.1872.
93. F to JLB, 3.5.1873 and 18.5.1873.
94. F to JLB, 24.1.1878.
95. *Norfolk County School Chronicle* I, 6 (Norwich City library).
96. *Illustrated London News*, Supplement (26.9.1874), p. 301; T Hugh Bryant, *Norfolk Churches—The Hundred of Launditch* (1903), p. 61.
97. *Illustrated London News, cit. supra.*
98. *Eastern Daily Press* (3.11.1955; 2.7.1921): items on school buildings.
99. HCBP, file 8009/1.
100. *Illustrated London News, cit. supra.*
101. Prospectus of the Norfolk County School, "founded 1871" (n.d.) (Norwich City library).
102. J. L. Brereton, Sermon: "Rugby and Elmham" (1883).
103. King's Lynn *Advertiser* (19.9.1874), quoted in N.C.S. Calendar, 1874.
104. J. L. Brereton, *County Education* (1874), pp. 122*ff.*
105. *Ibid.*, p. 119, Chapter X and *passim.*
106. *Prospectus of the County College, N. Devon* (n.d.), (HCBP) and *Address to the County Magistrates of Devon, Cornwall and Somerset* (n.d.), (HCBP).
107. J. L. Brereton, *op. cit.*, pp. 38–41, 48, 65.
108. *Times* (10.5.1873): "University Intelligence": report of a Memorial presented to the Vice-Chancellor against the proposed County College at Cambridge, signed by five headmasters:

    J. Merriman, Surrey County School, Cranleigh.

    Wm. Awdry, Hurstpierpoint.

    Wm. Jowitt, Schools of the Middle Class Corporation, London, E.C.

    P. Reginald Egerton, All Saints' School (Bloxham).

    R. G. Watson, Dorset County School.

109. F to JLB, 31.7.1876.
110. H.M.C. Report for 1876.
111. F to JLB, 26.7.1876 and 16.3.1877.
112. F to JLB, 1.9.1875.
113. F to JLB, 16.5.1877.
114. Duke of Devonshire to JLB, 6.3.1874 (HCBP).
115. Devonshire to JLB, 1873 (HCBP).
116. F to JLB, 10.12. 1891.
117. J. L. Brereton, *County Education* (1874), p. 60.
118. F to JLB, 10.2.1877. Fortescue explained to Brereton: "He (M. Arnold) had lost sight of you for so long, he said, that he enquired whether you were Ritualist or not, but I said the reverse, very broad but Evangelical. I think he will be a valuable ally, if we can secure him." To reassure Arnold about the presence of clergymen's sons at Cavendish, Fortescue mentioned to him JLB's two sons "and said many clergymen had spoken of it as a great boon, not only as to its cheapness, but its usefulness" (*Loc. cit.*).
119. Matthew Arnold to JLB, May 1874 (HCBP, file 8002).
120. Letter, T. J. Lawrence to Trustees and Directors of Cavendish College, 7.3.1877 (HCBP).
121. J. L. Brereton, *op. cit.*, p. 63.
122. Devonshire to JLB, 30.4.1878 (HCBP). On Cox and Asquith, see A. C. Douglas-Smith, *City of London School* (1965), p. 169.
123. Devonshire to JLB, 3.1.1877 (HCBP).
124. Devonshire to JLB, 29.1.1878 (HCBP).
125. Letter from Rev. F. Corfield, Heanor Rectory, Derbyshire, enclosed with letter from Morley to JLB, 22.3.1878 (HCBP).
126. See Sir J. J. Thompson, *Recollections and Reflections* (1936), pp. 78–9.
127. T. H. Simms, *Cavendish College* (typescript monograph, HCBP), p. 20.
128. G. C. T. Treherne, *Record of the University Boat Race, 1829–1883* (1884).
129. N. C. S. Calendar for 1881: report of Prize Day.
130. T. H. Simms, *op. cit.*, pp. 21, 44.
131. F to JLB, 1.12.1882.
132. *Pall Mall Gazette* (30.7.1874).
133. "Occasional Notes", *Pall Mall Gazette* (20.9.1887), p. 4.
134. "M.A. (Cavendish)" in *Pall Mall Gazette* (22.9.1887), p. 3; Simms (*op. cit.*) says that in 1887 the majority of students were drawn from business families in the rural counties, and those from professional families were of poor academic quality (p. 23).
135. *Private Schoolmaster* (August 1888), p. 211. Though, in fact, Flather

had a good degree.

136. F to JLB, 3.7.1891.
137. T. H. Simms, *op. cit.*, p. ii.
138. F to JLB, 10.12.1891.
139. *Spectator* (29.4.1876), quoted in C. E. Mallet, *History of the University of Oxford*, III (1927), p. 430.
140. C. E. Mallet, *op. cit.*, 425–6.
141. Reported by Devonshire to JLB, 27.3.1879 (HCBP).
142. F to JLB, 18.5.1878. But Fortescue's letter is rather ambiguous here: it is possible that this remark is his own judgment, in contrast to Morley's greater confidence in the success of the institution.
143. F to JLB, 18.4.1886.
144. These figures are cited in M. Grant, *Cambridge* (1966).
145. J. A. Venn, (charts, 1930).
146. Iris Morgan, *Memoirs of H. A. Morgan* (1927).
147. A. Attwater, *Short History of Pembroke College, Cambridge* (1936), pp. 117–18.
148. J. A. Venn, *Graph* (Cambridge, 1908) of entries to various colleges of the University of Cambridge 1544–1906, based on 10-year averages.
149. F to JLB, (undated) probably November 1887; also 12.10.1886.
150. J. L. Brereton, article in *Contemporary Review* (September 1878).
151. *Pall Mall Gazette* (20.9.1887); F to JLB, 22.4.1880.
152. For a favourable account of social and academic life at Cavendish, see W. M. Saunders, *art*: "Cavendish College, Cambridge: by one of its graduates" in *Cassell's Family Magazine* (1885), pp. 300*ff*. Saunders, who matriculated in 1877, claimed that he was neither extravagant nor unreasonably self-denying, and that with expenses at £105–120 for an academic year that included the long vacation term, Cavendish was at least £50 cheaper than other colleges. (Later in the 1880s Cavendish had to charge extra for the 4th term.)
153. F to JLB, 23.5.1882.
154. F. W. Pethick-Lawrence, *Fate has been kind* (1943), p. 32.
155. T. H. Simms, *op. cit.*, p. 9.
156. F to JLB, 11.1.1875.
157. The opinion of Frank Brereton (HM of North Eastern County School), quoted by F to JLB, 18.5.1887.
158. The Rev. Brereton L. Dwarris was a kinsman of J. L. Brereton. For the connexion, see the pedigree "The Breretons of Carrigslaney, Ireland, descended from the Breretons of Brereton Hall, Cheshire", which is the frontispiece to *A Memoir of the Brereton Family* (1848) by Sir Fortunatus Dwarris.

159. R. C. Hitchcock, *History of Barnard Castle School (1883–1933)* (West Hartlepool, 1933), esp. pp. 9–12.
160. F to JLB, 19.1.1881.
161. Gabbitas Thring and Co., scholastic agents (established 1873) had a special department for transfers and partnerships in schools. Their advertisements for schools (especially girls' schools) in the *Journal of Education* around 1889–1900 sometimes claim profits of up to £2,000 p.a., though £700–1,000 is more common. See also a valuable article on private schools in the *Victorian County History of Middlesex* (1969) by M. E. Bryant; and a reference to Leamington High School for Girls Co. Ltd in *Private Schoolmaster* (Dec. 1887), p. 28.
162. F to JLB, 17.7.1885.
163. Devonshire to JLB, 24.1.1881; see also his letter of 23.11.1880 (HCBP).
164. Devonshire to JLB, 15.9.1885 (HCBP).
165. Morley to JLB, 26.9.1885 (HCBP).
166. F to JLB, 30.9.1885.
167. See file B.5000 (HCBP) and *Autobiography of Elizabeth M. Sewell* (ed. Eleanor L. Sewell), (1907), pp. 191–2.
168. F to JLB, 8.1.1887.
169. F to JLB, 30.9.1885.
170. F to JLB, 12.1.1887.
171. By 1889 even Fortescue had so little faith in Brereton's new ventures that he refused to speak at the prize day at the Gloucester County School (F to JLB, 31.5.1889).
172. JLB to F, 1.8.1887 (HCBP).
173. F to Frank L. Brereton, 17.8.1887 and 27.8.1887 (HCBP).
174. F to JLB, 7.11.1886.
175. F to JLB, 8.1.1887. Also, F to *Mrs.* JLB, 20.9.1887 (HCBP).
176. F to JLB, 30.7.1887.
177. F to JLB, 6.6.1893. For Fortescue's opinion of the cause of the failure of the Norfolk County School, see F to JLB, 14.5.1891: "I am truly sorry to hear of the collapse of Elmham . . . It never had quite a fair chance. The foolish clergy shrank from it as not churchy enough, and the liberals as not secularist enough, and Lord Leicester never took it up energetically, though in the first place *patronising* it. The farmers, such as good Mr Brown and Mr Beck, etc., who really cared about it, were not strong enough to keep it up; indeed the Middle Class are easily cowed or unnerved by opposition . . ."
178. F to JLB, 5.5.1891; and 23.5.1892, which refers to fifteen students at Massingham, and to Brereton's expectation that numbers would increase.

179. In 1902 Harry succeeded JLB in the family living of Lt. Massingham.
180. F to JLB, 4.3.1891 and 21.8.1892.
181. F to JLB, 20.7.1885.
182. F to JLB, 12.10.1890.
183. F to JLB, 20.7.1892, 13.11.1892 and 20.7.1892.
184. F to JLB, 30.10.1892.
185. JLB to F, 31.1.1901 (HCBP).
186. F to JLB, 20.12.1893.
187. F to JLB, 23.7.1893 and 21.7.1894.
188. F to JLB, 30.5.1894.
189. F to JLB, 1.10.1899.
190. F to JLB, 14.8.1900.
191. F to JLB, 4.1.1900.
192. F to Frank L. Brereton, 12.10.1901 (HCBP).
193. F to JLB, 25.2.1900 and 9.3.1900; F to Frank L. Brereton, 10.6.1901 (HCBP).
194. F to JLB, 8.11.1900 and 14.3.1901.
195. J. L. Brereton, King's Lynn lecture.
196. F to JLB, 2.1.1901, 19.3.1901, also 8.1.1887.
197. *Cf.* F to JLB, 21.8.1892; 16.9.1886; 15.1.1901; 30.9.1885.
198. SIC VII, pt. 4, p. 14, quoted in J. A. Banks, *Prosperity and Parenthood* (1954), p. 192.
199. H. T. Garrans, Esq., Report on System of Secondary Education in Co. Devon: Bryce Comm. Report (1895), Vol. VI, p. 55.
200. Earl of Devon (Powderham Castle, Exeter) to JLB, Nov. 1864 (HCBP).
201. R. Duckworth to JLB, 14.11.1864 and 18.11.1864 (HCBP).
202. F to JLB, (undated) probably November 1895.
203. Bryce Comm. Report (Surrey) 1895, Vol. VI, p. 26.
204. *Letter to H. Chester, Esq., on Middle Class Education and the Society of Arts Public Local Examinations*, by Viscount Ebrington, M.P. (1855), pp. 90–3.
205. F to JLB, 5.7.1883.
206. F to JLB, 18.8.1864 (file B8000 HCBP); F to JLB, 8.10.1885 and 10.8.1879.
207. F to JLB, 7.8.1879 and 8.4.1886.
208. By E. G. West, *Education and the State* (1966), esp. part III.
209. F to JLB, 11.4.1881.
210. Prospectus of Norfolk County School (n.d.).
211. F to JLB, 13.1.1874.
212. F to JLB, 25.11. 1877.
213. F to JLB, 24.5.1880.
214. J. L. Brereton, *County Education* (1874) and F to JLB, 25.2.1900.

215. J. L. Brereton, *op. cit.*, p. 18.
216. F to JLB, (undated); transcriber's notes say probably March 1874.
217. F to JLB, 24.8.1875.
218. Rough notes by JLB (HCBP) show this was originally designed as £1300. In fact, the first warden got £500 and allowance for a house (Lawrence to Trustees and Directors, HCBP, 7.3.1877).
219. F to JLB, 12.5.1887.
220. *e.g.* pamphlets by H. A. Pottinger, M.A. (1871), etc.
221. See especially a correspondence in the *Times* (14.11.1866 and 16.11.1866) over the Keble Memorial College Appeal. The social assumptions of the correspondents "Presbyter Oxoniensis" and "Haud Immemor" are very revealing.
222. "Presbyter Oxoniensis" in *Times*.
223. Viscount Cecil of Chelwood, *All the Way* (1949), p. 26; Gwendolen Stephenson, *E. S. Talbot 1844–1934* (1936), pp. 22, 28, 31.
224. Lecturer and tutor of Keble, 1871–5. He was then in Holy Orders, which he relinquished in 1879 under the Clerical Disabilities Act of 1870.
225. G. Stephenson, *op. cit.*, pp. 27, 43.
226. F to JLB, 28.12.1874.
227. F to JLB, 11.10.1882.
228. M. A. J. Tarver, *Trent College 1868–1927* (1929), p. 4.
229. Woodard, *Plea for the Middle Classes* (1848); Heeney, (thesis) pp. 43*ff*.
230. Though Brereton was a frequent speaker at farmers' clubs. For Fortescue's view of Brereton as a writer, see F to JLB, 29.6.1899. For Woodard's qualities in these respects, as reflected in a press comment in 1853, see Heeney, (thesis), p. 40.
231. Heeney, (thesis), esp. pp. 73*ff*., and HCBP *passim*.
232. Sir J. T. Coleridge to W. E. Gladstone (BM: Gladstone Papers, Vol. LIII. Additional MSS. *44, 138* Fol. 484), quoted in Heeney, (thesis), p. 249.
233. F to JLB, 21.4.1873.
234. F to JLB, 26.9.1874.
235. F to JLB, 21.4.1883.
236. F to JLB, (undated), *c.* 21.1.1881.
237. Bishop Jackson to Lord Fortescue, 3.3.1879: the letter's contents quoted in F to JLB, 4.3.1879.
238. Woodard in 1885, quoted in Heeney, (thesis), p. 315.
239. Heeney, (thesis), p. 202.
240. *Ibid.*, p. 255.
241. Fortescue, *Public Schools for the Middle Classes* (1864), p. 92.
242. F to JLB, 17.12.1882.

243. F to JLB, 22.3.1868.
244. J. L. Brereton in *County Education* (1861)—a letter addressed to the Earl of Devon, p. 144.
245. Duke of Devonshire to JLB, Sept. 1872 (HCBP).
246. Incidentally, both Woodard (*cf. Lancing Register*, 1913) and Brereton used their schools for the education of their own sons.
247. Fortescue, *Public Schools for the Middle Classes* (1864), p. 22.
248. J. L. Brereton, article on Cavendish College in *Contemporary Review* (1878).
249. Heeney, (thesis), p. 362.
250. Also, of course, the products of his girls' schools.
251. L. R. Conisbee drew my attention to this possibility. (Author)
252. *Public Schools Cricket 1901–50* (1951), ed. W. N. Roe. The boy was W. E. C. Southwell, who made 107 against the M.C.C. (*Beds. Times and Independent*, 12.6.1931).
253. For Shirley's period at Elstow, see David L. Edwards, *F. J. Shirley, an Extraordinary Headmaster* (1969), p. 26.
254. *Beds. Times and Independent* (10.3.1916 and 12.6.1931).
255. Bryce Comm. Report, Vol. II (1895)—Minutes of Evidence, para. 4201. On railway stations located for school use, see A. K. Boyd (1948), p. 179.
256. T. H. Bryant, *op. cit.*, p. 61.
257. Item in *Eastern Daily Press* (16.5.1955).
258. Item in *Eastern Evening News* (12.12.1957).
259. *Eastern Daily Press* (10.1.1961 and 28.8.1967).

Chapter Three: The Development of the System

1. Diary of R. A. L. Nunns for 1851–52: entry for 22 September 1852 (Marlborough College archives).
2. A. G. B. Bradley *et al.* (1923), p. 168.
3. Note in early Prefects Record Book, Marlborough College Archives.
4. *Memoir of G. E. L. Cotton*, by his Wife (1871), p. 3.
5. An extract (preserved among the bursar's records at Marlborough) from a sermon preached at the school in 1896 by the Rev. J. S. Thomas (pupil 1848–55) suggests that the demand for organised games came from the boys themselves.
6. Cotton's circular to parents, June 1853 (copy in M.C. archives).
7. A. G. B. Bradley *et al.* (1923), p. 124 and Chapter IX *passim*.
8. L. Warwick James, MS monograph on the history of games at Marlborough.
9. Henry Palmer, MS diary: entry for 9 March 1854 (M.C. archives).

10. Eight articles: "Recollections of Marlborough College, by an Old Boy" [*sc.* C. W. Scott] in *Routledge's Every Boy's Annual* (ed. Edm. Routledge, 1869), pp. 246*ff.*
11. Henry Palmer, MS diary: entry for 6 March 1854 (M.C. archives).
12. D. L. Edwards (1957), p. 141.
13. *Speech at the Annual Dinner of Old Radleians* (1872), by the Founder, William Sewell (1873), pp. 73–4.
14. VCH Middlesex (1969), Vol. I, article on private schools by M. E. Bryant. See also C. Bibby, *art*: "A Victorian experiment in international education" in *B. J. Educ. Studies* V (1956), pp. 23*ff.*
15. A. C. Benson, *Life of E. W. Benson* (new edn., 1901), p. 68. A slightly different account is given in J. L. Bevir, *The Making of Wellington College* (1920), p. 2; G. F. H. Berkeley, *Wellington College: the Founders of the Tradition* (Newport, 1948), p. 23.
16. R. L. Hine, *Confessions of an Un-common Attorney* (3rd edn., 1945), p. 217.
17. A. K. Boyd (1948), pp. 198, 205.
18. D. H. Newsome (1959), p. 242.
19. E. Lyttelton (1925), p. 162; also, *Journal of Education* (March 1900), p. 235.
20. E. Lyttelton (1925), pp. 28*ff.*
21. Speeches at the Presentation of Dr Holden, 14 Sept. 1882 (*Durham Advertiser* pamphlet, Durham 1882).
22. C. C. Falkner, *History of Weymouth College to 1901* (n.d., *c.* 1928), Chapter II. "Praepostors" were established by his Old Rugbeian successor (see Chapter III, esp. p. 70).
23. See Minutes of Council, Marlborough College, for 1860, esp. from June onwards.
24. V. H. H. Green, *Oxford Common Room* (1957), p. 245.
25. *Ibid.*, pp. 37, 73; and D. A. Winstanley, *Early Victorian Cambridge* (1955 edn.), p. 387.
26. L. R. Farnell, *An Oxonian looks back* (1934), p. 59 and Chapter 6 *passim.*
27. *Loc. cit.*; C. M. Blagden (1953), p. 105.
28. D. H. Newsome (1961), esp. Chapter 4.
29. HMC Report for 1897, p. 78.
30. A. Lang, *Life of Sir Stafford Northcote* (new edn., 1891), p. 11.
31. R. H. Lyttelton, *Giants of the Game*, p. 22.
32. Geoffrey Faber (1957), pp. 328, 330.
33. G. B. Grundy (1945), p. 51.
34. R. H. Lyttelton, *op. cit.*, p. 23.
35. L. E. Jones (1955), p. 197; G. Kendall (1933), p. 59.
36. J. E. Morgan, *University Oars, a critical enquiry into the after health of the men who rowed in the Oxford and Cambridge Boat Race 1829–69*

(1873), p. 299 and *passim*; also, Sir P. H. S. Hartley and G. F. Llewellyn, *art*: "The longevity of oarsmen, a study of those who rowed in the Oxford and Cambridge Boat Race from 1829 to 1928" in *British Medical Journal* I (1939), p. 657.
37. W. C. Tuckwell (1893), pp. 32*ff*, 63.
38. J. D'E Firth (1954), p. 49.
39. Quoted in N. Annan (1965), pp. 10–11.
40. J. D'E Firth(1949), p. 174; also quoted in N. Annan (1965), p. 11.
41. J. D'E Firth (1954), p. 49.
42. J. D'E Firth, *Winchester* (1936), pp. 43–4.
43. Herman Merivale, *Autobiography—Bar, Stage and Platform* (1902), p. 189.
44. E. Graham (1920), pp. 267–8.
45. PSC I 253.
46. *Fettes College Register* (1933), p. xx.
47. R. H. Bruce Lockhart, *Friends, Foes and Foreigners* (1957), p. 11.
48. *Ibid.*, p. 75.
49. *Leys Fortnightly* I (1876–7), p. 184.
50. West Buckland "Register"; Letters of Lord Fortescue, Nov. 1867 and Feb. 1868.
51. O. Rysden, *The Book of Blues* (1900), p. viii; Sir J. J. Thompson, *Recollections and Reflections* (1936), pp. 70–1.
52. Quoted in P. C. McIntosh, *Landmarks in the History of Physical Education* (1957), p. 188.
53. *Cf.* S. H. Jeyes, *art*: "Our Gentlemanly Failures" in *Fortnightly Review* LXI (new Series, Jan.–June 1897), pp. 387*ff*.
54. *P.S. Mag.* III (1899), pp. 414.
55. A. K. Boyd (1948), p. 194.
56 Lord Chandos (1962), p. 9.
57. C. Alington (1943), p. 7.
58. *P.S. Mag.* II (1898), p. 284.
59. E. Lyttelton, *art*: "Athleticism in Public Schools" in *Nineteenth Century* (Jan. 1880), p. 55.
60. P. Woodruff, *Men Who Made India*, Vol. I, p. 282.
61. E. Lyttelton, *art. cit.*, pp. 44–5.
62. *Wisden* for 1879, p. 54.
63. E. Lyttelton, *art. cit.*, pp. 44–5.
64. G. L. Prestige (1935), p. 3; W. J. Ford, *History of the Cambridge University Cricket Club* (1902), p. 16.
65. J. H. Simpson, *The Public Schools and Athleticism* (Educational Times Booklets, No. 1, 1922), p. 5.
66. PSC I 56, etc.
67. *P.S. Mag.* II (1898), p. 283.
68. Rev. E. B. Hugh Jones (Marlborough boy 1875–9, HM of a

South African public school, 1903), *art*: "The Moral Aspect of Athletics" in *Journal of Education* (1900), p. 353.
69. *P.S. Mag.* II (1898), pp. 284–5.
70. F. W. Pethick-Lawrence, *op. cit.*, p. 35.
71. W. J. Ford, *op. cit.*, p. 22. Old Etonians had been prominent in the foundation of this club in the 1820s (p. 3).
72. Balfour, speech at Edinburgh, quoted in *Fortnightly Review* LXI (new series, 1897), p. 387.
73. C. E. Raven (1928), p. 13.
74. C. Hamilton, "Autobiography of 'Frank Richards'" (1952). 'Richards' wrote St. Jim's Stories for *Pluck,* etc. throughout the 1890s and after 1907 wrote of Billy Bunter and Greyfriars for *Gem* and *Magnet.*
75. A. F. Hattersley, *Hilton Portrait* (1945), Chapter 3 *passim.*
76. T. W. Dunn, privately printed memoir (1934), p. 13; *Marlborough College Register* (1952), p. 56.
77. *Malvern Register* (1925), p. xi; A. F. Leach (ed.), *History of Bradfield College, by Old Bradfield Boys* (1900), pp. 4, etc.
78. "Machinery, machinery, machinery, should be the motto of every good school. As little as possible ought to be left to personal merit in the teacher, or chance; as much as possible ought to rest on the system and appliances on every side checking vice and fostering good." (G. R. Parkin, 1898, Vol. I, p. 92).
79. A. B. Gourlay (1951), pp. 104, 107.
80. A. Macdonald, *Short History of Repton* (1929), Chapter 7.
81. L. P. Wenham, *History of Richmond School, Yorkshire* (Arbroath, 1958), pp. 68–9.
82. (ed.) N. G. L. Hammond (1962), p. 11.
83. C. Alington (1934), p. 68.
84. P. Grosskurth, *John Addington Symonds* (1964), pp. 26–7.
85. G. L. Prestige, *Life of Charles Gore* (1935), pp. 7–8.
86. J. D'E Firth, *Rendall of Winchester* (1954), p. 15; on the fragile authority of scholarly prefects of Wellington in the early years, see J. L. Bevir, *The Making of Wellington College* (1920), p. 73; G. F. H. Berkeley, *Wellington College, The Founders of the Tradition* (Newport, 1948), p. 55.
87. DNB (W. Leaf).
88. N. Annan (1965), p. 25; for a later example, see Charles Graves, *The Bad Old Days* (1951), p. 31.
89. (ed.) W. Holden (1950), pp. 19–20, 26.
90. G. H. O. Burgess, *Curious World of Frank Buckland* (1967), p. 21.
91. PSC I 143 (report on Winchester).
92. Minutes of Council of Marlborough College, 30 July 1890.
93. R. B. Gardiner and J. Lupton (1911), p. 121; V. M. Allom, *Ex*

Oriente Salus (Eastbourne, 1967), p. 67.

94. *Sam Brooke's Journal, the Diary of a Lancing Schoolboy 1860–65* (Lancing, 1953); *Lancing Register* (S. R. Brooke, No. 233); A. B. Gourlay (1951), p. 105.
95. S. P. B. Mais (1937), p. 40.
96. *Radley Register* (1947), p. xxxiv, and A. K. Boyd (1948), pp. 291, 324.
97. A. L. Irvine (1958), p. 93.
98. R. L. Ashcroft, *Haileybury 1908–61* (Haileybury, 1961), p. 20.
99. J. D'E Firth (1949), pp. 174–6.
100. M. C. Morgan (1968), pp. 79, 168; J. B. Hope Simpson (1967), p. 119. Malvern instituted a similar limitation of tenure in 1907: R. Blumenau (1965), p. 84.
101. Sir Edward May, *Changes and Chances of a Soldier's Life* (1925), p. 16.
102. J. H. Simpson (1954), Chapter 2 and p. 127.
103. Frank Fletcher (1937), p. 96.
104. W. F. Bushell (1962), p. 54.
105. G. St. Quentin (1956), pp. 150, 197.
106. G. R. Parkin (1898), Vol. I, p. 77.
107. A. F. Leach, *History of Winchester College* (1899), p. 416.
108. B. Simon, *Studies in the History of Education 1780–1870* (1960), p. 326.
109. F. R. Balls, *art*: "English Grammar Schools in the 19th century", II, in *Durham Research Review* V, 20 [1968], p. 223 and *passim*; for an account of H. D. Harper's effective suppression of the rights of Sherborne townsfolk, see G. G. Coulton (1943), p. 201.
110. H. W. Nevinson, *Changes and Chances* (1923), p. 31.
111. Bryce Comm. Report (1895), Vol. I, p. 210.
112. C. D. Linnell, *Dr. R. B. Poole* (pamphlet, Bedford, n.d.), p. 6.
113. J. Sargeaunt, *History of Bedford School* (1925), p. 114.
114. C. D. Linnell, *op. cit.*, pp. 5, 9.
115. Bryce Comm. Report (1895), Evidence, para. 6167–8.
116. See the thesis by Dr. D. P. Leinster-Mackay, "The English Private School 1830–1914, with special reference to the Preparatory School", (Ph.D., University of Durham, 1972).
117. J. Dover Wilson (ed.), *The Schools of England* (1926), p. 65; H. C. King, article in the *Journal Of Education* (1925), cited in J. Dover Wilson, p. 66. They differed from public schools in being in most cases privately owned, though some eventually became trusts.
118. HMC Report for 1890. Some preparatory schools specialised in preparing for particular public schools, which meant that the total of the numbers of prep. schools serving those public schools might be relatively smaller. Wellington, with a specifically military connexion, was served by thirty-three prep. schools in

1896: G. H. Wilson, *History of Windlesham House School* (1937), p. 58.

119. A. C. Ainger, *Memories of Eton Sixty Years Ago* (1917), p. 13.
120. G. H. Wilson, *op. cit.*, Chapter I. The school began with twenty boys in 1837 and ultimately numbered eighty (pp. 26, 31).
121. Lord Ernle, *From Whippingham to Westerminster* (1938), p. 20.
122. W. F. Bushell (1962), p. 134. A. Lubbock, author of *Memories of Eton and Etonians* (1899), was at the school from 1854–63.
123. MS letter, Rev. E. Coleridge to Dr Pusey, 10 January 1848 (Coleridge Letters, Pusey Library, Oxford) referring to a regulation "made about two years since".
124. Compiled by the author from the Marlborough, Lancing and Rugby Registers.
125. A. Esdaile (ed.), *Lancing Register* (1913), pp. 116–21; T. Pellatt, *Boys in the Making* (1937), p. 42.
126. *Lancing Register* (1913), p. 120: Moor.
127. L. E. Upcott in H. C. Brentnall and E. G. H. Kempson (eds.), *Marlborough College 1843–1943* (Cambridge, 1943), p. 24.
128. Marlborough College Council Minutes, November 1887 and February 1889.
129. Details can be found in the Chart (and accompanying Notes) at the end of the unpublished thesis: J. R deS. Honey, "The Victorian Public School, 1828–1902: the School as a Community" (D. Phil., Oxford, 1970).
130. G. L. Prestige (1935), p. 9.
131. (eds.) R. B. Gardiner and J. Lupton (1911), p. 124.
132. Sir E. Barker, *Father of the Man* (1949), p. 25.
133. (ed.) P. Cowburn (1964), p. 106; see also D. S. Colman, *Sabrinae Corolla* (Shrewsbury, 1950), p. 5.
134. M. R. D. Foot (ed.), *Gladstone Diaries* (1968–), Vol. I, p. 349.
135. H. S. Tremenheere, autobiographical MS, p. 17.
136. *Ibid.*, p. 15; SL I 118–19.
137. Pears' answer to SIC, quoted in B. Thomas, *Repton 1557–1957* (1957), p. 42.
138. PSC III 114, 3537; see also W. E. Bowen (1902), p. 137.
139. Lord Berners, *A Distant Prospect* (1945), p. 30.
140. SL I 119.
141. Report (1923), p. 7.
142. S. Rothblatt, *Revolution of the Dons* (1968), pp. 163–5.
143. R. Livingstone, *The Rainbow Bridge* (1959), pp. 117–18. (My italics—Author.)
144. D. L. Edwards, *Leaders of the Church of England* (1971), p. 187.
145. R. M. Ogilvie (1964), pp. 117, 121.
146. Sir Maurice Bowra, *Memories* (1966), p. 141.

147. *Ibid.*, p. 245.
148. R. M. Ogilvie (1964), p. 121.
149. On Greek and Latin authors and their "lessons of patriotism", "love of country" and readiness to defend her "to the death", see the introductions by J. A. Nairn, headmaster of Merchant Taylors' 1900–29, to his *Latin Prose Composition* (1925) and *Greek Prose Composition* (1927).
150. On the influence, particularly through Homer, of the cult of the warrior-hero, see R. M. Ogilvie (1964), p. 175.
151. A. L. Irvine (1958), pp. 78–9.
152. C. Neate, Fellow of Oriel, in PSC II 49.
153. M. I. Henderson on Murray in DNB 1951–60, p. 758.
154. Lord Chandos, *From Peace to War* (1968), p. 45.
155. According to Sir Oswald Mosley in (G. Tayar, ed.) *Personality and Power* (1971), p. 82.
156. Lord Chandos, *op. cit.*, p. 46.
157. PSC III §509, p. 345.
158. N. Nuttall, *Lift Up Your Hearts* (Hilton, Natal, 1971), p. 48.
159. *Rugby Magazine* I (1836), p. 361.
160. A. Amos, *Four Lectures on the Advantages of a Classical Education* (1846), quoted in M. L. Clarke (1959), p. 170.
161. D. Newsome (1959), pp. 74–7, etc.
162. M. L. Clarke (1959), p. 170.
163. R. C. Robertson-Glasgow, *46 Not Out* (1948), p. 60.
164. Lord Kilbracken, *Reminiscences* (1916), 1931 edn., p. 41.
165. Geoffrey Faber (1957), p. 222.
166. L. E. Jones, *Georgian Afternoon* (1958), p. 10.
167. W. F. Bushell (1962), p. 31; W. R. Holden (ed.), (1950), p. 35.
168. A. K. Boyd (1948), p. 264.
169. Sir Edward May, *op cit.*, p. 21. However, G. G. Coulton was tested for his French accent before being offered a post to teach languages at Sherborne in 1889 (G. G. Coulton, 1943, p. 201).
170. Lord Kilbracken, *op. cit.*, p. 105.
171. Kenneth Rose (1969), p. 279.
172. Lord Chandos, *op. cit.*, p. 45. For the history of the development of this attitude, see Desmond MacCarthy, *Memories* (1953), p. 38.
173. A version of the story is given in Evelyn Waugh, *Ronald Knox* (1959).
174. J. B. Hope Simpson (1967), p. 194.
175. A. L. Irvine (1958), p. 18.
176. PSC I 81.
177. A. K. Boyd (1948), p. 208.
178. G. B. Grundy (1945), p. 71.
179. A. K. Boyd (1948), pp. 183, 207.

180. C. Hollis, *Along the Road to Frome* (1958), p. 42; see also Lord Berners, *op. cit.*, p. 37.
181. L. E. Jones (1955), p. 208.
182. John Morris, *Hired to Kill* (1960), p. 145.
183. Article on Ridley in DNB 1951–60.
184. Article on Soddy, *ibid.*
185. R. W. Clark, *Tizard* (1965), p. 9; A. A. Milne, *It's Too Late Now* (1939), pp. 90, 102, 127.
186. Julian Huxley, *Memories* (1970), Penguin edn., 1972, pp. 45–6.
187. Article on Sir J. L. Simonsen, DNB 1951–60.
188. Speech of Glazebrook, head of Manchester Grammar School, in HMC Report for 1888.
189. E. D. Laborde, *Harrow School Yesterday and To-day* (1948), p. 50. For a thorough account of the Harrow Modern Side 1869–1881, and of the rift between Bowen and Welldon concerning it in 1893, see W. E. Bowen (1902), pp. 103–17.
190. W. F. Bushell (1962), pp. 46, 107.
191. A. E. Douglas-Smith (1965), pp. 161–3.
192. G. C. Beresford, *Schooldays with Kipling* (1936), pp. 168*ff*; R. Kipling, *Something of Myself* (1937), pp. 31–3 and Chapter 2 *passim.*
193. D. H. S. Cranage (1952), p. 34.
194. J. E. C. Welldon, *Gerald Eversley's Friendship* (p. 75) quoted in J. Fitch, *Thomas and Matthew Arnold* (1897), pp. 78–9.
195. J. H. Simpson (1954), p. 63.
196. G. W. E. Russell, *Sketches and Snapshots* (1910), p. 227.
197. R. Meinertzhagen, *Diary of a Black Sheep* (1964), p. 183: Harrow songs "have kept alive my love for the school".
198. W. E. Bowen (1902), p. 189.
199. L. C. M. S. Amery, *My Political Life* (1953), Vol. I, p. 38.
200. A. B. Gourlay (1951), p. 164.
201. A. H. Trelawny-Ross, *Their Prime of Life* (Winchester, 1956), pp. 14, 24.
202. F. C. Mackenzie, *William Cory* (1950), pp. 39–40.
203. R. Rhodes James, *Rosebery* (1963), p. 486. Mr Rhodes James doubts if the dying Rosebery actually heard "the haunting music, redolent of hot summer afternoons, the quiet laughter of friends, and the golden days of his young manhood".
204. C. A. E. Moberly (ed.), *Dulce Domum* (1916), pp. 131–2; C. Oman (1941), p. 87.
205. C. D. Linnell, *op. cit.*, p. 14.
206. Devon County School (West Buckland School) archives.
207. G. W. E. Russell, *op. cit.*, pp. 422–3.
208. C. E. Raven (1928), p. 28.
209. J. Marlowe, *Late Victorian* (1967), Chapter I and p. 353. Wilson's

biographer here specifically connects his school conditioning with his later flirtation, as a Conservative M.P., with Nazism.

210. Lord Chandos (1962), p. 14.
211. Quoted by Kenneth Rose (1969), p. 59.
212. Evelyn Waugh, *op. cit.*, pp. 53, 73, 79. Knox went to Eton in 1900.
213. L. E. Jones (1955), p. 240; see also Sir Julian Huxley, *op. cit.,* p. 59. for another Etonian's reactions to Oxford.
214. L. E. Jones (1956), p. 12.
215. For an account of Winston Churchill at Harrow, see Chapter II of *My Early Life* (1930–). He was school fencing champion of 1892 and in the same year won the Public School Fencing Championship (R. S. Churchill, *Winston S. Churchill*, 1966, pp. 177–9).
216. R. S. Churchill, *op. cit.*, p. 53.
217. Fortescue commented to Brereton on the favourable reception he heard had been given by the Clarendon Commissioners to the report by Dr Mortimer, HM of the City of London School, on the kind of *esprit de corps* which could be cultivated in a day-school. See PSC II, Appendix P, p. 579–81.
218. SIC Appendix VI, 150, 322, and PSC I 8, and III 502–3; quoted in R. H. Tawney, *art*: "The problem of the public schools" in *Political Quarterly* XIV (1943).
219. R. H. Tawney, *art. cit.*
220. A. C. Clutton-Brock, *Eton* (1900), p. 243.
221. PSC I 108.
222. Figures derived from PSC I 8.
223. PSC I 11.
224. M. C. Morgan (1968), p. 207.
225. Following the suggested 'public-school' ranking of schools around 1902 as set out in Chapter Four, these *very approximate* figures illustrate the general picture of growth for schools below Group I (leading public schools) between *c.* 1900 and the 1960s:

Group II:		*Group III:*	
Radley	200–470	Shrewsbury	280–560
Eastbourne	180–600	Leys	170–380
Felsted	245–500	Fettes	220–450
Lancing	100–410	Loretto	95–240
Hurst'p't	120–340		

Group IV:		*Others:*	
Dover	200–400	St Peter's, York	130–360
St. Edward's, Oxford	125–490	Bromsgrove	120–320
		Monmouth	150–550
		Sutton Valence	70–300

Two schools in Group III, Weymouth (106 around 1900) and Bath College (130) have not survived. Similar in size to Sutton Valence was Oakham, on the HMC by 1900 but not yet recognised as a public school, which grew over this period from seventy boys to three hundred and fifty before becoming a co-educational school of over six hundred at the end of the 1960s.

226. This word was actually used by the Victorians in connexion with school premises. For one example (Benson), see G. F. H. Berkeley, *op. cit.*, p. 74N.
227. G. G. Coulton (1943), p. 253.
228. *Ibid.*, p. 175 (Llandovery in 1885); on Marlborough *c.* 1895, the late F. B. Malim, private information to J. R. deS. Honey.
229. G. R. Parkin (1898), Vol. I, p. 79.
230. A. B. Gourlay (1951), p. 105.
231. V. M. Allom, *op. cit.*, pp. 47, 60.
232. R. D. Hill, *History of St. Edward's School, Oxford* (Altrincham, 1962), p. 106.
233. D. L. Edwards, *op. cit.*, p. 46–7.
234. G. H. Parkin (1898), Vol. II, p. 196.
235. T. W. Bamford, *art*: "Public Schools and Social Class 1801–50" in *British Journal of Sociology* XII (1961), p. 224.
236. Sir W. C. Dampier (formerly Whetham), *Cambridge and Elsewhere* (1950), pp. 15–16; D. H. S. Cranage (1952), p. 27. Sixty years after he matriculated at Oxford, Bishop Blagden could identify the public schools attended by each of his seventeen fellow-entrants to Corpus Christi College in 1892 (C. M. Blagden, 1953, p. 79).
237. Especially a boarding prep. school. See, for example, C. E. Raven (1928), p. 10 (on an entrant to Uppingham in 1898); Evelyn Waugh, *op. cit.*, p. 58 (on Shaw-Stewart at Eton); L. E. Jones (1955), p. 113; Viscount Cecil of Chelwood, *All the Way* (1949), p. 17.
238. See E. Lyttelton (then HM of Haileybury) in "Preparatory Schools for Boys: their place in English education" (*Special Reports on Educational Subjects*, ed. M. E. Sadler, Vol. 6, 1900). £100,000 was involved in the growth of the scholarship system in forty schools by 1895. See Bryce Comm. Report (1895), Vol. I, p. 173.
239. H. M. Butler, Master of Trinity, speech at 25th jubilee of headmastership of Millington at Bromsgrove, 1898 (*P.S. Mag.* II, 1898, p. 477).
240. SL II 79 (in 1837).
241. Printed copy of sermon delivered at Marlborough by J. Llewellyn Davies (M.C. archives).
242. Printed copy of sermon delivered at Marlborough in 1877 by E.

C. Hawkins, who had been one of the first pupils at Marlborough; HM of St John's Leatherhead, 1861–83.

243. Dr J. Phillips Kay (Shuttleworth), Asst. Poor Law Commissioner and Secretary to the Committee of Council on Education, in his Appendix II (Report on the Training of Pauper Children, and on District Schools) in *Report to the Secretary of State for the Home Dept., from the Poor Law Commissioners, on the Training of Pauper Children*, with appendices (1841). House of Lords Sessional Papers, XXXIII, 1 (1841). For a discussion of the theme of the elementary school teacher as a parent-substitute as a "key concept in Kay-Shuttleworth's educational thought", see Section V of Richard Johnson, "Educational Policy and Social Control in Early Victorian England" in *Past and Present* 49 (November 1970), pp. 110–16.

244. Pamphlet by Rev. Henry Hayman, B. D., then (1858) HM of St Olave's and St John's, Southwark, pp. 1, 6, 8. (My italics—Author.)

245. G. Stephenson, *E. S. Talbot* (1936), pp. 7–8. Also, *cf.* Benson's sermon references to the potentially "poisonous effects" of wealth (though "there are quite as many wise and good people among the rich as among those of the middle class"). Book I, Sermon x, of E. W. Benson, "Boy life, its trial, its strength, its fulness" in *Sundays in Wellington College 1859–73* (new edn., 1883), p. 70.

246. W. Temple (1921), p. 36.

247. A version of this is quoted in W. F. Bushell (1962), p. 23.

248. *The Book of the Repton Tercentenary* (Derby, 1857), pp. 72, 74–5.

249. A. C. Tait, notes for a sermon, in MS Tait Diaries, Vol. XII, p. 74 (Lambeth Palace Library). See also *Sketch of the History of Surrey County School, Cranleigh* (n.d.); Archbishop Tait's sermon at the dedication of the new Cranleigh chapel (1869): "The main idea running through it was family life, to which school life should be assimilated."

250. George Moberly's *Journal*, June 1849, quoted in C. A. E. Moberly (ed.), (1916), p. 92.

251. *Cf.* P. Sangster, *Pity my Simplicity* (1963), esp. Chapter IV; F. Musgrove, *art*: "Middle class families and schools 1780–1880" in *Sociological Review* VII (new series, Dec. 1959), pp. 169 *ff.*

252. See W. J. Reader (1966), pp. 85, 93 and Chapter 6 *passim.*

253. *Ibid.*, p. 98.

254. *Pall Mall Gazette* (15 October 1887): "The Public School Record, 1886–7"; and (17 October 1888).

255. "I have recently been found fault with by parents whose sons were being prepared for a competitive examination for wasting their time by giving them a Greek Testament lesson to prepare on

Sundays, because 'such subjects would not get them marks'." (Kynaston in *Pall Mall Gazette*, 20 Oct. 1887).

256. Leading article in *Pall Mall Gazette* (17 Oct. 1888).

257. Rev. D. Melvill, Principal of Bp. Hatfield's Hall, University of Durham, Evidence (pt. II) to Oxford University Commission: Report (1852), p. 51.

258. See J. L. Brereton's article in the *Contemporary Review* (September 1878).

259. Bryce Comm. Report (1895), Vol. XLVII, p. 152, referred to in S. Rothblatt, *op. cit.*, p. 69.

260. W. Temple (1921), pp. 36–7, 85–6.

261. J. L. Brereton, *The Comparative Advantages of Day and Boarding Schools* (International Health Exhibition Literature, London 1884), p. 312.

262. W. J. Reader (1966), p. 98. For some indication of the expenses of an officer, see R. S. Churchill, *op. cit.*, pp. 198, 203–4, 257.

263. Quoted by T. L. Hummerstone, *The Public Schools Question* (1944), p. 30. See also Stanley Committee Report on Officers' Expenses (1903: Cmd. 1421), x, 535; C. D. Otley ("The Origins and Recruitment of the British Army élite 1870–1959", Ph.D. Hull, 1965, pp. 104–5) states that private means were a necessity for most corps of the Home Army at least up to 1914.

264. For the foreign office and diplomatic service, "until after the Great War it was made a condition of nomination that candidates should possess a private income of not less than £400 p.a." (R. Nightingale, *American Polit. Sci. Review* XXIV, 1930, pp. 313–4).

265. T. J. H. Bishop and R. Wilkinson, *Winchester and the Public School Elite* (1967), pp. 93–4; T. W. Bamford in *Educational Review* X, 1 (Birmingham, 1957), p. 26.

266. Devon County School Old Boys held their first annual dinner in London in 1886.

267. Schools whose Histories happen to offer ready information on the foundation of Old-Boy associations indicate the following dates for these:

Aldenham	1902	Haileybury	1895	Sherborne	1896
Blackheath	1885	Malvern	1898	Shrewsbury	1886
Brighton	1882	Ipswich	1889	Tonbridge	1886
Bromsgrove	1898	Radley	1889	Worcester King's Sch	1894
Cheltenham	1868	Repton	1902	Weymouth	1886
Eastbourne	1895	Rossall	1894	Warwick	1895
Felsted	1900	St Paul's	1872		
Framlingham	1900	St Peter's, York	1886		

In many cases such institutions were predated by several years by the foundation of Old-Boy clubs for cricket and/or football.

268. A. K. Boyd (1948), p. 247. See also A. B. Gourlay (1951), p. 183.
269. *e.g.* Christ's Hospital. See H. A. Roberts, *Records of the Amicable Society of Old Blues and its predecessors* (Cambridge, 1924), p. 3. For similar 'benevolent' functions of Old-Boy associations at City of London School and Denstone, see *P.S. Mag.* II (1898), p. 286.
270 *Sketch of the History of the Surrey County School, Cranleigh* (Guildford, n.d.), p. 26.
271. *P.S. Mag.* I (1898), p. 473.
272. Evelyn Waugh, *op. cit.*, p. 81.
273. E. S. Turner, *Gallant Gentlemen* (1956), p. 241, quoted in C. B. Otley, *op. cit.*
274. *P.S. Mag.* VIII (1902), pp. 24, 358.
275. H. A. Sams, *Pauline and Old Pauline* (Cambridge, 1933), pp. 75, 77.
276. A. H. Tod, *Charterhouse* (2nd edn., 1905), p. 93.
277. Quoted in H. C. Barnard, *Short History of English Education* (1947), p. 283.
278. H. J. Laski in *American Polit. Sci. Review* (1928), p. 23.
279. Also referred to in Bishop and Wilkinson, *op. cit.*, p. 17. The minister concerned (de Freitas) had in any case strong claims to office, though these were rather pointedly passed over by the next Labour prime minister.
280. R. L. Ashcroft, *Haileybury 1908–61* (Haileybury, 1961), pp. 172, 176. In an 'In Memoriam' article on Attlee as he knew him after 1945 (*Spectator*, 13 October 1967), Christopher Hollis wrote: "His affection for Haileybury, his old school, was as intense as his devotion to cricket, and he would talk at length of the deficiencies of Haileybury's cricket team."
281. S. Haxey, *Tory M.P.* (1939), p. 180.
282. Aldis, Garnett and Gurney. See C. H. Whiting, *The University of Durham 1832–1932* (1932), and A. E. Douglas-Smith (1965), p. 543. The fact that this school produced many scientists is obviously relevant.
283. C. A. Evors, *Story of Highgate School* (2nd edn., 1949), p. 14.
284. *e.g.* at Rossall early this century. See S. P. B. Mais (1937), p. 59.
285. W. A. Darlington, *I Do What I Like* (1947), p. 66.
286. E. Lyttelton (1925), p. 174.
287. *Loc. cit.*; C. Alington (1936), p. 135.
288. C. Alington (1934), p. 82.
289. PSYB 1967, p. 337.
290. J. B. C. Grundy, *Life's Five Windows* (1967), p. 209.
291. E. Graham (1920), p. 291.
292. C. Alington (1934), p. 89.

293. See article on reference groups by N. P. Pollis in *British Journal of Sociology* XIX (1968), p. 300.
294. From a definition of reference groups by T. Shibutani, *American Journal of Sociology* (May 1955), quoted by Pollis.
295. E. G. Sandford, *Frederick Temple, an appreciation* (1907), p. xxix.
296. G. G. Coulton (1923), p. 21.
297. *Ibid.*, p. 136.
298. F. Fletcher (1937), p. 82.
299. F. B. Malim (1948), p. 15.
300. H. E. Luxmoore to K. H. Bruce in Luxmoore's *Letters* (Cambridge, 1929), p. 194.
301. Bernard Williams in a review of Rose and Ziman's "Camford Observed" in *New Statesman* (3 April 1964), p. 537.
302. S. P. B. Mais (1937), p. 65.
303. Evelyn Waugh, *A Little Learning* (1968), p. 223.
304. Item in *Evening Standard* (22 Dec. 1965), p. 16.
305. R. Hart Davis, *Hugh Walpole, a Biography* (1952), p. 23 etc.
306. E. Lyttelton (1925), pp. 20–1. An item in the *Observer* (Review, 1 June 1969) relates how the former newspaper tycoon Cecil H. King described (in his autobiography) his schooldays as the most unhappy time in his life. "But he sent his son to Winchester, to the same house that he was in," his daughter is quoted as saying. "Now his two grandsons are at Winchester."
307. Lady Gwendolen Cecil, *Life of Robert, Marquis of Salisbury* (1921), Vol. I, pp. 15–16.
308. J. D'E Firth (1954), pp. 17–18.
309. The *Lancing Register* (1848–1912) contains some very substantial cousinages. It also shows that twenty-five boys who entered the school in 1888 (only two of them the sons of Old Boys) had between them at least sixty-two Lancing brothers, cousins and nephews (A. J. K. Esdaile, *op. cit.*). (My arithmetic—Author.)
310. C. Alington (1934), p. 5.
311. T. J. H. Bishop, "Origins and Achievements of Winchester College Pupils 1836–1934" (Ph.D., London, 1962); and Bishop and Wilkinson, *op. cit.*, Appendix A.
312. *Fettes College Register* (Edinburgh, 1933).
313. Patrick Murray on Ian Hay (Beith) in DNB 1951–60.
314. H. J. Perkin, *The Origins of Modern English Society* (1968), p. 42.
315. Minutes of Council of Marlborough College 1902–06, esp. meeting for February 1906.
316. *Times* (30 May 1967), "Old Boy's V.C. given to school".
317. *Rugby Magazine* I (1835), pp. 247–9.
318. W. Temple (1921), p. 371.
319. Information from his grandson, Jonathan Aiken, 16 June 1969.

320. L. H. Gann and M. Gelfand, *Huggins of Rhodesia* (1964), pp. 18, 19, etc.
321. See, for example, L. E. Jones (1955), pp. 165, 244.
322. *Cf.* Lord Chandos (1962), p. xi.
323. Malcolm Muggeridge makes this point forcefully when describing his early days as an undergraduate (after a state-school education) at Cambridge in the 1920s, in his volume of essays *Tread Softly for you Tread on my Jokes* (1966): "Forgotten in Tranquillity".
324. See F. Musgrove, *art. cit.*; the critic J. G. Weightman has made the point about French literature.
325. J. A. Banks, *Prosperity and Parenthood* (1954), p. 168: "by the end of the century the small middle-class family had become the accepted norm."
326. For a discussion of some methods of family limitation which were widely available and perhaps widely used in pre-industrial European societies, see E. A. Wrigley, "Family Limitation in Pre-Industrial England", *Economic History Review* 19 (1966), pp. 102–5. For references to an unspecified form of birth control practised in the George Eliot circle in the first half of the Victorian period, see G. S. Haight, *George Eliot, a Biography* (Oxford, 1968), p. 205.
327. Sir O. Mosley, *My Life* (1968), p. 114.
328. T. H. Hollingsworth, "Demography of the British Peerage", (supplement to) *Population Studies* XVIII, 2 (1965).
329. SL I 285; also II 226, 235, 268.
330. G. R. Parkin (1898), Vol II, Chapters 1 and 2.
331. H. R. Pyatt (ed.), *Fifty Years of Fettes* (1931), pp. 93–100.
332. D. Newsome (1959), Chapter 6, esp. pp. 208–20; see also G. F. H. Berkeley, *Wellington College, the Founders of the tradition* (Newport, 1948), Appendix E.
333. G. H. O. Burgess, *op. cit.*, p. 57.
334. *Lancing Register 1848–1912* (1913), p. xxi.
335. G. A. E. Moberly, *op. cit.*, p. 75.
336. S. G. Checkland, *The Gladstones, a Family Biography* (Cambridge, 1971), p. 206.
337. Kilvert's *Diary*, Vol. I, pp. 72–3.
338. Dr C. Dukes, quoted in *The Private Schoolmaster* I (15 November 1887).
339. C. Creighton, *History of Epidemics in Britain* (Cambridge, 1894), Vol. II, pp. 723, 726 and Chapter VI *passim*.
340 *Ibid.*, pp. 726–36; G. F. H. Berkeley, *op. cit.*, p. 127.
341. R. L. Ashcroft, *op. cit.*, p. 157.
342. C. Creighton, *op. cit.*; P. J. Wormald, *The Epidemic nature of strep-*

tococcus pyogenes (M.D. thesis, Cambridge, 1954).

343. C. Creighton, *op. cit.*, p. 304; influenza had not been identified, or so named, by the 1880s: see Lord Kilbracken, *op. cit.*, p. 147.
344. A. L. Irvine (1958), pp. 20–1.
345. Goldwin Smith, *Reminiscences* (ed. A. Haultain), (New York, 1910), p. 104.
346. W. Benham (ed.), *Catherine and Crauford Tait, a Memoir* (1879), pp. 272–391.
347. G. F. Browne, *Recollections of a bishop* (1915), p. 56. For an Oxford don's obsessive fear of infectious disease (around 1890), see C. M. Blagden (1953), p. 67.
348. HMC Report for 1875; also, S. G. Checkland, *op. cit.*, p. 164.
349. G. F. Browne, *op. cit.*, p. 55.
350. J. H. Simpson (1954), p. 124.
351. P. Laslett, *The World We Have Lost* (1965), p. 221.
352. For a good account of the changing problems facing a late Victorian public-school doctor and his twentieth-century successors, see R. L. Ashcroft, *op. cit.*, Chapter 8.
353. F. Temple, *Sermons Preached in Rugby Chapel 1856–60* (new edn., 1867), p. 300 and *passim*.
354. *Cf.* C. Alington (1934), p. 41.
355. *Cf.* J. Marlow, *op. cit.*, p. 36; see also Geoffrey Faber (1957), p. 144.
356. The age of consent was only twelve in the 1860s: see *e.g. Times* (27 Nov. 1866), p. 11.
357. On after-dinner conversation, see *e.g.* Viscount Cecil of Chelwood, *op. cit.*, p. 36; *Collections and Recollections, by One Who Has Kept a Diary* (1898), p. 233; R. C. Robertson-Glasgow, *op. cit.*, p. 57.
358. J. M. Tanner, *Education and Physical Growth* (1961), Chapter 7; A. Comfort, article in *Times Educational Supplement* (2 December 1960).
359. (ed.) N. G. L. Hammond (1962), p. 30; L. E. Jones (1955), pp. 159, 223; Rugby house photographs *c.* 1868, etc.; A. K. Boyd (1948), p. 162.
360. E. Lyttelton (1925), pp. 44, 80.
361. *Ibid.*, p. 30.
362. Diary of Henry Palmer, entry for 5 March 1854 (M.C. archives).
363. Thomas Steele, *Musings of an Old Schoolmaster* (1932), p. 16; A. Whitridge, *Dr Arnold of Rugby* (1928), p. 143; T. W. Hutton, *King Edward's School, Birmingham* (Oxford, 1952), p. 137.
364. A. B. Gourlay (1951), p. 128.
365. J. Booth, *Framlingham College, the First 60 Years* (1925), p. 61.
366. A. K. Boyd (1948), p. 17; L. J. Ashford and C. M. Haworth,

History of the Royal Grammar School, High Wycombe (High Wycombe, 1962), p. 99N25; F. Locker-Lampson, *My Confidences* (1896), p. 109.

367. A. Comfort, *The Anxiety Makers* (Panther edn., 1968), Chapter III.
368. This is the interpretation given by the editor of *The Gladstone Diaries* [ed. M. R. D. Foot, Introduction (1968), p. xl] to entries for 17 Nov. 1829 and 1 April 1831. See also S. G. Checkland, *op. cit.*, pp. 207, 240.
369. Preface to E. B. Pusey's edition of the Abbé Gaume's *Manual for Confessors* (London and Oxford, 1878), pp. xxi*ff*. See also G. R. Parkin (1898), Vol. II, p. 158.
370. E. B. Pusey, Letter to *Times* (15 December 1866), p. 12, part of a correspondence on Ritualism, Confession and Sin, in the *Times* (19 November to end of December 1866).
371. Clement Dukes, *The Preservation of Health as it is affected by personal habits* (1885), esp. pp. 144, 145, 158, 166.
372. Barrington Kaye, *Bringing Up Children in Ghana* (1962), p. 124.
373. E. Lyttelton, *Training of the Young in the Laws of Sex* (1900), p. 55. etc. and his preface to the tracts "Kirk Sex Series" (ed. E. B. Kirk), (1905), Vol. I: For Boys, and p. 34 for this tract.
374. H. Verrier Elwin, *The Tribal Life of Verrier Elwin* (Oxford, 1964), p. 8.
375. F. W. Farrar, *St. Winifred's, or the World of School* (1910 edn.), pp. 230–1.
376. Farrar's printed sermons (M.C. archives), esp. sermon: "The Objects of School Life" (9 May 1875), "printed at the request of the Sixth form". See also A. Comfort's treatment of *Eric* in *The Anxiety Makers* (Panther edn., 1968), pp. 98–100.
377. E. Thring, *Uppingham Sermons* (1886), Vol. II, p. 15.
378. Rev. W. Watson, sermon (Feb. 1873) in N.C.S. *Chronicle*.
379. N.C.S. *Chronicle* I (August 1872).
380. A. K. Boyd (1948), p. 42. Among schools which copied Radley was King's School, Canterbury, in the 1860s (D. L. Edwards, 1957, p. 136; H. S. Goodrich, *op. cit.*, p. 14).
381. D. Newsome (1959), p. 109.
382. C. Dukes, *op. cit.*, p. 159. (My italics—Author.)
383. G. R. Parkin (1898), Vol. II, p. 157.
384. C. Dukes, *op. cit.*, pp. 150–1, 159, 216.
385. C. Dukes, *Health at School* (3rd edn., 1894), p. 77; (4th edn, 1895), pp. 85–8, 345.
386. E. Lyttelton, *Mothers and Sons* (1892), p. 101.
387. Quoted by Sir T. Acland in *International Health Exhibition Literature* (1884), p. 321.
388. J. G. Cotton Minchin (1898), p. 33; E. Graham (1920), p. 138; E.

D. Rendall, *Recollections and Impressions of the Rev. John Smith* (1913), pp. 9–10, 53, 109.

389. L. E. Jones (1955), pp. 153, 200.
390. See H. Macan, *art*: "In loco parentis" in *Journal of Education* (Nov. 1900), p. 672.
391. J. H. Bradley, *Memories and Reflections* (1955), p. 55.
392. G. R. Parkin (1898), Vol. II, pp. 157–8, 161.
393. *Cf.* T. Steele, *op. cit.*, pp. 14–18.
394. J. E. C. Welldon, *art*: "The Religious Education of Boys" in *Thirteen Essays of Education, by Members of the Thirteen*, 1891, p. 79.
395. HMC Report for 1890, and G. H. Wilson, *Windlesham House School 1837–1937* (n.d.), pp. 56–7.
396. Pusey, preface to Gaume, *op. cit.*, p. xxii*ff.*
397. Heeney, (thesis), p. 164.
398. Pusey to Tait, Tait Papers (Lambeth Palace Library), Vol. 97 (1877), pp. 217*ff.* This source is also cited in P. T. Marsh, *The Victorian Church in Decline* (1968), p. 234N.
399. T. Steele, *op. cit.*, Chapter II.
400. C. E. Raven (1928), p. 16; R. Kipling, *Something of Myself* (1937), pp. 23–4.
401. E. Lyttelton (1925), pp. 166, 170, 140.
402. C. C. Cotterill, "The Prospective Character of School Training" in *Thirteen Essays* (1891), pp. 133–41.
403. R. J. Mackenzie, *Almond of Loretto* (1905), pp. 95, 282.
404. Charles Kingsley, *Health and Education* (new edn., 1887), esp. p. 5 and Chapter I *passim.*
405. Pusey, preface to Gaume, *op. cit.*, p. xxiii.
406. *e.g.* F. W. Farrar, quoted in G. W. E. Russell, *Sketches and Snapshots* (1910), pp. 236*ff.*
407. W. Tuckwell (1893), p. 130. See also *Boys and Their Ways, by One Who Knows Them* (1880), pp. 11–14.
408. (1860): one million copies sold, its popularity only to be outdone by that of her daughter's *Black Beauty* (1877).
409. MS diary of Henry Palmer (M.C. archives), entry for Sunday, 5 Feb. 1854: "We found out afterwards it was Rigden."
410. *Cf.* Welldon, *art. cit.*, p. 60.
411. Edith Lyttelton, *Alfred Lyttelton* (1917), pp. 19–21.
412. Viscount Cecil of Chelwood, *op. cit.*, p. 16.
413. C. Dukes, *Preservation of Health* . . . (1885), p. 150. Unfortunately he does not give references to the other (unnamed) sources.
414. Lord Pethick-Lawrence, *op. cit.*, p. 23.
415. G. F. H. Berkeley, *op. cit.*, pp. 33–6; D. Newsome (1959), pp. 166–70. According to Benson, this was one of "only two cases of V.D. since the school started" (Berkeley, *op. cit.*, p. 37N).

416. J. M. Wilson, "Morality in Public Schools, and its Relation to Religion" (supplement to *Journal of Education*, 1881, pp. 253*ff*).
417. One of Bishop Hensley Henson's letters refers to his first hearing "active discussion of the problem how best sexual morality should be taught to the young" in the 1880s. Henson was an undergraduate at Oxford when this national press controversy took place. But he may have been referring to a renewed phase of the controversy, around 1888 (E. F. Braley, ed., *More Letters of H. H. Henson*, 1954, pp. 113–14).
418. *Journal of Education* (Dec. 1881 and Jan–April 1882).
419. "Olim Etonensis", letter in *Journal of Education* (March 1882), p. 85.
420. Lord Berners, *op. cit.*, p. 50.
421. E. Graham (1920), p. 264.
422. F. D. How, *Bishop Waltham How* (1898), pp. 320–1.
423. *e.g.* C.E.P.S. Papers for Men (1885) and C.E.P.S. tract: "Letters to a Lad" referred to in a letter in *The Private Schoolmaster* (April 1888) as "not for boys under 15".
424. *Cf. The Private Schoolmaster* (March 1888), letter from E. H. Daw, M.A.
425. HMC Report for 1884, p. 34.
426. HMC Report for 1890, p. 52.
427. *e.g.* Thring's speech to Church Congress in Carlisle (1884) on "The Best Means of Raising the Standard of Morality" (G. R. Parkin, 1898, Vol. II, pp. 153–4).
428. G. R. Parkin (1898), Vol. II, p. 161.
429. H. Lee Warner, *art*: "House Boarders and Day Boys" in *Contemporary Review* XLVI (1884), pp. 364*ff*.
430. G. G. Robinson in M. E. Sadler (ed.), *Moral Instruction and Training in Schools* (1908), Vol. I, p. 165.
431. "Olim Etonensis" in *Journal of Education* (March 1882), p. 86.
432. W. S. Grignon, letter in *Journal of Education* (1882), p. 113.
433. Circular to parents (revised, 1885) of Haileybury boys, signed Rev. J. Robertson (HM). Copy in archives of St Edmund's College, Ware, Box E3 (124).
434. R. L. Ashcroft, *Random Recollections of Haileybury* (Haileybury, 1956), p. 20.
435. W. Temple (1921), pp. 100, 110, 115–16; J. H. Simpson (1954), p. 63. See also Sir Edward May, *op. cit.*, p. 15. Curiously enough, it would seem that Percival had not introduced this during his earlier headmastership of Clifton (1862–79), since its introduction was one of the first acts of a later Clifton headmaster (Glazebrook, a former Harrow housemaster) around 1891—exactly the period when Percival was beginning to enforce

it at Rugby (Sir Harold Morris, *Back View*, 1960, p. 90). This lends support to the argument that headmasters were being overtaken in the 1880s and 1890s by an obsession of which they were innocent in the 1860s and 1870s.

436. L. E. Jones (1955), pp. 152–3; Lord Berners, *op. cit.*, p. 38; R. Meinertzhagen, *op. cit.*, p. 178; J. H. Simpson (1954), pp. 61–2.
437. C. Dukes, *Health at School* (3rd edn., 1894), p. 108; (4th edn., 1905), p. 127.
438. HMC Report for 1877, discussion on day boys.
439. C. E. Raven (1928), p. 28.
440. C. Alington (1934), p. 5.
441. (ed.) N. G. L. Hammond (1962), p. 10.
442. A. A. Milne, *op. cit.*, p. 98; R. W. Clark, *op. cit.*, p. 9.
443. R. Meinertzhagen, *op. cit.*, p. 192.
444. Lord Berners, *op. cit.*, pp. 79–82.
445. R. C. Robertson-Glasgow, *op. cit.*, p. 52; C. Graves, *op. cit.*, p. 39.
446. J. H. Simpson (1954), p. 75.
447. R. H. Bruce-Lockhart, *My Scottish Youth* (1937), p. 324. At Oundle, the sudden discovery of cases of 'vice' among boys sleeping in unsupervised boarding-house annexes in 1883 led to modification of the house system, to new school rules inhibiting friendships across houses, and to the specification "no study door shall on any pretence be locked" (W. G. Walker, 1956, pp. 440, 443–6).
448. T. C. Worsley, *Flannelled Fool* (1967), p. 94; *Memorials of Lionel Helbert* (1926), p. 15; Lord Charnwood (ed.), *Discourses and Letters of H. M. Burge* (1930), p. 32.
449. H. Nicolson, *Some People* (1927), pp. 31–2; C. E. Raven (1928), pp. 26–9, makes a similar point concerning Uppingham around 1898.
450. Desmond MacCarthy, *op. cit.*, p. 209–11.
451. C. Hollis, *op. cit.*, pp. 46–7.
452. C. R. L. Fletcher, *Edmond Warre* (1922), pp. 135, 212.
453. *Cf.* H. E. Wortham, *Victorian Eton and King's* (new edn., 1956), p. 97.
454. See, for example, Sir Julian Huxley, *op. cit.*, p. 41; Viscount Cecil, *A Great Experiment* (1941), p. 14; *Memorials of Lionel Helbert* (1926), p. 7; C. Graves, *op. cit.*, p. 27.
455. MS diary of Henry Palmer (M.C. archives). W. S. Smith later became Archbishop of Sydney.
456. G. E. L. Cotton, *Marlborough Sermons 1852–58* (Cambridge, 1858), pp. 336, 337–8. (My italics—Author.)
457. *Tom Brown's Schooldays*, Chapter VIII: "Tom's Last Match" (Dent edn., 1949), pp. 328–9.

458. *Rugby Magazine* I, 4 (1835), pp. 348–50.
459. Thomas Hughes, *Tom Brown at Oxford* (1895 edn.), Chapter 20, pp. 193–4; Chapter 22, p. 206.
460. D. Newsome (1961), p. 112.
461. F. W. Farrar, *op. cit.*, pp. 31, 41, 237–53.
462. See, for example, p. 345 of Clement Scott, *Recollections of Marlborough* (1869).
463. W. Tuckwell (1893), p. 143; also pp. 63–4, 66, 122. At Harrow in the 1830s, "boys with a very fair complexion usually received a feminine name, e.g. Polly, Sukey, Fanny, Dolly . . ." (H. J. Torre, *Recollections of Schooldays at Harrow*, Manchester, 1890, p. 15).
464. W. Sewell, *A Year's Sermons to Boys* I (1854), Sermon 2 (1853) and Sermon 12, pp. 171–3.
465. *Sam Brooke's Journal, the Diary of a Lancing Schoolboy 1860–65* (Lancing, 1953), pp. 58, 68, 70–1, 82, 84, 88, 96, 99–100.
466. Rev. Francis Close, Inaugural meeting of Cheltenham (Proprietary) College (29.7.1841), reported in local paper, preserved in Cheltenham College archives.
467. W. Sewell, *op. cit.*, Sermon 13.
468. F. N. Maude, *War and the World's Life* (1907), pp. 381–2. I owe this reference to Professor G. F. A. Best.
469. See Geoffrey Faber (1957), pp. 84, 140, 144–5, 450, etc., and Geoffrey Faber, *Oxford Apostles* (1935), *passim.*
470. B. Disraeli, *op. cit.*, p. 36.
471. R. Blake, *Disraeli* (1966), p. 14.
472. They await the removal in 1976 of Symonds' executor's embargo on publication of the Symonds Memoirs. See P. Grosskurth, *John Addington Symonds* (1964), p. ix. For an account of the Vaughan affair and of the state of 'morality' at Harrow in the 1850s, see Grosskurth, pp. 32–41.
473. *i.e.* Symonds *Memoirs* (P. Grosskurth, *op. cit.*, p. 39).
474. R. Croft-Cooke, *Feasting with Panthers* (1967), p. 107.
475. E. Wingfield Stratford (1945), p. 126.
476. H. E. Wortham (1956), esp. Chapter VIII.
477. David L. Edwards, *Leaders of the Church of England 1828–1944* (1971), p. 50. He cites no authority for this statement.
478. P. Grosskurth, *op. cit.*, p. 114.
479. W. Temple (1921), p. 103.
480. For Symonds' discussions with Percival on this, see P. Grosskurth, *op. cit.*, pp. 114–15. For Symonds' exploitation of this situation, see pp. 128*ff.*
481. P. Hinchliff, *The Anglican Church in South Africa* (1963), p. 80.
482. *Cambridge Independent Press* (28 Feb. 1875), items on bishops. I owe this abstruse reference to the annotated copy of *Crockford*

bequeathed by J. E. B. Mayor to the Cambridge University Library.

483. D. Newsome (1959), p. 109.
484. S. G. Checkland, *op. cit.*, pp. 207–8.
485. Kenneth Rose (1969), p. 34.
486. E. Lyttelton (1925), pp. 23, 28–36.
487. E. Lyttelton, published works for the young on sex, cited above.
488. *Letters* of H. E. Luxmoore (Cambridge, 1929), p. 261.
489. Augustus Hare, *Story of My Life* (1896), Vol. I, pp. 422, 440.
490. G. G. Coulton (1923), pp. 28–9.
491. See, for example, V. H. H. Green, *Oxford Common Room* (1957), p. 137N. For the fortunes of a school friendship of his late teens, for which Sir A. Quiller-Couch uses the word "love", see his *Memories and Opinions* (1944), p. 64. For a classic statement of the conception of "passionate friendship" between Oxford undergraduates around 1870, see S. Paget (ed.), *Henry Scott Holland* (1921), pp. 94–6, also pp. 36, 43, 64.
492. W. Sewell, *Speech* to Old Radleians (1872), pp. 34–5.
493. A. K. Boyd (1948), pp. 98–9.
494. *Ibid.*, p. 193; D. Newsome (1961), p. 163. For tearful scenes involving both Benson and one of his assistant masters, see J. L. Bevir, *The Making of Wellington College* (1920), pp. 30, 82–3.
495. H. Nicolson, *Good Behaviour* (1955), p. 261.
496. R. S. Churchill, *op. cit.*, Vol. I, p. 250.
497. On the influence of Edward Carpenter at Cambridge *c.* 1885, see Virginia Woolf, *op. cit.*, pp. 46–7; on his general influence, see E. Delavenay, *D. H. Lawrence and Edward Carpenter* (1971), pp. 8, 17 and *passim.*
498. For details, see Brian Reade (ed.), *Sexual Heretics* (1970), and T. D'Arch Smith, *Love in Earnest* (1970).
499. M. Holroyd, *Lytton Strachey* (1967), Vol. I, p. 137.
500. H. A. Vachell, *The Hill* (1905), quoted in G. W. R. Russell, *op. cit.*, p. 228.
501. *Harrow Register* (1800–1911): for H. A. Vachell, 1876.
502. E. F. Benson, *David Blaise* (1916), esp. Chapter VIII.
503. E. F. Benson's own attitude to homosexuality can be gauged from his *As We Were* (1930), pp. 147, 227, 239. For other indications, see B. Reade (ed.), *op. cit.*, p. 36 and T. D'Arch Smith, *op. cit.*, p. 7.
504. G. L. Prestige (1935), p. 23.
505. SL I 157.
506. S. P. B. Mais (1937), p. 56.
507. PSC IV 287, §1539, 1540.
508. *The Educational Magazine* I, pp. 197–201, quoted in J. H. Carr, *art:*

"Lancasterian Schools: a reappraisal" in *Durham Research Review* V, 24 (1970), p. 430.

509. Richard Johnson, *art*: "Educational Policy and Social Control in Early Victorian England" in *Past and Present* 49 (November 1970).
510. E. C. Mack (1938), p. 217, quoting the *Journal of Education* (July 1835), p. 99.
511. Arnold, SERM II 33–5; also quoted in T. W. Bamford (ed.), *Thomas Arnold on Education* (Cambridge, 1970), pp. 52–3.
512. Letters between Dr Pusey and Rev. E. Coleridge (Nov. 19, 1846), Pusey Library, Oxford.
513. F. W. Farrar, *op. cit.*, p. 242.
514. Copy Letter, Matthew Wilkinson to Rev. G. Simpson, re the boy Twyford (8 November 1851) in Wilkinson's carbon letter-book (M.C. archives). This is the clear implication of Wilkinson's letter.
515. T. W. Bamford (1960), Chapter 6.
516. Anon., *The Story of St. Bees 1583–1939* (1939), p. 95.
517. J. B. Oldham, *Headmasters of Shrewsbury School 1552–1908* (Shrewsbury, 1937), p. 76.
518. W. F. Bushell (1962), p. 38; C. Alington (1936), p. 140N.
519. E. Wingfield-Stratford (1945), p. 128.
520. G. Kendall (1933), p. 47.
521. *Ibid.*, p. 38; J. Amery, *Approach March* (1973), p. 55 (on 1930s).
522. E. Wingfield-Stratford (1945), pp. 128–9.
523. Virginia Woolf, *op. cit.*, p. 33. The passage quoted goes on to describe, with appalling detail, what happened when one victim evacuated in the course of being flogged.
524. Kenneth Rose (169), pp. 23–4.
525. A. K. Boyd (1948), pp. 243–4.
526. Sir Charles Oman (1941), pp. 32, 34.
527. A. A. Milne, *op. cit.*, p. 98.
528. C. J. Vaughan, *A Letter to Viscount Palmerston on the Monitorial System at Harrow School* (1854) and other pamphlets on this case cited by G. G. Coulton (1923), p. 72N.
529. Sir C. Oman (1941), pp. 36–9.
530. For one notorious case, see R. Croft-Cooke, *Feasting with Panthers* (1967), p. 28.
531. Marlborough College Council Minutes, May 1893 meeting, and *Marlbrough College Register* (ed. L. Warwick James), 9th edn., 1952: entrant no. 6326.
532. Sir C. Oman (1941), p. 34.
533. E. Wingfield-Stratford, (1945), p. 121.
534. C. S. Lewis, *Surprised by Joy* (Fontana edn., 1959), pp. 30–1.

535. W. F. Bushell (1962), p. 43; C. Graves, *op. cit.*, p. 29.
536. Lord Berners, *First Childhood* (1934), pp. 133, 159–60.
537. C. S. Lewis, *op. cit.*, pp. 27–8.
538. V. Woolf, *op. cit.*, pp. 32, 35.
539. E. Wingfield-Stratford (1945), p. 128.
540. Sir C. Oman (1941), p. 38.
541. W. E. Bowen (1902), p. 369.
542. Place Papers, Vol. 35 (British Museum Add. MSS 27823), p. 25.
543. The Place Correspondence. Vol. I, 1810–1816 (BM Add. MSS 35152), p. 41; letter to Mr Wakefield, London (March 25, 1814). I owe the location of these references to Mr J. R. Carr, an authority on Lancasterian shools.
544. Place Papers, Vol. 35, p. 25. 'Sopha' was, presumably, a common spelling: see R. Blake, *op. cit.*, p. 103, quoting a letter from Lady Sykes in 1833. These facts about Lancaster have been neglected even by modern historians of education. See, for example, M. Sturt, *The Education of the People* (1967): "Lancaster was one of the great schoolmasters, and his understanding of children, his humanity, his zest, and his most unquakerlike love of jollity, display, and even extravagance, must have made his school very different from others of similar pretensions" (p. 20). "As a Quaker, Lancaster disapproved of corporal punishment" (p. 25).
545. R. Croft-Cooke, *op. cit.*, pp. 20–6 and Chapter I *passim*.
546. R. Kipling, *op. cit.*, Chapter II.
547. Sir C. Oman (1941), p. 57.
548. P. Laslett, *op. cit.*, (1965), pp. 13–14, 65.
549. *Ibid.*, p. 69. For one example of this traffic, see J. M. Osborn (ed.), *The Autobiography of Thomas Whythorne* (1962), pp. 3–4. The views of Whythorne, a Tudor musician, on the upbringing of children are themselves noteworthy (pp. 2–3).
550. P. Ariès (1962), p. 365.
551. A. K. Boyd (1948), p. 35; H. B. Gray, *The Public Schools and the Empire* (1913), p. 235.
552. P. Ariès (1962), p. 400.
553. One of many possible examples was the young Curzon's sadistic governess, Miss Paraman. See Kenneth Rose, *op. cit.*, p. 20.
554. E. Wingfield-Stratford (1945), p. 119.
555. F. Musgrove, "Population Changes and the Status of the Young" in *Sociological Review* II (1963), reprinted in P. W. Musgrave (ed.), *Sociology, History and Education* (1970), p. 41.
556. S. G. Checkland, *op. cit.*, p. 85.
557. F. Henriques, *Modern Sexuality* (*Prostitution and Society* III, 1968), Chapter 6.

558. P. Ariès (1962), p. 400; see also F. M. L. Thompson, *English Landed Society in the 19th Century* (1963), p. 85.
559. F. M. L. Thompson, *op. cit.*, pp. 85–6. For parental concern over servants' sexual behaviour, see also S. G. Checkland, *op. cit.*, p. 88.
560. W. Tuckwell (1893), p. 57; C. Hollis (1960), p. 212; H. J. Torre, *op. cit.*, pp. 43–7, etc.
561. I have paraphrased P. Ariès (1962), p. 413 and *passim*.
562. For a full discussion of this theme, see D. Newsome (1961), Chapter 4, Section 2.
563. L. M. Quiller-Couch (ed.), *Reminiscences of Oxford by Oxford Men* (1892), p. 378; G. B. Grundy (1945), p. 53. See also Augustus Hare, *Story of My Life* (1896), Vol. I, p. 498. For a transvestite tennis tournament around 1900, see E. Wingfield-Stratford (1945), p. 79.
564. Kenneth Rose (1969), p. 284.
565. R. S. Churchill, *op. cit.*, p. 124.
566. R. St. C. Talboys, *A Victorian School* (Oxford, 1943), p. 51.
567. C. Dukes, *Health at School* (3rd edn., 1894), p. 107.
568. A. H. Trelawny Ross, *Their Prime of Life* (Winchester, 1956), p. 210; see also J. H. Simpson (1954), p. 64.
569. D. Newsome (1961), p. 211.
570. Barbara Wootton, *In a World I Never Made* (1967).
571. D. McIntyre, *A Century of "Bishops"* (Cape Town, 1950), p. 39 and Chapter 6 *passim*; J. R. deS. Honey, *Tom Brown in South Africa* (Rhodes University, Grahamstown, 1972), pp. 16–17.
572. D. Newsome (1961), p. 211.
573. C. S. Lewis, *op. cit.*, p. 30.
574. *Times* (9 Oct. 1857), p. 10. I owe this reference to Mr Patrick Scott.
575. G. R. Parkin (1898), Vol. I, pp. 23, 135.
576. Sir C. Oman (1941), p. 39.
577. Letters between E. W. and M. W. Benson, quoted in Newsome (1961), p. 176.
578. E. Wingfield-Strafford (1945), p. 113.
579. F. Musgrove, *art. cit.*, p. 39.
580. *Ibid.*, pp. 39–40.
581. A. K. Boyd (1948), p. 230.
582. R. St. C. Talboys, *op. cit.*, p. 57; and D. Newsome (1959), p. 285 N41, referring to evidence from 1901, 1907 and 1914.
583. R. Kipling (1899), Chapter 3.
584. *Memorials of Lionel Helbert* (1926), p. 9.
585. Quoted in D. Newsome (1959), p. 284.
586. W. F. Bushell (1962), pp. 41–2.
587. W. Tuckwell (1893), pp. 51–2.
588. Sir C. Oman (1941), p. 47.

589. A. A. Milne, *op. cit.*, p. 100; Lord Berners, *A Distant Prospect* (1945), p. 22. See also R. Meinertzhagen, *op. cit.*, p. 193.
590. Radley in the 1890s was perhaps exceptional: the school "had an addiction to washing which not all schools at that time could claim" (A. K. Boyd, 1948, p. 238).
591. A. E. Shipley, "*J, a Memoir of J. Willis Clark*" (1913), p. 56.
592. Sir C. Oman (1941), p. 30.
593. A. M. Powell in W. H. Holden (ed.), (1950), pp. 13–14.
594. W. F. Bushell (1962), p. 41.
595. A. K. Boyd (1948), p. 247.
596. Sir Francis Chichester, *The Lonely Sea and the Sky* (1964), p. 26. For a similar account of cold, hunger and lack of privacy at Marlborough by a boy who entered six years after Chichester, see T. C. Worsley, *op. cit.*, pp. 38–9. For an account sixty years earlier of the "paralysing" publicity and lack of privacy, the hunger, and the "real suffering caused by the intense cold of a Wiltshire February" at Marlborough, see Lord Ernle, *Whippingham to Westminster* (1938), p. 39.
597. A. M. Powell in W. H. Holden (ed.), (1950), p. 14. (My italics—Author.)
598. R. Meinertzhagen, *op. cit.*, pp. 192, 195, 223.
599. Sir C. Oman (1941), p. 31.
600. G. H. O. Burgess, *The Curious World of Frank Buckland* (1967), p. 22.)
601. Sir C. Oman (1941), p. 31; boys up early to fag at Winchester had to wait nearly two-and-a-half hours for breakfast in the 1890s (Herbert Asquith, *Moments of Memory*, 1938, pp. 94–5). As late as 1913 numbers of boys at Charterhouse would faint in Chapel for lack of breakfast (C. Graves, *op. cit.*, p. 41).
602. Sir C. Oman (1941), p. 31: A. M. Powell in W. H. Holden (ed.), (1950), p. 13.
603. A. A. Milne, *op. cit.*, p. 92. (Sir) Colin Coote entered Rugby in 1907: "I was perpetually ill or hungry or both during the whole of my four years at Rugby." (Sir C. R. Coote, *Editorial*, 1965, p. 22)
604. Private information, Rev. F. A. Simpson to J. R. deS. Honey, (Cambridge, 1.5.1969). Admittedly. the Rossall bursar of the time was said to have been later exposed as an embezzler.
605. Marghanita Laski, in S. Nowell-Smith (ed.), *Edwardian England* (1964), p. 205.
606. *Loc. cit.* The term 'public school' is not defined, nor are details given of the research which was the basis of this comparison.
607. See Appendix by J. M. Tanner and H. Goldstein in Gerald W. Murray and T. A. A. Hunter, *Physical Education and Health* (1966),

pp. 174*ff*.
608. PSC I 44.
609. W. Tuckwell (1893), pp. 162–4.
610. For two of many possible examples, see W. H. Holden (ed.), (1950), p. 22, and W. F. Bushell (1962), p. 44.
611. For a description of this structure, see M. E. Sadler (ed.), *Moral Instruction and Training in Schools* (1908), Vol. I, pp. 110–11.
612. E. D. Laborde, *op. cit.*, pp. 209–14; on Rugby *c.* 1900, J. H. Simpson (1954), p. 78; Meinertzhagen, *op. cit.*, p. 192 (Harrow in the 1890s); Lord Berners, *op. cit.* (1945), p. 27. On "descending terraces of sartorial privilege as intricate as a suit in Chancery" at Charterhouse around 1910, see R. C. Robertson-Glasgow, *op. cit.*, p. 52.
613. Goldwin Smith, *Reminiscences* (ed. A Haultain), (New York, 1910), p. 369. There is an account of such practices in South African universities in Dan Jacobson's novel, *The Beginners* (1966).
614. P. Lubbock (ed.), *Diary of A. C. Benson* (n.d.), p. 150.
615. D. Newsome (1959), p. 271.
616. E. C. Mack (1938), p. 187.
617. J. B. C. Grundy, *op. cit.*, p. 119.
618. W. J. Ong, "Latin Language Study as a Renaissance Puberty Rite" in *Studies in Philology* (Vol. 56, 2, April 1959), pp. 103–24, reprinted in P. W. Musgrave (ed.), *op. cit.*, part IV, Chapter 5.
619. A. van Gennep, *The Rites of Passage*, trans. Vizedom and Caffee (London, 1960); (Introduction by S. T. Kimball), pp. vii, 65*ff*, 81, 87–8.
620. W. J. Ong, *art. cit.*, p. 234; A. van Gennep, *op. cit.*, p. 75 and Chapter VI *passim*.
621. R. H. Bruce-Lockhart, *My Scottish Youth* (1937), p. 339.
622. Sir Ian Hamilton, Introduction, p. x., to J. L. Bevir, *op. cit.*
623. A. K. Boyd (1948), p. 190.
624. *Lancing Register* (1913), p. xviii.
625. *Ibid.*; see also W. Tuckwell (1893), p. 15 etc.
626. Herbert Asquith, *Moments of Memory* (1938), p. 92.
627. R. St. J. Ainslie, *Sedbergh School Songs* (Leeds, 1896), p. 21.
628. R. R. Marett, *A Jerseyman at Oxford* (1941), pp. 144, 304, 322.
629. *Cornhill Magazine* 27 (March 1873), p. 284. I owe this reference to Mr J. A. Mangan.
630. For two post-Victorian examples of this reticence, see F. J. Stiglingh, "A Comparative Study of the Public Schools of England and the Anglican Schools in Cape Province" (unpublished B.Ed. thesis, University of the Cape Town, 1957), p. 106; D. Newsome (1959), p. 361.
631. See also Lord Berners, *op. cit.*, p. 26, writing about Eton *c.* 1897.

632. *Ibid.*, pp. 29–30; W. H. Holden (ed.), (1950), p. 26; C. Graves, *op. cit.*, p. 33. Radley around 1860, with some one hundred and fifty boys aged eight to nineteen, had forty-one servants, of whom all but seven were male. Much of the domestic work and waiting at table was done by "servitors", a category of boys (the first of them, recruited at St Columba's, were "five little naked Irish boys") intended by the schools' founder to double up as choristers and, if of academic promise, to pass into the main school, though none ever did. In the First World War most of them were replaced by maids (A. K Boyd, 1948, pp. 10, 25, 156, 301; and Lord Kilbracken, *op. cit.*, p. 22). So this school at least was one which offered little relief from contact with servants—though by now such contact was formalised and controlled. For servants at Haileybury before 1908, see R. L. Ashcroft, *op. cit.*, pp. 51–2, and L. S. Milford, *Haileybury College* (1909), Chapter VI; at Charterhouse, W. Veale (college servant 1880–1945) *From a New Angle* (Winchester, 1967), *passim.* At Malvern around 1910 two house prefects were demoted for "meeting and talking with girls on Sundays", an offence which in the prefects' minute book was rated as "immorality", along with smoking, swearing, "lewd talk", and "spreading scandal" (R. Blumenau, 1965, pp. 72–3). See also C. Graves, *op. cit.*, p. 41.
633. J. H. Simpson (1954), p. 76.
634. Lord Ernle, *op. cit.*, p. 39.
635. R. Meinertzhagen, *op. cit.*, p. 192. In his short story "The Man who Kept His Form" (1920, published in *Caravan*, 1925), John Galsworthy, who had been at Harrow in the 1880s, described a house prefect's embarrassment at seeing the pictures of a junior boy's parents and sister (p. 188). See also Lord Berners, *First Childhood* (1934), p. 123.
636. E. H. Ryle (ed.), *A. C. Benson* (1925), p. 47, referring to Eton. E. F. Benson, who had been at Marlborough, makes the hero of *David Blazie* refer to it as "a sort of disgrace to have your Christian name known", even more so at prep. school than at public school (p. 143).
637. T. Pellatt, *Boys in the Making* (1936), p. 58; J. R. Ackerley, *My Father and Myself* (1968), pp. 79–80.
638. Lord Berners, *A Distant Prospect* (1945), p. 44.
639. *Memoir of T. W. Dunn* (1934), p. 95.
640. A. H. Trelawny Ross, *op. cit.*, p. 298.
641. H. W. Nevinson, *More Changes and Chances* (1925), p. 262.
642. "Toyeite" [A. N. Palmer], *Winchester 1900–1905* (Winchester, 1954), p. 33.
643. N. Monsarrat, *Life is a Four-Letter Word* (1966), Vol. I, p. 172.

644. Sir F. Chichester, *op. cit.*, p. 29.
645. P. Ariès (1962), p. 328.
646. R. C. Robertson-Glasgow, *op. cit.*, p. 58.
647. F. Fletcher (1937), p. 19.
648. R. C. Robertson-Glasgow, *op. cit.*, p. 58.
649. See, for example, P. Cowburn (1964), p. 236, on Shrewsbury in the 1930s. But Col. R. Meinertzhagen, analysing his experiences of Harrow in the 1890s, later wrote: "In Victorian days uniformity was aimed at and even insisted on at public schools. Individuality and personality were driven underground when they should have been encouraged" (*op. cit.*, p. 220).
650. J. M. Compton, "Open Competition and the Indian Civil Service, 1854–1876" in *English Historical Review* 83 (1968), pp. 273–5.
651. *Ibid.*, pp. 271, 278.
652. *Ibid.*, p. 271.
653. *Ibid.*, pp. 271, 274.
654. W. E. Bowen, *Edward Bowen* (1902), pp. 164–70.
655. P. Cowburn (1964), p. 237.
656. Dufferin Military Education First Report 1868–9 [4221], xxii, 1 (My italics—Author), quoted in C. B. Otley, "The Origins and Recruitment of the British Army Elite" (Ph.D., Hull, 1965).
657. G. F. H. Berkeley, *op. cit.*, pp. 25, 62, 41, 73 (My italics—Author).
658. A. W. Potts (HM Fettes 1870–89), Speech to an Edinburgh Company dinner, quoted by T. R. Butchard, unpublished script, *The Fettes Masque* (1970).
659. Quoted in Sir C. Harington, *Plumer of Messines* (1935), p. 295 (My italics—Author).
660. W. Sewell, *Speech to Old Radleians* (1872), p. 59.
661. T. H. S. Escott, *English Society in the Country House* (1907), pp. 17, 72*ff*.
662. J. H. Newman, *Rise and Progress of the Universities* (1854), quoted in W. R. Ward, *Victorian Oxford* (1965), p. 156.
663. United University (1822), Oxford and Cambridge (1830). See T. H. S. Escott, *Club Makers and Club Members* (1914), pp. 238–9.
664. Advertisement: "Masterships Wanted" in *The Private Schoolmaster* (Jan. 1886).
665. C. B. Otley, thesis cited, p. 185.
666. *Clifton Register* (1948); C. G. Martin (18), E. L. Harrison (17), W. H. Pexton (17).
667. *Public Schools Winter Sports Club Who's Who* (1909): *Rules* of the Club.
668. *P.S. Mag.* II (1898), p. 558.
669. N. Annan (1965) p. 31.
670. R. W. Chapman, *Oxford English* (S.P.E. Tract No. 37, 1932), p.

561; H. C. Wyld, *History of Modern Colloquial English* (3rd edn., 1936), p. 6; H. C. Wyld, *The Best English* (S.P.E. Tract No. 39, 1934), p. 614; Raymond Williams, *The Long Revolution* (1961), Chapter IV *passim.*

671. G. N. Clark, *The Bulls Bellow* (S.P.E. Tract No. 33, part I, p. 417); and DNB (for 15th Earl).
672. R. Blake, *op. cit.*, p. 544.
673. Sir E. W. Hamilton, *Mr Gladstone, a monograph* (1898), p. 2. G. W. E. Russell, *op. cit.*, p. 127; W. C. Wyld, appendix (on Mr Gladstone's accent), to S.P.E. Tract No. 39 (1934); Lord Kilbracken, *op. cit.*, pp. 109, 113. Gladstone lectured to the bewildered Eton boys on "Oomy" (Homer): M. R. James (1926), p. 56.
674. F. J. Snell, *Blundell's, a short history* (1927), p. 149; G. F. Browne, *Recollections of a Bishop* (1915), p. 342.
675. J. B. Hope Simpson (1967), p. 123.
676. D. L. Edwards (1957), p. 137.
677. (ed.) N. Hammond (1962), p. 6.
678. W. Temple (1921), pp. 21, 29, 102.
679. Maurice Davidson, *Memories of a Golden Age* (Oxford, 1958), p. 42.
680. L. Magnus, *Herbert Warren of Magdalen* (1932), p. 13. For Warren's humble social origins and entrance to Clifton, see Sir C. Mackenzie's autobiography, *Octave III*, p. 64.
681. C. M. Blagden (1953), p. 67; G. B. Grundy (1945), p. 102. For the social implications (in the Victorian period, as now) of the misplaced aspirate, see A. Hare, *op. cit.*, Vol. I, p. 281N1; E. Sewell (ed.), *op. cit.*, p. 111.
682. F. M. L. Thompson, *op. cit.*, pp. 85–6.
683. MS letter, T. Arnold to Rev. Geo. Cornish (23/24 February 1820, BCAP).
684. M. R. James (1926), p. 85; see also A. Lubbock, *op. cit.*, p. 171.
685. G. G. Coulton (1943), p. 291.
686. L. E. Jones (1955), p. 185.
687. C. B. Linnell, *Dr R. B. Poole* (pamphlet, Bedford, n.d.), p. 8.
688. L. E. Jones (1956), pp. 8–9; *cf.* also the account in W. Elmhirst's *Diary* (Oxford, 1969) of his freshman year at Oxford of a tea party with a fellow Worcester undergraduate: "A black man from Keble there, Bruce-James, a prince of the blood royal of Demarara in British Guiana. He has evidently been to an English Public School because if you hadn't seen his face you wouldn't have known you weren't speaking to an Engish chap. Not the least trace of any accent" (p. 62). Elmhirst's assumption about the public school as the necessary agent in the transformation is all the more notable since the *Keble Register* (1927) lists this man as

having attended Queen's College, British Guiana, and he is unlikely to have concealed any English public-school attendance from the Keble authorities.

689. C. B. Fry, *Life Worth Living* (1939), p. 79.
690. Sir Ernest Barker, *Father of the Man* (1949), p. 24, reprinted in *Age and Youth* (1953), p. 257.
691. Sir Maurice Bowra, *op. cit.*, p. 104.
692. (eds.) R. B. Gardiner and J. Lupton (1911), p. 128.
693. C. Norwood, *The English Tradition of Education* (1929), p. 131.
694. S.P.B. Mais (1937), pp. 40, 54.
695. *Winchester College Notions, by Three Beetleites*, 2 vols. (1901); Sir C. Oman (1941), p. 30; see also W. H. Holden (ed.), (1950), p. 28; A. K. Boyd (1948), pp. 445–9.
696 Quoted in D. Newsome (1961), p. 176.
697. W. H. Blanch, *The Blue Coat Boys* (1877), Chapter 12.
698. *P.S. Mag.* VIII (1901), pp. 69, 297.
699. J. R. Ware, *The Passing English of the Victorian Era* (1909): *Rudders*.
700. Eric Partridge, *Dictionary of Slang* (1949), p. 596.
701. E. B. Poulton, *Life of Ronald Poulton* (1919), p. 85.
702. L. E. Jones (1955), p. 222.
703. *Letters of H. E. Luxmoore* (Cambridge, 1929); *Durham University Journal* (2 July 1881), p. 117; Viscount Cecil of Chelwood, *op. cit.*, p. 28; M. Marples, *Public School Slang* (1940), p. 68; *Oxford English Dictionary* (Supplement, 1933) on "Oxford-*er*".
704. Countess of Munster, *My Memories and Recollections* (2nd edn., 1904), pp. 176–7.
705. Nancy Mitford, *art*: "The English Aristocracy" in *Encounter* (Sept. 1955), based on a paper by Prof. Alan Ross on "Upper-class English Usage" published in Helsinki in 1954.
706. M. R. James (1926), p. 47; L. E. Jones (1955), pp. 152, 177; A. Lubbock, *op. cit.*, p. 171.
707. L. E. Jones (1955), p. 177.
708. W. C. Tuckwell (1893), p. 146; O. Mosley, *op. cit.*, p. 112.
709. A. L. Irvine (1958), p. 2; Lord Chandos (1962), p. 27; Goldwin Smith, *op. cit.*, p. 12; G. G. Coulton (1943), pp. 253, 158. For Gladstone—private information from Dr G. Kitson Clark (1969).
710. *Cf.* Harold Nicolson, *op. cit.*, p. 266; K. H. Abshagen, *King, Lords and Gentlemen,* Influence and Power of the English Upper Classes (English edn., 1939), pp. 145–51, 174–5.

Chapter Four: The Public-Schools Community

1. Lord Ernle, *op. cit.*, p. 31.

2. Francis Hope, in Miriam Gross (ed.), *The World of George Orwell* (1971), p. 10.
3. Ian Weinberg, *The English Public Schools: the Sociology of Elite Education* (1967), Preface, pp. x–xii. T. W. Bamford identified the public-school system in 1962 as consisting of between 84–106 schools, depending on minima accepted for numbers of boarders, and on inclusion or otherwise of Direct Grant schools: (1967, pp. 268–70 and Appendix, pp. 331–35). Another recent book on the public schools, J. Wakeford's *The Cloistered Elite* (1969), deals with eighty-two independent (*i.e.* non state-aided) boarding public schools in 1963 (Chapter I and p. 213).
4. Board of Education, The Public Schools and the General Educational System [Fleming Report] (1944), Appendix A, *passim*; PSC II 47 (Sir J. W. F. Herschel). Soon after the establishment of the HMC, the Harrow housemaster Edward Bowen wrote that he defined public schools to include "all schools which may choose to adopt the title": "Essay on proposed control of the public schools by the universities" (April 1872) in W. E. Bowen (ed.), (1902), p. 316.
5. PSC I 1 and *passim*. The "Clarendon seven" refers to these schools with the exclusion of the predominantly day schools, St Paul's and Merchant Taylors'.
6. H. McKenna and M. L. Gwyer, *Westminster Athletic Records* (1898), quoted in *P.S. Mag.* II (1898), p. 554.
7. (pseud.) "Martello Tower", *At School and at Sea* (1899), p. 25.
8. *M.C.C. Cricket Scores and Biographies from 1855–75*, Being a Continuation of F. Lillywhite's Scores and Biographies 1772–1854 (1877), Vol. IX, pp. 469–70.
9. *Times* (3.2.1865), p. 4.
10. Though information is not available from the Public Schools Club (at 100 Piccadilly) about the original criteria for membership, it seems that in the 1920s the Club's proposal form contained a list of schools which the Club was prepared to accept as public schools for puposes of membership; this list contained about seventy-five schools at a time when the PSYB, reflecting the membership of the HMC, contained about one hundred and twenty (private information from Mr Gerald W. Murray of Marlborough College, a member of the Club in May 1925).
11. Grant Duff, quoted in the Fleming Report, p. 121.
12. PSC I 25–6; II 11, 23, 83 (W. Lethbridge), Appendix P; IV 412–16.
13. H. Staunton, *Great Public Schools of England* (1865), p. 481.
14. (pseud.) "Martello Tower", *op. cit.*, p. 25.
15. T. H. S. Escott, *England, its People, Policy and Pursuits* (2dn edn.,

1881, 3rd edn., 1885), p. 289.
16. Figures extracted from Education Department, *Return of Pupils in public and private secondary schools . . . in England . . . on 1.6.1897* [C. 8634], (1898).
17. *Ibid.* See also J. R. deS. Honey, *The Victorian Public School . . .*, Appendix C, Table 1.
18. The fact that scholarships were 'closed' (*i.e.* available only to pupils from certain named schools or localities rather than 'open', might increase, not diminish, the attractiveness of the school to parents.
19. *Pall Mall Gazette* (18 Oct. 1888), p. 2.
20. *Ibid.* (17 Oct. 1888).
21. G. Baron, *art*: "The origins and early history of the HMC 1869–1914" in *Educational Review* VII (Birmingham, 1955), p. 3.
22. Dulwich, Charterhouse, City of London, and Haileybury were exceptions whose absence from the lists was a matter of comment in, for example, the PSYB.
23. MacDonnell Comm. Report [*c.* 6209/10], (1912), §335–46.
24. Jessop, HM of Ipswich, quoted in G. Baron, *op. cit.*
25. *Ibid.*, p. 230.
26. G. Baron, *art. cit.*
27. HMC Report for 1871.
28. G. Baron, *art. cit.*
29. PSYB 1896, p. 325.
30. *Fleming Report*, p. 34.
31. Figures fromHMC Reports for 1871 and 1876 and from Fleming Report, p. 35.
32. HMC Report for 1876, p. 61.
33. G. Baron, *art. cit.*, and HMC Report for 1895.
34. *P.S. Mag* II (1898), p. 558.
35. In (*e.g.*) 1886, only 53% of member headmasters actually attended; heads from schools with long-established and active HMC representation, like Harrow and Sherborne, were absent for all six years 1898–1903.
36. Prefatory note, PSYB (1889).
37. The PSYB wording was ambiguous as to whether the exceptions were among the schools they included or those they omitted.
38. G. Baron, *art. cit.*, pp. 233–4.
39. G. Baron, *loc. cit.*, indicates a membership of 101 in 1902, the SMYB gives 105. B. Simon quotes the HMC itself as authority for his statement that there were 102 schools in membership of the HMC in the summer of 1903: these schools are identified by Simon as "a recognizable 'system' of public schools" (*Education and the Labour Movement*, 1965, pp. 97–8).

40. For full details, see Honey, (thesis), Appendix C.
41. *P.S. Mag.* I (1898), p. 493.
42. *Ibid.*, p. 546 and III (1899), p. 391. Farrar as HM of Marlborough had felt obliged to ban the participation of his boys in athletic events organised for the townsfolk which had given rise to similar suggestions of betting (Red Book: Colton, Bradley, Farrar; M.C. archives).
43. *P.S. Mag.* VII (1901), p. 412. See also *Times* (22.4.1901), p. 11.
44. C. M. Blagden (1953), pp. 36, 38, 44–5. Similarly, for an indication of the importance to Clifton of the winning of the Ashburton Shield in the early 1880s, see Virginia Woolf, *op. cit.*, p. 37.
45. *Cf. Times* (13.7.1900) report of Ashburton Competition.
46. Honey, (thesis), Appendix C, Table V, column 6.
47. *P.S. Mag.* II (1898), p. 209.
48. *Ibid.*, p. 306. Just after the end of the Victorian period a stranger in Bolton told Howson of Gresham's School, Holt, that he was sending his son to Gresham's because "my other sons who are at X (a well-known public school) tell me that the Holt boys are the best behaved at Camp" (H. H. Simpson, 1925, p. 51). The originator of the Public Schools Camp in 1889 was the Haileybury housemaster A. F. Hoare (N. C. King (ed.), *Haileybury Register 1862–1946*, 7th edn., Haileybury, n.d., p. 2).
49. *Cf.* Honey, (thesis), Appendix C, Table VI. For L.R.B., see *History of the London Rifle Brigade 1859–1919* (1921), p. 61.
50. *Wisden* (1900): "Public School Cricket in 1900", p. lxxvi.
51. Some schools in Group 2 played schools in Group 3.
52. W. N. Roe, *Public Schools Cricket 1901–50* (1951).
53. Radley had its own distinctive football code until 1881 when it changed to soccer specifically because of its failure to find other leading schools willing to play according to Radley Rules (A. K. Boyd, 1948, pp. 192, 433–4).
54. *P.S. Mag.* I–IX (1898–1902), *passim; Encyclopedia of Sport* (ed. Earl of Suffolk and Berkshire, *et al.*) II (1898), pp. 139–54, 515–6.
55. *P.S. Mag.* II (1898), p. 297, IX (1902), p. 100.
56. Honey, (thesis),Appendix C, Note Va and VIa; also Note 7 of Table 2.
57. See below, Chapter Five (reference to W. E. Gladstone at Glenalmond), in apparent support of the boarding schools of Group I and, with the one qualification, of Group II.
58. A. K. Boyd (1948), pp. 91, 96, 121, 273, 278. When, after altering its proprietary character in order to qualify, Monkton Combe School was elected to the HMC in 1903, the school proceeded to found a cadet corps—"to put it on the same footing"as other public schools (A. F. Lace, *A Goodly Heritage,* Bath 1968, p. 117).

59. Chapter I of the official biography of F. A Lindemann (Lord Cherwell) gives details of parental income, and also of the brothers' schooling at Blair Lodge (Lord Birkenhead, *The Prof. in Two Worlds*, 1961). There is an account of this school in the useful thesis by I. Thomson, *Almond of Loretto, and the Development of Physical Education in Scotland during the 19th Century*, M.Sc. (Soc.Sc.) Edinburgh, 1969.
60. J. H. Simpson (1954), p. 92, indicates that "the lemon-coloured back and plump body of *Wisden*" were a common sight around public schools at the very beginning of this century.
61. For the public-school and cricketing credentials of W. J. Ford (1853–1904), author of several *Wisden* articles on "Public Schools Cricket" around the turn of the century, see his entry in Venn, *Alumni Cantabrigienses*, pt. II.
62. E.H.A. in *P.S. Mag.* II (1898), p. 471.
63. For details, see Honey, (thesis), Appendix, C, Table V, column 6.
64. *P.S. Mag* II (1898), pp. 472, 550.
65. A few minor participants in Public School Rowing have been similarly excepted. See *Table 2*, Note 1.
66. Though the PSYB for 1902 included Loretto as if it were HMC.
67. HMC Report for 1904, p. 55.
68. *Journal of Education* (Sept. 1900), p. 550.
69. B. C. W. Johnson, *Wrekin College 1880–1964* (Shrewsbury, 1964), p. 80.
70. 1(a). H. Laski, *art*: "The Personnel of the English [*sic*] Cabinet 1801–24" in *Amer. Journal of Pol. Sci.* XXII, 12 (Feb. 1928).

    1(b). H. Laski, *The British Cabinet 1801–1924, a study of its personnel* (Fabian Pamphlet No. 223, 1968).

    2. H. R. G. Greaves, *art*: "Personal Origins and Interrelations of the Houses of Parliament" in *Economica* (June 1929), pp. 173*ff*.

    3. R. T. Nightingale, *art*: "The Personnel of the British Foreign Office and Diplomatic Service 1851–1929" in *American Political Science Review* XXIV (1930). Nightingale also published a Fabian Pamphlet (No. 232) with the same title.

    4. R. H. Tawney, Halley Stewart Memorial Lecture 1929, published as *Equality* (1931), esp. Appendix I.

    5. L. J. Edwards and G. M. Jeeves, Appendix II of (anon.) W.E.A. Educational Pamphlet No. 5, *The Public Schools and the Educational System* (1943).

    6. G. J. Z. Bereda-Fijalkowski (later Prof. George Bereday of Harvard), *art*: "The Education of Prominent Men" in *Pilot Papers* II, 4 (Dec. 1947).

    7. J. F. Ross, *Parliamentary Representation* (2nd edn., 1948), pp. 41*ff*, etc.

8. N. Hans, *art*: "Independent Schools and the Liberal Professions" in G. B. Jeffery *et al.* (eds.), *Yearbook of Education* (1950), Section II, Chapter 4, pp. 219–38.
9. H. Jenkins and D. Caradog Jones, *art*: "The Social Class of Cambridge University alumni of the 18th and 19th centuries" in *Brit. Jnl. Sociology* I (1950), pp. 93–116.
10. J. A. Banks, *Prosperity and Parenthood* (1954), listing the seven Clarendon boarding schools (p. 189) and, in List R (pp. 228–9) seventy public schools founded, or remodelled as public schools, in the Victorian period. Though Banks himself nowhere states that this is a list of schools which would necessarily have counted as public schools within the Victorian period, other writers have used his list as if it were. In some sense this is true of G. Kitson Clark, *The Making of Victorian England* (1962), p. 272N2; and of S. Rothblatt, *op. cit.*, p. 57N2. If the inclusion of Banks, Kitson Clark and Rothblatt is in any way unfair to those scholars, at least it may warn future researchers off making any such use of List R for the Victorian period.
11. G. H. Copeman, *Leaders of British Industry* (1955), p. 101, etc.
12. Acton Society, *Management Succession* (1956), p. 8, etc.
13. J. A. Thomas, *The House of Commons 1906–1911: an analysis of its economic and social character* (Cardiff, 1958).
14. R. V. Clements, *Managers: a Study of their Careers in Industry* (1958).
15. R. K. Kelsall, *High Civil Servants in Britain from 1870 until the present day* (1958).
16. Raymond Williams, *The Long Revolution* (1961), Chapter 5: The Social History of English Writers.
17. Richard D. Altick, *art*: "The Sociology of Authorship: the social origins, education and occupations of 1,100 British writers 1800–1935" in *Bulletin of New York Public Library* 66, 6 (June 1962).
18. W. L. Guttsman, *The British Political Elite* (1963).
19. D. H. J. Morgan, *Social and Educational Background of English Diocesan Bishops in the Church of England 1860–1960* (M.A. Hull university, 1963–4). The same author contributed an article on this theme to the *Brit. Jnl. Sociol,* 20, 3 (1969).
20. C. B. Otley, *The Origins and Recruitment of the British Army elite 1870–1959* (Ph.D., Hull, 1965). The same author has also published an article on this theme in the *Sociol. Review* 18, 2, (Keele, 1970).
21. Diana F. Laurenson, *The Social Situation of British Writers 1860–1910* (Ph.D., London, 1966). The same author has an article on this theme in *Brit. Jnl. Sociol.* 20, 3 (1969).
22. David Butler and Jennie Freeman, *British Political Facts*

1900–1967 (2nd edn., 1968), pp. 65 *ff*.
23. J. M. Compton, *art*: "Open Competition and the Indian Civil Service 1854–76" in *Eng. Hist. Rev.* 83, 327, April 1968, p. 279*ff* Compton's period barely overlaps with that covered by my suggested later Victorian community of public schools, but his second short list, of eighteen "newer" schools (*c.* 1845–76), "recognised at the time as based on the Clarendon prototype" contains at least four whose standing, especially in the 1840s and 1850s, could hardly have borne the distinction Compton makes between them and his contrasted category of grammar and proprietary schools, etc.
24. A. W. Coats and S. E. Coats, *art*: "The social composition of the Royal Economic Society and the beginnings of the British economics 'profession' 1890–1915" in *Brit. Jnl. Sociol.* 21 (1970), pp. 75*ff*. In addition to the above, H. Glennerster and R. Pryke, in the Fabian Society's publication, The Public Schools (1964) reprinted in J. Urry and J. Wakeford, *Power in Britain: sociological readings* (1973) give a rehash of more than a dozen of the above studies, plus a few more, but without any definition of the term 'public school' which is the basis of the analysis. *Élites and their Education* (1973) by David Boyd is an elaborate comparative analysis of almost all these surveys, and several more: again, he falls into the same traps. If his article in *Sociology* (vol. 1, No. 1, January 1967) is representative, Professor A. P. M. Coxon's analyses of the background of Anglican clergy, involving the classification of 'public schools' since 1870, almost certainly suffer from the same defective research procedures.

71. R. H. Tawney, *op. cit.*, p. 74.
72. G. J. Z. Bereda-Fijalkowski, *op. cit.*, p. 83.
73. Acton Society, *op. cit.*, p. 8.
74. (My italics—Author). *Cf.* N. Hans, *op. cit.*
75. All of his Group A (975 out of 2522, or 39%) plus some of Group B entered secondary school before 1902 (N. Hans, *op. cit.*, pp. 221, 224–5).
76. Jenkins and Jones, *op. cit.*, pp. 108, 93–116 *passim*.
77. See *Table I* above: column A (22 schools) plus Bristol Grammar School at head of column B. For expensiveness in 1902, see Honey, (thesis), Table D following p. 272.
78. *e.g. op. cit. supra:* Acton Society (1956), Kelsall (1958), Clements (1958), Guttsman (1963), Morgan (1963–4), Coats (1970).
79. W. L. Guttsman, *op. cit.*, p. 100.
80. *Ibid.*, p. 290N1: "Those who do not give their education, or declare that they were educated 'privately', can generally be assumed to have had 'inferior' schooling."

81. For example, Bereday's élite studied are the 750 whose education can be traced out of a total sample of 1000: the other 250 may have consisted (and on Guttsman's argument *would* have) overwhelmingly of non-public school men, constituting a proportion which, if retained in the analysis, could have run a coach and horses through Bereday's statistical conclusions.
82. To underline the social distinction between the two group II schools, Radley and Merchant Taylors', we notice that in 1913 the Rev. J. A. Nairn, HM of Merchant Taylors', was an unsuccessful candidate for the headship of Radley (A. K. Boyd, 1948, p. 288). The first volume of Gerald Brenan's autobiography contains a chapter on his schooldays, around 1908, at Radley—"a sort of annexe of Eton, a poor relation of it. Many of the boys who set the tone at Radley had elder brothers there" (*A Life of One's Own*, 1962, Chapter VII, p. 80).
83. G. G. Coulton (1943), pp. 101*ff*; W. E. Heitland, *After Many Years* (1926), pp. 72–102.
84. The list is cited in V. Ogilvie (1957), p. 180. All thirty-four schools named are in my groups I to III (*i.e.* what in Section 9 of this chapter are called Class A) except the following: City of London (my Group IV); Manchester Gr. School, King Edward's, Birmingham, Mill Hill, Stonyhurst (all on my *Table* 5, as is also Christ's Hospital, by 1905 re-established in the Sussex countryside).
85. Sir Michael Sadler's *Report on Secondary Schools in Liverpool* (1904) wrote of Greenbank School in Sefton Park as preparing boys "for the great Public Schools". The school was founded in 1888 and expired in 1912. Its second headmaster, C. C. Cotterill (1890–98), formerly a master at Haileybury and Fettes, was the author of several works on education, including an essay noticed in Chapter Three above; its third headmaster, R. St. J. Ainslie (1898–1903) had been a housemaster at Sedbergh and was author of *Sedbergh School Songs* (1896). Dr D. P. Leinster-Mackay drew my attention to the memoir *Greenbank School, Liverpool* (1939), which indicates that, between 1888 and the end of 1901, boys leaving Greenbank (to enter their public school by 1902) went on to the following schools (schools with three or more entrants listed): Sedbergh (53), Rugby (38), Charterhouse (15), Eastbourne (15), Loretto (14), Shrewsbury (14), Uppingham (14), Eton (11), Fettes (9), Harrow (6), Wellington (5), Bedford, Liverpool College, Haileybury and Marlborough (3 each). Yet Sedbergh as a first-grade classical school had almost expired in 1870; its Old Boys at Cambridge in 1888 chose to join up with those of Giggleswick and the Royal Grammar School, Lancaster,

to form the 'Triad' social and athletic club. Before 1906 Sedbergh played only Giggleswick at cricket, and before 1902 only Giggleswick and Loretto at football. It was under Henry Hart's successor, Charles Lowry (HM 1900–07), that a school corps was immediately instituted (1901), and it attended Camp at Aldershot in 1902; and a Shooting VIII competed at Bisley in 1905. E. A. Bell, *History of Giggleswick School* (1912), pp. 174–6; A. L. Murray, *The Royal Grammar School Lancaster* (Cambridge, *c.* 1952), p. 190; H. L. Clarke and W. N. Weech, *History of Sedbergh School* (Sedbergh, 1925), p. 163; *Sedbergh School Register* (Leeds, 1909), pp. 51–2, 654–6.

86. V. Ogilvie (1957), p. 168.
87. See *Table 2* Note 1 and *Table 6*.
88. On the origins of the foundation scholarship system at Fettes, see D. Crichton Miller, "The Public Schools and the Welfare State" in *Brit. Jnl. Educ. Studies* (1954), esp. pp. 14–16; also R. H. Bruce-Lockhart, *op. cit.*, pp. 259–60.
89. *P.S. Mag.* II (1898), p. 481.
90. See Education Department *Return* (1898), cited above; and Section 6 of Chapter Three above; on the expansion of numbers of pupils after 1908, see S. Foot, "An Educated Democracy" in *Nineteenth Century* 107 (1930), pp. 23–4; see also "Public Schools Statistics for Five Years", in *Times Educ. Supp.* (5 March 1912).
91. Personal communication from Dr J. Kitching of the University of Durham; G. Scott, *The RCs* (1967), p. 142 and Chapter 8 *passim.*
92. See, for example, Elizabeth Isichei, *Victorian Quakers* (Oxford, 1970), Section V and *passim.*
93. Public Schools (Newsome) Commission Report 1968: Appendices, Vol II, pp. 4–6, 11.
94. W. A. Guttsman, *op. cit.*, p. 98. By contrast, J. M. Compton states, of a period which overlaps with Guttsman's, "A public school education was valued for the training it imparted and the character-value that it instilled rather than as an index of social status" (*op. cit.*, p. 279 N1).
95. Viscount Simon, *Retrospect* (1952), Chapters I and II; C. Hollis, *The Oxford Union* (1965), pp. 140–1.
96. See, *e.g.*, R. Jenkins, *Asquith* (1964), Chapter I.
97. F. Campbell, "Latin and the élite tradition in education" in *Brit. Jnl. Sociol.* 19 (1968), p. 308.
98. Including the first Lord Chalmers, C. E. Montague, Sir Frederick Gowland Hopkins, O.M., Sir William Huggins, O.M., Sir William Parkin, F.R.S., Sir George Newnes, C. T. (Lord) Ritchie (Chancellor of the Exchequer), etc.
99. W. L. Guttsman, *op. cit.*, p. 98.

100. Sir Ernest Barker, *Age and Youth* (1953), pt. II, Chapters 1 and 2.
101. Insofar as Oxford and Cambridge themselves constitute an élite, all schools when they become HMC schools demonstrate their power to equip some of their pupils to enter élites, since one of the criteria for HMC membership is the representation of the school's Old Boys at Oxford and Cambridge.
102. T. J. H. Bishop has suggested that in the early decades of the twentieth century Old Wykehamists who had not been to university had at least no less success than those who had, in entering élites. See p. 385 of T. J. H. Bishop, *Origins and Achievements of Winchester College Pupils 1836–1934* (Ph.D., London, 1962), rewritten by Bishop and R. Wilkinson as *Winchester and the Public School Elite: a statistical analysis* (1967), esp. Chapter 6.
103. A. G. Ives, *Kingswood School* (1970), p. 168.
104. David L. Edwards, *op. cit.*, esp. Chapters 5 and 6.
105. W. S. Maugham, *Of Human Bondage* (1915), Penguin edn. 1963, Chapter 36, p. 159.
106. S. W. Brown, *Leighton Park* (Reading, 1952), pp. 32–3, 95. See also H. Wilson Harris, *Life So Far* (1954), p. 75.
107. S. W. Brown, *op. cit.*, pp. 128, 147.
108. J. H. Simpson, *Schoolmaster's Harvest* (1954), p. 79.
109. T. Pellatt, *Public School Education and the War* (1917), p. 55.
110. D. Newsome (1959), p. 276.
111. C. P. Hill, *History of Bristol Grammar School* (1951), pp. 118, 164, 184 and *Table 1* above.
112. T. C. Worsley, *op. cit.*, p. 40.
113. P. Levi, *Beaumont* (1961), pp. 25, 30–2; F. Devas, *History of Beaumont* (1911), p. 52–3.
114. L. Hudson and B. Jacot, "Education and Eminence in British Medicine" in *Brit. Medical Journal* (18 Oct. 1971).

Chapter Five: Scholars and Gentlemen

1. Quoted in C. H. P. Mayo, *Reminiscences of a Harrow Master* (1928), p. 168.
2. H. W. H. Hiley, *Memories of Half a Century* (1899), p. 329.
3. Peter Hinchliff, *John William Colenso* (1964), p. 31.
4. On the stipends of fellows, see H. F. Howard, *Finances of St. John's College, Cambridge 1511–1926* (Cambridge, 1935), pp. 182, 207.
5. Those were the fees charged by his successor in the living (another former fellow of St. John's). See F. S. de Carteret-Bisson (ed.), *Our Schools and Colleges* (n.d.), p. 622.
6. P. Hinchliff, *op. cit.*, pp. 51, 95–6.

7. PSC I 81.
8. PSC I 294.
9. A Trollope in *Fortnightly Review* II (1865), p. 476, quoted in W. J. Reader (1966), p. 106.
10. See Appendix I in J. B. Hope Simpson (1967).
11. *e.g.* A. H. F. Hyslop, a Harrow assistant master in 1893 but not a housemaster by 1902, so that he could therefore afford to go off without great loss in the latter year to the headmastership of Glenalmond, then worth not much more than £1,000.
12. Sir A. Quiller-Couch *et al.*, *T. E. Brown, a Memorial Volume 1830–1930* (Cambridge, 1930), pp. 29–31.
13. *Table 11* and J. D'E. Firth (1949), p. 242.
14. J. D'E. Firth (1954), p. 115, writing of the conditions in 1911.
15. *Journal of Education* (July 1900), p. 425.
16. H. E. Wortham (1956), pp. 146, 159. For Browning's expenditure on books, see K. Rose (1969), p. 30.
17. J. D'E. Firth (1954), p. 68, writing of the year 1867.
18. J. D'E Firth (1949), p. 242.
19. Marlborough Council Minutes, Weds. 6 Feb. 1867.
20. R. Farrar, *Life of F. W. Farrar* (1904), p. 218.
21. *Whitaker's Almanack* (1897), p. 241.
22. J. B. Blakeway *et al.*, *History of Shrewsbury School* (1889), pp. 144–5.
23. Advertisement in *Journal of Education* (July 1900), p. 449 (My arithmetic—Author).
24. *Journal of Education* (August 1900), p. 519 (My arithmetic—Author).
25. J. Booth, *op. cit.*, pp. 60–1.
26. Fortescue to J. L. Brereton in 1894 and 1895 (HCBP, Rev. P. Brereton's transcription), pp. 321, 326.
27. G. P. Burstow and M. B. Whittaker, *History of Brighton College* (1957), p. 70.
28. L. A. G. Strong, *Green Memory* (1961), p. 155.
29. H. D. Harper, speech quoted in HMC Report for 1876.
30. HMC Report for 1876, p. 62.
31. J. E. C. Welldon, quoted in *The Private Schoolmaster* (March 1888).
32. *Cf.* Dr Carver's speech in discussion on salaries, HMC Report for 1876. Reforms of the Alleyn Foundation, discussed in Chapter II (*supra*) would have effected some improvement in the pay of Dulwich masters by 1888.
33. Bryce Comm. Report (1895), Vol. I, p. 304 and Vol. IV, p. 539.
34. *Journal of Eduation* (December 1900), p. 737.
35. W. H. D. Rouse, article in *Contemporary Review* 78 (August 1900), pp. 275–80.
36. Charles Wordsworth, *Annals of My Early Life, 1806–46* (1891), pp.

160, 170.

37. Charles Wordsworth, *Annals . . . 1847–56* (1893), p.23.
38. A. Westcott, *Life and Letters of B. R. Westcott* (1903), Vol. I, pp. 37, 195, 273, 275.
39. G. L. Prestige (1935), p. 10.
40. A. Westcott, *op. cit.* 274; W. F. Bushell (1962), p. 18.
41. H. E. Haig-Brown (ed.), *William H. Haig-Brown of Charterhouse* (1908), esp. p. 15 and Chapter III.
42. Venn, *Alumni Cantabrigienses*, on J. E. B. Mayor.
43. For an account of Mayor's lecture course at Cambridge in 1885, see M. R. James (1926), pp. 181–2.
44. E. W. Watson, *Life of Bishop John Wordsworth* (1915), pp. 31–7, 47. See also G. B. Grundy (1945), pp. 80–1.
45. G. F. Browne, *op. cit.*, Chapters III–V.
46. DNB: W. M. Ackworth (1850–1925).
47. G. G. Coulton (1943), *passim.*
48. *Journal of Education* (November 1900), p. 669.
49. Rupert Martin, *H. A. P. Sawyer, St Bees and Shrewsbury, a Memoir* (Shrewsbury, n.d.).
50. A. K. Boyd (1948), p. 181.
51. Speech of S. R. James, HMC Report for 1907.
52. Letter signed "One of the Profession" in *Pall Mall Gazette* (6 Oct. 1891).
53. *The Private Schoolmaster* (March 1888).
54. *Pall Mall Gazette* (2 Oct. 1891), p. 7 and (14 Oct. 1891), p. 3.
55. Computation from identities of members actually attending HMC in 1898–1903 inclusive, according to HMC Reports for those years (See Chapter Four). (My arithmetic—Author)
56. F. Fletcher (1937), p. 108.
57. J. Sargeaunt, *History of Bedford School* (1925), p. 11.
58. MS letter from young H. W. Badger to his mother, from Rugby 25 August 1865, in the possession of the Mr H. Badger, lately assistant master at Barnard Castle School.
59. J. M. Wilson (1932), Chapters 4 and 5.
60. G. G. Coulton (1923), pp. 80–2.
61. Speech of Bishop of Worcester at silver jubilee of Millington's headmastership (*P.S. Mag.* II, 1898, p. 476).
62. *Journal of Education* (December 1900), p. 760.
63. F. Fletcher (1937), pp. 105–6.
64. J. D'E. Firth (1949), p. 286.
65. A. B. Gourlay (1951), p. 107N.
66. S. R. James, *Seventy Years* (1926), p. 208. Until 1912 the school's constitution required the headmaster to be ordained: the next appointee (1914) was a layman (R. Blumenau, 1965, p. 86).

67. For the attitude of Durnford, Bishop of Chichester, around 1894, see G. H. Wilson, *History of Windlesham House School 1837–1937* (n.d.), p. 58.
68. HMC Report for 1907.
69. F. Fletcher (1937), p. 105.
70. Lady Grogan, *Reginald Bosworth Smith, A Memoir* (1909), p. 258.
71. F. Fletcher (1937), p. 107.
72. B. W. T. Handford, *Lancing 1848–1930* (Oxford, 1933), p. 220.
73. *Pall Mall Gazette* (6 Oct. 1891), letter signed "One of the Profession". His estimate of a quarter was supported by figures for assistant masters and housemasters of Eton, Harrow, Winchester and Charterhouse.
74. J. E. C. Welldon, essay in *Thirteen Essays, by Members of The Thirteen* (1891), p. 70.
75. R. Wilkinson, *The Prefects—British Leadership and the Public School Tradition* (1964), p. 202. For an extended and perhaps over-severe critique of this book, see J. R. deS. Honey, review *art*: "Schooling and Ruling, a critical notice" in *Durham Research Review* IV, 15 (1964).
76. *Cf.* accounts of Eton sermons from the 1840s to the end of the century in, *e.g.*, A. D. Coleridge, *Eton in the Forties* (1896), pp. 94–5; L. E. Jones (1955), p. 207 etc.; Evelyn Waugh, *op. cit.*, p. 57; C. Alington, *op. cit.*, (1934), p. 41; Lord Chandos (1962), p. 14; E. Lyttelton (1925), p. 37; T. Balston, *Dr Balston at Eton* (1952), p. 86.
77. For schoolboy reaction to the sermons of Benson, Temple, and Farrar, see D. Newsome (1961), p. 30; for a powerful impression of Temple in the Rugby pulpit, see also Lord Kilbracken, *op. cit.*, p. 37 and J. H. Wilson (1932), p. 73. On reaction to sermons at other schools, see Virginia Woolf, *op. cit.*, p. 39; J. H. Simpson (1954), p. 65; M. E. Sadler (e.d.), *Moral, Instruction and Training in Schools* (1908), Vol. II, p. 96; R. Jasper, *A. C. Headlam* (1960), p. 27; C. M. Blagden (1953), pp. 42–3; R. H. Bruce-Lockhart, *op. cit.*, pp. 268–9.
78. Minutes of meeting of Council of Marlborough College, September 1851.
79. E. Graham (1920), p. 126.
80. *Ibid.*, p. 288.
81. H. H. Henson, *Retrospect of an Unimportant Life* (1943), Vol. I, pp. 20, 24.
82. *Pall Mall Gazette* (2 Oct. 1891), p. 7.
83. *Pall Mall Gazette* (6 Oct. 1891): "One of the Profession".
84. Hart to Fowler (13 June 1898) in Hart-Fowler Correspondence, 1898–99, St Johns' College Library, Cambridge; parts of this were quoted by G. G. Coulton in his S.P.E. Tract (No. 43): "H.

W. Fowler" (Oxford, 1934).
85. *e.g. The King's English* (1906).
86. W. F. Bushell (1962), p. 20.
87. G. Kendall (1933), p. 57.
88. C. Alington (1934), pp. 33, 62.
89. Harold Nicolson, *Some People*, pp. 43*ff*; D. Newsome (1959), p. 234.
90. F. Fletcher (1937), p. 107.
91. N. Woodard to C. Lowe (Nov. 1864), quoted in Heeney, (thesis), p. 243.
92. G. St Quentin (1956), p. 82.
93. *Sanderson of Oundle* (1923), pp. 4–6.
94. E. G. Sandford, *Frederick Temple, an appreciation* (1907), pp. xviii, xxvi.
95. D. L. Edwards (1957), pp. 134–8.
96. F. Fletcher (1937), p. 263.
97. E. Lyttelton (1925), p. 135.
98. Bryce Comm. Report (1895), Vol. I, p. 238, evidence of Warren of Magdalen; see also A. L. Irvine (1958), p. 43.
99. L. E. Upcott (Marlborough assistant master 1878–1911 and 1917–19), writing of his days as a member of staff at Marlborough in H. C. Brentnall and E. G. H. Kempson (eds.), *Marlborough College 1843–1943* (Cambridge, 1943), p. 24. *Cf.* also (Sir) Shane Leslie's note in his "Eton novel based on memories of boys and masters at the turn of the century" that "a Music master is a little lower than a French master in the Eton hierarchy" (*The Oppidan*, 1922, 1969 edn., pp. vii, 42).
100. *e.g.* Sherborne under J. R. Sterndale-Bennett and L. N. Parker in the 1870s and after. See A. B. Gourlay (1951), pp. 124–5.
101. A. L. Irvine (1958), p. 63, on Bradfield before 1910; p. 24 on Winchester before 1901.
102. *Ibid.*, p. 62.
103. For some of many possible examples, see A. L. Irvine (1958), p. 79; D. Newsome (1959), pp. 225, 264; A. K. Boyd (1948), pp. 212, 243, 266; J. H. Simpson (1954), pp. 63–4.
104. J. D'E. Firth (1954), pp. 70–1.
105. *Journal of Education* (July 1900), p. 425, referring to speculation in the *Morning Leader* and *Outlook*. In 1902 Warre was offered the Deanery of Salisbury (C. R. L. Fletcher, *Edmond Warre*, 1922, p. 166).
106. E. Lyttelton (1925), p. 65.
107. Lord Chandos (1962), pp. 9–10; Evelyn Waugh, *op. cit.*, p. 57.
108. M. C. Morgan (1968), p. 33.
109. *Journal of Education* (July 1900), p. 425.

110. R. B. Gardiner and J. Lupton (1911), p. 126.
111. J. B. Oldham, *Headmasters of Shrewsbury School* (1937), p. 78.
112. Quoted in F. B. Malim, *Almae Matres* (1948), p. 51.
113. R. J. Mackenzie, *op. cit.*, p. 227.
114. A. F. Leach in *Cyclopaedia of Education* (1913), quoted in T. W. Bamford (1967), p. 186.
115. See, For example, H. S. Goodrich, *Thomas Field, D. D., A Memoir* (1937), p. 80.
116. Viscount Simon, *Retrospect* (1952), p. 45.
117. D. Newsome (1961), p. 3.
118. *e.g.* Jex-Blake, Benson, Temple, Ridding, Percival, Moberly, Tait.
119. *e.g.* Mitchinson, Colenso, Chapman, Rigaud, Awdry, Cotterill, Abraham, Cornish, Westcott.
120. Longley, Tait, Benson, Frederick Temple, William Temple, Fisher.
121. As above, except Longley and Fisher.
122. *e.g.* Tait, Benson, Wordsworth, Jeune, Moberly.
123. *e.g.* Wynne-Willson, Pollock, David, Williams, Gorton, Leeson.
124. Quoted in G. K. A. Bell, *Randall Davidson* (1935), Vol. II, p. 1240–1.
125. D. Newsome (1961), pp. 126–8; H. Henson, *Retrospect of an Unimportant Life*, Vol. I, p. 225.
126. *Journal of Education* (1881), p. 26
127. Private information from the late F. B. Malim.
128. *P.S. Mag.* III (1899), p. 13.
129. H. A. James, "Some Autobiographical Notes" (typescript) in Library of St John's College, Oxford, p. 52.
130. Durham University Library: Thorp Correspondence: W. van Mildert to Archdeacon Thorp (21.4.1834), Vol. I, p. 175; and Thorp to W. van Mildert (23.4.1834). The prospect of a Durham professorship for Sidney Smith was also mentioned.
131. G. G. Coulton (1943), p. 142.
132. G. R. L. Fletcher, *op. cit.*, p. 108; Professor Robinson Ellis to Percival (18.11.88), quoted in W. Temple (1921), pp. 91, 94.
133. H. A. James, *op. cit.* (typescript notes). Section III.
134. For a comment on the state of Charterhouse in Haig-Brown's "declining years", see G. B. Grundy (1945), p. 45.
135. H. A. James, *op. cit.*, p. 55.
136. G. G. Coulton (1943), p. 222.
137. *Journal of Education* (September 1900), p. 529.
138. W. Temple (1921), p. 101.
139. M. C. Morgan (1968), p. 82.
140. Details of the workings of the fund and the investments involved

can be found in the Marlborough College Council Minutes from 1874 onwards.

141. M. C. Morgan (1968), p. 81.
142. C. A. Alington (1936), p. 140; Sir Harold Morris, *Back View* (1960), p. 91.
143. *Journal of Education* (January 1900), p. 75.
144. HMC Reports for 1873, 1876, 1892, 1897, etc.
145. HMC Report for 1892, p. 63.
146. Sanderson of Lancing, HMC Report for 1873, p. 36. (My italics—Author)
147. W. E. Bowen (1902), pp. 363–5. (My italics—Author)
148. *Loc. sit.* (November 1900), p. 667.
149. S. P. B. Mais (1937), p. 38.
150. J. H. Simpson (1954), p. 115.
151. D. H. S. Cranage (1952), pp. 30–1; *Journal of Education* (October 1900), p. 619 and (November 1900), p. 681.
152. L. Tomlinson, *art*: "Oxford University and the Training of Teachers 1892–1921" in *Brit. Jnl. Educ. Stud.* 16 (1968), pp. 292–307.
153. G. Kendall (1933), p. 52.
154. Inge had been no more successful previously at Winchester. See A. Fox (1960), pp. 34–44.
155. A. Fox (1960), p. 42.
156. *Journal of Education* (November 1900), p. 609.
157. J. B. Hope-Simpson (1967), p. 90. For an account of the Hayman case, see below in this section.
158. C. Hollis (1960), p. 116.
159. F. Fletcher (1903), p. 136.
160. *Quarterly Journal of Education* (1835), pp. 85–9, quoted in E. C. Mack (1938), p. 218.
161. A. K. Boyd (1948), Chapter XII; D. L. Edwards (1957), p. 137; H. S. Goodrich, *op. cit.*, Chapter I, etc.
162. *P. S. Mag.* II (1898), p. 576.
163. F. Fletcher (1937), p. 80.
164. *Cf.* Chapter VI of T. W. Bamford (1967) where many kinship links among Victorian public-school staff are plotted.
165. H. S. Tremenheere, typescript autobiography at present in the possession of Professor E. L. Edmonds of the University of Prince Edward Island.
166. According to F. A. Y. Browne in *Family Notes* (privately printed, Genoa, 1917).
167. C. M. Bowra, *Memories 1898–1939* (1966), p. 29.
168. W. S. Maugham, *op. cit.*, pp. 58, 60 and Chapter XV; H. S. Goodrich, *op. cit.*, pp. 74–5; A. K. Boyd (1948), p. 285.

169. "and eleven of whom are of strong Tory politics," (according to a correspondent in the *Rugby Advertiser* for 22 November 1869). This account of the Hayman case is based on J. B. Hope Simpson (1967), Chapter III *passim*; James M. Wilson (1932), Chapter IV; Benson Papers, Trinity College, Cambridge: Private letters, volume for 1869–72; file of press-cuttings on Hayman case in Temple Reading Room, Rugby School. Some parts of this book's account have appeared in J. R. deS. Honey, *art*: "Towers of Men: the Victorian Headmaster and his Successors" in *Listener* LXXVII, 1967 (27.4.1967).
170. Benson to Lightfoot, "December 1869"; Benson to Mrs E. Wordsworth, 23.12.1869: Benson Papers, Trinity College, Cambridge.
171. W. E. Bowen (1902), p. 175; for Thompson, see A. K. Boyd (1948), p. 224. For C. J. Vaughan's tactful dissimulation of his political views, see G. G. Goulton (1943), pp. 142–3.
172. W. Temple (1921), p. 303; D. H. S. Cranage (1952), p. 62.
173. T. W. Bamford (1967), p. 143.
174. C. Hollis, *op. cit.*, (1965), p. 69; H. A. Morrah, *The Oxford Union 1823–1923* (1923), p. 298 and Chapters VI and VII. Temple, for example, had been a member of the Union and had delighted in its debates.
175. C. E. Mallet, *History of the University of Oxford* (1927), Vol. III, p. 395.
176. Correspondence in Hayman case press-cuttings file, Temple Reading Room, Rugby School.
177. J. M. Wilson (1932), p. 73.
178. T. L. Bloxam, *Companion to Rugby School Register 1675–1870* (Rugby, 1871), p. 61; see also leading article, *Rugby Advertiser* (27 November 1869).
179. Hayman press file, Temple Reading Room, Rugby School.
180. J. S. Watson, *Life of Richard Porson* (1861), pp. 154, 172.
181. R. M. Ogilvie (1964), p. 87.
182. J. M. Wilson (1932), pp. 72–3.
183. Sir Edward May, *op. cit.*, p. 16; G. B. Grundy (1945), p. 13. May stated that Hayman was a Conservative, "and the masters at Rugby at that time were mostly Radicals." (*loc. cit.*)
184. Marlborough College Minutes, special meeting to appoint Master, 16.1.1871.
185. J. B. Hope Simpson (1967), p. 134.
186. Rev. James Robertson to Rev. G. C. Bell (Master of Marlborough), from Haileybury, 14 February 1884. Original in Marlborough College archives.
187. This school cannot now be identified.

188. See E. Marjoribanks, *Life of Lord Carson* (1932), Vol. I, Chapter 32.
189. This account of the Hutt case draws on information supplied by Mr F. R. Thompson and Mr D. Hunt of Haileybury College. See also *Haileybury Register 1862–1946* (ed. N. C. King), Hertford, n.d.), p. 115; E. Lyttelton (1925), p. 153.
190. G. G. Coulton, (1943), p. 204. This account of the Young affair is based on Coulton, Chapter XXI, and on A. B. Gourlay (1951), Chapter XVII.
191. S. Cloete, *A Victorian Son* (1972), pp. 155–6.
192. G. G. Coulton (1943), p. 204; A. B. Gourlay (1951), pp. 166–70.
193. G. G. Coulton (1943), p. 205.
194. G. B. Grundy (1945), pp. 34–5.
195. M. Craze, *A History of Felsted School* (Ipswich, 1955), p. 191, Chapters 16 and 17.
196. I. E. Gray and W. E. Potter, *Ipswich School* (Ipswich, 1950), Chapter 10, For the enforced 'retirement' of a headmaster of Oundle in 1883, and for an account of the dismissals and 'resignations' by which Sanderson engineered a 'clean sweep' of the majority of the staff he took over in 1892, see W. G. Walker (1956), pp. 430–42, 486*ff*.
197. *Journal of Education* (March 1900), p. 168.
198. For Sargeaunt, see also M. Craze, *op. cit.*, p. 216.
199. *Cf.* J. D'E. Firth (1949), pp. 242–3; R. Blumenau (1965), pp. 84, 94.
200. W. F. Bushell (1962), p. 18.
201. A. Fox (1960), p. 17; W. F. Bushell (1962), p. 211.
202. On the quality of social life at schools with (or without) Masters' Common Rooms, see, for example, C. Alington (1934), p. 36; H. E. Luxmoore, *op. cit.*, p. 6; J. D'E. Firth (1949), p. 176; S. P. B. Mais (1937), p. 60; G. G. Coulton (1943), pp. 175, 206–7; F. Fletcher (1937), p. 83; C. Alington (1936), pp. 80–1; J. H. Simpson (1954), pp. 113–14; A. L. Irvine (1958), p. 80. On the 'shoppiness' and other aspects of common-room society at Victorian Wellington (compared to Eton), see E. Lyttelton (1925), pp. 102–6, etc.
203. G. St Quentin (1956), p. 68.
204. G. F. Browne, *op. cit.*, p. 53.
205. Farrar's answer to the Rev. C. E. Thorpe was confirmed by the Council's resolution (Minutes, 15 November 1871): "In answer to Mr Thorpe's application the Council do not wish to sanction the principle that a master's salary should be increased when his services are diminished by ceasing to assist in the internal discipline of the college." The headmaster in 1902 (Bell) was still maintaining that "Marriage here is a privilege of long service." (G. Kendall, 1933, p. 170)

206. C. Alington (1943), p. 58.
207. W. Temple (1921), pp. 12, 16.
208. M. Craze, *op. cit.*, pp. 225–6, 244; M. C. Morgan (1968), p. 66. (By contrast Laffan's successor's wife was a distinct asset. See C. M. Bowra, *op. cit.*, p. 43.); W. F. Bushell (1962), p. 71; J. G. C. Minchin (1898), pp. 27–8.
209. G. B. Grundy (1945), pp. 68–9. True, Mrs Wickham was an invalid during her last three years at Wellington, but Grundy's judgment applies for the whole of her twenty years. See also G. F. H. Berkeley, *My Recollections of Wellington College* (Newport, 1945), pp. 43–4.
210. Private information to the author from the late F. B. Malim.
211. A. K. Boyd (1948), p. 273.
212. Abbot Sir D. Hunter-Blair, *In Victorian Days* (1937), p. 28.
213. For examples of varying conceptions of such roles, see F. B. Malim (1948), p. 21; F. Fletcher (1937), pp. 95–6; W. F. Bushell (1962), pp. 42–3, 135; N. G. L. Hammond (1962), pp. 8–10; A. L. Irvine (1958), p. 82; J. H. Simpson (1954), p. 75; (anon), *Memorials of Lionel Helbert* (1926), p. 8; (ed.) W. H. Holden (1950), p. 20.
214. H. E. Wortham (1956), p. 47; W. Temple (1921), p. 20; O. Browning, *Memories of Sixty Years* (1910), p. 258.
215. See preface to *Thirteen Essays on Education* . . . (1891); and H. S. Goodrich, *op. cit.*, pp. 30–1.
216. C. Alington (1934), pp. 38–9, 94; A. K. Boyd (1948), p. 258.
217. Quoted in G. G. Coulton (1943), p. 127.
218. Benson to Westcott, 18.4.1870: Benson Papers, Trinity College, Cambridge.
219. Benson to Jex-Blake, 7.1.1873: Benson Papers, Trinity College, Cambridge.
220. *Loc. sit.*, chapter "The Flag of their Country".
221. J. E. C. Welldon in his article "The Religious Education of Boys" in *Thirteen Essays on Education* . . . (1891), p. 61.
222. Viscount Simon, *op. cit.*, p. 28.
223. Also partly on Hilton's father, an elementary school headmaster.
224. This point is developed by J. R. deS. Honey, *art. cit.*
225. This point is well made by W. B. D. Heeney in articles on Edw. Monro in *Canadian Journal of Theology* XIII, 4 (1967), and XIV, 1 (1968).

Select Bibliography

C. A. Alington, *Lionel Ford* (1934)
C. A. Alington, *Things Ancient and Modern* (1936)

C. A. Alington, *Edward Lyttelton* (1943)
N. Annan, *Roxburgh of Stowe* (1965)
P. Ariès, *Centuries of Childhood* (trans. R. Baldick, 1962)

T. W. Bamford, *Thomas Arnold* (1960)
T. W. Bamford, *The Rise of the Public Schools* (1967)
C. M. Blagden, *Well Remembered* (1953)
R. Blumenau, *A History of Malvern College* (1965)
W. E. Bowen, *Edward Bowen* (1902)
A. K. Boyd, *History of Radley College 1847–1947* (Oxford, 1948)
A. G. Bradley, A. C. Champneys and J. W. Baines, *A History of Marlborough College* (1923)
W. F. Bushell, *School Memories* (Liverpool, 1962)

Lord Chandos, *Memoirs* (1962)
M. L. Clarke, *Classical Education in Britain* (Cambridge, 1959)
G. G. Coulton, *A Victorian Schoolmaster: Henry Hart of Sedbergh* (1923)
G. G. Coulton, *Fourscore Years* (Cambridge, 1943)
P. Cowburn, *A Salopian Anthology* (1964)
D. H. S. Cranage, *Not Only a Dean* (1952)

A. E. Douglas-Smith, *The City of London School* (2nd edn. Oxford, 1965)

D. L. Edwards, *History of King's School, Canterbury* (1957)

Geoffrey Faber, *Jowett* (1957)
J. D'E. Firth, *Winchester College* (1949)
J. D'E. Firth, *Rendall of Winchester* (1954)
F. Fletcher, *After Many Days* (1937)
Adam Fox, *Dean Inge* (1960)
W. Furness (ed.) *Centenary History of Rossall School* (Aldershot, 2nd edn. 1946)

R. B. Gardiner and J. Lupton (eds.) *Res Paulinae* (1911)
A. B. Gourlay, *A History of Sherborne School* (Winchester 1951)
E. Graham, *The Harrow Life of H. M. Butler* (1920)
G. B. Grundy, *Fifty-Five Years at Oxford* (1945)

N. G. L. Hammond (ed.), *Centenary Essays on Clifton College* (Bristol 1962)
Brian Heeney, *Mission to the Middle Classes* (1969)
W. H. Holden (ed.), *The Charterhouse We Knew* (1950)
C. Hollis, *Eton* (1960)
J. B. Hope Simpson, *Rugby Since Arnold* (1967)
Thomas Hughes, *Tom Brown's Schooldays* (1857)

H. E. M. Icely, *Bromsgrove School Through Four Centuries* (Oxford 1953)
A. L. Irvine, *Sixty Years at School* (Winchester, 1958)

M. R. James, *Eton and King's* (1926)
L. E. Jones, *A Victorian Boyhood* (1955)
L. E. Jones, *An Edwardian Youth* (1956)

G. Kendall, *A Headmaster Remembers* (1933)
Rudyard Kipling, *Stalky & Co.* (1899)

E. Lyttelton, *Memories and Hopes* (1925)

P. C. McIntosh, *Physical Education in England since 1800* (2nd edn. 1968)
E. C. Mack, *Public Schools and British Opinion, 1780 to 1860* (1938), *Since 1860* (New York, 1941)
S. P. B. Mais, *All the Days of My Life* (1937)
F. B. Malim, *Almae Matres* (Cambridge, 1948)
J. G. C. Minchin, *Old Harrow Days* (1898)
M. C. Morgan, *Cheltenham College, the First Hundred Years* (Chalfont St Giles, 1968)

D. Newsome, *History of Wellington College* (1959)
D. Newsome, *Godliness and Good Learning* (1961)

R. M. Ogilvie, *Latin and Greek* (1964)
V. Ogilvie, *The English Public School* (1957)
Sir Charles Oman, *Memories of Victorian Oxford* (1941)

G. R. Parkin, *Life and Letters of Edward Thring* (1898)
G. L. Prestige, *Life of Charles Gore* (1935)

C. E. Raven, *A Wanderer's Way* (1928)
W. J. Reader, *Professional Men* (1966)
Kenneth Rose, *Superior Person* (1969)

G. St. Quentin, *History of Glenalmond* (Glenalmond 1956)
J. H. Simpson, *Howson of Holt* (1925)
J. H. Simpson, *Schoolmaster's Harvest* (1954)
A. P. Stanley, *Life and Correspondence of Thomas Arnold* (1844 etc.)

William Temple, *Life of Bishop Percival* (1921)
W. Tuckwell, *The Ancient Ways: Winchester Fifty Years Ago* (1893)

W. G. Walker, *A History of the Oundle Schools* (1956)
James M. Wilson, *Autobiography 1836–1931* (1932)
E. Wingfield-Stratford, *Before the Lights Went Out* (1945)
H. E. Wortham, *Victorian Eton and Cambridge* (1927, new edn. 1956)

Index